An image of the pre-Columbian god of the Solar Moon in the underworld.

The Olmec Riddle

The Olmec Riddle:

An Inquiry into the Origin of Pre-Columbian Civilization

by James C. Gruener

Library of Congress Catalog Number: 87-50370

ISBN: 0-942185-56-0

Post Office Box 1085
Rancho Santa Fe, California 92067

To Florence.

ACKNOWLEDGMENTS

This book could not have been written without the help and guidance of David H. Kelley of the University of Calgary; and Gordon Ekholm of the American Museum of Natural History, who started me on the trail leading back to the origin of pre-Columbian civilization. I wish also to acknowledge the assistance given me by Fred Laughter and Barbara Brennan Laughter, who edited, designed, indexed, and produced this book, as well as accomplishing the color photography; Patrick Whelan, who read the manuscript and made substantive comments and suggestions; Hasso Von Winning, consultant to the Southwest Museum, Los Angeles, who read the manuscript and gave me critical advice concerning my conclusions from the archaeological evidence; and Frances Brainerd, who read and helped edit the first drafts of the manuscript and without whose encouragement I would not have brought this work to completion; and William M. Holmes of Case Western Reserve School of Medicine, who drew the illustrations for this book and whose infinite care and drawing ability ensured their accuracy.

— James C. Gruener

PREFACE

Thoughtful consideration of the mythology and literature of ancient Sumer and Babylon reveals that: Creation and the universe were pictured in the minds of the people in the third and second millennia B.C. differently from our conception of them today. To the Sumerians and Babylonians, the universe was divine. In its divinity, the universe was personified as the progenitor couple combined as a sea of mingled salt and fresh waters filling a limitless void. In their union, salt water was the goddess and fresh water her divine consort. Their progeny became the sky, the earth, and the life of the earth. The life of the earth was created and constituted by the Moon and the Sun following their monthly and seasonal course throughout the year.

The world came into existence through the sacrifice of the progenitor couple. In the beginning, the shape and life of the world were inchoate; when the progenitor couple died, they returned to a state of nonbeing and inchoate life, in which state they surrounded the existing world. In the created world, the earth was half underworld and half the world of living man. The underworld was a region of death and returning life, and time was a succession of cycles. When a cycle ended, life ceased until a new cycle began. The new cycles were formed in the outer universe and they came into existence in the underworld where earthly forms of life were created. The life created in the underworld came on earth as annual cycles of vegetation and animal life.

Creation was viewed as the new Moon appearing in the evening. Its motion was life. The process of creation was imagined as the formation of

its motion. The process progressed in four stages, each constituted by the Moon of a quarter. The first stage was the last quarter, in which the lunar cycle ended and the Moon vanished. The Moon was inchoate in that stage. The second stage was the new Moon, in which the Moon's motion began. The third stage was the first quarter when the Moon waxed toward the full, and the fourth stage was the full Moon which, having become full, began to wane.

The Moon was both male and female. Its divinity was the Sun, its mortality, vegetation and the forms and products of earthly life. These elements of its divinity were distinguished as gods and were the source of the Moon's motion. Together they functioned as the power of creation and the cycles of earthly life.

The Sumerians and the ancient Babylonians devised a calendar to record the progress of creation and of life, and they held that the divinity of the Moon was incarnate in the king.

In ancient Mexico and Central America, the same concepts of creation, the universe, and the divinity of the ruler were part of the religious culture. For instance, the Aztecs called the god who was the universe Ometeotl, which literally means "Two-God." In his dual form, he was the primordial couple. In a creation myth, Ometeotl's issue were four Tezcatlipocas. They were distinguished by color and world direction: one was red and east, the next black and north, the next white and west, and the fourth blue and south. Tezcatlipoca had different aspects, but he was essentially the Moon. We know from the *Codex Fejérváry-Mayer* that his divinity was male and female and was composed of the Sun, the mortality of the Moon, vegetation, and the fertility of the earth. These elements of divinity were gods and the means of lunar motion.

The four Tezcatlipocas functioned as Ometeotl's power in the creation of the world. Their directions identify them as the four stages of the Moon's cycle; their colors, directional identities, and function mark them as the last quarter, new Moon, first quarter, and full Moon, respectively.

Their function was to create the life of the world and bring it into existence.

The Aztecs called the world as it existed in their time the Fifth Sun, or Sun of Movement. The Sun of Movement was not the Sun as such, but the cycle of time which delimited the length of the world's existence. In the cycle, the Sun was the compound divinity of the Moon and its movement was the Moon's motion.

This concept was universal in Mesoamerican religion. The peoples of Mesoamerica used a calendar to register the progress of creation and life. Its structure was the same as that of the Sumero-Babylonian calendar.

The Sumero-Babylonian doctrine of the nature of the universe and the creation was the part of the religion of the Great Goddess which spread universally across Eurasia. Although the metaphors which gave them expression were different, the religious beliefs and practices which were part of the Mesoamerican civilization were essentially the same as those of the Great Goddess religion.

However, they have not been recognized as such because the interpretation of mythology and art has been made on the assumption that, as in modern thought, there was a single creation; the universe was distinct from any god; time was infinite; and the underworld was part of an afterworld where the souls of the dead were lodged.

In this assumption, the afterworld was separated and permanently sealed off from the world of life. It has been thought, therefore, that the scenes of mythology and of religious dramas were laid in the world of real life during historical periods of time.

The following pages describe the origin and development of the doctrines and practices of the Great Goddess religion; their diffusion through Asia during the second millennium B.C., eastward to the Pacific Ocean; and their sudden appearance in that millennium in the Olmec culture of Mexico.

In considering the mythology of Mesoamerica, we should bear in mind that, like the peoples of Eurasia who worshiped the Great Goddess, the

people of Mesoamerica had many gods.

The gods, however, were all functional aspects of the divinity of the Moon and the universe of which the Moon was its life-giving agent. As men still appeal to different saints in the Christian religion, men formerly looked to the particular gods whose functions were in accord with their particular needs. This individualizing of the Moon's divinity as gods obscured the gods' relation to the Moon itself.

Some of the interpretations presented in this study differ from the traditional views held by those who specialize in the cultures considered, nevertheless, they make intelligible otherwise inexplicable features of mythology and religious rites. The different approach which has been followed should stimulate a reevaluation of the spread of ancient religious systems and the consequent development of Mesoamerican civilization.

TABLE OF CONTENTS

TABLE OF CONTENTS

ILLUSTRATIONS

ILLUSTRATIONS

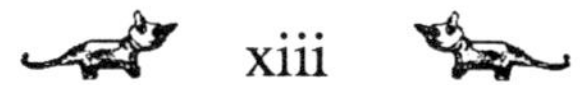

INTRODUCTION

Mesoamerican civilization began with the culture of the Olmecs in the later centuries of the second millennium B.C. It lasted for nearly three thousand years. The Olmecs lived in Guatemala and southeastern Mexico on the southern borders of Mesoamerica.

Mesoamerica is that part of Central America which lies between central Honduras and northwest Costa Rica on the south, and an east-west line across Mexico a little above the tropic of Cancer on the north. Olmec culture flowered in the midst of a primitive civilization. There is no evidence of any period of development and its seemingly spontaneous appearance is the "Olmec riddle." This book is a study which solves the riddle. The culture which formed as Mesoamerican civilization evolved in Eurasia.

Spades have found no answer to the riddle in the soil of Mesoamerica. Spades unearth material objects from which students can reconstruct the evolution of the ways in which men developed their culture. The Olmec civilization which suddenly blossomed was singularly spiritual. The place to dig for the answer, therefore, is in the mystic past; the search should begin with the study of the religion of Mesoamerican civilization. The first part of the following work describes the doctrines and rituals which form the cultural foundation of that civilization.

Mesoamerican religion has features of the Great Goddess religion, which originated in southwest Asia and subsequently evolved in Mesopotamia and the eastern Mediterranean. The doctrines of the Great

Goddess religion have not been fully defined in the studies of the culture of southwest Asia, hence the focus of the search must be on the mythology and rituals of the Mesopotamian peoples who adopted the religion. The next part of this study describes the search and its findings.

In order to interpret the mythology and understand the rituals of the Great Goddess religion, we must trace its development. Its genesis was in the early hunter societies sometime before 15,000 B.C. In southwest Asia, agriculture displaced hunting as the basic economy and the Great Goddess religion evolved with the social changes which resulted. It reached full development in the course of the urban revolution which followed during the fourth and third millennia B.C., and which evolved the ancient civilization.

From the Sumero-Babylonian center, the Great Goddess religion was carried into the Eurasian steppes. During the second millennium, it spread westward from the steppes, until it eventually reached the Atlantic Ocean, and eastward across Asia through India, to China and the Pacific Ocean. It left its trace in China at the time of the Shang dynasty in the fourteenth century B.C. and, perhaps as early as that same century, it was in some way carried across the ocean and appeared abruptly in the Olmec region of Mesoamerica.

The doctrines of the Great Goddess religion may be described briefly as follows: The Supreme God was the Earth Mother, whose consort was the sky. Together they were one. They were the universe and their manifestations were its elements. The forms of the elements are constantly changing and the changes were the supreme god's movement as life and time. In the imagery of this movement, the elements were formed in progressions which were personified as the generations of the goddess and her consort. The earth, into which all life returns and from which it springs, formed as the gods of death and new life. The sky, which is the realm of air and water, formed as the gods of life.

The manifestations of the Supreme God as all forms of life were the

Moon and the Sun and the planetary star Mercury. The Moon was mortality and the substance of life, and the Sun and Mercury were immortal. The Sun was the spirit of life and Mercury was the Moon's spirit of motion. The Moon was the life body of the spirit and, therefore, the Sun and the Moon were one and their motion was the cycling of the Moon. The Moon's diurnal motion was the manifestation of the Supreme God as life, and its retrograde motion from new Moon to new Moon was the Supreme God's working as creation.

In her form as goddess of death, the Great Goddess was the Earth Mother. The underworld was a region of death and the womb of the Earth Mother. Therefore, life formed in the underworld and its return as vegetation in the fields each spring was the offspring of the goddess. The world of life was thus divided into two parts: the underworld where life formed, and the world above where it matured and ended. The cycles of life were created as years, but the life of the world did not end each year, rather it endured for a cycle of years. Just as life in the created world formed in the underworld region of death and came into being on earth, a new cycle of years formed in the regions of nonexistence and, when a cycle of years ended, came into existence as a new world of life.

The universe of the Supreme God was thus divided into three spheres: one beyond the outer limits of the world, one in the earth underworld, and one on the surface of the earth. The first two were spheres of life creation. New life rose from the death of precedent life, the medium of resurrection was sacrifice, and the source of resurrection was the Moon's power of regeneration. In each stage of its motion, the Moon formed as a planetary god manifest as a planet star. When its motion completed the creation of a new cycle of world life, the gods of its motion all united and died in a single sacrifice. In their common death, they formed as the divinity of a new Moon and took the cosmic shape of a world-man. Their resurrection was in the underworld where they formed as the Moon's movement with the Sun. There each god formed as a day and all moved together as cycles of days.

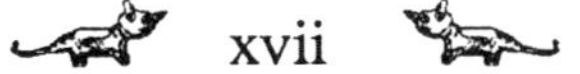

In the course of their cycles, life formed in the underworld.

The gods died again when the cycles of days had formed a year and returned on earth as a new year of life. In their new resurrection, they were incarnated in the persons of the Queen and her consort the King, the rulers of the land. During the year which followed, the Queen and King were the earthly forms of the Great Goddess and her consort, and the source of life on earth.

The creed of the Great Goddess as the Creator and Maker was put into the form of a calendar which described her movement as the Moon and Sun creating the days of the cycles of world life.

The foregoing description of the Great Goddess religion, with certain changes to account for national and sectarian differences, is a description of Mesoamerican religion. The universe of the Mesoamerican civilization was called the "Sun of Movement." The movement was the motion of the Moon as the incarnation of the Sun. The moving spirit of the Moon was the planet Venus.

Our study in the search for the answer to the origin of Mesoamerican civilization follows the diffusion of the Great Goddess religion across Asia to China, and describes its appearance on the opposite side of the Pacific Ocean in the Olmec region. How it was carried across the ocean is a riddle within the riddle. The last chapter suggests a solution, but still leaves unanswered that part of the riddle.

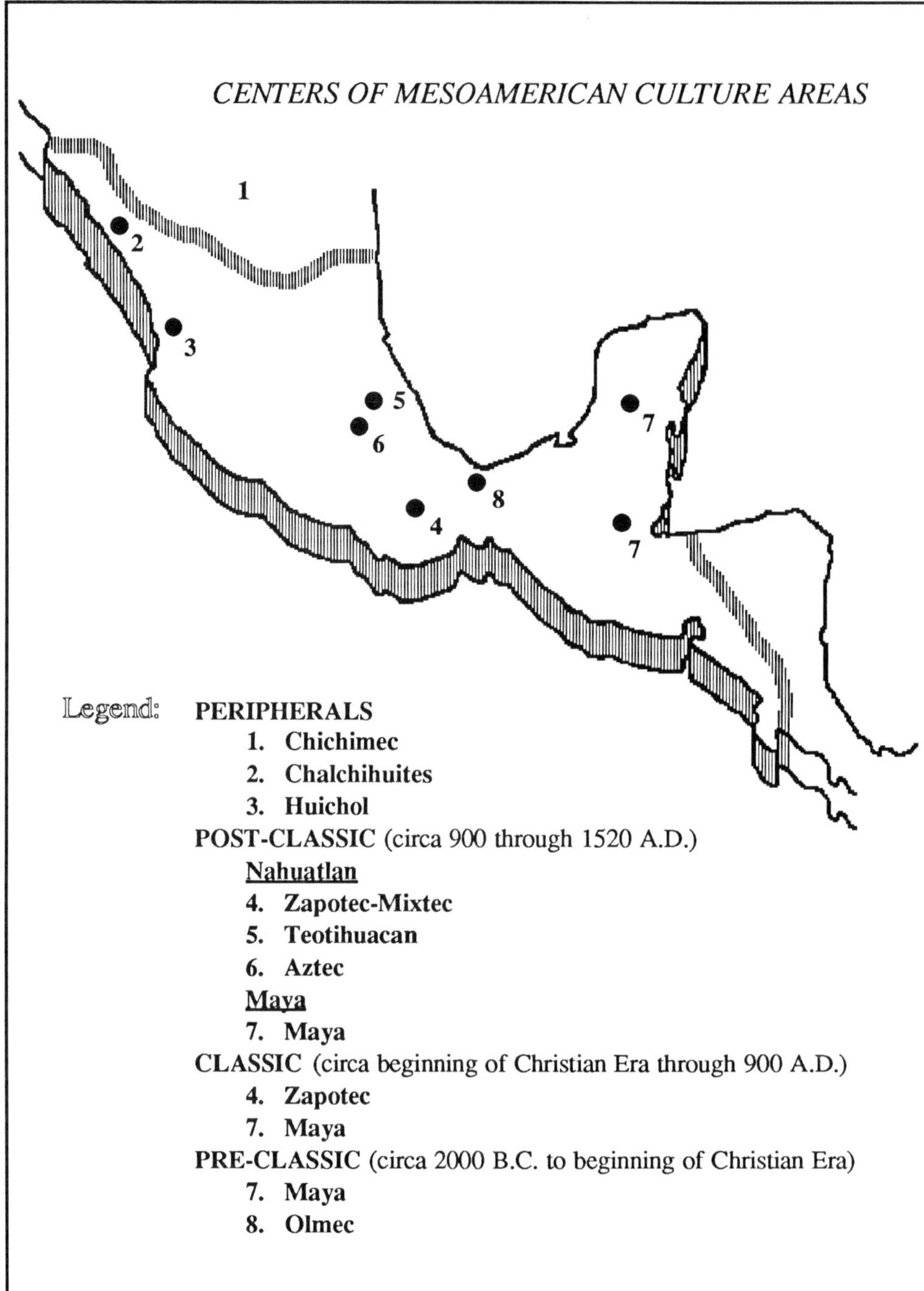
CENTERS OF MESOAMERICAN CULTURE AREAS
1
2
3
5
6
7
8
4
7
Legend:
PERIPHERALS
1. Chichimec
2. Chalchihuites
3. Huichol
POST-CLASSIC (circa 900 through 1520 A.D.)
Nahuatlan
4. Zapotec-Mixtec
5. Teotihuacan
6. Aztec
Maya
7. Maya
CLASSIC (circa beginning of Christian Era through 900 A.D.)
4. Zapotec
7. Maya
PRE-CLASSIC (circa 2000 B.C. to beginning of Christian Era)
7. Maya
8. Olmec

PART I

CHAPTER 1

The Doctrine of Sacrifice

prior to 15,000 B.C. through 1900 A.D.

The origin of Mesoamerican civilization is an enigma — established by the Olmecs who appeared in what is now central and southern Mexico and adjacent Guatemala in the latter half of the second millennium B.C., Mesoamerican civilization was formed by religion. Fundamental to the religion was the doctrine of sacrifice, which also is the core of the Judeo-Christian religion on which western civilization was formed. But the two civilizations developed very differently. To understand the religion of the ancient Americans, we shall have to look back to a time before the Olmecs. Our window opening onto this past is the culture of the Huichol Indians who live in western Mexico in the state of Nayarit.

Before the rise of Mesoamerican civilization, the people were village farmers. At the turn of the nineteenth to the twentieth century, the Huichols were representative of a village farming culture, as described in *Unknown Mexico* by Carl Lumholtz, who lived with the Huichols at the turn of the present century. He wrote that they "belong to the tribes which remained in barbarism while the main stock of the family developed and reached a state of culture culminating in the establishment of the Aztec empire."

The Huichols live in a region of rugged mountains where the valleys are narrow. Their food staple is corn, or maize as it is called in Mexico, and they supplement their diet with game, chiefly deer which abound in the region. Their homes are in tiny villages built on the mesas of the mountain ridges, and they make their fields on the surrounding steep slopes. At the time of Lumholtz' study, their clothing and pottery had been changed only

to a small degree by Western influences, and their way of life was largely unchanged.

The Huichols have not always lived in the country which is now their home. Around the beginning of the Christian era, their ancestors were among the peoples living in western Durango in the foothills of the Sierra Madre Occidental — all of whom were related groups belonging to the Uto-Aztecoidan linguistic stock, whose culture was a desert culture, although they had begun to depend in part on simple farming for subsistence. At this time, traits of Mesoamerican civilization (such as simple ceramics and basic platform architecture) were diffused northward to these peoples; under these influences, the desert culture evolved into a village farming culture with characteristics distinguishing it as the Loma San Gabriel culture.

Later, around 200 A.D., Mesoamerican civilization spread to western Durango in the form known as Chalchihuites and reached its classic development there around 300 A.D. The Chalchihuites peoples remained concentrated around their ceremonial centers, leaving the Loma San Gabriel peasants more or less untouched, although those closest to the Chalchihuites' occupation were more culturally related to the higher civilization. The Chalchihuites' culture ended around 1000 A.D. when the power of the central Mexican states declined and their boundaries receded under the pressure of the barbarian Chichimecs who were invading from the north; but the Loma San Gabriel farmers remained.

The desert culture was a food-gathering continuation of the hunting cultures. The Loma San Gabriel culture added planting and villages to the desert culture and adapted hunting religion to the uses of farming. The religious culture of the Huichols is the Loma San Gabriel, slightly modified by the Chalchihuites' influence. While the precise origin of the Huichols is not known, they belong to the Uto-Aztecan linguistic stock to which the Loma San Gabriel peoples belonged. Their language and their heritage mark the Huichols as descendants of the Loma San Gabriel peoples of western Durango.

The Doctrine of Sacrifice

The Huichols inherited their religious practices from Mesoamerican civilization and partly from the village farmers who preceded them. However, the Mesoamerican part was considerably diluted; the ancestral Huichols lived outside the pale of higher culture and in the course of time the elements of the higher civilization degenerated such that their culture reverted to the village agricultural level. In its surviving form, the religious practices of the Huichols are, or were at the time of Lumholtz' study, essentially the same as those of the hunter societies of Eurasia from which the village farming culture evolved.

The Huichols build their temples and god houses in ceremonial centers away from their villages. Each ceremonial center serves the people living in the surrounding area. A typical ceremonial center consists of a tiny collection of huts with adobe or rough stone walls and thatched roofs, hardly distinguishable from the ground. The huts stand on a high mountain spur or at a place surrounded by a superb prospect of nature where the gods are believed to live. The largest hut, usually round, is the temple where religious ceremonies are performed. In the center of the temple is a fireplace; around the walls are little chairs on which the images of the gods sit during the rites. Between the ceremonies, each of the dieties is kept in his own house, where a rude altar has been set up on the dirt floor.

The chief god of the Huichols is the Fire God, Tatevale, who is manifest as deer, the Sun, and maize. The Earth Goddess is Nakawe, who is maize and vegetation, and whose cosmic form is the Moon. She, likewise, is manifest as deer. The principle rite is the deer sacrifice.

The sacrifice rite begins with a hunt which is a sacred ritual. The hunters set out behind three or five leaders who walk abreast and impersonate different gods; the leader who walks in the center is the Fire God. The hunters drive the deer until one is caught in a snare previously set on the trails which the deer follow. When a deer has been killed, a piece of its intestine (which has been filled with blood and tied at both ends) is sent by a special runner to the shamans and the principal men of the tribe, who

have been waiting at the temple. When the runner draws near, a woman fills her mouth with sacred water from a drinking gourd and squirts it upon the runner. The runner then gives the intestine of blood to the shaman, who smears daubs of blood on the gods' chairs, which are believed to be occupied by the gods, although they are invisible. He also smears it on his drum, on the chairs of the principal men of the temple, and on the ceremonial objects being used in the feast. This ritual is followed by the return of the hunters with the dead deer, which is carefully laid on straw in front of the temple entrance with its legs turned toward the east. Offerings of food and tresvino, the Huichol corn beer, are then placed before the deer. The Indians go up, one by one, and each strokes the deer with his right hand while addressing it as "Elder Brother" or "Elder Sister" (the title given to the gods), thanks it for being caught, and bids it rest. In the meantime, the deer's blood has been collected, boiled in a jar, and eaten by the people. Then the deer is skinned and its hide is carefully preserved.

The Huichols regard the deer sacrifice as the rite most valued by the gods, since without it rain and good crops, health and life cannot be had; and they look upon the deer as the incarnation of all the divine powers which combine to provide the corn harvest. They believe that the killing of the deer makes their crops swell and that by their eating the meat broth of the sacrificed deer, the corn will be made to grow.

The rite is essentially the same as the Bear Cult rites performed by hunting tribes in Asia who worship the bear as a god. The Ainu, who are one such tribe, fasten the skull of the sacrificed bear on a pole which is part of an altar. The altar consists of a row of poles set in the ground, one next to the other, and fastened by a cross-pole which holds them together. The altar looks like a ragged pale fence. The Gilyaks, another tribe, take the skull and bones of the sacrificed bear to the forest. In the forest, they cut down a small tree and make a notch in the stump; then they place the skull in the notch and bury bones in the earth beside it.

In the doctrine of the Bear Cult, the spirit of the Bear God descends

through the pole into the earth where it unites with the Earth Goddess. The Ainu Earth Goddess is the Fire Goddess, Fuji. As a result of the union, the Earth Goddess releases the food animals on which the hunters live and the Bear God returns to the earth in a new body, bringing the food animals with him. Thus, the purpose of the bear sacrifice, like the Huichol deer sacrifice, is to ensure the food supply.

The communion meal was originally an essential part of the sacrifice rite because the hunters regard their animal god as a kindred member of their hunting group, and the bond of kinship prohibited one kinsman from killing another. When the hunters kill the bear, the kindred bond is broken and the communion feast is the means of renewing it. In the sacrifice rite, the bear does not die, but lives as a god-spirit that is present in the parts of the bear which the people eat in their communion meal. The bear spirit enters into all those who consume the flesh, thus all become one with each other. In the Bear Cult communion, the bear joins in the feast, as the deer does in the Huichol rite — in the atonement, the kinship bond is renewed.

This belief in the transmigration of the spirit and in the kindred nature of the animal god is apparent in the Gilyak belief that if a man falls in combat with a bear, his soul goes into the bear. In some rites, one of the women dons the skin of the bear in symbolism of the bear's union with the Earth Goddess.

While the ritual of the Huichol deer sacrifice follows the Bear Cult form, the Huichol religion evolved as a syncretism of the Bear and Deer Cults. The early hunters of northern Europe depended on the deer herds for their food and their animal god was the deer. In the Deer Cult, as in the Bear Cult, sacrifice was the means of creating life on which the hunters depended, and the sacrifice doctrine was essentially the same; but the deer hunters conceived of the Earth Goddess as uniting with the Sky Father to constitute a progenitor couple. Their union constituted a single god which we may properly call the "Creator-Maker."* In the sacrifice, the deer

*This is the term used by the Quiché Maya in their sacred book, the *Popol Vuh.*

became one with the pair and the new life which returned to the earth was procreated in the union.

The earliest evidence of the rituals of the Deer Cult dates back to the late Magdalenian Period between 15,000 and 10,000 B.C. at the Meiendorf and Stellmoor sites near Hamburg in northern Germany. Ancient lake beds at these two sites yield evidence that reindeer hunters sacrificed two yearling does. The growth of the antlers shows that the deer were killed before the fawns were born in the spring, when they had returned to the summer pasture. The finds indicate that the deer were killed during the course of a hunt as shown by the mark of a projectile point which had pierced the shoulder bone of one of the animals. For the sacrifice, the dead deer was taken to the camp where the hunters cut open its body and wedged one or more stones into the cavity of the thorax. The cut was then sewn together and the body submerged in the lake. The lake bed represented the Earth Mother and the Sky Father united as the progenitor couple and the stones were the embryo forms of life which would quicken in their union.

Changing geological conditions at Meiendorf caused the lakes to silt up, but several thousand years later, Mesolithic hunters were again sacrificing does in the same manner at the Stellmoor site where melting glaciers had formed new lakes. These men, known as the Ahrensburg hunters, also left evidence of another form of sacrifice. A pole was found with the head of a fifteen-year-old deer mounted at the top. This pole evidently had been set upright in the water close to the shoreline. Other large skulls of older animals were found in the lake bed. The pole, like the pole altar of the Bear Cult, served as the pathway for the deer spirit's journey through the underworld.

We may be sure that the Deer Cult hunters sacrificed deer because they believed that sacrifices made the herds produce young, just as the Huichols, whose rituals were those of the Bear Cult, believed that sacrifice made the corn grow. We may also be sure that they sewed stones in the bodies of does and submerged them in the lake, and that they fastened the heads of

male deer on poles set in the water, because they believed that thereby the fertility of the Earth Mother and Sky Father was imparted to the herds. That they held these beliefs becomes apparent when we consider the nature of the doctrines of the Deer Cult, and the mythology and institutions that evolved within it.

The Deer Cult hunters sewed stones in the bodies of does to identify them with the Earth Mother. On the soft bottoms of the lakes, the land becomes ooze and swamp where earth and water mix. This mixture of water and earth — together with the water of lakes and streams — was the primary earth form of the Sky Father. In his earth form, he united with the Earth Mother; through this union, they became the Creator-Maker.

The Creator-Maker as the progenitor couple and the god-spirit returning through the underworld bringing new life on earth evolved into a doctrine of the universe and creation which became the fundamental doctrine of Mesoamerican religion. The formation of the doctrine began with a new image of the animal god-spirit moving through the underworld in the creation of new life. When the new image first formed, it was purely phallic. It then reformed as a serpent, which later became the animal form of the Moon, and finally evolved into the planetary form of either Venus or Mercury. This development has been obscured by the fact that the anthropologists of the nineteenth century were obsessed with the idea that primitive hunters lacked the information to connect sexual intercourse and pregnancy; but the cave paintings of southern France make it abundantly clear that those ancient hunters understood very well the procreative purpose of intercourse.

When they imagined the spirit of the animal god traveling through the underworld and returning on earth with new life, these ancient hunters pictured the spirit as a phallus being changed into the things on which they lived, or as the spirit traveling along a phallic pathway and changing its forms into that of animals which were god-forms of life on earth.

The evolution began with the lakes where the hunters sacrificed the deer. In the imagery of the union of the progenitor couple, waters falling from the sky were manifestations of the fertilizing seed of the Sky Father and the hollow in the earth in which waters formed as a lake was the vaginal opening of the Earth Mother. The progenitor couple, or Creator-Maker, were the female and male principle of procreation and, in the sacrifice, the spirit of the animal god united with the Creator-Maker. This union is described in the Trickster mythology of the Winnebago Indians of North America.

Trickster was the primordial form of the spirit of the animal god which is found in some form in the mythologies of all early civilizations. He evolved from the doctrine of the sacrifice of the animal god when men began to speculate on the metaphysics of creation and to imagine the god renewing his bodily form as he returned through the god-world, bringing game to the hunting grounds. Men invented the adventures which befell him during his journey, and added humor for embellishment. The North American Trickster myths form a group known as a cycle. They tell how Trickster goes on a journey to gather food animals and meets with many adventures. He has a remarkable penis of such length that he carries it coiled in a box.* At one point, he sees the daughter of a chief and has an adventure with her which is described as follows:

"Trickster walked down a slope and finally came to a lake. On the opposite side, he saw a number of women swimming, the chief's daughter and her friends. 'Now,' exclaimed Trickster, 'it's the opportune time; now

*In Greek mythology, Trickster was Hermes, who was first represented as a stone phallus in which form he was worshiped in early Greece. Graves describes this early Hermes as the "totemistic virtue of a phallic pillar" — a description which also fits Trickster. Hermes' journeys through the underworld made him god of travelers and stone phalli were set up to mark the trails. In later Greek religion, he became guide to the underworld and the planet Mercury. His sign was the caduceus, a staff with two serpents coiled around it. The staff, like the poles of the Bear and Deer Cults, represented his path through the underworld, and the serpents were his spirit image as the Evening and Morning Stars.

I am going to have intercourse.' Thereupon he took his penis out of the box and addressed it, 'My younger brother, you are going after the chief's daughter. Pass her friends, but see that you lodge squarely in her, the chief's daughter.' Thus speaking, he dispatched it. It went sliding on the surface of the water. 'Younger brother, come back, come back. You will scare them away if you approach in that manner.' So he pulled his penis back, tied a stone around its neck, and sent it out again. This time it dropped to the bottom of the lake. Again he pulled it back, took another stone, smaller in size, and attached it to its neck. Soon he sent it forth again. It slid along the water, creating waves as it passed along. 'Brother, come back, come back! You will drive the women away if you create waves like that!' So he tried a fourth time. This time, he got a stone, just the right size and just the right weight, and attached it to its neck. When he dispatched it, this time it went directly toward the designated place. It passed and just barely touched the friends of the chief's daughter. They saw it and cried out, 'Come out of the water quick!' The chief's daughter was the last one on the bank and could not get away, so the penis lodged squarely in her. Her friends came back and tried to pull it out but to no avail. They could do absolutely nothing. Then the men who had the reputation for being strong were called and tried but they, too, could not move it. Finally all gave up. Then one of them said, 'There is an old woman around here who knows many things. Let us go and get her.' So they went out and got her and brought her to the place where this is happening. When she came there she recognized immediately what was taking place. 'Why, this is First-born, Trickster. The chief's daughter is having intercourse and you are all just annoying her.' Thereupon she went out, got an awl and straddling the penis, worked the awl into it a number of times singing as she did so:

"'First-born, if it is you, pull it out. Pull it out.' Thus she sang. Suddenly in the midst of her singing, the penis was jerked out and the old woman was thrown a great distance. As she stood there, bewildered,

Trickster, from across the lake laughed loudly at her. 'That naughty old woman! Why is she doing this when I am trying to have intercourse? Now she has spoiled all the pleasure.'"

The meaning of the metaphor is clear: Trickster and the pool represent the Sky Father, the old woman and the chief's daughter represent the Earth Mother.

In the development of the doctrine, the phallus becomes the providence which the Creator-Maker sends on earth with the returning god-spirit. Another episode in the Trickster cycle describes this development.

The Winnebago tell how one day, when Trickster was pursuing his adventures, he came upon Chipmunk who ran into a hollow log. Trickster set about dislodging him and to do so he took his penis out of the box and, using as a probe, stuck it into the hollow of the log. Chipmunk retreated farther and farther in and Trickster was unable to force him out. Finally, in exasperation, Trickster kicked the log until it broke open. He then discovered that Chipmunk had gnawed his penis into many pieces. He looked at them ruefully and said, "Oh my, of what a wonderful organ he has deprived me! But why do I speak thus? I will make objects out of the pieces for human use."

Trickster threw the pieces into a lake nearby. One turned into the lily-of-the-lake, another into artichokes, and others into potatoes and so on until he had created plants out of all the chewed-up pieces of his penis. One part remained, however, which Chipmunk had not chewed up; this was just the size of a man's organ and so Trickster fastened it onto himself where it belonged and thus acquired a sex organ of the proper size.

In the cycle, Trickster begins as an amorphous being which forms into human shape from a phallus. He is an anthropomorphized animal god-spirit. In the Deer Cult, the route of the spirit's descent was the pole set in the lake, and this also was the route of ascent to the world of life on earth. In the metaphor of the episode, the log was the pole in the lake and the Chipmunk in the log was the symbol of sacrifice and resurrection.

The Doctrine of Sacrifice

The next stage in the development of the doctrinal image was the transformation of the phallus into a serpent. For this we may cite a Polynesian myth.

In the islands of Polynesia, eels take the place of serpents. One myth concerns an eel named Te Tuna, which means phallus. One day a maiden bathed in a pool where Te Tuna was swimming. Te Tuna turned himself into a man, naturally a handsome one, and made love to the maiden, who responded with a willingness and who thereafter returned regularly to Te Tuna's pool. Te Tuna continued to live as an eel; but when the maiden came, he always changed his form into a beautiful youth and in that form made love and was accepted by the maiden. One day he told her that their happiness would have to end; that he would come to her in a flood in the form of an eel; and that afterward she should cut off his head and bury it. Thus, he came to her, and afterwards she obediently decapitated him and buried the head as he had bidden her to do. A coconut tree thereupon grew out of his head.

In a further development, the food supply which formed from the serpent was identified with the Sun and the serpent returning from the union with the progenitor couple was imagined as the Sun-bearer. The doctrine evolved in the northern hemisphere where life as vegetation dies in the winter and revives with the return of the Sun in the spring. Spring, also, is the season when the young are born in herds. The Sun thus came to be associated with returning life and, consequently, the returning animal god. In Eurasia, the phallic image of the god returning through the underworld must have been formed early in the development of the doctrine. When the returning god-spirit came to be imagined as a serpent, the life which he brought was pictured as the Sun with the serpent carrying it. The Sun setting in the west and rising in the east was thought to travel through the underworld and, in the imagery of the serpent carrying the Sun, its movement came to be represented as a serpent with the head of the Sun God or carrying the Sun in its mouth.

In this Eurasian evolution, when the god-spirit traveling with the Sun through the underworld took the serpent image, it retained its character as vegetation and in its serpent body it became an animal form of the Moon. This was a natural development. The Deer God was, from early times, identified with the Moon because the Moon, which appears to die and revive regularly, was associated with mortality. This association was extended to plants and in its common identity with the Moon as vegetation, the serpent was identified with the Moon. This identity was made complete by the nature of the serpent, which periodically casts its skin and so appears to renew its life.

Time was measured by the Moon and, in its serpent image, the Moon came to be imagined as carrying the Sun through the underworld during the winter death of vegetation and bringing it back to the world of life to begin a new year on earth. The phallic image of the animal god-spirit as exemplified by Trickster was probably brought to America by migrating hunters; its further development into serpent form may have taken place in the New World, but in any case, the serpent form of the animal god is commonly found in Amerind primitive religions, and shows that the evolution of the Deer Cult had followed the same course, or at least a parallel course, in the Americas.

The religious beliefs of the Huichols show that their culture was formed in the stages of this evolution. The Huichols equate the Sun and maize with deer as manifestations of the same god. Nakawe is the Earth Goddess, the Corn Mother, goddess of growth and vegetation, and the Mother of the Gods. Tatevale, whose name means "Our Grandfather," is the Fire God who is particularly powerful as the god of the underworld and is the chief of the Huichol gods. Nakawe is the creator-half and Tatevale is the maker-half of the Creator-Maker. All of the gods are subject to the power of the Nakawe and Tatevale, and are in fact part of their combined divinity.

The idols of Nakawe show her an an old woman whose face and body are covered with spots of different colors of the corn which the Huichols

grow: red, black, and yellow. She leans for support on four crooked canes: the first two are her hands, and the third and fourth are fastened to the front and back of her skirt. The canes represent serpents. Some idols show Nakawe with naked breasts and with her hair and feet painted black. These idols have a serpent represented on each shoulder, a butterfly on the upper part of her chest, a grasshopper on her stomach, and corn symbols on her skirt. In this representation, she is the Corn Mother, and she is further associated with the serpent by the serpent-stick in her hand and the plumed serpent on her back. Nakawe is also a two-headed serpent which the Huichols believe girdles the earth.

Both Nakawe and Tatevale are underworld and upperworld gods. In her upperworld form, Nakawe is known as Tate Velika Uimale, which means "Mother-Eagle-Young-Girl." Her animal form is a two-headed eagle with four serpents as appendages — these are the rain-serpents and each relates to one of the four directions. They have the same significance as the four serpents belonging to Nakawe's underworld form, and the Huichols say that the plumed serpent on Nakawe's back flies in rain. Nakawe is the mother of the Sun, which she conceived in her aspect as "Mother-Eagle-Young-Girl." In Huichol mythology, both are described as the Sun God's mother and both are worshiped as the Corn Mother.

Nakawe was the mother and Tatevale the father of the Sun in Huichol mythology. While still a boy, the Sun was thrown in an oven; but he escaped and, traveling underground, rose full-fledged as the Sun. In the symbolism of the myth, the Sun was created in the physical union of Nakawe and Tatevale, for it is clear that the oven was the Fire God's heat and the darkness was the interior of the Earth Goddess' body.

The story of the boy thrown into the oven and escaping to become the Sun is the Huichol story of creation, and shows that creation is the result of sacrifice. Lumholtz records it as follows: [in the beginning there was only the light of the Moon] "The principal men came together to see what could be done to give the world better light. They asked the Moon to lend them her only son, a limp, one-eyed boy. She first objected, but at last consented. They gave the boy a full ceremonial dress with sandals, plumes, and tobacco-gourds, and painted his face. Then they threw him into an oven where he was consumed; but the boy revived, ran under the earth, and 5 days later rose as the Sun." As the Sun, he became lord of the western part of the Huichol country, and was named Ta-Yau which means "Our Father."

Nakawe, the Moon, was a Serpent Goddess. As mother of the boy who became the Sun, she carried the Sun in her womb and kept him with her after he was born. Thus she conforms to the imagery of the serpent as the Sun-bearer. The boy was limp, because the action was in the underworld which was the region of death and so he was lifeless; his eye was his being as the Sun and, when the principal men threw him in the oven, their act was the sacrifice which gave him life. When he rose as the Sun, he also rose as maize growing in the fields.

In the development of the doctrine of the Deer Cult in Eurasia, the life returning with the resurrection of the god came to be identified with the Sun. The annual cycles of the Sun made the process of creation a continuing succession of cycles in which, each year, life was created in the underworld and rose with the Sun of the new year on earth. In this cosmic image of the cycle of creation, the Moon lost its image as the serpent bringing the Sun as new life on earth, because of the difference in time cycles of the Sun and Moon, and the serpent image of the Sun-bearer was transferred to Venus (or in the Sumerian form of the doctrine, to Mercury), as the Evening and Morning Stars which accompanied the Sun into the underworld and led it back into the sky over the earth. Theologically, the change did not alter the lunar nature of the serpent. The planets move in the same path with the Moon and, like the Moon, they seem to die and revive periodically; consequently, the planet carrying the Sun was seen as a sort of arm by which the Moon held and moved the Sun.

The creation of continually repeating cycles of life naturally led the

formulators of religious thought to apply the doctrine to the original creation of the universe. The concept of the progenitor couple was expanded into the divinity of a universe which came into being spontaneously as an all-embracing Supreme Being, a creator and maker of life on earth, and of the two worlds of nonexistence and existence. In the world of existence, the divinity was constituted as the world of life on earth and the underworld beneath. Its existence began, not on the surface of the earth where living things have their being, but in the underworld. To the ancients, life was manifest as vegetation. Animal and human life perished without vegetation, which grew from the soil and returned to the soil in death. In its world of existence, the underworld was the region in which it took earthly form as created life, and the world above was where it was life in being. In its divinity as life, it was mortal and its living and underworld forms came alternately to mortal ends. As each cycle of creation ended in the underworld and came on earth as a new cycle of life, the divinity began the creation of a new cycle in the underworld.

In a further development in Eurasia, the Deer Cult evolved into a cult of a Divine King. When the economy changed from hunting to farming, political units formed as matriarchies ruled by queens who were believed to be incarnations of the Earth Goddess. Queens took new consorts each year who, by virtue of the union, became gods of vegetation and domestic animals. Theologically, their divinity evolved from the Deer God and the consummation of the union of the queen and the consort fertilized the fields and livestock. Each year the consort was sacrificed and his resurrection came as the produce of the land and livestock. In the course of time, the consort took the queen's place as the ruler and the sacrificial rite was abandoned; but the consort retained his divine nature and, as the ruler, became the medium in which the god who was the year-Sun lodged in order to dispense the providence which he brought on earth.

In Mesoamerican religion these doctrines appear in a form essentially the same as the Eurasian; moreover, there are elements of Huichol religion which suggest these advanced doctrines of creation and a Supreme God.

The idols of the Fire God, for instance, in his underworld and upperworld forms, are set up in twos, one above the other. The lower one stands on a little god chair in a hole dug into the floor beneath the altar and covered by a round stone, and the upper one is set on the stone which covers the one below. The lower one is the more reverenced and the more carefully guarded of these idol manifestations. The forms of the idols are not identical in appearance.

The stone which separates the over and under idols of the Fire God shows the godhead escutcheon formed as a two-headed eagle portrayed in front view, standing erect with legs and talons apart, wings unfolded, and the heads turned in opposite directions, one to the left and the other to the right. On the eagle's breast is a stylized toto, a little white flower which blooms in the wet season and which symbolizes rain and maize. Mother-Eagle-Young-Girl has the same double-eagle for her emblem and symbols for rain and maize; and her power as the center of the four rain-serpents is controlled by Tatevale who can hold back the rains when he wills.

The two-headed eagle is a metaphorical image of the Sun as the symbol of life which the gods sent on earth as maize and other food crops growing in the fields. One head represents the rising Sun returning from the underworld as new life, the other represents the descending Sun of the west and the harvest which is the bounty of the dying plants.* On the stone between the double idols of the Fire God is the emblem of Mother-Eagle-Young-Girl who, as Nakawe is combined with the Fire God as the Creator-Maker — thereby denoting their function as the creators of life.

*The two-headed eagle is particularly an Eurasian device. It was the emblem of the Hapsburgs, inherited from the time when their ancestors were divine rulers on the Eurasian steppes. The Hapsburg Charles V was the Holy Roman Emperor and King of Spain whom Cortez served when he conquered Mexico and, when the Spaniards who were his followers carved the two-headed eagle on the wall of the church which they built in Tlaxcala, the two-headed eagle came full circle around the world.

The Doctrine of Sacrifice

When they adopted features of Mesoamerican civilization, the forebears of the present day Huichols probably failed to comprehend fully the complexities of Mesoamerican religion and, so, made a rough imitation of the sky and earth forms of the underworld creator and life forms of the Mesoamerican Supreme God, and set up their images as underworld and upperworld forms of the Mesoamerican god of the universe.

Huichol religion, as it is described by Lumholtz, is a religion which is partly one of village farming culture and partly one of Mesoamerican civilization. The deer sacrifice and the belief that the communion meal makes the maize grow is a feature of village farming religion; it is a doctrine which came directly from the hunting cultures as they evolved in America. The doctrine of time and creation — which held that the Moon, Venus, and the Sun moved uniformly together and created repeated periods of world existence — which evolved in Eurasia from the same doctrine, became the foundation on which Mesoamerican religion was formed. Let us now turn to the study of Mesoamerican religion and its origin in Eurasia.

CHAPTER 2

Nahuatlan Religion

ca. 900 through 1500 A.D.

When the Spaniards conquered Mexico at the beginning of the sixteenth century, Mesoamerican civilization had evolved into what is known as its Postclassic Period. Although generally identified as being Aztec, *Nahuatlan* is the more proper term for identifying the culture of the Postclassic Nahua speakers of central highland Mexico.

The Supreme Being in Mesoamerican religion was the universe, whose Nahuatlan name was Ometeotl. As the universe, he was the progenitor couple, the Creator-Maker. He had many names and, as the Creator-Maker, he was called Xiutecuhtli, which means "Fire God," as well as Huehueteotl, which means "Old God." These names denoted his masculine side. His feminine side was the Death Goddess and Earth Mother, and was called Tlazolteotl.* In his abstract geophysical form, he was an "otherworld" divided into two parts: one a region of death and creation, the other a region of created life forms and the world of life. As Creator-Maker and life, he was all the gods.

In the creation of life and as life in being, he was called the Fifth Sun, the Sun of Movement. In the work of creation, he moved through the otherworld as the Moon and the serpent Venus with the Sun, continually creating a succession of new years of life on earth. His movement on earth was the life which, as the year, died continually and continually came into being. Thus, he was time.

*Other names were: Coatlicue, Chicomecoatl, Cihuacoatl, Illamatecuhtli, Ixcuina, Teteoinnan, Toci, Tonantzin.

He was manifest as the sky and the earth, as the Moon and the Sun, and as vegetation and living things on earth. In all these manifestations, he was continually changing; his image was fluid in the Nahuatlan theology. Thus he was the night sky when there was no Moon, and he was the Moon. In this image, when the Moon waned and vanished, he appeared as the sky and the stars, and when the Moon revived, he appeared as its changing face. In this aspect as the sky and the Moon, he was called Tezcatlipoca. In the otherworld, he moved as Tezcatlipoca with the Sun in a counterclockwise direction through the cardinal direction points, beginning in the east and moving north, then west, south, and so back to the east. In this movement, he created the new year which would come as a new Sun on earth. The four stages of direction were Ometeotl as the Creator-Maker, consequently, as the Fire God he was also called Tezcatlipoca.

Ometeotl's image as the Sun likewise was a changing one. Implicit in this image was Ometeotl's Moon divinity in a different form. Theologically the Moon was a life form of the earth and, since the life of earth was manifest as vegetation, vegetation was a transubstantiated form of the Moon. The life which the Sun brought on earth was particularly in the form of vegetation and, more specifically, in the form of maize; the divinity of vegetation was implicit in Ometeotl's image as the Sun. He was the rising Sun in the east, and he was the descending Sun in the west. The west was the female side of Ometeotl as the universe — when he entered the west as the Sun, the nature of his being as the progenitor couple made the Sun the consort of the Earth Goddess. The Sun was the universe in existence and it was called the Fifth Sun, or the Sun of Movement. In this form, he was a fertility god with the nature of the Sky Father. When the Sky Father fertilized the Earth Mother, he descended as rain and lightning; Ometeotl as the descending Sun was a Storm and Rain God and was called Tlaloc. Because of his identity with Ometeotl as the progenitor couple, Tlaloc was also a name for the Fire God.

The Sun and Moon were, therefore, combined as a two-fold being and

together formed Ometeotl, whose name means Two-Lord, as the Sun of Movement. The movement was created by the twin fire-serpents, the animal forms of the planet Venus. One serpent was the Evening Star, Xolotl; the other was the Morning Star, Quetzalcoatl. The Moon, like vegetation which was the emanation of its divinity, was mortal; the planet was its immortal spirit which animated it and gave it motion. Consequently, the Moon's motion created the Sun's motion and the two serpents were pictured in Mesoamerican mythology as Sun-bearers: Xolotl, the Evening Star carrying it through the underworld of death, and Quetzalcoatl carrying it through the regions of life.

The Moon nature of Venus is evident in the mythology and iconography of the Mesoamerican religion which identifies it with vegetation. In the Nahuatlan creation myth, Xolotl appears as both maize and maguey, and Quetzalcoatl's image is a plumed serpent. His plumes are quetzal feathers. The quetzal, a forest bird with brilliant green plumage, represents the Sun. In the symbolism, the bird is the Sun, the green plumage is maize, the serpent is Venus as the Sun-bearer, and the trees are paths through which the serpent rises bringing the Sun from the underworld where it is created. In this image, Quetzalcoatl is both the Sun as it was formed in the life region of the underworld and as it came into being as the new year of life on earth; consequently, Ometeotl was sometimes called Quetzalcoatl.

In this image of Quetzalcoatl, maize was identified with the Sun of each year of life on earth and, when the Sun rose and began a new year, it rose as the new maize planted and growing in the fields. Its divinity as maize was the nature of the Moon and, in its annual course as the Fifth Sun in the created world, it was equally a form of Tezcatlipoca — who reversed the direction in which he had moved during its creation, and moved clockwise through the cardinal points from east to south, west, north, around to east.

Nahuatlan mythology and the religious dramas performed by the Aztecs, as they have been described by the Spaniards, give a picture of the Mesoamerican concept of the otherworld beyond the world of life, and the movement of the Fifth Sun as the creation of life and as life on earth. The otherworld had many facets and was formed as an Above and Below. In the Above, there were 13 heavens. Their relation to each other has been variously conceived; one of the codices pictures them one above the other, separated by celestial crossbars, and shows the different levels as passageways through which the heavenly bodies moved, each level being assigned to different celestial bodies. This image is only one facet and is misleading because the movements of the Sun, Moon, and Venus were combined, and the 13 heavens were 13 forms of Ometeotl as time which came as the firmament of night and enveloped the earth. The Below was formed by nine underworlds, but we do not have any description of their physical relation to each other.

The Above and Below were also divided horizontally into the East and North, and West and South. The East and North were the abode of Ometeotl in his masculine aspect as the Fire God. The West and South were his abode in his feminine aspect as Tlazolteotl, the Death Goddess and Earth Mother.

The created world of life was the earth which was divided into two parts: one was the underworld, the other was the plane of the earth's surface with the atmosphere which supported the life of man. The plane was a great disk entirely surrounded by water. At its center, set in the earth's navel, stood a world pillar* — or a gigantic tree — which supported the heavens. From his dwelling place in the navel, it was said that Ometeotl "endows the earth with solidity" and "covers the earth with cotton" — which is to say that from there he brought the things of the earth and sky into being through the world pillar or tree of life. The navel, therefore, was the division point between existence and nonexistence.

There are two myths which describe the original creation of the Fifth

*A huge wooden column or pillar was set up in the Temple of Quetzalcoatl at Teotihuacan. Its purpose could only have been to represent a world pillar supporting the heavens. This pillar is preserved in the museum in Teotihuacan.

Sun. In one, the process of creation began when Ometeotl formed in the void which was before the beginning and, in his dual sex as Ometecuhtli and Omecihuatl, generated four Tezcatlipocas, each with its own direction and color. Tezcatlipoca was the Moon compounded with the Sun.* In the Nahuatlan form of Mesoamerican religion, the divinity of the Sun was the source and spirit of life, and the divinity of the Moon was the body and substance of life. The Moon was the governor of time and, hence, it governed the cycles of life which were manifest as its changing phases. Because of its nature as body substance, it incarnated the Sun and its motion, and combined its own and the Sun's motion into a single movement which created the days, months, and seasons of the year. This combined motion constituted the source of continuing life; it was divided into four stages constituted by the four Tezcatlipocas; and it was the motion which made the Fifth Sun the Sun of Movement.

The quarterly phases of the Moon's cycle were the manifestation of life. The four Tezcatlipocas were Xipe, the red Tezcatlipoca of the east; Tezcatlipoca, whose color was black and whose province was north; Quetzalcoatl, the white Tezcatlipoca of the west; and Huitzilopochtli, the blue Tezcatlipoca of the south. Their directional provinces and their colors identify them as the four phases of the Moon's motion; but their directional sequence beginning in the east and moving around through the north to the west, a course counter to the diurnal course of the Sun, is the direction of life creation.

Creation begins in a state of nonexistence. In the last quarter of its cycle through the month, the Moon vanishes in the Sun rising in the east. The rising Sun was seen as the coming of life; but, without the Moon, the Sun's appearance was thought of as being in a world of nothingness. Nonexistence, therefore, was in the east and it was in that direction that creation was believed to begin. In the cycle of the Tezcatlipocas, nonexistence was the death state of the Moon and the Sun within it was

*See Chapter 3.

imagined as potential life in the cosmic body of the dead Moon. The Moon's compound divinity makes Xipe potential life in the dead and vanished Moon of the third quarter; Tezcatlipoca is life forming as the new Moon; Quetzalcoatl is life coming into being as the first quarter; and Huitzilopochtli is the maturity of life as the full Moon.

Thus the cycle of the four Tezcatlipocas begins in death and ends in life and reverses the order of life which ends in death. The reversal shows them as the cycle of creation. The myth records that Ometeotl delegated the function of bringing the world into existence to Quetzalcoatl and Huitzilopochtli. Fire and a half-Sun were created first. Next the gods created man and woman, to whom they gave maize. Then they created the calendar, that is, the movement of the Fifth Sun as the continuation of life. Lastly they created the Below, the 13 heavens and the waters, and the earth, which they formed as a monster alligator or fish called Cipactli.

In the cycle of the four Tezcatlipocas, Xipe and Tezcatlipoca were the gods of creation and prelife, while Quetzalcoatl and Huitzilopochtli were gods of the created life, hence they were charged with bringing the world into existence. In creating fire and a half-Sun, they formed the pattern of continuing life through the cycle of the four Tezcatlipocas. The world had the two divisions of the underworld and the earth above. The underworld was a place of night and winter where earthly life ended and began again before coming on earth. The world above was where the course of life in being began and ended — a place of daytime and summertime. Fire, which was the source of renewal of life, burned in the underworld. In the cycle of the four Tezcatlipocas, the underworld was the province of Xipe and Tezcatlipoca. The Sun was the life which brought day and summer to the world of life on the earth above. It was the world of Quetzalcoatl and Huitzilopochtli and the half-Sun of their creation. Thus, they first created life and time, then they formed the frame of the world to contain it to make their works of creation complete.

The second myth describes the creation as a succession of four stages

or Suns, and the created world of the Fifth Sun as a final stage. The details differ as they were described by the Spanish chroniclers, but the myth is generally in accord with the version which follows:

There were four Suns, or eras, in the world before the present Sun was created. The first Sun was Tezcatlipoca, the Fire God (Ometeotl) in his aspect as the Supreme Lord of Night. Before he appeared spontaneously to begin the Fire God's self-creation as the universe, there was nothing. The next Sun was Quetzalcoatl, who struck down Tezcatlipoca so that he fell into the cosmic waters. Turning into a jaguar in his fall, he devoured all the men in the world who were giants. Quetzalcoatl reigned as the second Sun until Tezcatlipoca struck him down with his paw; then all men were turned into monkeys. After a prodigious wind destroyed the world, Tezcatlipoca called Tlaloc as the third Sun. His era ended in a storm of fiery rain when Quetzalcoatl deposed him and replaced him with his sister-wife, the Earth Goddess Chalchiuhlicue. At the end of Tlaloc's Sun, men were turned into birds. Chalchiuhlicue's Sun was destroyed by a flood and men were turned into fish.

Then there was no god to be the Sun. The world was in darkness and in the darkness the gods considered and said to each other: "Who will be the Sun?"

A god possessing great riches, named Tecuciztecatl, offered himself. The gods then asked: "And who else?"

None volunteered, so the gods chose one who had taken no part in their discussion. Nanauatzin, scabby and covered with pustules, was very poor. They said to him, "Thou shall be the one, oh Nanauatzin." He accepted, saying, "It is well, oh gods; you have been good to me."

Now, to become the Sun each god had to hurl himself into a fire which had been burning for 4 days. So, after Tecuciztecatl and Nanauatzin had made due penance for 4 days, the rest of the gods lined up, leaving space for them to run and leap into the flames. Tecuciztecatl was to go first and, taking his place, he ran toward the fire; but when he felt the fierceness of the

heat, he turned back. Four times he tried, but each time he stopped and refused to jump. After the fourth try, it was Nanauatzin's turn. Closing his eyes and screwing his courage to the sticking point, Nanauatzin rushed toward the fire and cast himself into the flames.

When Nanauatzin's burning body "crackled and sizzled," Tecuciztecatl gathered his courage and followed him into the fire. In this manner, the two gods died. And thereupon, an eagle and a jaguar appeared and one after the other entered the fire.

The gods sat down and waited to see where the Sun would rise. When they had waited for a long time, the sky all around began to redden. Some gods expected the Sun to rise in one direction, others in another, and so they took places looking in all different directions. Quetzalcoatl and Xipe-Totec watched toward the east.

Nanauatzin rose in the east and Tecuciztecatl appeared following him. The two Suns were equal. The gods decided that this should not be. One of them came running and threw a rabbit in the face of the second Sun, which so darkened it that Tecuciztecatl became the Moon, and the rabbit became its animal form.

But the Sun did not move, neither did the Moon. They just hung where they had appeared in the sky. So the gods took counsel and it was decided that they all must die and in their sacrifice they would give life and motion to the Sun. The god who was the wind, Ehecatl, was appointed as the sacrifier. When he came to the god Xolotl, Xolotl tried to escape death by first turning himself into two young maize stalks growing from a single root (which the peasants called *xolotl*), and then into a maguey plant formed in two parts (called *mexolotl*), and finally into a small fish (called an *axolotl*). Each time Xolotl was discovered, and finally he was sacrificed with all the others. But when all had died, the Sun still did not move and the Moon remained in the place where it had stopped behind the Sun. Ehecatl then blew and set the Sun in motion. When it had reached the place where it set, the Moon moved. Here the myth continues, "So there they passed each other and each one went his own way. Thus the Sun cometh forth once and spendeth the whole day (in his work); and the Moon undertaketh the night's task, he worketh all night."

The creation myth is obviously constructed on the doctrine of sacrifice. This is the significance of the transformations at the end of the first four Suns, as well as the sacrifices necessary for the creation of the Fifth Sun. During each Sun, a part of the Fifth Sun's being was created. In the first: the jaguar, Tezcatlipoca, was the Fire God come into being as the end and beginning of life. The jaguar was the sign of Tezcatlipoca as the night sky and the Moon in its changing form from the beginning of life to death, and the fire of the Sun, which was the source of life. It was his sign as the lord of death and creation. The jaguar symbolized Tezcatlipoca because, as a carnivore, he was death — while as a hunter, he was life. His nocturnal nature identified him with the underworld and the darkness of night. In the imagery of Mesoamerican religion, the spots on his pelt were the sign of the stars in the sky. In theology, the Moon was the manifestation of the life of the earth and the Sun was the source of that life, so Tezcatlipoca was equally the Sun and, since the Moon of creation was in the underworld of the earth, his sign as the jaguar was his sign as the Earth Sun. In Mesoamerican iconography, the divinity of vegetation was represented in human form; when Tezcatlipoca became a jaguar and ate the giants, he combined the nature of vegetation with his Moon and Sun natures.

Quetzalcoatl's Sun was the era in which the Fire God became the Sun as the life principle and the power of creation. The wind at the end of his Sun symbolizes the breath of life and the transformation of men into monkeys, which were symbolic of sexual intercourse, symbolizes reproduction. Tlaloc's era was the creation of the earth body of the Sun as vegetation. The fiery rain which marked its end symbolizes the procreative union between the Sun as Sky Father and the Earth Mother. The feathered serpent of the underworld sky was the Sun in the life stage of vegetation; the transformation of men into birds thus symbolizes the Fire God's sky body as the Sun. Chalchiuhlicue's Sun, allied to Tlaloc's, constituted the stage in the creation in which the life form of the Sun was created. The fish into which men were transformed symbolize the vegetal body of the Sun.

Only by the process of incorporation through sacrificial death could the Fifth Sun, the present era, come into being. The events which followed the destruction of Chalchiuhlicue's Sun do not describe the creation clearly. The Fifth Sun was forming as the underworld and the world of life; in the stage which followed the flood, the Fifth Sun had not yet come into existence and the gods who gathered together were but potential life forms. To come into being, they had to die. Tecuciztecatl was the conception of the Moon as the divinity of life which would come on earth and which was signified by his riches. Nanauatzin was the conception of the serpent Venus, and his scabby skin was the dead skin which covered live skin beneath, in which he would emerge into existence; he was poor because he was the Moon spirit outside of his life body which would form as Tecuciztecatl. When Nanauatzin and Tecuciztecatl rose as two Suns, they were formed by the elements of Venus and the Sun. Venus was the Moon's moving spirit which combined with the Sun as a life spirit. The rabbit gave the spirit a Moon body.

Together the two Suns were the Sun of Movement and their combined motion in the underworld created the life which came on earth. Nanauatzin was the Sun moving in its course through the year; Tecuciztecatl was the Sun as the life spirit of the Moon moving in the Moon's course through the month. The course of the Sun through the year and of the Moon through each month was the circuit of the sky; so it was said that "the two passed each other and went his own way." But, although the Moon completed the circuit in the course of a month and continually passed the Sun, the movement of the two was the movement of time as days so that the two moved together as one. In the following narrative, the Sun is the combined form of the two Suns.

Nahuatlan Religion

Nanauatzin's Sun was the half-Sun which Quetzalcoatl and Huitzilopochtli created because as the Sun he lacked the Moon body which was the divinity of life created by the movement. Xipe and Tezcatlipoca were the Suns of Nanauatzin and Tecuciztecatl as the life formed in the underworld, and Quetzalcoatl and Huitzilopochtli were those same two Suns as life on earth. It was for this reason that Ometeotl charged them with the creation of the half-Sun.

In ancient Mexico, the life of the day began at midnight and the Moon's work of creation began at noon. This time relation reflected the doctrine of sacrifice. From noon until midnight was the period of the Sun's descent to the death region, and midnight to noon was the period of its return from death. Associated with this time division was the belief that the souls of warriors who died in sacrifice or battle accompanied the Sun rising to the meridian. These warriors were believed to have become one with the Morning Star, Quetzalcoatl. In this belief, the souls of women who died in childbirth met the Sun on the meridian and accompanied it on its descent. The west was Tlazolteotl as Death Goddess and Earth Mother and the souls of the women were held to be her spirit forms.

Although it traversed the realm of death each day, the Sun did not die until the end of the year on earth. During the year, life was forming as a new Sun in the underworld. This new Sun matured in the life region and when the Sun died on earth, it rose and became the new year which followed. But, it could only come on earth through death and the death and ascension were imagined as the death of the Moon and the journey of its spirit through the underworld. The spirit departing from its Moon body was the god Xolotl, the Evening Star of Venus which was transformed by death into Quetzalcoatl, the Morning Star.

A series of pictographs in the *Codex Borgia* show the journey which Edouard Seler, who interpreted the codex,* calls "the voyage of the Planet

*A codex is a picture-manuscript in which the text consists of a series of graphic images painted on a folding screen.

Venus across the Underworld." The symbolism of the pictographs connects the transformation of Xolotl into Quetzalcoatl with his journey through the underworld. The first pictographs show the death of the Sun. Xolotl is shown entering the underworld; then he is shown entering a temple and paying homage to the Lord of the Night, the Fire God Xiutecuhtli.

The next figures symbolize Xolotl's imminent transition from death to rebirth. A mantle covering a mummy bundle is decorated with figures of the Wind God and a skeleton. The meaning of these figures is explicable by reference to the myth of the creation of the Suns. The figures of the skeleton with the Wind God symbolize Xolotl's sacrifice by the Wind God Ehecatl. Xolotl's attempts to escape death by turning himself into a double-maize plant and a double-maguey plant identified him with maize and vegetation. The twin plant forms were Xolotl and Quetzalcoatl; when Xolotl died as one part of the plant, he came to life in the other part as Quetzalcoatl. These figures thus signify the death of Xolotl and his resurrection as Quetzalcoatl.

The actual transformation of Xolotl into Quetzalcoatl is depicted in the next pictures in the *Codex Borgia.* Two Quetzalcoatls, according to Seler, are shown leaving the temple. One is the Quetzalcoatl who is to be killed, that is, Xolotl, and the other is the Quetzalcoatl who will return as the rising Sun. The two play a ball game, after which the victor sacrifices the vanquished. The next plate, showing Xolotl burning in a pot set over a fire, symbolizes the reincarnation of the Fire and Sun spirit in the body of Xolotl-Quetzalcoatl by the Fire God's act of creation. The final ascension of the Sun, which brings with it the cycle of vegetation, is symbolized in the last plate, in which Xolotl is shown as a hummingbird in a flowering tree which grows from a human heart. The heart is Quetzalcoatl's, and thus the Morning Star; the tree constitutes the pathway to created life, and its flowers represent returning vegetation; the hummingbird, as Xolotl transformed into Quetzalcoatl, represents the rising Sun.

Nahuatlan Religion

In the voyage of the planet Venus, Xolotl is pictured in human form. He had three animal forms: a serpent, a dog, and a jaguar — sometimes he was pictured as the three together or as a composite of the three. The serpent was his planetary being as Venus, the dog was his spirit being as the corporeal nature of the Moon, and the jaguar was the underworld form of the Sun which he carried through the region of death. When he became the Morning Star, his dog and jaguar natures were transformed into a quetzal bird whose feathers formed him as a plumed serpent.

The movements of the two Suns were termed *Ollin.* Ollin was practically identical with Venus. The usual sign for the planet Venus is a curved line forming a double-u with an eye enclosed in the curve of each single-u [**Figure 1**]. The two u's represent the twin serpent forms of Venus. In the imagery of religious thought, Venus was the eyes of the Sun, which explains the significance of the eyes in the curves of the u's. The association of eyes with the Venus serpents was natural since the serpents as the carriers of the Sun were its guides and seeing eyes. Nor was it unique — the ancient Egyptians pictured Venus as a serpent and called him

Figure 1. Aztec sign for the planet Venus.

the Eye of Horus. Horus was the Sun on the horizon — at rising and setting when the morning and Evening Stars were its guide to the sky above and the underworld below. In the symbol of the double-u, the serpents are joined at their tails which are twisted together. In its simplest form, the ollin sign is a twist section of the two tails, although it is sometimes elaborated and changed so that it is not always recognizable [**Figure 2**].

Ollin was a doctrine of creation of life and sacrifice was necessary to maintain it. Mesoamerican civilization was urban and, in the transition from farming to urban culture, men anthropomorphized their gods to a greater and greater extent and humans came to replace animals as gods of sacrifice. Victims were secured by raiding, which led to the rise of a martial cult and a ritual of warfare that came to be known as Flowering War.

Figure 2. Ollin signs.

Nahuatlan Religion

In its essential form, the Flowering War was a limited military engagement between two states which was fought by mutual agreement and in which each side took captives for sacrifice and returned to its home base. It was a mystic rite in which the warriors were identified with Venus and the Sun, either as jaguars or eagles (the animal form of the Sun in the sky), and so they were known as jaguar or eagle knights. In the fighting and sacrifices which followed, the captors and captives were endowed with the same divinity and men were said to be in "Flood and Fire," a term which referred to the flood that followed Chalchiuhlicue's Sun and the fire of the Fire God in which Nanauatzin and Tecuciztecatl were created as the two Suns.

CHAPTER 3

Toxcatl
AZTEC PERIOD

ca. 1350 through 1520 A.D.

The sacrifices were not confined to captive warriors. Slaves were often sacrificed and young men and women were chosen from the populace. The sacrifices were part of religious dramas of creation performed at feasts and celebrated every month, or on particular occasions. The drama of the Feast of Toxcatl portrays the underworld Sun creating the Sun of life, which rises as the new year on earth. The underworld Sun is constituted as the Moon, Tezcatlipoca, with Venus as the Sun-bearer. In the drama, Venus is called Ixteucale.

The feast was celebrated every year and at its conclusion the drama of the year's next feast began, for the action lasted a whole year. A physically perfect youth was chosen for the part of Tezcatlipoca. He was dressed in rich clothing with a net cape and a mantle of flowers. His jewelry included shell earrings with turquoise plugs, and a shell necklace and pectoral. Gold bracelets and bells were fastened to his legs. He wore sandals with jaguar skin ears and a long and costly breechclout. His face was painted black and his hair was allowed to grow so that it fell to his loins. He was crowned with a headdress of eagle down and a circlet of flowers. Dressed and adorned in this fashion and attended by eight young men, he went about playing a flute and smoking a pipe. At this time, a youth representing Ixteucale was chosen to accompany him at all times.

Tezcatlipoca and Ixteucale lived together until the next feast of Toxcatl. Twenty days before the feast, Tezcatlipoca was married to four young women who represented the Maize and Earth Goddesses: Xochiquetzal,

Xilolen, Altatonan, and Huixtociuatl. Upon marriage, he discarded his ornaments, his hair was cut and dressed in the fashion of a war captain, and his crown was changed to a forked heron feather with single quetzal feathers attached. He lived with the four Earth Goddesses during the last 20 days before the feast. He spent the first 4 of the last 5 days with his four wives and attendants in rituals of dancing and singing and went to a different place each day. On the fifth and last day, all crossed a lagoon by canoe and came to a pyramid. There, Tezcatlipoca's wives left him. Breaking his flute on the first step, Tezcatlipoca climbed the pyramid alone. At the top, priests seized him, cut out his heart, and raised it as an offering to the Sun. They carried his body down the steps, cut off his head, and hung it on the skull rack.

The sacrifice of Ixteucale followed as the second act of the drama. The first scene was the raising of the Huitzilopochtli's image on a serpent bench to the pyramid top. Huitzilopochtli was the Sun of the new year on earth. His idol was placed on a platform ornamented with serpents and called a serpent bench. The idol was made of fish amaranth dough held on a frame of mesquite wood and dressed in a jacket painted with human bones and covered with a net mantle and a cape ornamented with the red feathers and a golden Sun disk. The idol was crowned with a feather headdress ornamented with a blood-colored sacrificial knife also made of feathers. Bones made of fish amaranth dough were then piled in front of the image; and a mantle painted with bones to represent Xolotl as the Skeleton God with fleshed hands and feet, materializing as the Sun in life form, was spread over the bone pile. Finally, a strip of heavy paper was unrolled in front of the idol. It was of great length and, stretched out before him, represented his breech clout. The serpent bench with the idol and the breechclout were then carried to the top of the pyramid. Those who carried the breechclout supported it with ceremonial arrows hardened in a fire for the purpose. The length of the breechclout was such that it trailed down the side of the pyramid and as the serpent bench was moved to the top, some of the men carrying the breechclout rolled it up, collecting the arrows as they did so, and fastened the roll in front of the idol of Huitzilopochtli.

On the following day, quail were sacrificed and a great fire was kindled and dedicated, and incense was cast into it in offering to Huitzilopochtli.

The quail sacrifices were followed by a dance called "the leap in the month of Toxcatl" which the women began, holding in both hands canes to which sacrificial banners were fastened. The banners were paper and were painted with black scroll designs. The women leaped as they danced. Joining the dance, the priests wore white feathers fastened to their heads and paper rosettes on their foreheads, and they smeared their lips with honey. They carried staves with a cup and ball made of black feathers fixed on the base and decorated with papers painted with black scrolls. As they danced, they struck their staves against the ground, making circles as they did so.

The circles which the dancing priests made on the ground with their staves, and their action in striking the earth in the circles signified the union of Ometecuhtli and Omecihuatl as the progenitor couple. In the symbolism of the dance, Ometecuhtli was portrayed as Tezcatlipoca, and Omecihuatl as Coatlicue. The feather ball was an emblem of Tezcatlipoca and the cup was a variant for the symbol which was the traditional sign of the Earth Goddess.

This symbolism of the feather cup and ball has its explanation in the myth of Huitzilopochtli's birth. Once, when Coatlicue was cleaning her temple, she found a feather ball. She picked it up and tucked it inside her bosom. As a result, she conceived the Sun Huitzilopochtli. When her children, the stars, discovered her pregnancy, they resolved to kill her because of her apparent adultery.

But Huitzilopochtli sprang from her womb, brandished the fire-serpent as a weapon and slew the stars. In the pantomime of the dancing priests, the circles portrayed the Earth Goddess and the staves striking the ground portrayed her impregnation.

During the dance, warriors and youths danced a serpent dance in another dance place, moving back and forth and from side to side, and meeting each other face to face. Also young women danced a popcorn dance in which they appeared with their bodies covered with feathers from their arms to their thighs, and wearing garlands of popcorn on their heads. These women were said to have "embraced Huitzilopochtli."

On the next day, all danced the serpent dance again and then Ixteucale was sacrificed. His heart was lifted up in offering to the Sun, and his head was placed on the skull rack. When Ixteucale was dead, two youths were consecrated and became the new Tezcatlipoca and Ixteucale for the ensuing year.

The youth who had been consecrated as Tezcatlipoca was regarded as a god, the common people bowed and kissed the earth in reverence to him. When we consider the symbolism, we see that he was the incarnation of the divinity of life which supported them. Ixteucale was not accorded the same honor, although, when we inquire into his identity, we find that he was the planet Venus and, so, was the immortal spirit of Tezcatlipoca's Moon nature. Torquemada describes Ixteucale as the "eyes of the Lord of the Divine House, or of the Divine Lord of the House" and states that he was Huitzilopochtli's younger brother. The eyes of the Sun were the Morning and Evening Stars, therefore, the Lord of the Divine House was clearly the Sun. The Sun and Venus were brothers in Mesoamerican mythology, consequently, since Huitzilopochtli was the Sun, Ixteucale must have been Venus.

After the death of Tezcatlipoca and before his own death, however, Ixteucale was both the planet star and the earth Sun. Torquemada says that the youth who took the part of Ixteucale was dedicated to Huitzilopochtli. When he was sacrificed, he was dressed in a net cape and other accoutrements which were associated with Huitzilopochtli, and wore a paper crown set with eagle feathers and flint knife made of red feathers. This headdress was like Huitzilopochtli's and identified him with the rising

Sun. The headdress was in disorder, presumably to indicate the struggle in which he broke free from the death forces of the underworld. His identity with the Sun was further confirmed by his raiment which was of paper and painted with black disks symbolic of the spots of the jaguar. Thus, Ixteucale represented the jaguar becoming the eagle — which is to say, Xolotl becoming Quetzalcoatl, and thus, the new year Sun.

The black paint on Tezcatlipoca's face showed that he was in the underworld. His mantle of flowers and rich adornment symbolized the life which was forming in the underworld as maize and other life-sustaining crops and which would come on earth for a year with the Sun God, Huitzilopochtli. When Tezcatlipoca discarded his adornments, dressed as a war captain, and had his hair cut, the symbolism was his death as the Moon (his hair symbolized vegetation). The action denoted that the year Sun had been created mortal; it also identified Venus as the immortal spirit of the Moon. When warriors were sacrificed, they rose as the Morning Star and, dressed as a war captain, Tezcatlipoca was the Morning Star.

At this point in the drama, the two stars of Venus have come together as two forms of the Moon spirit: Tezcatlipoca, who would become the Moon divinity as plant life, was a corporeal spirit; Ixteucale, the source of the Moon's motion and carrying the Sun, was incorporeal. While as the planet they were one spirit, they were portrayed as two to distinguish the dual nature of the Moon as life and motion, the one mortal, the other immortal. This dual nature was the essential nature of the Fifth Sun and in the action of the drama portraying its rise bringing a year of life on earth, the two roles combine as one.

The act began with the arrival of Tezcatlipoca at the foot of the pyramid, which he climbed to meet his death. During the year in which he had lived with Ixteucale, he had gone about playing a flute. The music symbolized the harmony of Ollin; when he broke the flute as he started up the steps of the pyramid, his act signified that the work of creation had been finished. His ascent signified that the Sun of the new year was rising. Although he

was the life which it would bring, he could not come into being except through death. Therefore, he was sacrificed at the top of the pyramid, which was the gateway to the earth above, and his body was carried reverently to the base of the pyramid, back to the region of death, because his body was the Moon spirit which would become the maize and the other plants which provided men's life on earth. His body had to be preserved.

His resurrection is portrayed in the drama by the raising of Huitzilopochtli's image to the top of the pyramid on the serpent bench and the dances that followed. In the drama of Toxcatl, the Sun rising as the new year was Xolotl, who appeared as Ixteucale and who would come on earth incarnate as the divinity of the Moon. When Tezcatlipoca died as the Morning Star on the summit of the pyramid and was carried to its base in the underworld, he became the life form of Ixteucale and the two were united as one.

But here, again, to come into being on earth, a god had to die. Ixteucale, who now combined the Moon life of Tezcatlipoca with his spirit being with Sun, had to die. He was sacrificed and when he rose transformed into Huitzilopochtli he was the Moon, Venus, and the Sun.

The doctrine of the Deer Cult in the theme of the drama is interesting, as is some of the symbolism of the ritual. The sacrifice of the Deer God and the descent of his spirit to a union with the Earth Mother is enacted in the death of Tezcatlipoca as the Moon and his transformation into the Morning Star symbolized by his warrior haircut and his marriage to the four Earth Goddesses. In the sacrifice rites of the Deer Cult, the union with the Earth Goddess was in the lake where the sacrifices were performed and which identified the god-spirit with the Sky Father united with the Earth Mother as the progenitor couple. The lagoon that Tezcatlipoca crossed when he went to meet his death served as the lake where the Deer Gods were killed. The canoe in which he made the crossing was a latter-day substitute for the poles on which the hunters set the heads of their sacrifices. Finally, the resurrection of Ixteucale as Huitzilopochtli was the ancient Mexican

portrayal of the Deer God returning from the god world bringing food animals for the hunters' subsistence.

The symbolism becomes clear when Venus' nature as the two fire-serpents and the nature of the Moon's death are considered. We saw in the development of the Deer Cult doctrine that the Moon's disappearance and regeneration was represented as a serpent sloughing its skin, and that the Moon had an animal form as a serpent. In the drama of Toxcatl, when Tezcatlipoca died, he became the Morning Star fire-serpent and in their two roles he and Ixteucale became one.

As for the symbolism, the heron-and-quetzal-feather crown which Tezcatlipoca wore when he died symbolized his resurrection as the lunar half of the Sun. The association of the heron with the ascension of the Sun bringing life on earth came from its nature as a fish-eating bird of the marshes and shore. Herons feed where alligators and other amphibians live, and these animals are representatives of the earth monster which rose as the earth from the universal sea in the myth of creation. In the creation, fish were the embryo bodies of the Sun; herons, eating fish in the marshes and along the shores, which were themselves symbolic of the earth rising out of the water during the act of creation, came to represent the transformation of the fish as the Sun's earth body form to a bird as its sky body form.

In the drama of Toxcatl, the symbolism of the serpent and his transformation into the Sun of the new year on earth is implicit in the nature of Ixteucale as Venus and is explicit in the raising of the serpent bench and the serpent dance, which was danced twice.

One action in Toxcatl shows the doctrine of the Divine King. The supreme Aztec chief was believed to be an incarnation of the Sun God, Huitzilopochtli. At the end of each year it was believed that Huitzilopochtli died and his divinity left the person of the ruler. The god's death occurred at the end of 360 days of each year and, during the remaining 5 days, the Sun was believed to be dead; at the end of 5 days, the Sun revived and rose out of the underworld. These 5 days were the last days before Tezcatlipoca's death, and during that length of time, the Aztec ruler remained in his palace in symbolism of the Sun's death. When the new year of Toxcatl began, the ruler resumed his place among the people.

The 5-day seclusion of the ruler also shows a doctrine of time as divine. The Aztecs called time the Sun of Movement and rituals of Toxcatl enacted the joint movement of the Sun and Moon as a year-cycle of time. In the year-long drama of the Feast, Tezcatlipoca was the Moon and, because as the Moon he constituted the maize and other life forms which were the staples of the peoples lives, he was especially reverenced. Ixteucale was the planet Venus, the force which gave the Sun its motion, and so, in his role, he was also the Sun. As the planet, he was the mortal or corporeal spirit of the Moon. He was Tezcatlipoca's companion, and so together they constituted a solar Moon.

They were not the only actors. Tezcatlipoca also had eight other companions. Four were warriors and four were slaves. These eight were not identified in the description of the feast, but if we consider their number and relation to Tezcatlipoca, we will see that they represented stages in the cyclical motion of the Moon. We will find later in our study that there were nine stages in the cycle. The first was that in which the Moon and its motion were generated by the Fire God. In the next four, the Moon rose and became full; in the last four, it waned and vanished. The cycle then repeated and created the months of the year. The nine stages were represented by nine gods known as the Lords of the Night who were lords of the succession of days in the 360-day year. The god of the first stage was the Fire God, Xiutecuhtli.

Tezcatlipoca and Ixteucale together represented the Fire God. This is clear because Ixteucale with the Sun was fire and motion, and Tezcatlipoca as the Moon was the substance of life. The two were chosen together, remained together throughout the year, and were one in their deaths when they rose together as the two Suns. The four warriors represented the life stages of the cycle because, as warriors, they were identified with the Morning Star and, hence, the ascension of the Moon; the four slaves represented the waning stages of the Moon because they were sacrificed in the ceremonies which ended and began the year. Furthermore, as captives, each slave was an alter ego of his warrior captor. This identity becomes apparent in the Feast of Tlacaxipeualiztli, which will be described in Chapter 5, and it was a doctrine of hunters which held that when a man is killed in combat with a bear, his soul goes into the bear and the two thus become one.

CHAPTER 4

Ochpaniztli
AZTEC PERIOD

ca. 1350 through 1520 A.D.

The drama of Ochpaniztli is another drama of the underworld which portrays the Mesoamerican doctrine of a yearly creation of the Sun. The feast of Ochpaniztli, which means "The Sweeping of the Way," was celebrated in the eleventh month, which corresponded to the time from the end of our month of August through September 19. The Ochpaniztli was a new year celebration; but since it was held at the end of summer, it could not have been the new year on earth, since the year had begun some 10 months earlier — there were 18 months in the Nahuatlan calendar. The year being celebrated was in the underworld and the scenes of the drama were laid first in the region of death and then in the region of life.

The Aztec feast opened with a ritual dance, after which there was a mock battle between women. The women were divided into two groups: one, which included the old medicine women, represented the Earth Mother, and the other represented the young Moon and Maize Goddess. The Earth Mother group chased the young goddess group and pelted it with flowers, balls of Spanish moss, and cactus leaves. This mock battle lasted 4 days and seems to have symbolized the cyclical transformation of the young Moon and the Maize Goddess into her Earth Mother form.

When the battle was concluded, a young woman who took the part of Toci joined the old medicine women. Toci was one of the names of the Death Goddess and Earth Mother who was also the old Moon Goddess. Moctezuma, as the Aztec ruler, was regarded as the Sun's earthly form. The old women told Toci that Moctezuma would sleep with her, but at midnight they took her to a pyramid temple where one priest held her addorsed on his back while another cut off her head. Then they flayed her and cut a piece of skin from her thigh; after which, a very strong priest dressed himself in her skin.

Toci died as the Moon. The Moon was Ometeotl moving as the Fifth Sun in a cycle of creation and in that form his sex was dual and he combined the life-giving power of the Sun and the moving force of Venus in his person. When the priest put on Toci's skin, he became Toci and the reviving Moon, and in her skin he was primarily the goddess.

The skin cut from Toci's thigh was made into a mask and given to a warrior who impersonated Centeotl, to wear. Centeotl was the Maize God and son of Toci. The thigh was a symbol for reproduction and the mask was made from Toci's thigh to symbolize the birth of Centeotl.

A procession of chiefs and nobles in war array led the priest, whom we will now call Toci, to the pyramid of Huitzilopochtli where Centeotl was waiting. As the procession advanced, the men alternately ran and stopped and wheeled. They clashed their shields together, waved a straw broom which had been soaked in blood, and chased all who happened to be along the way. In the death and life symbolism of the ritual, the road to the pyramid of Huitzilopochtli was the underworld road from death to the beginning of life. The warriors whirling backwards and forwards pantomimed death and new life. The bloody broom symbolized new life, for the broom was straw which symbolized dead vegetation and the blood was the medium through which life was transmitted through death to Centeotl as the new crop cycle. The fighting on the way to the pyramid was called "fighting with grass" and symbolized the struggle of the forces of creation against the forces of death and nonexistence. Toci and her vanguard of chiefs were opening the way through the roadblock of death to return to life.

When they reached the temple, Toci faced the pyramid and raised and spread her arms and spread her legs. Then she turned and stood beside

Centeotl who put on a "peaked cap which was curved back and serrated." In the cap, Centeotl became Itztlacoliuhqui, which means "Curved Obsidian Knife," whose form as a Death God was frost and dead maize. This transformation signifies the death of vegetation in the fall when the Ochpaniztli was celebrated. Then Toci and her attendants returned to the temple. They were accompanied by Itztlacoliuhqui who wore the mask fashioned from Toci's thigh.

The next act of the drama began in the morning when the Sun had risen, and Toci and Centeotl had returned to the temple. Toci climbed to the top of the pyramid where a group of nobles were waiting. The nobles pasted an eagle crown on her head, painted her face, dressed her in a shirt decorated with an eagle design and a skirt, and performed other ceremonies. Afterwards, she was further attired with rich vestments and a paper crown. The feathers and eagle shirt identified her with the Sun. The rich vestments and the crown identified her with the riches of the earth: maize and vegetation.

In her new array, Toci sacrificed four captives. Then she left with a number of priests for Huitzilopochtli's temple. Toci's old medicine women and some old priests joined this group. As they moved along, the old priests beat on a horizontal drum on which a water gourd was hung. The water gourd probably symbolized the flood of creation.

Toci's route led past the skull rack and when her party reached it, Centeotl, wearing Toci's thigh mask, was waiting with a band of warriors. The party stopped and Toci's drum was brought to her. She tramped on it and Centeotl departed with his warriors to climb a peak of one of the mountains which rim the Valley of Mexico, to set the mask on the summit. The peak was on land belonging to an enemy tribe and enemy warriors were waiting when they reached the top.

A fight ensued in which men on both sides were killed. Then Centeotl and his Aztec warriors fastened the mask to a wooden frame and returned to Tenochtitlan. The mask symbolized the dead maize in the fields and

Centeotl, returned to Tenochtitlan, was the maize spirit which would come to life.

Centeotl and his warriors began their ascent of the mountain at the skull rack because it was the point at which the spirits of men, sacrificed as the Sun, began their resurrections as spirits of the Morning Star. In the symbolism of the drama, the summit of the mountain was the life region of the underworld. Centeotl's ascent was the Sun rising out of the region of death and nonexistence, and coming into existence as a summer of prelife before rising as a new year on earth. The enemy which Centeotl encountered was the host of death which sought to hold him bound in death by preventing him from leaving his mask on the mountain top.

Centeotl led his warriors up the mountain called Ixtacihuatl, which rises to a height of nearly 17,000 feet and is southwest of ancient Tenochtitlan. As this was the direction point at which creation began in the Nahuatlan religion, the peak on Ixtacihuatl where Centeotl engaged the enemy must have been regarded as sacred. The way to the ancient center of Cholula passed over the flank of Ixtacihuatl and we can guess the Cholulans, with whom the Aztecs were often at war, provided the force which met Centeotl.

The battle was clearly arranged as a rite in the Flowering War. The battle involved no military objectives for either side and was followed by a ceremony in Tenochtitlan in which chiefs and warriors were enlisted in anticipation of arranging a return engagement. In the ceremony, Moctezuma sat on a throne called an eagle mat which had a seat made of the skin and feathers of an eagle, and a back made of jaguar skin.

From this throne, he bestowed gifts and honors upon the chiefs and warriors which bound them to fight when the time came. The nature of the anticipated conflict is shown by laments of the women who wailed and cried, "These are our beloved sons whom we see here; if, in five or ten days, word comes — [we are] in flood and fire [that is, at war] — is it possible that they will return again? Will they find their way back? Verily they will be gone forever!"

Ochpaniztli

After the Flowering War ceremonies, the action returned to Huitzilopochtli's temple. Priests of Chicomecoatl, the Maize Goddess 7-Serpent, who was an aspect of Toci, climbed the pyramid. The priests wore the skins of captives who had been sacrificed and flayed during the ceremonies, or they served as proxies for the men who wore the skins. By putting on the skins of dead warriors, the priests became the beings of the warriors. Warriors were incarnations of the Venus Morning Star with the Sun and as such we may refer to warriors as Suns. The priests were assisted by priestesses whose arms and legs were pasted with feathers and who had strands of seven maize ears tied to their backs. The priests threw grains of maize which were avidly gathered by the people who were waiting below. The action of the priests and the strands of the seven maize ears which the priestesses wore signified the harvest of the underworld summer which would come with the Sun of the new year when it rose on earth.

When the seed had been distributed, chalk and white feathers were brought down from the pyramid top and placed at the base. A number of chiefs who had been waiting at a distance raced forward. The first to arrive threw feathers in the air and those who followed gathered what they could and did the same. In the rituals of the Flowering War, the captor of a sacrificed victim was called the white earth — the feather — because he was whitened with chalk and decked with feathers. Since both captors and victims were Suns, the actions symbolize sending the Sun upwards on its return through the underworld to the sky. When the chiefs had thrown the feathers into the air, they ran down the pyramid and continued running for some distance.

Moctezuma ran with them and it was said that "sometimes he quickly entered [his] treasure room, sometimes he quickly entered [the district of] Tecanman." This run symbolized the beginning of the Sun's summer course through the underworld. Moctezuma was the Sun; his treasure room was his aviary; and Tecanman was the temple of Chantico, the Fire Goddess. Thus, when Moctezuma entered his treasure room, the Sun entered the sky of the underworld; when Moctezuma entered Tecanman, the Sun entered the underworld earth. Moctezuma represented the Sun moving in its diurnal course in the process of creation in the underworld. Toci followed, dropping behind with the priests who accompanied her. When she came to a place called Tocititlan (presumably her temple), she took off the skin of the slain Toci, stretched it flat, and left it on a wooden frame with the "head" looking out. Then she departed, leaving her other adornments.

The first part of the drama portrays the death region of the underworld with the pyramid on which Toci died on one side of the stage and Huitzilopochtli's temple pyramid on the other side, with the skull rack in the center.* The flower battle between the women signified the spontaneous formation of the Moon in the person of Toci. To come into existence, Toci had to die; her creation as life began with her sacrifice and resurrection in the priest as Toci. The procession which the resurrected Toci led to the temple of Huitzilopochtli was an abstract portrayal of the process of life regenerating in death. The procession ended at the point of beginning life when Toci raised her arms to hail the new year Sun before the temple. This point was also the point at which Centeotl stood wearing the mask from Toci's thigh and put on his hat which he wore in the guise of Itztlacoliuhqui. It was the guise in which he would begin his journey to life on the peak of Ixtacihuatl.

From there the action returned to the first pyramid where Toci appeared on top, dressed as the rising Sun, and sacrificed four warriors to signify the creation of its annual course. The action then moved to the skull rack which was the place where the Sun began its journey of life creation in the underworld. Toci's son, in his Itztlacoliuhqui hat and wearing the mask from her thigh, took the part of the Sun in the course of its journey. In this

*This, of course, is not necessarily the actual arrangement since the stage was the center of Tenochtitlan and the precise location of the temples in their relation to the skull rack is not known.

part of the drama, the scene changed to the life region of the underworld with the peak of Ixtacihuatl on one side of the stage and the temple of Huitzilopochtli on the other, and with the martial field where the ceremonies of the Flowering War were held in the center.

In the composition of the drama, the action in the underworld life region, like the action in the underworld death region, was divided into three parts. Where the warriors "fighting with grass" in their procession portrayed the creation of life in death, the Flowering War ceremonies (i.e., rites of the doctrine of Ollin) portrayed the maintenance of life through death. The last scene in the drama portrayed the harvest from the maize crop which Centeotl created on the mountaintop, and the ascension of the Sun as the means of its becoming the earth's new crop of maize. Because of Ochpaniztli's date, this would not be until the following summer.

Thus, Ochpaniztli dramatized the doctrine of the underworld, with its regions of death and creation and of life, in which life formed as a Sun which rose each year bringing a new year of life on earth. The process of creation was the movement of the Moon carrying the Sun, and the symbol of creation was a serpent renewing its life by casting its dead skin. The serpent was depicted in the drama by the priest in Toci's flayed skin and Centeotl's mask, and by the priests of Chicomecoatl, the goddess 7-Serpent, in the flayed skins of warriors.

If we look at this serpent image in the light of Toxcatl, we can understand the meaning of the concluding scene. In Toxcatl, Tezcatlipoca (the Moon) was transformed into the Morning Star when he was sacrificed on the pyramid and so became one with Ixteucale. When Toci took off the skin of the slain Toci, he was like Tezcatlipoca leaving his wives behind; when he went to die and rise as the Morning Star, and Toci's act of leaving the skin stretched on the rack in such a fashion that it looked out — forward in the direction in which he had been following behind Moctezuma — symbolized his transformation into the Morning Star in the person of Moctezuma as the Sun which would bring new life on earth.

CHAPTER 5

Tlacaxipeualiztli
AZTEC PERIOD

ca. 1350 through 1520 A.D.

There is one other drama which we should consider because the rituals portrayed the ascension of the Sun created in the underworld, bringing the maize crop of the new year. This was the Feast of Tlacaxipeualiztli. As it was described by the early Spaniards, the feast was held when spring first comes to the Valley of Mexico and flowers burst from the soil. This was the second month of the Aztec calendar* which fell on our calendar during the first weeks of March. The symbolism was spectacular but gruesome.

The mythology of the underworld — picturing the different forms of Xolotl traversing the underworld and being created into a new Sun as the cycle of vegetation — explains the meaning of the sacrifice which was the first act of the drama. The sacrifice took the form of a combat between five jaguar-and-eagle knights and a captive. First, the knights dedicated their captive to the Sun. Then a number of men, impersonating gods, took their places as actors in the drama. The ritual of the sacrifice symbolized Xolotl as a dog bringing the Sun into the region of death, Xolotl's own sacrifice in the "voyage of the planet Venus across the underworld," and his revival as Quetzalcoatl. In the drama, Xipe was identical with both Xolotl and Quetzalcoatl.

For the main action, there was a large circular stone with a rope attached to its center. A priest called "Old Wolf" tied the captive to the stone by fastening a rope around his waist. Four of the knights, alternately masked

*No correction was made for the leap year, consequently, the months gradually moved forward in the year.

as jaguars and eagles, circled him and slashed him with pointed weapons while he defended himself with a blunt club and blunt missiles. Finally, after the first four had wounded and weakened the captive, a fifth knight, masked as a jaguar and impersonating Opochtli, an aspect of Huitzilopochtli, stepped up and finished the fight by wounding the captive in the arm and knocking him out. A priest then cut out the captive's heart and offered it to the Sun, and Old Wolf held up the rope which had bound him to the stone, wept, howled, and dedicated it to the four directions.

The circular stone represented the death region of the underworld where the new year Sun was held bound in the underworld until it was released through sacrifice. The Old Wolf represented the dog Xolotl. The captive whom Old Wolf tied to the stone was the god who had been created as the new year Sun. In the symbolism of the drama, he was Xipe who had descended as Xolotl from the life region of the underworld with the newly created yearly crop of maize. The four knights represented the four Tezcatlipoca Suns of the creation myth. The fifth knight, who was masked as a jaguar, represented the jaguar Xolotl as the underworld Sun who would become Quetzalcoatl as the reincarnation of the captive bound to the stone. When the captive was sacrificed, he revived in the person of the fifth knight. His dead body was flayed and his captor's proxy put on the skin. Thus, both the captor and his proxy became incarnations of the sacrificed warrior, Xolotl-Xipe. When the proxy took off the skin of the dead warrior, the fifth knight, the captor, and his proxy all became incarnations of the living Xipe as Quetzalcoatl.

One more act was needed before the sacrificed captives could join the Sun and the transformations of the jaguar knight and the captor would be complete. The complete enactment of the original creation was believed necessary to the fullness of life of the new cycle of vegetation which Xipe brought when he rose on earth. In the creation myth, all the gods were sacrificed in order to put the Sun in motion. In the rituals of the Tlacaxipeualiztli, the sacrifice was enacted in the dance of the severed

heads. When it was time for the dance, many captives had been sacrificed and decapitated. Each of the god impersonators took one of the heads and all danced, each holding the head which he had taken. Dancing signified coming to life and, holding the severed heads, the dancers became Suns in resurrection.

The rope which bound the captive as a Sun to the death region of the underworld was also the means of imparting life. When the warrior died, the maize spirit of Xolotl-Xipe lodged in the rope. When Old Wolf raised the rope and dedicated it to the four directions, the spirit was released to become incarnate in the new year Sun. When Old Wolf wept and howled, he was acting as a priest placating the spirit of the god on behalf of the people by showing remorse for having killed him.

The drama lasted throughout the month; the stage was the public part of Tenochtitlan; and the actors included certain numbers of the people and others who attended the feast or chanced to become involved in the action. Among them were men who had skin diseases. Captive warriors, who were sacrificed, were flayed and these men put on their skins and wore them for the duration of the feast. In the skins of the dead warriors, they were beings of Xipe-Totec and were called *xipeme* and *tototecti.* They did not bathe, because water symbolized resurrection and return to life and the scene was the underworld death region. When they finally took off the dead skins, they covered themselves with cornmeal and scrubbed themselves with it. The symbolism is clear: the xipeme and tototecti, by putting on the skins of the warriors, became beings of the warriors who were Suns. When they took off the skins and covered themselves with cornmeal, they were the Sun renewing its maize body by casting off its dead skin.

In the creation myth, when Ehecatl sacrificed all the gods, Xolotl turned himself into different forms of his being as vegetation and Ehecatl found him as a double-maize stalk. The xipeme and the tototecti were, in effect, constituted as double-maize stalks. In their borrowed warrior skins when they did not bathe, they were the Xolotl Maize-stalk God of the underworld; in their skins covered with cornmeal, they were the Quetzalcoatl maize stalk of the rising Sun. But they were also men covered with pustules from their skin diseases and thus, living counterparts of the scabby Nanauatzin who, in the creation myth, died and rose from death as the Sun and who was, in reality, the fire-serpent Venus-Xolotl as the Evening Star sloughing its skin and rising as the Morning Star Quetzalcoatl.

In Nahuatlan theology, captors and captives were equally Suns. In death, they were called "eagle men" and the sacrifice was called "the sending upward of the eagle man." In their resurrection, they became one with the Morning Star and the Sun as it rose in the sky. The Morning Star was Quetzalcoatl who, in that form and as a warrior, was called Tlahuizcalpantecuhtli. In that form, he was also represented as a butterfly. The symbolism was resurrection from death and in this symbolism, Xolotl was sometimes represented as a larva which enters an apparent death stage as a chrysallis from which it emerges transformed into a butterfly. When warriors died and rose as beings of the Morning Star, they were imagined as butterflies.

The identification of the warriors with the Sun explains the ritual of sacrifice. As the women wailed in the Flowering War ceremonies in Ochpaniztli, the men were in "Flood and Fire" and, so, in the midst of creation of the Sun as a new cycle of vegetation. Accordingly, the captives were ritually bathed in a baptismal rite representing the flood. In the sacrifice, their backs were arched over the sacrificial stone (representing the death region of the underworld?) while the sacrificers cut out their hearts and then, as Sahagun described it, "They lifted them up to the Sun, the turquoise prince, the soaring eagle. They offered it to him; they nourished him with it." The captives' hearts merged into the Morning Star and, as nourishment, augmented its motion. Their bodies rose to become the new spirit bodies of the Sun. The doctrine was symbolized by a glyph denoting a curving band of water. Streams of water spring from the side, and fire

issues from the end [**Figure 3**]. The symbol was a sign of resurrection, like the Christian sign of the cross.

The bodies of the captives were maize incarnations of the Sun and were of the substance of the earth, so the sacrifices returned them to the earth by

Figure 3. Flood and Fire creation symbol issuing from death skull with smoking mirror sign of Tezcatlipoca on the temple [after Covarrubias, *Indian Art of Mexico and Central America*, Plate LXI].

rolling them off the pyramid where they were sacrificed. At the bottom of the pyramid, each captor took up the body of his captive. The captive's flesh was cooked in a stew of dried maize and eaten as a communion meal with the captor's kinsmen. The captor did not, however, partake of the cannibal meal because he held himself to be the father of his victim. This relationship was established before the sacrifice when he took a lock of his captive's hair at a midnight ceremony before the Fire God's fire.

The sacrifices of the Tlacaxipeualiztli adhered to the sacrifice doctrine of the ancient hunters who killed their Bear and Deer Gods in the belief that the animal gods would return bringing new food animals or increase in the herds. The elaboration of the rites into a religious drama obscures the simpler forms of the hunter rituals which crop out in the communion meal of the sacrificed warriors and in a ritual performed at the conclusion of the feast. In this ritual, the captors fastened masks of the slain captives to the captives' thigh bones and hung them on poles outside their houses. They called these the "poles of the flaying of men" and the trophies which they hung on them were called the "god captives." The setting up of the poles on which the mask and the thigh bone of the god captive were hung echoes the ritual of the Deer Cult sacrifice in which pole altars were the pathway by which the animal gods made their way into the underworld and returned with new life.

In the rituals and sacrifices, the warriors were incarnations of Xipe or Xolotl-Quetzalcoatl. Their nature and his is described in the Song of Xipe which follows:

> O Iouallauan, why dost thou mask thyself?
> Put on thy disguise. Don thy golden cape.
> My god, thy precious water hath come down
> from Coapan. It hath made the cypress a quetzal.
> The fire-serpent hath been made a quetzal-serpent.
>
> Want hath gone from me. Mayhap I shall
> die and perish — I, the tender maize.

Tlacaxipeualiztli

Like a precious green stone is my heart;
(yet) I shall see gold in it. I shall be content
if first I mature. The war chief is born.
My god, (give me) in part plenteous tender maize.
My worshiper looketh toward the mountain.
I shall be content if first I ripen.
The warrior chief is born.

The sense and most of the meaning of the song is clear, but we have to interpret the probable meaning of certain phrases. The warrior is addressing Xipe who is called Iouallauan. The mask should be a jaguar mask such as that worn by the fifth knight in the gladiator combat and, as such, represents his form as Xolotl in the underworld. The disguise is probably the maize plant which became Xolotl-Xipe's embodiment as vegetation. The golden cape would be the Sun which, as the quetzal serpent (Quetzalcoatl) he would carry through the sky; precious water would be the flood of creation; the cypress is the symbol of the tree life in the underworld region of death; and the quetzal is the Sun's life form as maize. The fire-serpent is Xipe as Xolotl and the quetzal-serpent is Xipe as Quetzalcoatl.

In the last part of the song, the warrior identifies himself with Xipe as maize. The precious green stone is jade which is the underworld form of maize. Thus, the warrior sees himself as the underworld Sun Xolotl whose heart is the planet Venus. The gold which the warrior will see in his heart is his identification with the Sun through his resurrection as the Morning Star, after his death. The mountain is the point at which Xolotl becomes Quetzalcoatl; that is, where Xipe rises as the new year Sun. The warrior chief is Xipe himself as the Morning Star Quetzalcoatl.

In the song, therefore, the warrior hails Xipe as the Sun who brings maize to the earth. He then resigns himself to death as the maize Sun, either in the battlefield of the Flowering War or by sacrifice. There was glory in sacrificial death but the warrior captor received great honor and kept his life, so it was obviously more desirable to return from the war with a captive

than to be killed or taken prisoner. Accordingly, the warrior looks toward the mountain as his salvation in death because of his identity with Xipe, but he wants Xipe to know that he would be glad to live the fullness of life.

The story of the birth of Huitzilopochtli, whom the Aztecs identified with Quetzalcoatl, helps to explain the warrior nature of Xipe. Huitzilopochtli was the son of the Earth Goddess Coatlicue. He sprang from her womb brandishing the fire-serpent and vanquished the Moon and stars. The Moon and stars were the Fifth Sun moving in the underworld in the work of creating a new Sun to be a new year of life on earth. They were prenatal forms of Huitzilopochtli, but could only come into being as a new year of life through death. The slaying of the Moon and stars was the Fifth Sun's self-sacrifice and resurrection as life on earth. The killing is comparable to the end of the gladiator combat in which the fifth knight killed the captive bound to the round stone in the underworld, and the Old Wolf howled and threw the rope which bound the captive to the four winds.

Xipe personified the symbolism of the serpent bringing the Sun out of the underworld with a new year of life on earth. His image was formed as a man wearing the flayed skin of another who dies in sacrifice. It was the image of a serpent with its scaly dead skin still clinging to it, but the sloughing of the skin and renewal of life is implicit in the image. Thus Xipe was represented wearing a crown of flowers and his image is explicitly described in the Song of Xipe as "the fire-serpent hath been made a quetzal-serpent."

CHAPTER 6

The Ceremonies of the Calendar Round
AZTEC PERIOD

ca. 1350 through 1520 A.D.

In Nahuatlan theology, the underworld process of creating Suns which rose each year bringing new life on earth, was a 52-year cycle which has been called a Calendar Round. When a Calendar Round ended, there was no certainty that a new one would begin. Accordingly, the end of the Calendar Round was a time of foreboding and fear. In order to allay the fears of the people, when the end of a Calendar Round was approaching, the priests watched for a sign that a new one would follow and, when the sign appeared, performed a special sacrifice to ensure its continuance. Their ceremony for the sacrifice was called the New Fire Ceremony and was associated with other rites in which the people prepared for the new Calendar Round. These were the Binding of the Years and the Fifty-Two-Year Atonement.

The New Fire Ceremony was held when the constellation of the Pleiades was due to cross the meridian at midnight. If the constellation made the crossing, it was the Fire God's sign that the Calendar Round would begin again. In the dramas of the feasts which have been described, we saw that the life which each new year Sun brought on earth was created by the Moon, moving through the four quarters of the underworld with the Venus serpent and the Sun. In Toxcatl, we saw that the Venus serpent was actually an instrumental part of the Moon by which it kept the Sun in motion in uniformity with its own motion. The Moon was Tezcatlipoca and when the Pleiades gave the signal that a new Calendar Round would begin, the doctrine of Ollin required that an earthly god form of Tezcatlipoca had to be

sacrificed. The sacrifice was the requisite feature of the New Fire Ceremony.

As the New Fire Ceremony was celebrated by the Aztecs, all fires were put out on the night of the anticipated sign. A procession of fire priests left Tenochtitlan and, moving through the darkness, made its way to a hill in the center of the valley. The procession climbed the hill and stopped. On the summit, the priests waited and watched the stars wheel imperceptibly overhead. All around the valley, people watched the hilltop. The sign was the transit of the Pleiades across the meridian at midnight and when they crossed, the fire priests sacrificed a man whose mother had carried him in her womb when the Calendar Round had begun. Then they kindled a fire in the dead man's breast and with its flame lit a bonfire on the hilltop. The people watching in the valley saw the blaze and, rejoicing, went back to their homes. Then they made new fires on their hearths, kindling them from brands which runners took from the bonfire and carried everywhere through the valley.

The *Codex Borbonicus* pictures the Binding of the Years as a rite of the New Fire Ceremony. Bundles of reeds representing the years of the Calendar Round were sacrificed as effigies of the Sun. The codex pictures 4-year bundles representing the four 13-year quarters being cast into a fire by four priests.

At the time of the Spanish conquest, the Pleiades were on the meridian at midnight in November. Consequently, the beginning of the Calendar Round then did not coincide with the beginning of the calendar year, which was the first day of Atlcoualco which fell toward the middle of February on our calendar.* The annual calendar, however, did not allow for leap year, while the Pleiades marks the length of the year precisely. Hence the calendar gradually moved ahead of the Pleiades and the calendrical new year and the New Fire Ceremony fell at different times.

*Scholars are not in agreement as to which month was the first, nor on the precise date on which it began.

The Ceremonies of the Calendar Round

The ceremony of the Fifty-Two-Year Atonement was held in order to enable the people to purge their old mortality and prepare themselves for the sacredness of the returning Calendar Round. It was held after the close of Izcalli, the last month of the calendar and, therefore, related to the beginning of the new Calendar Round. By our calendar, it was the period between January 18 and February 6. Between Izcalli and the first month of the new year were five Nemontemi days, as they were called. These were not counted as true days and were thought of as the period during which the Sun rose bringing the new year cycle of vegetation.

When Izcalli ended and the Nemontemi days began, the people fasted and made offerings before their idols. They let the fires die on their hearths and renewed the stones on which they built them. They destroyed the pestles with which they ground their corn and made new ones. They replaced their ceremonial belongings and put on new clothes. Even the ceremonial centers were renewed. New idols were set up in the temples and new pyramids were built to cover and enlarge the old. Finally, when the Nemontemi days were over and the noon of the new day had come, the priests killed their sacrifices. According to the chronicler Sahagun, "Then all rejoiced and there was feasting. Then once again, fires were newly laid and placed."

CHAPTER 7

The Tepantitla Tlaloc
CLASSIC PERIOD

300 through 700 A.D.

There is a fresco picturing the lord of the universe in the underworld, painted on a wall of the remains of the palace of Tepantitla at Teotihuacan, an ancient city situated north of the Valley of Mexico, a few miles from modern Mexico City, the Aztec Tenochtitlan. The painting is from an earlier period known as the Classic to distinguish it from the cultures of the Postclassic Period which included the Nahuatlan. The Classic Period began in Teotihuacan a century of so before the beginning of the Christian era, and ended generally in the tenth to the eleventh centuries. But Teotihuacan, which was the primary cultural center of Mexico during the Classic Period, was destroyed by fire about 750 A.D.

Nahuatlan culture was a continuation of Teotihuacan culture with stylistic and sectarian changes. As he is represented at Teotihuacan, the lord of the universe has been identified with Tlaloc, although Pasztory has distinguished him from the typical Rain God Tlaloc; Furst identifies the central figure of the fresco as Tlaloc's sister-spouse Chalchiuhlicue.* But the Rain God was an aspect of Tlaloc as the Supreme Being of the universe and we may properly refer to the god pictured in the Tepantitla fresco by the name Tlaloc, as the Classic Teotihuacan equivalent of Ometeotl.

The painting portrays Tlaloc's underworld, Tlalocan, which is composed in two parts arranged one above the other. The scene in the lower part is the death region. Human and animal forms appear

*Pasztory, *The Iconography of the Teotihuacan Tlaloc*; Furst, "The Tepantitla Mural," pp. 193 *ff* in *Mesoamerican Archaeology, New Approaches.*

haphazardly without any particular relation to each other. Some of the humans are dancing and singing or otherwise disporting themselves amidst butterflies and flowering plants.

A mountain dominates the scene. Tlaloc was worshipped by the Aztecs at their Feast of Atemoztli as a mountain, and was pictured in the codices with all the insignia of Tepeyolotl, the Jaguar God known as "Heart of the Mountain." Therefore, we recognize the mountain as Tlaloc in the aspect of the lord of the underworld.

A river — flowing from the summit of the mountain — branches into two streams, one flowing into a lake and the other into a sea. There are plants growing on the banks of the river and human figures appear swimming in the stream. The symbolism of the branching river is not evident in the picture. Tlaloc was a god of waters and fire and, as the lord of the underworld, he was a god of death and a creator of life. Water was associated with life; but the scene is in the land of death, so the water flowing down the mountain must represent life, or its spirit being, returning to earth in death. This meaning brings the symbolism of the two branches into focus.

The sea, into which one of the branches flows, is the creation flood of Chalchiuhlicue which appears in the upper half of the painting. In the doctrine of sacrifice, life returned to the living world through death. The river branch flowing into the sea, therefore, was life returning to a new existence and flowing from the power to creation of Chalchiuhlicue and Tlaloc as the Creator-Maker. The branch to the sea was a river of life.

The other branch flowing into the lake was a river of death. This death symbolism comports with the doctrine of the earth as the death-and-life-mother goddess in one, a doctrine which was so fundamental in pre-Columbian Mexican religion that it surely was part of the Classic forms of Teotihuacan. According to this doctrine, the Creator-Maker was also the progenitor couple and, consequently, the lake would represent their procreative union in which the goddess took part in her life aspect and

immediately reverted to her death aspect. In her reversion, she brought forth new life which flowed in the stream of the life river.

When we now consider Tlalocan with the mountain and the river, we see that it was the god world part of the underworld where new life was formed. Souls specially chosen by Tlaloc went to Tlalocan. The categories of chosen souls must have included Teotihuacan warriors because Tlaloc appeared as a warrior in the wall paintings of that city. The butterflies in the picture of Tlalocan were symbols of the Morning Star. In death, warriors arose in resurrection as spirit forms of the Morning Star and returned to earth as butterflies. In the painting, some of the figures of men are catching butterflies, an act symbolizing their transformation into that form. Besides warriors, men who died in sacrifice returned to the earth as maize and other plants and some of the figures hold branches of vegetation as though they were being reincarnated for their return to life in that form. Other figures are ball players; ball players (like warriors) were sacrificed and returned to life as beings of the Sun, presumably in the form of butterflies.

In the upper part of the fresco [**Figure 4**], Tlaloc is pictured on the waves of a boundless flood. This is the underworld region of life. Tlaloc wears a mask representing the Fire God and a huge feather headdress with a bird head in the center. His arms are extended outward to the side and drops of water fall from shells in his hands. A divine attendant stands on each side facing Tlaloc with arms held out toward the god. Each holds an object that looks like a stylized butterfly in one hand, while a stream of water falls downward and a volute curves upward and outward from the other. Shells spray from the streams of water and in the stream flowing from the hand of the attendant on the left, there are jade symbols which represent maize and the earth's abundance as Tlaloc's gift to man. The other stream which flows from the hand of the attendant on the right, is filled with shells symbolizing the fertility of Tlaloc as the Sun. The volutes which curve upward at the source of the streams gushing from the hand of each attendant divinity, spray lotus blossoms or other flowers and they, too,

symbolize the abundance of Tlaloc's power of life creation; and the remnant of the fresco repeats the symbols of the earth's abundance as though to venerate Tlaloc as the creator god. The two attendants are aspects of Tlaloc at the Fifth Sun. They represent the life created in the underworld which will come into being as the new year Sun on earth.

The hands of the two attendants are emphasized as the sources of the earth's abundance and fertility. In Mesoamerican theology, the maize plant was divine; when it died and returned to earth it was transformed into jade. The hand symbolized sacrifice and the jade symbols in the stream flowing from the hand of the attendant on the left represent the new maize which the returning Sun will bring on earth. This sign of sacrifice in relation to the figures in resurrection on the Tlalocan mountain below, identify the left attendant as the Morning Star rising with the Sun.

Figure 4. Tlaloc [upper panel], Palace of Tepantitla, Teotihuacan.

The Tepantitla Tlaloc

The shells in the stream flowing from the hand of the attendant on the right symbolize fertility and birth and, hence, the flood crops which the fields will bear and which were associated with the Moon. In Toxcatl, the food crops were symbolized by the jewels and adornment which Tezcatlipoca wore. The attendant on the right, therefore, represents the divinity of the Moon which will come with the Sun as a year of life on earth. The left one, who is the Morning Star, is the Moon spirit which, in Toxcatl, appeared when Tezcatlipoca died as the Moon. He will combine with the one on the right and the two will rise as the new year Sun on earth, as Tezcatlipoca and Ixteucale combined and rose on earth as Huitzilopochtli.

Kubler identifies the bird head in the center of Tlaloc's headdress as an owl. The owl is a bird of the night sky which was associated with the underworld of creation and marked Tlaloc as the Creator-Maker god of the underworld. Tlaloc, thus, was like Ometeotl as the progenitor couple, Ometecuhtli and Omecihuatl. This dual sex role appears in his position on the waves, which places him in union with his Earth Goddess spouse, Chalchiuhlicue; and the dress of the figure itself seems to represent him as a female.

A border framing the picture of Tlalocan separates the upper and lower panels. It is composed of two entwined serpents with a mask of Tlaloc at the center and Tlaloc heads in the coils. They are the fire-serpents which gave the Sun its motion. One has earth-monster-shaped markings on its body; these markings show it to be the serpent which moves the Sun through the underworld. The other is marked with stars which, according to Séjourné, symbolize water. In any case, they would be symbols of the sky, and hence life, and show it to be the fire-serpent of the sky and Quetzalcoatl as the Morning Star. The entwining of the serpents forms them into signs of Ollin as the movement of the Fifth Sun. The mask of Tlaloc at the center of their movement clearly marks him as the creator of its movement and the Tlaloc heads in the coils can only represent the life which is being created and which will come on earth as the Sun of the new year.

In Mesoamerican theology, the serpents represented the movement of the Fifth Sun in the creation of life and in the passing of life. They were the symbol of both immortality and mortality. They carried the Sun and were the life spirit of the Moon; the Moon was the manifestation of the workings of the Fifth Sun as the universe.

Let us now turn to the religions of the ancient East before the beginning of Mesoamerican civilization, and see how they form a base for the doctrines and beliefs which we have found in the religion of ancient Mexico, and how the fundamental doctrines of those religions came to ancient Mexico. We will begin with southwest Asia.

Plate I – Mother Goddess. This stone figure is an abstraction of the Mesoamerican belief that life formed in the underworld. The earth is portrayed as the Mother Goddess; the Sun's motion is portrayed as the open jaws of a serpent-bird, bringing the human head of the Sun from the underworld, which was the Earth Mother's womb. The bird is symbolized here by the hood, which is constituted by feathers spread into a fan, and a bird beak which, coupled with the serpent's head, crowns the hood. The forked tongue of the serpent is fused and curves over the lower jaw. In the underworld, the Sun was a jaguar; in this figure, the jaguar's ears are represented by the rounded protrusions on the sides of the serpent's upper jaws. *Classic Period, Mexico* [27.5 inches, height; 13.5 inches, width]

Plate II – Tlaloc. A Mexican creator god, manifest as rain and the mountain on which the rain clouds form. The stone figure shows him as an ax, signifying sacrifice and the resurrection of life. The fire of the Sun was held to be the animating spirit which gave life and Tlaloc, as the bringer of life, was associated with the Sun. The Sun had no movement of its own, but was carried by the planet Venus through the sky and through the underworld at night and during the winter. Venus' animal form was a serpent, which is represented in the figure by the circles around the eyes. *Classic Period, Gulf Coast* [15 inches, height; 9 inches, width]

Plate III – Pelican. Water birds were associated with the annual cycle of vegetation because they were fish-eaters. Water was the medium of creation, fish were embryo Suns as the divinity of the maize plant. The birds' flight symbolized the Sun's course through the sky. *Classic Period, Gulf Coast* [1·6 inches, height; 3.75 inches, width; 7.5 inches, depth]

Plate IV – Xipe. Terra-cotta figure of the god of life returning from winter death. He wears the skin flayed from a human sacrificed as his godhead of the preceding year; in his own skin, he is god of the new year of life and will cast off the flayed skin as a serpent sloughs its skin. *Classic Period, Mexico* [17 inches, height; 12 inches, width]

Plate V – Olmec Supreme God. Serpentine figurine of the Supreme God in the form of a human jaguar, part-man, part-feline. *Preclassic Period, Olmec culture* [4.25 inches, height; 1.75 inches, width]

Plate VI – Mayan Warrior. When warriors died, they were believed to be translated into the Morning Star. This terra-cotta figure is from a burial; the shield represents the Maya Supreme God, Itzam Na, who is pictured symbolically as the universe which he created. *Classic Period, Mexico* [6.75 inches, height; 3.5 inches, width]

Plate VII – Earth Goddess with Alligator Headdress. Mesoamerican beliefs held that the earth first appeared from primordial waters as an alligator, and that life was given by the Sun which circled the earth through the underworld and the sky, carried by a feathered serpent. The underworld was a region of death where new life was continually created as the Sun moved through it and returned to life. The black paint on the mouth of this terra-cotta figure identifies the goddess with the underworld and her headdress, which has both serpent and alligator characteristics, shows her to be the Earth Goddess. *Classic Period, Gulf Coast* [28 inches, height; 12 inches, width]

Plate VIII – Mayan Vase. In Olmec and succeeding cultures, death was believed to be the source of life. The underworld was a region of death where life formed and its elements were created and from which they were released by the lords of the underworld. The Mayans imagined these lords as fabulous beings with human attributes. This terra-cotta vase depicts one of those lords. *Classic Period, Mexico* [9.75 inches, height; 4 inches, width]

Plate IX – Nayarit House. Terra-cotta figure depicting village life. *Preclassic Period, west Mexico* [7.5 inches, height; 5 inches, width; 3.75 inches, depth]

Plate X – Priest and Two Maidens. Terra-cotta figures of priest leading two maidens to be sacrificed as Maize Goddesses. *Classic Period, Gulf Coast, Mexico* [Priest: 23 inches, height, 9.75 inches, width; maidens: 20 inches, height]

PART II

CHAPTER 8

The Sumero-Babylonian Creation

ca. 3000 through 600 B.C.

The supreme deity of southwest Asia was the Great Goddess. She was the Death Goddess and Earth Mother, the life of the earth and the region of the sky where she was Queen of Heaven, and she was the Moon and the planet Venus. In her different aspects, she was called by different names. In Sumer, as Death Goddess and Earth Mother, she was Ereshkigal, or as the Earth Mother, Ninhursag. The Babylonian name of the Earth Mother was Damkina. As the Sumerian life of the earth and Queen of Heaven, she was Inanna (known to the Babylonians as Ishtar), this was also her name as Venus; but as the planet she was distinguished from the Moon in which her name was Ningal. She had other names, too, but in her different aspects, she comprised the life of the universe and the source of its continual renewal.

In the Sumero-Babylonian religion, the Great Goddess was not dual in sex. She had god consorts for her different aspects, who were regarded theologically as separate god forms of the Sumero-Babylonian universe. As Ninhursag, her first consort was the Sky Father An (Anu), but in the course of time, Enki (Ea), who was the Sky Father's water and earth form, was worshiped as her consort; her consort as the life zone of the universe was the Storm God Enlil; and when she was life on earth as the products of the fields and domestic animals, she was Queen of Heaven and her consort was Dumuzi (Marduk). Dumuzi had the same life nature as Inanna, but he was mortal as a living god. Life on earth formed from the soil which was Inanna's being as the earth and so, as the creator of life, she was Queen of the Underworld and her consort was Dumuzi's alter ego. In this form, as Lord of the Underworld, Dumuzi was immortal.

The universe of the Great Goddess was the union of the Earth Mother and the Sky Father of the Deer Cult divided into its constituent world regions and personified as goddesses and gods. The creation myth, which has survived in its Babylonian form but which is Sumerian in origin, describes the regions of the world descending as a lineage of gods from the union of the Earth Mother and the Sky Father. Creation began with Apsu and Tiamat — the universal waters from which the world and its life emerged. Apsu was the primeval Fresh Waters of the Abyss, and Tiamat was the Ocean. As they mingled, Mummu, the creative life force, appeared and their mingling was the first stage of creation. In the second stage, Lamu and Lahamu, a pair of serpents rose from the waters. Lamu and Lahamu were procreant spirits which formed into Anshar (*An* = Sky) and Kishar (*Ki* = Earth), the god and goddess who were the elements of the sky and earth in the space which was on the waters.

The lineage of the regional gods of the universe began with Anshar and Kishar, who ruled the third stage of creation. In these stages, time moved in eons. They were followed by the generations of Anshar and Kishar who begot Anu, the sky. Anu was the god of the fourth age; he begot Ea, the Earth and Water God.

At this point in the creation, Apsu found the comings and goings of the gods annoying and decided to destroy them. But the gods learned his plans and killed him before he could accomplish his purpose. Ea then took his seat in the Abyss of Apsu and, as consort of the Earth Mother, Damkina, ruled the fifth age. Ea begot Marduk, the tutelary god of Babylon, whom the Babylonians, in recording the creation myth, substituted for the Sumerian Air and Storm God Enlil. The Babylonians were a Semitic people whose social structure was patriarchal and they gave the gods preeminence over the goddesses; but each was, nevertheless, the consort of the Great Goddess as she developed into the earth regions of the universe.

Tiamat now turned against the gods, as Apsu had, and created a force of dragons and monsters to destroy them. The gods, fearing Tiamat and her dragons, called on Marduk to defend them. Marduk agreed on the condition that he be made king, and the gods consented. Marduk then challenged Tiamat to single combat. Their battle was furious. Tiamat came as a monstrous serpent, and Marduk was armed with seven winds. When Tiamat opened her mouth to eat Marduk, he filled it with Bad-wind so that she could not close it. Then he killed her by sending furious winds and inflated her belly, which he then burst open with an arrow shot. Having thus overcome her, he cleaved her in two as though separating the two halves of a shell fish. He then raised up one of the halves to contain the sky and set the other half for the world to rest on — fixing it so that the waters could not flow out.

Marduk's disposition of Tiamat fixed the frame of the world as it had been created in the sixth stage. Lamu and Lahamu, in the god forms of Anshar and Kishar, constituted the source of life and the remaining gods formed the regions of the universe in which the life of the earth was generated, took earthly form, and matured. Marduk, or Enlil (to give him his Sumerian name which appears in the related creation myths), was the region of life between An/Anu and Enki/Ea. It was the region of air which supports life and the upper layer of the earth in which vegetation grows. Hence, in his being, Enlil included all the life forms of the earth.

At this point, the world was static and to give it motion, Enlil created the lunar cycle and the quarterly phases of the Moon. The myth which describes Enlil's act is an allegorical anecdote of human passion. The world was peopled by gods. Among them was a virgin maiden named Ninlil whose mother was set on her marriage to Enlil.

To further her purpose, she sent Ninlil to bathe in a stream where Enlil would see her and be so filled with desire that he would make her his wife. When Enlil saw Ninlil, he proposed intercourse instead of marriage. Ninlil refused his proposal, but she got into a boat with him; while they were sailing on the stream, Enlil raped her.

For this act, the gods banished Enlil to the region of death, even though he was their king. But his banishment was only temporary and, Ninlil, captivated by love, followed him. Ninlil was now pregnant with the Moon God Nanna-Sin and Enlil wanted to be sure that Nanna, as we may properly call him, would be born in the region of life which he, Enlil, ruled. The way through the death region was in three stages and Enlil was determined to father a Moon God in each stage, and so delay the birth of Nanna. The first stage began at the Nippur Gates. Enlil changed himself into the gatekeeper and, when Ninlil passed through, had intercourse with her. The next stage crossed the "man-devouring river." There Enlil changed himself into the "man of the netherworld river" and when Ninlil came to cross, had intercourse with her. The third stage was across the waters which separated the region of death from the region of life; there he transformed himself into the ferryman and when Ninlil entered the ferry, he had intercourse with her for the third time. He then returned to the life region followed by Ninlil where Nanna was born.

The myth, as it is recorded by Sumerologists, does not record the birth of the other three gods. But it is obvious that, because Nanna, who was begotten first, was born last, the other three Moon brothers were born in the order of their begetting. Thus the first Moon born was begotten by Enlil as the ferryman, he was the waning Moon of the third quarter entering the region of death. The second Moon was Enlil's son begotten where the road crossed the "man-devouring river," the river of death flowing through the Abyss; this Moon was the new Moon. The third birth was the Moon begotten at the gates of Nippur. Nippur was the Sumerian city where Enlil was the tutelary god and the gates metaphorically denoted the entrance to life; Nanna was the full Moon.

The order in which the Moons were born recorded the act of their creation which, in the doctrine of sacrifice, began in death and so proceeded contrary to the process of life which ends in death. By creating the Moon

and its cycle, Enlil and Ninlil created the means by which life would be maintained in the universe. This life was the product of the Moon and was formed as the gods Utu (the Sun whom the Babylonians called Shamash) and Inanna (whose cosmic being was the planet Venus). Nanna was the consort of the Moon Goddess Ningal, and Utu and Inanna were their offspring.

In its Babylonian form, the myth records that when Enlil's "age" had come, Marduk set the constellations in the sky and set the stations of the heavenly bodies; then the gods made man and built a temple in Babylon, the Esaglia, as a home for Marduk.

The age of Enlil was a golden one in which death was unknown. As a Sumerian poet described the golden age,

> "The lion does not kill, the wolf does not touch the lamb...."

Except that there was no death and all things were ideal, life was the same as life on earth; but life had not yet come into being there, for the creation of the universe was not complete. Enlil ruled in the person of a god-king named Utnapishtim, whose name in Sumerian times had been Ziusudra. But the creation of the universe, once begun, had to continue to completion and the gods were "driven" to send a deluge which would destroy the life which had been created. They delegated the task to Enlil.

Ea was well disposed towards Utnapishtim and contrived to warn him and instruct him to build an ark and go on board with his family and possessions, kinsmen, craftsmen, and all the animals. Utnapishtim did as he was instructed and, with the ark's cargo, rode out the Flood. When the Flood receded, Enlil was furious to find that Utnapishtim had survived with life which the gods had intended to destroy. But Ea appeased him and Enlil gave Utnapishtim and his wife eternal life and let him live with Ea in the Abyss.

The deluge which destroyed the golden age was the final act of creation. Doctrine held that life is created out of sacrifice. Therefore, when Enlil, who was the golden age itself, sent the Flood, he was destroying himself by an act of self sacrifice and so bringing himself into being as the world of life on earth. Thus, the seventh age was created as the existing world of Sumer and Babylon. It was an age to which Enlil had, by his death, given mortality.

Sumero-Babylonian belief held that the universe was formed as two worlds — one as the underworld where life was created and to which it returned in death, and the other as the world of life on earth. The underworld was divided into two regions — one was the death region where life was generated, and the other as the life region where life took the forms in which it came into being on earth. The two regions were separated by a "lapis lazuli" mountain; the death region was Apsu, the Great Abyss, which was beneath the mountain; the life region, which was above, was a replica of the world on earth. When the Sun set on earth, it rose in the underworld where it returned to rise over the earth in the east.

The universe, which was created in seven stages as it is described in the creation myth, conforms with that belief. The doctrine of sacrifice determined the course of its creation. Life in the form of Mummu appeared spontaneously in the primordial waters and formed as the serpent couple Lamu and Lahamu. These two, being procreant spirits, took bodily form in the darkness which covered the primordial waters when nothing existed, as Anshar and Kishar (the outer sky and unformed earth). Anshar and Kishar begot the Sky and Earth as the life-giving gods of the universe. But, as elements of the universe, these gods were only forms and could not come into existence and so bring life into being without passing through the state of death.

In the following discussion when the Babylonian name of a god is used, it refers equally to his Sumerian antecedent. Similarly, the Sumerian name denotes the same god in Babylonian mythology. In general, the

version of the myth determines which name will be used.

When the gods killed Apsu, they created that death state in the Abyss and, when Apsu died, Mummu remained with him. Thus, when Ea succeeded Apsu, the Fresh Waters which became his being formed a sea of death; but they contained the seed of life and, with Damkina, the Earth Mother, they became the power of regeneration of life. At that point, Marduk killed Tiamat. Her death was a sacrifice and when Marduk set her body to contain the universe, his action was her resurrection as the universe, and the gods who were only forms came into existence as part of her being.

Tiamat was the Great Goddess and the form of the two parts of her body above and beneath the sky and the earth, and the manner in which she was killed, symbolize the nature of creation. In ancient cultures, shells were universally symbolic of birth. The placement of the two parts of Tiamat's body fixed them as her vulva. The stages of creation were phallic. First came Mummu as the seed, then the serpents, Lamu and Lahamu, symbolizing the organs of copulation. That the serpent should represent the female organ may be surprising at first; but Joseph Campbell in *Occidental Mythology* as part of his work, *The Masks of God*, describes the concept as follows: "The phallic suggestion (of the serpent) is immediate, and, as swallower, the female organ is also suggested; so that a dual image is rendered... ."*

In the next two stages, the physical nature of the universe was formed as the sky and earth, Anshar and Kishar, to become, probably, the death region; and Anu and Damkina, the life region. These were two stages of procreation. Lastly, Ea formed as the self-regenerating power of the universe, a power which, by its nature, lodged in the waters of Apsu. Damkina, who as the Great Goddess herself as Death and Earth Mother, had the same self-regenerating power and so she combined with Ea.

*Page 10.

The god forms who constituted these elements of the universe were all contained in the womb of Tiamat. The arrow which Marduk shot into her belly was a symbol denoting sacrifice and, as Tiamat died, they came into being through the natural channel of birth. But, as they came into existence, they all merged in Apsu and so formed, first, as the death region around Ea, and then, forming into life, as the region surrounding Enlil/Marduk.

The doctrine of the Deer Cult is obvious in the creation myth. The union of the Sky Father and Earth Mother, imagined as the lakes where the hunters sacrificed their Deer Gods, is repeated as Ea and Damkina in the Abyss with Mummu. Their state is the death state into which the Deer Gods descended and entered the union. The sacrificed deer, as they were combined in the union, are pictured as Enlil raping Ninlil in the boat on the river where she went to bathe. In the mythological picture, the poles which the hunters set in the lakes to make the path for the gods' descent to the underworld have been changed to a boat sailing on the water. The returning spirit of the Deer God has been changed to the Moon which Enlil begot of Ninlil, and the life which the Deer Gods brought back on their return to earth has been personified as the Sun God Utu and the goddess Inanna.

The mythology of the creation of the world continues along the line of the Deer Cult doctrine. When the spirit of the returning Deer God reached the hunting grounds, it became incarnate in the living deer. The returning spirits were bucks and does, and the divinity of the mating deer constituted the food source of the hunters. In the final stage of the Sumerian creation, the Moon spirit, with the Sun and Inanna, came as life on earth incarnate in the King and Queen of Sumer. The Queen became Inanna's incarnation and the King became the living form of the mortal Moon with the Sun incarnate, and the consort of the goddess. We can reconstruct this final stage in the following way.

The golden age was an immortal age because Tiamat failed to destroy Marduk; but Enlil created the Flood and destroyed the golden age and, thereby sacrificed himself, and rose bringing the world of life into being as

a mortal age. Enlil's path through death was the path which he had taken when Ninlil followed him and they begot the three Moons of the death region, thus, it led him through the Abyss where he was united with Ea. Ea renewed Enlil's life and sent him on to establish the world above. Sumerian myths describe Enlil as the god who planned for the welfare of man and Enki as the god who carried out the plans and had charge of the decrees of the gods which governed men; thus, with Ea-Enki, Enlil was a joint maker of the world on earth.

The product of creation was not only the physical state of the universe and the life within it, it was also time. The stages of creation were time eras. In the first stages, the universe was nonexistent. In the final stages, the form of the world and the life within it came into existence as the underworld where life continually took form and then, through the sacrifice of Enlil as all the gods, as the world of life on earth. Life is inseparably coupled with time and the mortal age which Enlil brought on earth was believed to have a finite existence. The world in creation had begun forming as a series of eons of nonexistence which ended when it first came into existence. The division between nonexistence and existence was death. The world which Enlil brought on earth began with life. Life ends in nonexistence and the division between the two states is death.

Life is the state of the world, and to ancient peoples it seemed that the end of life which sustained them would be the end of the world. Their lives were determined by the rhythm of time — to the hunters, it had been the return of the deer herds to their summer pasture, and to the Neolithic farmers, it was the annual grain crop. As a practical matter, therefore, the worlds of those early peoples ended when their food supply failed and so they sacrificed their gods to renew the cycle of life. With the advance of civilization, the ancients identified their food supply with time and their kings as its divine source, and at the end of each year sacrificed their kings to bring the food crop of the new year. From this, there arose the idea that the world of life was created for finite periods of time and that when the

period ended, the world would cease to exist unless a new-year Sun rose to begin a new period of world existence.

At first, the time period was a year which was measured by the Moon. The Sumerians evolved a theology of time which they developed into a sacred calendar. The Sumerian year was divided into two seasons — summer as the first half, and winter as the last half. The summer was the season of life which had been created in the underworld and, because of the inversion which distinguished life on the earth from life in creation in the underworld, when it was summer on earth, it was winter in the underworld and vice versa.

When the hunters sacrificed their deer, they did not attach a time interval to the god's return, but counted on a relatively early one; so they were not concerned with how the life was created which the god brought back. But when the god which the later peoples sacrificed was the King, and the life which he was believed to bring back contained an appreciable time element, it had to have been formed when he died and his god spirit descended to the underworld. The Sumerian theologians resolved this problem by extending the doctrine of creation to include a cycle of Moon generation in which the life of the underworld summer was created in Nanna and Ningal as King and Queen of the life region of the underworld. This life was recreated as the offspring of their union, Utu and Inanna, the Sun and Venus, respectively. When the sacrificed King reached the region of death in the underworld, the summer had ended and Nanna and Ningal as the Moon were dead, and the King's spirit and Nanna's spirit were joined as one. In her death, Ningal brought forth Utu and Inanna. The Moon God spirit, which was the King's spirit because his and Nanna's spirit were the same, returned on earth with Utu and Inanna.

It is not clear at what point the Sumerians ceased sacrificing their Divine Kings; but when they abandoned the practice, the King simulated death by ritually entering the earth in order to receive the spirit of the Moon God and bring a new year of life on earth.

The Sumero-Babylonian Creation

Here we must remember that we are piecing together fragments of mythology from Sumerian and Babylonian records and that, while they give us a fairly complete picture of the history of the Sumerian creation mythology, the exact details are obscure. The Sumerian records identify the King with the god Dumuzi, but although Dumuzi was not one of the original Sumerian creator gods, he appeared as a god in the course of a sectarian reformation which did not change the fundamental doctrine. Dumuzi was a Moon God and his mythology is pertinent to the reconstruction of the early Sumerian creation theology. The following reconstruction projects him back into the place of the original Moon God without changing the fundamental mythology.

In the mythological imagery, the Moon God was a bull and his spirit was a serpent. At the end of the underworld summer, the Moon God died and his spirit descended to the Abyss in the region of death. In the rituals which were performed in lieu of the sacrifice in the later Sumero-Babylonian period, a bull was sacrificed as the Moon God at the same time. We know from doctrine that its Moon spirit met the Moon God of the underworld in the Abyss and, because both were the same spirit, it became part of the serpent which had come from the life region of the underworld. In the Abyss, Enki gave the Moon spirit its earthly body as the King of Sumer and sent it on its way to the earth above.

The medium through which Enki reembodied the Moon God's spirit as the King was Utnapishtim, whom the Sumerians called Ziusudra. This is recorded in the myth of the Flood. Since the Babylonian version of the myth is fully recorded, we will use it here to explain the metaphysics of the Moon spirit's reincarnation.

During the golden age, Enlil had dispensed life through Utnapishtim as the King and, since the Moon was the medium through which Enlil dispensed life after the universe came into being, certainly Utnapishtim was a personification of the Moon. The golden age was resurrected as the mortal age of life on earth with all that was in it changed into mortal form;

and the king, who had been the Moon in the underworld, came into mortal form as the medium through which Enlil sent life on earth.

That Utnapishtim had two beings is in keeping with the nature of the Moon which was imagined as dying and becoming the new Moon, and returning to life to become the full Moon; and in its cycle of death and life it was accounted the governor of time. Utnapishtim in Ea's house was the new Moon and was immortal; the king as Utnapishtim's life being on earth, was the full Moon and was mortal. Utnapishtim's immortality was his power of regeneration. Once regenerated, he had to go on to the full state, but it would be in the body of another Moon, for Utnapishtim was bodiless. The Moon God coming to the Abyss and ascending to the earth was that mortal body.

In this light, the account of the Flood has a secondary meaning which relates it to the Deer Cult doctrine. The survival of the ark with Utnapishtim and its cargo established the annual passage of the Moon God bringing life from the underworld onto the earth. The ark was the way by which Utnapishtim was united with the Sky Father and Earth Mother as Ea and Damkina in their death union in the underworld. It was also the way by which he ascended bringing the ark's cargo of life on earth. This meaning is attested by the structure of the ark which was built in the form of the ziggurat, the temple where Marduk lodged on earth.

The Moon Goddess was usually imagined as human, but her spirit had the animal form of a serpent. Being the Moon, she descended to the Abyss of Death at the end of the underworld summer. There is a Sumerian myth which is part of the Dumuzi cult which describes the goddess' descent and so is pertinent to the early theology. It is called "Inanna's Descent to the Netherworld," but before considering the myth, let us see how Inanna was imagined in the early period.

A vase from Khafaje in Sumer dating from the beginning of the third millennium (2900-2800 B.C.) portrays Inanna as a woman standing with each foot near a lion and holding a serpent in each hand [**Figure 5**]. The

two lions are facing in opposite directions. Inanna was the Great Goddess in her aspect as the life and abundance of the earth. She was the life which formed first in the underworld and then rose to the world above. This aspect of the earth was identified with the Moon throughout the ancient Near East, both as goddess and god, and the figure of the woman on the Khafaje vase represents Inanna as the Moon in the life region of the underworld.*

The waning Moon was declining and dying life, and in the underworld the Moon Goddess in this stage descended to death in the Abyss. She descended as a spirit leaving her dying Moon body and, in the same spirit form, rose from the Abyss to a new life in a new Moon body. Her spirit had the form of a serpent and the serpents which the goddess holds in each hand represent her descending and rising spirit. The goddess' spirit was a combined body and life spirit formed by the planet Venus and the Sun. In

*In the mythology of Inanna, on the eve of her marriage to Dumuzi, the goddess sings ecstatically that she is at Ningal's gate, meaning that she is about to become the Moon Goddess with the Moon as her consort.

Figure 5. Decorative detail from the 5,000-year-old steatite vase found at Khafaje [after Frankfort, *Art and Architecture*, p.19, Fig. 9].

the life region, the goddess as Ningal cohabited with her consort Nanna, and when she descended to the Abyss she was pregnant. She died in the Abyss and afterwards returned to the life region, where she put on a new Moon body and renewed her union with the Moon God.

The myth will enable us to understand the significance of the lions at the goddess' feet on the Khafaje vase. In the myth, Inanna descended to the region of death dressed in her state robes and jewels with the intention of visiting her elder sister Ereshkigal. Ereshkigal was the Death Goddess who is also described in the myth as "the birth-giving mother." There were seven gates to Ereshkigal's domain and, at Ereshkigal's instructions, at each gate the gatekeeper took away part of Inanna's jewelry and clothing until she entered before Ereshkigal stark naked. When Inanna presented herself, Ereshkigal fixed her eye of death upon her and Inanna died. Her dead body was hung on a stake.

In the iconography of ancient religions, clothes denote the nature of a deity and Inanna's rich finery represented her Moon body. As the gatekeeper took off her jewels and clothing, she died as the Moon and appeared naked as the Moon spirit Venus. The identification of Ereshkigal and Inanna as sisters is a mythological device for describing them as two time aspects of the same goddess. Ereshkigal was the elder because, as the Death Goddess and Earth Mother, she was the same as Ninhursag, Enki's wife as the Queen of the Abyss and the mother of Ninlil. She was also the same as Ninlil who followed Enlil through the Abyss and became the mother of Ningal, who was Inanna as the Moon in Enlil's life region in the underworld.

This cycle of generations, which related the present to the past, was a natural construction resulting from combining the passing of time with the continual repetition of the same pattern of life on earth. The Moon waxes and wanes and vanishes and another Moon comes and follows the same cycle; the seed sprouts, the plant matures and produces seed and dies and a new plant appears and grows and produces its seed. This rhythm of life

and death and returning life was the changing nature of the Moon Goddess and her Moon consort, and their cycle continually returned to death.

Inanna — dead and hanging on a stake — and Ereshkigal were one. When Ereshkigal hung Inanna on the stake, she fell ill and the myth tells how Enki cured her and revived Inanna. He fashioned two spirit messengers from the earth beneath his fingernails. To one, the *kurgarra*, he gave the food of life. To the other, the *kalatur*, he gave the water of life, and sent them to attend Ereshkigal.

The *kurgarra* and *kalatur* followed instructions and found Ereshkigal crying, "Woe! Oh my inside!" They said to her, "From my inside to your inside. From my outside to your outside." These words cured her and she gave them Inanna's body. The *kurgarra* then sprinkled food of life on her body and the *kalatur* sprinkled water of life on it and Inanna revived. But she could not leave Ereshkigal's realm of death without a substitute to take her place and she returned to the life region whence she had descended and where she found her Moon consort Dumuzi lording it in her absence. Outraged by his conduct, she turned him over to demons which had come with her to bring back the substitute. Trying to avoid them, Dumuzi turned into a snake, but the demons caught him and took him to the Abyss.

This scene in the underworld is obscure because of the fantastic images which appear, but it clears when we see that it is the center of the universe in the Abyss where the Sky, Apsu, and the Earth, Tiamat, are united in the void of death and nonexistence in which the universe began forming. The scene is fluid and the death union merges into a life union. The death scene is characterized by Ereshkigal as the Death Goddess; but she is also "the birth-giving mother" whose consort is Enki and, as the scene changes from death to life, she becomes the Earth Mother in union with Enki as the Sky Father. Her illness then appears as Ereshkigal-Inanna in labor. The *kurgarra* and *kalatur* are metaphorical images of Enki's fingers shaping new life for Inanna, and their words are Enki's words describing his complete union with Ereshkigal as the Earth Mother.

The fantasy is the imagery of the Deer Cult. Inanna's descent to Ereshkigal is a late version of the sacrificed doe goddess of the hunters descending through the water to the lake bed beneath. The stake which was the path of the doe goddess had become the stake on which Inanna was hung, and the waters of the lake where the doe goddess was sacrificed had become the waters of the Abyss which, although they are not described in the myth, were an integral part of the death region. In the imagery of the Deer Cult, the doe goddess became one with the Earth Mother in her union with the Sky Father, and Inanna became one with Ereshkigal in her union with Enki.

The children of the Moon were Venus (Inanna) and the Sun (Utu). Enki gave life to their embryo forms in the body of Ereshkigal-Inanna by the food of life and water of life which the *kurgarra* and the *kalatur* sprinkled on her body — life substance to the embryo Inanna and fertility to the embryo Utu. Inanna returning from her visit to her sister returned as a New Moon with the Sun.

To the ancient Sumerians, the food which the gods sent was constituted by the fruit which their plants bore and the milk products which their domestic animals produced. The food divinity was not only the plant and the animal — it was equally the seed and the product. The theology of those ancients was largely determined by agriculture, and the grain which they harvested from their plantings was a product of the plants' death. Consequently, the theologians formed their image of the Great Goddess as both mother and offspring and they formed Inanna in the underworld as plant life and harvest, the one as Ningal-Ereshkigal, the harvest as Inanna and Utu. Thus, Inanna and Utu came on earth incarnate as a new generation in the plants and livestock.

The myth is not complete, and Inanna's return apparently left Dumuzi in the Death Goddess' clutches. But Dumuzi was a Moon God and the godhead of the King, and the divinity of the Moon was constituted by the god and goddess combined. We will see that Dumuzi received a dispensation that permitted him to come on earth each year as consort of Inanna. This brings us back to the lions with which the Khafaje image of Inanna stands. They are symbols denoting the Sun which was the life spirit joined to her body spirit. The body of a living being is the vehicle containing and moving the spirit within, Inanna's planetary spirit Venus, being her body spirit, was the moving force of the Sun. Her two-fold spirit was contained in her Moon body represented by her human figure standing with the lions. Feet are the means of movement and the goddess' feet near the lions symbolized her movement with the Sun. They faced in opposite directions because her movement was the cycle of generation of life in which the directions change from descent to death to return to life.

In the reformation, the cycle of the Moon moving in creation was reconstituted as a planetary year cycle with seven stages. Dumuzi became Inanna's Moon consort with Mercury as his Moon spirit, and the Sun was separated from Inanna's spirit as Venus and joined to the Moon spirit Mercury, which became the Sun-bearer. We will consider these changes in the course of this study.

The doctrine of the Deer Cult and the creation myth has enabled us to define the Sumero-Babylonian doctrine which held that the years of life on earth were formed in the underworld by the movement of the Moon with Venus, and Mercury with the Sun, and that the years came on earth as an earthly incarnation of the Great Goddess and the King as her consort. The supporting mythology has required a new interpretation, but if we look at Divine Kingship in a different perspective and follow its development along another line of study, we reach the same definition of the doctrine.

CHAPTER 9

The Divine King

The Great Goddess was worshiped universally in southwest Asia and the eastern Mediterranean. The cult of the Divine King with regional variations was part of her religion. The Sumerian theology of kingship which we have just studied was constructed on a doctrine that formed naturally and directly from the sacrifice rites of the hunters, for the Divine King and the Deer God were theologically identical with each other. With the advent of agriculture, societies are thought to have developed along matriarchal lines, and we find that at an early time political units were formed under the rulership of queens. These queens were believed to be the incarnations of the Earth Mother. The old religious beliefs of the hunters did not change materially; the domestic animal, usually a bull, was substituted for the buck as the life form of the god and the staple crop was regarded as one of its incarnate forms; but the ritual of sacrifice continued to be the means of ensuring the creation of life. Although domestic animals were sacrificed as the god, for various reasons men came to be substituted for animals in sacrifice. In the substitution, the man received the full divinity of the god in his person, sometimes by being costumed as a stag before the immolation.

In death, the human god form made the descent and union with the Earth Mother and Sky Father and the journey of return, bringing new life on earth just as had his animal predecessor. The stag, which had been his predecessor, returning as a god on earth mated with a doe which was the animal form of the Earth Mother. In a society in which the queen was the

life being of the Earth Mother, the man who took the animal-god's place in the drama of life became the queen's consort and, by virtue of that relation to her, he became the human form of the god.

The queen's consort thus became a god king; but he had to die in sacrifice each year in order to bring new life on earth and so the queen had to espouse a new consort each year. When the doctrine of the Divine King was evolving from the image of the Deer God, the Deer God had become identified with the Moon because its changing nature made it seem mortal and, as the governor of time, it marked the seasons. Therefore, the Moon marked the life cycle of the deer herds. Also, in the course of this development, the Deer God became identified with the Sun as its life spirit.

When the world economy changed to agriculture, the Sun became the cosmic body which marked the seasons. This development brought about a change in the ritual and theology of Divine Kingship. The Divine King, who was identified with the Moon, and a co-king, who was identified with the Sun as his life spirit, were considered two companion beings. Each year, therefore, when the Divine King was chosen and became the queen's consort, a companion was chosen to represent his spirit. The divine nature of the king was the life which his Moon body had brought back to earth. Thus, when vegetation died at the end of the summer, it manifested the god's death. Accordingly, the time of the king's sacrifice was changed to conform to the seasonal life of the staple crop and the king was sacrificed at the end of a half-year.

When the Divine King died, his spirit passed to the companion. The Moon spirit and the Sun were thus combined in the companion who made the journey of death through the underworld. Mythological evidence shows that he also became the queen's consort in her being as the Death Goddess and Earth Mother, and in the ritual of Divine Kingship, he was the successor king. Robert Graves, in *The White Goddess*, has termed this companion and successor king a *tanist,* a term taken from an Irish survival of the institution of Divine Kingship.

The Divine King

The cosmic image of the Divine King was the Moon, with his spirit formed as a serpent. Since the tanist was his death companion, he likewise was imagined as a serpent. The serpent was the Moon's corporeal spirit and the Sun its life spirit. The fire of the Sun was immortal and, while the spirit body died, it came to life again as did the Moon. The cosmic image of the tanist as the Divine King spirit came to be Venus or Mercury because, like the Moon's, their brilliance increased and diminished; as evening stars, they disappeared in an apparent extinction of death, and reappeared as morning stars.

In the course of time, the dominant power of the matriarch declined and the ruling authority passed to her consort as king. With this change, the rite of sacrificing the king was abandoned. The ancient Egyptian theology of Divine Kingship furnishes an example of this stage of development, and is clearly recorded in the ancient documents. We should consider the Egyptian example because of its relationship to the Sumero-Babylonian theology, which has survived in fragmentary records.

The god Osiris was the first king of Egypt. He was the Moon and his brother Seth was the tanist. Seth killed Osiris. In the orthodox form of sacrifice, the tanist killed the Divine King because it was an ancient hunter belief that the spirit of the animal-god lodged in the person of the man who killed it, and when the tanist killed the king, his corporeal Moon spirit combined with the life spirit. Seth became king and Osiris descended to the underworld where he became the Lord of Death and creator of new life. Osiris then mated with the goddess Isis. In Egypt, the roles of the Earth Mother and Sky Father were reversed because the life-giving waters came from the Nile flood which seemed to flow out of the earth. Isis was a Sky Goddess and Osiris, at the center of the death region in the underworld, was an Earth God.

The offspring of the union was Horus. When Horus was grown, he deposed Seth and became king. Horus was the Sun in the daytime and Venus in the twilight, and he was the life and the world of Egypt. His divinity lodged in an image of a serpent which was fixed in the headdress, called the uraeus, worn by the kings of Egypt as his successors. The uraeus was the *zet*-serpent and was called the Eye of Horus. It was the divinity of the Moon and also the planet Venus, and its possessor became the King of Egypt.

The rituals of the ceremonies which were performed when a king died and new one was acclaimed follow the doctrine of Divine Kingship as it had developed from the Deer Cult. When the king died, he ceased to be Horus and became Osiris in the underworld. In the ritual of the new king's accession, Seth, or an actor playing his part, took the uraeus and became Horus' successor and the life of Egypt. But in Egyptian theology, life left the land of Egypt when the king died, which meant that Seth had gone to the underworld with the uraeus.

He was performing his tanist role, which was to carry the Sun through the region of death and bring it back with new life for Egypt. We find Seth pictured in a boat carrying the Sun in the underworld, therefore Seth returned to the land of Egypt.

In the underworld, a new Horus appeared as the child of Osiris and made his way to the world above. There Horus, grown to manhood, met Seth. The two fought and Horus, the victor, took the uraeus from Seth.

In the ritual of succession, when the time came to acclaim the new king as Horus, the new king wrested the uraeus from Seth and placed it on his own head and the dead king's (Osiris') head. By this act, he became Horus and the life created by Osiris, thus life was restored to Egypt. This ritual in which Seth took the uraeus from the dead king and the new king took it from Seth, symbolically portrayed the *zet*-serpent casting off its dead body and putting on a new one. The *zet*-serpent was the Moon, so it was also an abstract portrayal of the New Moon forming as new life. The new life was Horus. Horus was the Moon's son, begotten in death in the womb of the sky. In the less complicated form of the Deer Cult theology, he was the life formed in the death union of the Earth Mother and Sky Father. In the changing imagery of the doctrine, the god spirit descending into the earth had become the evening star in the dying body of the *zet*-serpent, and the new life had become the morning star in its new body.

The life which the god spirit brought in his return was no longer imagined as new life in the deer herd following the train of the returning god, but it was the Moon itself as the living earth and was embodied as a serpent which came bringing the food of life which the earth produced. In this imagery, the returning god was manifest as the things which sustained life, it was the Moon and the Sun and the evening and morning stars, and it was present in the ruler. Its image was a serpent being transformed into the new-year Sun, its life line was the uraeus which joined the king to Osiris in the underworld and, in the king, it was the Moon and Sun combined in a uniform cycle of time.

In its Egyptian form, Horus' sovereign divinity did not depend on his marriage to the Earth Goddess; but this did not mean that Egyptian Kingship was unorthodox, it was simply a peculiarity of the development of Egyptian religion around the annual flooding of the Nile. If we recall the basic theology of the Deer Cult and consider the nature of the tanist, we will see how the Divine King's marital relation to the goddess was a fundamental tenet of the Egyptian theology.

In the Deer Cult, the spirit of the dead deer buck became part of the progenitor couple and lodged in the being of the Sky Father in his union with the Earth Mother. The spirit was a life spirit endowed with the procreative power of the Sky Father. The consequence of the union was the life which he brought back on earth. When the god returned in life form, he mated with the does; the consequence of the union was the fawn crop of the herd. Just how the life returning from the underworld related to the life begotten on earth is not clear, but almost certainly the returning life was of a divine nature which became incarnate in earthly forms and gave them vitality and reproductive power. In the cycle of creation, however, there were two matings, one in life on earth, the other in death in the underworld.

In the coupling of the Divine King and tanist, the Divine King's marriage formed the first union; the tanist, in his succession as king and consort, formed the second. The tanist represented a spirit endowed with the reproductive power which had been the fundamental part of the Divine King's nature. Thus, in the orthodox sacrifice rites when the tanist killed the king, he castrated him because his power of generation was part of the tanist's own spirit being; therefore, he took it as he departed from his Moon body.

Osiris' sacrifice was an original sacrifice of world creation in which Osiris became a fixed part of the earth region of the universe as the fertility of the earth and as growing grain and vegetation; therefore, he did not return to the earth above as the living form of the Divine King. Instead, Horus came as the Divine King and mythology records ritual fights between Horus and Seth in which Seth wrests the Eye of Horus, i.e., the uraeus, from Horus and castrates him. In the theology of the Divine King, the life of Egypt is renewed in the union of Osiris and Isis and returns on earth as their child Horus when he secures possession of the uraeus. However, there was no earthly form of an Earth Goddess for Horus to espouse because Osiris had taken that place; but by putting the uraeus on his own and the dead king's head in the ritual of accession, the king became Horus and united himself to Osiris and, through Osiris, to Isis. Thus, the two matings were merged in the underworld union of Osiris and Isis, and life on earth continued to flow from their union.

The Sumerian doctrine was essentially the same as the Egyptian. The tanist, like Seth, was a figure of the underworld who translated the Moon God of the underworld into the Divine King on earth. Like Seth, he was a serpent as the Moon spirit and his divinity was a planet combined with the Sun. Between Ea and Osiris, there were only Sumerian and Egyptian sectarian differences. As sovereign of the Abyss, like Osiris, Ea was Lord of Death; through his proxy, Utnapishtim, he was the Moon. In his function as organizer of world order and executor of the gods' decrees, he sent the Moon on earth to become incarnate in the King, and so bring a renewal of life on earth. Both the Sumerian and the Egyptian underworlds were worlds where life formed and where death reigned, but there was a difference in their physical natures. The Sumerian underworld was divided into two regions by the lapis lazuli mountain, but in the Egyptian underworld, the life region merged into the death region in the person of Osiris who, besides being the Lord of Death, was vegetation and growing grain.

There was also a time difference. The life of Egypt as it was created in Horus was the natural life of the King; while the life of Sumer was a fixed length of time and the King was either sacrificed at the end of the period or underwent a ritual death. The length of the Sumerian King's life probably conformed to the orthodox doctrine of Divine Kingship as it developed in the Great Goddess religion, generally, and at first was a year. Later the King's life was extended to eight years, a period which is thought to have been determined by the near coincidence of a full Moon and the end of the eight year period. It is more probable that this period was established by Sumerians who discovered that a conjunction of the Sun and Venus occurred every eight years at the same time of the year and that the conjunction was triple, or nearly so, with the Moon as the third celestial body. At such a time, the Moon would be new and disappear from the sky and the evening star of Venus would appear to be moving into the Sun and, after disappearing in it, leaving it and reappearing as the morning star. In the mystic imagery of the Moon, Venus, and the Sun, the triple conjunction would appear as the Moon spirit leaving the dying body of the Moon descending into the death region of the underworld and beginning its return to life in the body of a new King and god on earth. It would signal the time for the Divine King's death.

The discovery must have been accidental, but the triple conjunction would not have reoccurred often because the time coincidences are inexact. When they ceased to occur, the eight-year period would have lost its mystic significance. In any event, the Sumerians invented a different celestial combination which fixed the length of the King's reign and the period of world existence at seven years.

The Sumerians made the doctrine of the Divine King a doctrine of world order which they called the *me's* and which had its counterpart in the Egyptian doctrine of *maat.* In Sumerian theology, the god was Dumuzi, who in Egypt was Horus. On earth, like Horus as the king, Dumuzi was mortal, but unlike Horus, his life span was contained within a single year. Dumuzi was incarnate in the person of the king, but the Sumerian kings differed from the Egyptian kings in that their divinity was coupled directly to the Earth Goddess through the sacred marriage rite. The historians of this ancient time consider that the Egyptian kings had the full divinity of a true god, but the Sumerian kings' earthly relation to the government of the people was more human than divine. The reason is that Sumerian cities fought for supremacy as rulers of Sumer and, in the pragmatic theology of their contests, the Sumerian king was divine as the medium through which the gods sent life on earth; the divinity which flowed through him was complete.

Just as a new Horus came into being when Horus as the living King died, each year a new Dumuzi came into being in the person of the king as a new year of life on earth. In the underworld, he was the consort of Inanna in her triple form. He was the Moon divinity of the King and each year he died; but each year, in the underworld, a new Dumuzi formed as the Moon and when the Dumuzi incarnate in the king died, the new Dumuzi came on earth as his successor.

The *Epic of Gilgamesh*, which was the Bible of the Sumero-Babylonian cult of the Divine King, in the religion of the Great Goddess, describes the creation of the new Dumuzi in the underworld. Each year he appears as a new Moon and on becoming full, dies and rises on earth as the new incarnation of the king. In the epic, Dumuzi is named Gilgamesh as the consort of Inanna, who is called by her Babylonian name, Ishtar.

The Divine King

On earth, Dumuzi was the Divine King, but the new Dumuzi who appeared as the new Moon in the underworld was his tanist spirit whose body, materializing and becoming full, formed the life of the new year coming on earth. In the Egyptian theology of kingship, Horus became King of Egypt by overcoming the tanist Seth and wrestling the uraeus from him. The uraeus was the divinity of the Moon and transformed Horus into the Moon God. In the theology of Dumuzi, his death as the tanist in the underworld was a sacrifice from which he rose translated into the Divine King of Sumer.

The epic adds a new dimension to the doctrine of Divine Kingship which is a departure from the Egyptian theology. The universe of the Deer Cult was the world of the earth and the underworld. The two worlds of the hunters were worlds in existence; but as the Sumerians evolved their religion they wondered what brought the worlds into existence, and they evolved the concept of creation which we considered in Chapter 8. They held that life in the created universe was finite and they came to believe that, like the gods who formed the elements of the universe, new eras of world life were continually created in the regions where nothing existed, and that these new eras came into existence when the worlds in which men lived ended, thus forming a continuation of life on earth.

The theme of the epic is the creation story of new eras and their coming into existence in the underworld where they form as the years of life on earth. The epic reveals a cultural change in theology. In the theology of the hunters, the hunters themselves created the life which the Earth Mother and Sky Father formed in the underworld and then brought into being on earth. The process of life formation was the sacrificial killing of the animal-god and the communion meal in which all the people became one with the god. When the god descended to its death mating with the Earth Mother and Sky Father, it was the life spirit of the hunters' community and it returned to earth as the life of the land and the people.

In agricultural economy, the nature of the god changed from the animal

killed in the hunt to the fruits of the field and, with the growth and dispersal of the population, the community lost its cohesion. The sacred state of the people became diluted and their divinity became concentrated in the king as the representative of the people. Then, as men ceased to sacrifice the king and his tanist, and substituted animals and mock death, the concept of the community as the instrument of creation lost validity. In reformulating appropriate doctrine, the theologians substituted the process of the original creation as the means by which the new eras of life were formed.

In the old theology, the god that was sacrificed gave the people the food on which they lived, and the people, in their sacred state of communion with the god, were one with the god. The sacrifice was the death and rebirth of the people as the god and the life which the sacrificed god brought. In the new theology, the god that died combined the divinity of the Moon and Sun, with its planetary carrier, united as a cycle of time. The god returned in death to a world of nonexistence to come again into being in the underworld of the earth as a new cycle of time. When that cycle ended, it was renewed as in death and came again on earth bringing the life of a new cycle. The new theology, however, did not discard the old; within each new cycle the Moon and Sun, with its planet carrier, moved in the lesser cycle of single years, and as gods, died each year and revived to give the people the annual renewal of the food sources on which they lived.

In this way, the formation of the years of the new era began as the new Moon in death. Its life and motion were constituted by the gods of the Sun and Moon; and the cycles of its motion were solar years. As the Moon moved through each year cycle, when it waxed it formed the summer and the life of the year. Being earthly life, its body was mortal, but its life spirit was immortal. The Moon body constituted the divinity of the king, and the spirit the divinity of his tanist. Thus, in the theology of the Moon's movement, the waxing Moon was the god incarnate in the king and, when it became full, it sacrificed itself and the gods of its mortal nature rose bringing a new year of life on earth — while the god spirits returned to the

death state of the new Moon to form the new year of life as the Moon of the following year.

The idea of eternal existence without beginning and without end was implicit in the hunter doctrine. The reform necessarily changed that to a belief in a finite world with a beginning and end.

CHAPTER 10

The Epic of Gilgamesh

ca. 3000 through 600 B.C.

The epic begins with a description of life in Erech where Gilgamesh as king was oppressing the people by taking the son from the father, and the maiden from her lover. The scenes of the story are laid in the underworld and world of nonexistence beyond. The situation in Erech symbolizes the chaos which was before the beginning of ordered life. The epic is a Babylonian version, but the theme was an original Sumerian composition.

Erech was a Sumerian city-state where Gilgamesh ruled as king of Sumer circa 2600 B.C. But the Erech in the opening scene is a projection of the city in the world of creation, and Gilgamesh is Mercury as the life spirit of the Moon and divine spirit of the Sumerian King. The Moon is called Enkidu.

While the epic does not specifically identify Gilgamesh and Enkidu as Mercury and the Moon, it is clear from the text that they were those cosmic bodies, as we shall see.

The story begins beyond the created world when Enkidu first appeared out of the steppes as a monster wildman who lived with animals and whose hair grew like barley. He was transformed into normal human form when a harlot seduced him and he spent six days and seven nights copulating with her. The harlot was Ishtar who had been sent by Gilgamesh. Enkidu was the new Moon taking form and in his union with Ishtar, he became her consort. Ishtar clothed Enkidu in one of her garments and took him to Erech where Gilgamesh met him and the two wrestled until Gilgamesh overcame Enkidu. They then became inseparable companions.

In their first adventure, Gilgamesh and Enkidu left Erech and set out to kill the monster Huwawa who was the guardian of the cedar forest in the land of life formation. This land was in the world of nonexistence, which in the Sumerian version of the epic is called the *Land of the Living*. Huwawa's face had the features of a lion combined with those of a serpent or dragon. His breath was death, his mouth was the Fire God, and his voice was the rush of an onrushing flood. The cedar forest was a metaphorical elaboration of the tree of life and Huwawa was the opposing life-giving and destructive power of the Sun manifest in the fields of ripening grain and in the devastation of the desert steppes. When Gilgamesh and Enkidu arrived in the cedar forest, Gilgamesh cut down a great cedar and so came into the presence of Huwawa whom they killed with the aid of the Sun God Shamash. When Huwawa died, he became one with Gilgamesh, who thus became Mercury as the Sun-bearer.

The wrestling match between Gilgamesh and Enkidu united the two as the Moon; the killing of Huwawa added the Sun to their combined being. This is more clearly apparent in an older Sumerian version called *Gilgamesh and the Land of the Living*, in which they cut off Huwawa's head and gave it to Enlil who decreed a fiery fate for them with the words:

> "May your faces be scorched,
> May the food you eat be eaten by fire,
> May the water you drink be drunk by fire."

Huwawa's face was a lion's face with the teeth of a dragon (i.e., serpent); in the Babylonian version, his mouth was fire. These features show that he was the Sun in the mouth of the serpent Sun-bearer.

The two then returned to Erech where Ishtar, seeing and admiring Gilgamesh in the fullness of his new power, proposed marriage. But Gilgamesh spurned her saying that she destroyed her lovers. Furious, Ishtar appealed to her father, Anu, who sent the Heavenly Bull to avenge the insult. Enkidu held the bull while Gilgamesh killed it and tore out the heart which he gave to Shamash. Then he tore off the thigh bone and threw it at Ishtar. Gilgamesh was well advised to reject Ishtar for she was a goddess of death and her advances were an invitation to die.

The bull which was the Moon's animal form as the Lord of Vegetation, was Enkidu's alter ego and an archetype of the Divine King. When Gilgamesh killed it, his act was that of the tanist killing the Divine King. The bull's thigh bone was a euphemism for his genitals and Gilgamesh's act in hurling it at Ishtar symbolically meant that he had changed his mind and had ravished her. The act symbolized the mating of the tanist as the divine spirit with the Earth Goddess. When the bull died, Enkidu became sick and died on the twelfth day after the bull's death.

When Enkidu died, Gilgamesh wept bitterly and for seven days and nights, ran about the steppe land. While Gilgamesh wept, the scene changed to the underworld of the earth where the gods came into being. Then Gilgamesh buried Enkidu and started out to find Utnapishtim.

First he passed through the gate of the cosmic mountain Mashu. The gate was guarded by the Scorpion people, but they allowed Gilgamesh to pass because he was two-thirds immortal. With the death of the Heavenly Bull (which was Enkidu's Moon form), Enkidu's Moon divinity lodged in Gilgamesh, but it was the mortal divinity of the dying Moon. In the death region, Gilgamesh followed the road of the Sun which led to the house of Utnapishtim, who lived in the center of the Abyss. He wore old skins which gave him an odd appearance. These skins represented the dead Moon.

The road brought Gilgamesh to the waters of the Great Abyss where he found the lady Siduri who kept an inn by the side of the waters. She directed him to Utnapishtim's servant, the ferryman Urshanabi, who agreed to take him across. Urshanabi instructed Gilgamesh to go to the forest and cut punting poles. Urshanabi put the poles on the boat and they set out across the waters. When they reached the waters of death, Urshanabi told

Gilgamesh to punt the boat across and, as he made each thrust, to throw the pole away and use another so that no drop of the waters of death should touch his hands. In this way, they crossed to the house of Utnapishtim.

Gilgamesh slept six days and seven nights at Utnapishtim's house. Each night Utnapishtim's wife baked a loaf of bread and when Gilgamesh awoke she showed it to him to prove how long he had been sleeping. The Sun had staled the loaves as she had set them out so that only the last baked was fresh. Astonished, Gilgamesh began the return to Erech with Urshanabi. Utnapishtim directed Urshanabi to wash him and give him a new garment. Bathed, Gilgamesh discarded the old skins which he had been wearing and put on new clothes which Utnapishtim supplied for him.

Utnapishtim also told him the secret of a magic plant that renewed youth and which grew among thorns at the bottom of the sea. The plant was called "old man becomes young." When he was on the waters which lay beyond Utnapishtim's, Gilgamesh tied stones to his feet and, letting himself out of the boat, submerged and gathered the plant. With the plant in hand, he kicked off the stones and was cast up by the sea onto the shore where Urshanabi joined him. The two then walked until they came to a pool and Gilgamesh stopped to bathe, leaving the plant on the bank. A snake smelled the scent of the plant, rose out of the water and, taking it, disappeared into the depths; then reappeared and immediately sloughed its skin. Gilgamesh called the snake the "earth-lion." The two then went to Erech.

Let us now see how the myth identifies Enkidu with the Moon. From the context of the epic, clearly the route that Gilgamesh followed — first with Enkidu and then to the house of Utnapishtim — formed the annual route followed by the Moon with the Sun through the underworld. Until Enkidu's death, Gilgamesh's way was the road of the waxing Moon, but then it changed to the road of the waning Moon and the path through death. His journey along the road of the waxing Moon describes the creation of life; the path of death was the way of resurrection of life as the new Moon. The epic describes the way across the Abyss as the way where only the Sun could go, and when Gilgamesh reached the death waters of the Abyss, he crossed as the Moon spirit carrying the Sun, for Gilgamesh was under the protection of the Sun God Shamash throughout the entire journey. But Gilgamesh as Mercury was immortal and part of the Moon, and the Sun's route was the Moon's route. It was marked by seven constellations which formed a lunar zodiac.

When we follow the narrative of Enkidu and Gilgamesh in relation to the seven constellations, we see that it describes the development of Enkidu into the Moon moving through the circle of the zodiac. Along with their belief that the Sun returned to the east through the underworld at night, the Sumerians held that once each month the Moon joined the Sun there. They would naturally have related this event to the nights of the new Moon when the waning Moon's disappearance in the Sun at sunrise and its reappearance at sunset signalled the meeting. The belief proves the Sumerians understood that in the relative motions of the two bodies, the Moon and Sun were in conjunction at new Moon and in opposition at full Moon. At new Moon, the constellations were fully visible at night and revealed the place of the meetings of the Moon with the Sun in the underworld. The nights of the new Moon, therefore, marked the Moon's course through the stars.

The steppe was a wilderness associated with death and, in the metaphor of the epic, it was the void of night in which the new Moon appeared seemingly from nowhere. Ishtar was a Moon Goddess with a dual nature. One was her spirit nature as the planet Venus. As Venus, she and her brother (the Sun) were consorts; together they were a compound spirit of plant and animal life. Her other nature was her life form as the body of the Moon.

When she met Enkidu on the steppe and embraced him in coition the two became one. Their relationship identifies the semihuman wildman Enkidu emerging from the steppe as the unformed new Moon. The six days and seven nights during which they were united in embrace formed Enkidu into the life cycle of the Moon's motion.

In the symbolism of the myth, clothes denote the life body of a god. When Enkidu and Ishtar met, Ishtar took her clothes off and Enkidu had none. When they embraced, therefore, they were the body and life spirit combining in the formation of the new Moon. The animal form of the embryo body of the Moon was symbolically represented as a fish. The fish constellation is Pisces, and the story begins in its stars [**Figure 6**].

The union humanized Enkidu. Ishtar gave him one of her garments to wear, and the two dressed and made their way to Erech. Traveling with Ishtar in her dress, Enkidu was the male element of the Moon as it formed its cosmic shape. In its animal form, the Moon was a bull. The route of Ishtar and Enkidu was through the constellation the Sumerians identified with the bull, which we know as Taurus.

Gilgamesh who, as Mercury, was the spirit of the Moon as it followed the annual course of the Sun. When Enkidu and Gilgamesh wrestled and Gilgamesh won, Enkidu became Gilgamesh's Moon body and, in consequence, they became inseparable companions. Their companionship was formed in Gemini and together they set out to find Huwawa in the cedar forest.

Huwawa was a metaphorical configuration of the Sun. When they found him, they killed him. Thus Gilgamesh, the planet Mercury, became the spirit Sun-bearer and Enkidu, in his form as the Moon, became the Sun's incarnation. Enkidu's form was now the Moon in the fullness of life. The cedar forest in which they found and killed Huwawa was in the constellation of the lion, Leo.

After Enkidu had become the full Moon, the two companions met Ishtar who offered herself to Gilgamesh as his wife. Gilgamesh perforce refused; he and Ishtar were embodied in Enkidu as his life spirit and they could only wed by leaving his body in death. The Heavenly Bull, which Ishtar in her fury at Gilgamesh's refusal called down, was the full Moon descending to death. Its death was the self sacrifice of Enkidu and Ishtar as the Moon, and it freed Gilgamesh to his union with Ishtar. When Gilgamesh ravished

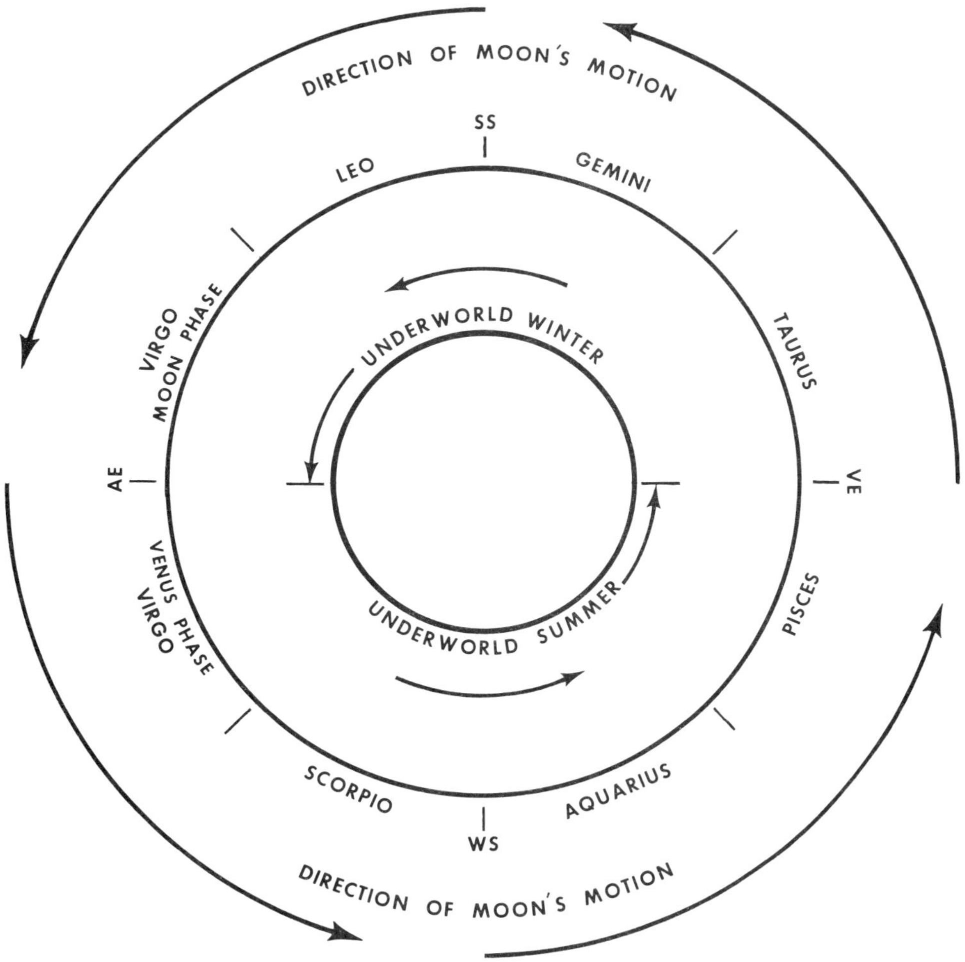

DIRECTION OF MOON'S MOTION
SS
LEO
GEMINI
VIRGO MOON PHASE
TAURUS
UNDERWORLD WINTER
AE
VE
VENUS PHASE VIRGO
PISCES
UNDERWORLD SUMMER
SCORPIO
AQUARIUS
WS
DIRECTION OF MOON'S MOTION

Figure 6. Sumerian zodiac of the underworld sky.

her, the union was consummated. Deserted by Ishtar, Enkidu sickened and died.

The meeting with Ishtar and the death of the Heavenly Bull were two stages in the cycle of Enkidu as the Moon. In the first stage, the Moon was full before it becomes gibbous; the second was the waning stage which ended as a half Moon. The constellation Virgo contained both stages.

When, after Enkidu's death, Gilgamesh began his descent to the Abyss where Utnapishtim lived and passed through the gate guarded by the Scorpion people, his journey was obviously in the constellation Scorpio.

Utnapishtim lived on an island in the waters of the Abyss and on coming to his house, Gilgamesh was in the constellation Aquarius. Aquarius completed the circle of the zodiac which began in the constellation Pisces.

The Moon's meetings with the Sun, as its month cycles advanced it through the year, formed the zodiac as the Moon's course through the year. The course had been set by Enlil and Ninlil in their journey through the region of death in the underworld. Thus, by virtue of its creation, the zodiac was a feature of the underworld and the constellations formed it as a circuit of the heavens which, at night, were imagined as its manifestation. The course was half in the underworld death region and half in the underworld life region. The stages of death were the second phase of Virgo, Scorpio, Aquarius, and Pisces; the life stages were Taurus, Gemini, Leo, and the first phase of Virgo.

The movement of the Moon through the zodiac created the life which came on earth each year. The source of creation was the new Moon which formed in each constellation when the Moon joined the Sun, and life was the divinity of the full Moon which grew from it and rose in the opposite constellation of the zodiac. When the new Moon formed in the life constellations of Taurus, Gemini, Leo, and the first stage of Virgo, it was summer on earth; but it was winter in the underworld and the full Moon formed successively in the second stage of Virgo, Scorpio, Aquarius, and

Pisces. These were the constellations of death and the Moon formed as a lifeless body.

The summer ended on earth and began in the underworld when the Pleiades rose in Taurus at sunset. The Sun was then entering the second stage of Virgo where the dying Moon joined it and revived in the formation of a new Moon. The full Moons in this stage of the year cycle rose in the constellations of life: Taurus, Gemini, Leo, and the first stage of Virgo. The divinity of those Moons formed as the life of summer which followed on earth.

The doctrine of the inversion of the seasons in the underworld must have evolved from the alternations of the Moon between conjunction and opposition. A corollary to the doctrine was a tenet that the underworld region of life was a mirror. The gods worked in the mirror creating the shapes of life before bringing them on earth. This tenet is clearly stated in a Hittite direction for the ritual erection of a king's palace. The king was a Divine King. The primeval goddesses are described as holding "filled mirrors" and "spinning the king's years."* The filled mirrors are pans of water which make a reflection. The years, of course, are not the years of the king's life as the ruler, but his life as the god bringing life on earth.

Now let us confirm the cosmic nature of Gilgamesh. We will see in a later chapter that the Sumerian astronomer priests associated the planets with stages of the Moon. The Moon God was the god of vegetation and so they made the Moon the vehicle of the Sun's motion through the year. But the motions of the two bodies were so obviously distinct that, to give the imagery theological reality, they identified the Sun's motion with the Moon's planetary aspect as Mercury and made that planet the Sun-bearer. The reason for this identification was certainly the nearness of Mercury to the Sun, for Mercury seems to travel constantly with the Sun, appearing now as an evening and again as a morning star.

*H.G. Güterbock, "Hittite Mythology," *Mythologies of the Ancient World*, Doubleday & Co., 1961, pg. 149.

A number of Greek myths identify Hermes, the Greek Mercury, as the Sun-bearer. His appearance alone is sufficient. Wings were fastened on his hat, his sandals were winged and of gold, and two serpents were entwined at the top of his staff. The wings represented motion, the golden sandals were the moving Sun, and the staff — which was called a caduceus — the Sun's path in its diurnal and annual cycles. The serpents would be the evening and morning stars of the planet.

The myth of Ixion confirms this image of Hermes as the source of the Sun's motion. Ixion was a Divine King; at Zeus's command, Hermes fastened Ixion spread-eagled to a fiery wheel and sent it rolling continuously through the sky. Ixion rolling around on the fiery wheel is also a metaphorical statement of the doctrine of the Moon and Sun moving together in the creation of annual cycles of time.

In Gilgamesh's journey through the death region of the underworld, the theme of the Deer Cult doctrine is repeated three times. It appears first when Gilgamesh punts the boat across the waters of the Abyss of Death. This episode corresponds to the descent of the sacrificed deer down the pole set in the lake bed. The union of the Deer God with the Earth Goddess is implicit in the account of Gilgamesh asleep at the house of Utnapishtim, for he and his wife correspond to the progenitor couple. Utnapishtim was the new Moon of death and new life, and Gilgamesh was the spirit of the dying and reviving Moon.

The theme of the Deer Cult sacrifices is repeated again in the incident in which Gilgamesh recovers the magic plant. The Deer Cult hunters had sewn stones in the bodies of sacrificed deer and sunk them in lakes in a rite that would ensure the return of the deer as new food animals or an increase in the herd. The stones tied to Gilgamesh's feet correspond to the stones in the body of the deer; the deer's revival corresponds to the magic plant.

The theme appears for the third time in the symbolism of the earth-lion serpent which is in itself a sort of visual summary of Gilgamesh's underworld journey. The serpent represents the Moon spirit renewing its

Moon life in the death region of the underworld.

In the Sumero-Babylonian mythology of creation, life began in the serpent Tiamat; the serpent renewing its skin in the *Epic of Gilgamesh* symbolizes the creation of life from the extinction of death. Hence the serpent, as a symbol of the renewal of life, came to be identified as the animal form of the dying and reviving Moon. Gilgamesh called it the earth-lion because the lion was the animal form of the Sun and the serpent carried the Sun through the underworld. The Heavenly Bull was the Moon in the death region of the underworld. When the Bull died, the serpent, which was its life spirit, left its dead body and rose in a new body, after crossing the waters of the Abyss of Death.

As a god, Gilgamesh was one-third mortal and two-thirds immortal. When he awoke at the house of Utnapishtim, he realized that death had claimed his mortal part, which he accepted as his lot.* Yet death was the prelude to resurrection as life on earth, for as a god he had not as yet lived on earth. His acceptance of mortality was followed by his return to Erech as the godhead of the King of Sumer. When his mortal being rose on earth, his immortal being began a new cycle of creation in the underworld. The episode in which the serpent stole his old-man-becomes-young plant shows the separation of his two identities. The earth-lion represented Gilgamesh's immortality. By taking and eating the plant, the serpent left Gilgamesh to his destiny as the Divine King on earth.

*The interpretation of the epic given here differs from the usual view that the epic is a philosophical essay on the fatality of life. This view is based on Gilgamesh's statement that the purpose of his journey was to learn from Utnapishtim how to achieve immortality. Utnapishtim told Gilgamesh that when the gods created the world "they set out death and life" and that there were no gods to change the world which they had created. Utnapishtim's answer reveals the dual nature of the Sumero-Babylonian universe. Gilgamesh's immortality shows that time was infinite and would continually create years of life in the underworld; but on earth, time was finite and the life which it created would continually end.

Although Gilgamesh's two immortal parts are not identified in the epic, they must have been the dual nature of his Moon spirit which combined the immortal Sun with the power of regenerating his body, imaged as Mercury. The two immortal parts were symbolized by the earth-lion. When Gilgamesh killed the Heavenly Bull, he sacrificed Enkidu as the Moon, and the Divine King's form in the underworld of creation. As the Moon spirit, Mercury, and Enkidu's tanist successor, he was about to begin his descent into the Abyss of Death. In the moment of his succession, he ravished Ishtar and became her consort. Therefore, in this relation to her, he passed through the gate of the Scorpion people and made his way to the house of Utnapishtim.

Here we should pause and anticipate the next chapter. The Gilgamesh epic is a complex metaphor which describes the coming into existence of seven years of life. The death of Enkidu divides it into two parts. The first part describes the completion of the formation of seven years outside the limits of world existence as the life cycle of the Moon, personified as Enkidu and Gilgamesh; the second part describes the seven years coming into being as Gilgamesh and forming in the underworld as the godhead of the king. Gilgamesh began existence in the underworld region of death when he ran about the steppe for seven days and nights and formed himself into the joint movement of the Moon and Sun. Then he started on his way to Utnapishtim and passed through the scorpion gate of death to begin the journey through the Abyss to life.

The Abyss was where death merged into life, and the Babylonian Death Goddess and Earth Mother was called Damkina whose spouse was Ea, who had a servant named Isimud. Isimud had two faces, each on an opposite side of his head because he performed errands for Ea on two sides of the Abyss. Being Ea's servant and doing his work, he was actually a part of Ea. Utnapishtim, who lived where Ea lived, was Ea's protégé and Urshanabi was his servant and a part of his being. When Utnapishtim gave Gilgamesh new garments and sent him back to the world of life, he performed Ea's function. When Utnapishtim's wife baked the seven loaves of bread, she was performing Damkina's function. Utnapishtim and Urshanabi were, in mythical actuality, special forms of Ea and Isimud.

Thus, in the Sumero-Babylonian form of the Divine King cult as it evolved from the Deer Cult doctrine, Utnapishtim and his wife personified the union of the Sky Father and Earth Mother of the hunter's underworld. When Gilgamesh ravished Ishtar on the threshold of the death region, he became her consort during the remaining stages of his journey through the underworld. When he and Ishtar arrived at the house of Utnapishtim, they were the Sumero-Babylonian successors of the Deer God and Goddess in the cosmic union of creation.

When Gilgamesh left Utnapishtim's house with Urshanabi, a new Ishtar accompanied them as the goddess of life of a new Moon. Although the epic does not mention her in this last part of the journey, Gilgamesh and Ishtar were following the footsteps of Enlil and Ninlil in their journey through the underworld when they procreated the stages of the Moon.

CHAPTER 11

Enkidu and the Planetary Gods

ca. 3000 through 600 B.C.

The zodiac was the road of the Moon, and the constellations were the stages of its motion. The Moon moved in two courses along the road: one as the month, the other as the year. The Moon's motion was created by the planetary god Mercury, who carried the Sun along with it. The ancient Sumerians came to think of the stages as planetary forms of the Moon. They substituted the planets for the constellations and formed the planetary cycle as the changing stages of the Moon in its monthly cycle. This development may have been as follows:

By the middle of the second millennium, the Sumerians had identified the five visible planets: Venus, Mercury, Mars, Jupiter, and Saturn. Venus had long been recognized as a planet in the sense that it was different from the other stars and, like the Moon, it was seen to follow the path of the zodiac and periodically "died" and came to life again. In the divine nature of the universe, the planet Venus had been linked to the Sun and, with the Sun, had been regarded as the life spirit of the Moon. When the Sumerian theologians found that the planets were all like Venus in their courses through the sky, they held that they also were Moon spirits.

As spirits, they were body spirits with the Sun as the life spirit. The Sumerians associated them with the progressive phases of the Moon. They held that the Moon was the life body of the Sun and moved it through the year. The Sumerians evolved the planetary cycle to describe the path of the Moon in its motion around the circuit of the underworld, bringing each new year of life on earth. The nearness of Mercury to the Sun and the

consequent frequency of its conjunctions gave it a closer relation to that body than Venus. The theologians reformed the orthodox doctrine to transfer the function of the Sun-bearer to Mercury as the male Moon spirit and united him with Venus as her consort.

When Enlil was banished for his rape of Ninlil and the two traveled through the death region of the underworld, they begot three Moons before they returned to the life region where Ninlil gave birth to Nanna-Sin who had been begotten in the rape. In establishing the planetary cycle, the reformers related the planets to these four Moon offspring. Only Nanna was begotten and born in the life region, the other three were begotten and born on Enlil's and Ninlil's circuit through the underworld region of death. Nanna, therefore, was counted as the full Moon, and the other three were the waning third quarter,* the new Moon, and the waxing first quarter. Jupiter, which rivals Venus in brightness, was naturally identified with the full Moon; Saturn was imagined as the spirit form of the waning Moon; and Mars, the spirit form of the waxing first quarter. The new Moon, which formed as a crescent, vanished at sunrise, and reappeared at sunset, was like the disappearing morning star and the returning evening star of Venus and was itself counted as a planet.

The Sun, as the life spirit of the Moon, was identified as Mercury. Mercury as the Sun-bearer was the moving spirit which changed the phases of the Moon, hence, Mercury was all the planets one at a time. The motion of Mercury with the Sun formed the planetary cycle as the Moon. It evolved out of the Deer Cult doctrine of sacrifice, which began with the descent of the god spirit to a death union in the underworld, and ended in the return of the spirit on earth, bringing fertility to livestock and the soil, and the harvest. In the planetary cycle, the descending spirit was Saturn and the new life began when Mercury changed from the evening star to the morning star in the Abyss of Death and began its ascent to life. At that

*The third quarter ends at conjunction of the Moon and Sun, hence, it is commonly called the last quarter.

point, the body of the Moon vanished, leaving the Sun to animate the new Moon beginning to form around Mercury's morning star. This was the planetary Moon spirit which in the next stage of the cycle became Mars and then rose as Mercury's morning star bringing the Sun, thus bringing the Moon into the fullness of life as the incarnation of the spirit Jupiter. Both sexes were combined in the Moon so that Venus and Mercury were united as consorts and Venus combined with each of the other planet spirits in turn. After her union with Jupiter, the cycle ended with Venus as the Death Goddess and Earth Mother giving birth to a new cycle of Moon life, which on earth came as the harvest of the land and the increase of flocks and herds.

The planetary cycle was thus constituted as Saturn-Sun-Moon-Mars-Mercury- Jupiter-Venus. Each of the planets was a god with the combined divinities of the Moon and Sun and an aspect of the Great Goddess and her consort.

The planets in the cycle correspond to the constellations of the Sumerian zodiac; their god identities relate them to the theme of *Epic of Gilgamesh.* The planetary elements of the cycle were introduced in the opening scenes.* Gilgamesh appears as Mercury. Enkidu, emerging on the steppe from the forest where he lived as an animal, comes as the new Moon. The harlot whom Gilgamesh sends to tame Enkidu is Ishtar, the planet Venus, and when Enkidu copulates with her, he becomes her consort and the changing form of the Moon. Huwawa is the Sun.

The scene is the nonworld of the creation region in which Gilgamesh, Ishtar, Enkidu, and Huwawa (as Mercury, Venus, the Moon, and the Sun, respectively) combine to form the planetary cycle. Gilgamesh brings them all together by uniting Ishtar and Enkidu, defeating Enkidu in the wrestling match, and capturing Huwawa with the help of Enkidu. Thus, the planetary cycle is composed of Gilgamesh (Mercury) with the Sun and Enkidu (the

*The planetary gods are not mentioned specifically in the epic, but they are implicit in the natures of Gilgamesh and Ishtar, and in the combining of the 7 days of succession.

Moon in its changing planetary forms), united with Ishtar (Venus) who form in combination as the full Moon to constitute the divinity which will come on earth as the god of a new year of life.

The life formed in the planetary cycle was a year in which the planetary gods, being divisions, were gods of time. Based on the planetary cycle, the Sumerian theologians constructed a sacred calendar. Each day was counted as one of the planetary gods beginning with Saturn representing the genesis of life; then the Sun as the life spirit; then the Moon as life substance; Mars, the god of growth; Mercury, time; Jupiter, maturity; and finally Venus, decline and death. In the calendar, the gods combined as units of 7 days.

The year was divided into 13 months of 4 weeks, or 28 days, which made the length of the year 364 days. This year was one day shorter than the actual year, which was counted as 365 days. The theologians, therefore, combined the years into 7-year cycles with 7 intercalated days at the end, which conformed them into actual years. The life which formed in these years of creation came on earth in the person of the Divine King. Thus, the 7-year cycle was certainly an extended planetary cycle in which each year was a god in the planetary order.

The evidence for attributing the development of the calendar to the Sumerians is partly presumptive since no Sumerian clay tablets have been found recording this planetary calendar. There is evidence of a planetary week in Babylon and Palestine early in the second millennium B.C. and, at about the same time in Greece, the seven Titans and Titanesses were made the rulers of the planetary days. By that time, the Babylonians had supplanted the Sumerians; but the planetary calendar was certainly a Sumerian invention.

The story of the epic is divided into two parts. The first part recounts the civilizing and death of Enkidu; the second part describes Gilgamesh's journey through the underworld. Enkidu personified the creation of the 7-year cycle as the Moon's motion with the Sun and his death was the means of bringing the planetary gods into existence as the life which came on

earth. He was the archetype Divine King, and Gilgamesh was his tanist. The tanist, as his life spirit, departed at the death of the Divine King and, carrying the divine life through the underworld, brought it to the world on earth where it lodged in the successor king. When Enkidu died, Gilgamesh entered the underworld as the planetary gods, each in succession, and brought them through the underworld to the gateway to life in the city of Erech.

There were thus two time cycles of creation, each of seven years. The first proceeded outside of the world of existence in the void of infinity in which the world was created. The time and the life created in that cycle were potential and came into being as the second cycle through death. Death was the gateway between nonexistence and existence. The power of creation was the divinity of the Moon which, in its cyclical manifestation, disappears into an apparent state of nonexistence and then reappears. To the ancients, the disappearance and reappearance were sacrifice and resurrection, and the 7-year time cycles were imagined as extended cycles of the Moon. The first cycle was the Moon forming into seven planetary years in a process of creation comparable to that by which the world was originally created.

When the world came into existence in the original creation, it was a world in which the earth was divided into an underworld and the world on the surface above. Life rose out of the earth through the soil. In the sequence of creation, the underworld formed first; when the 7 years came into existence, they came as creation years in the underworld of the earth and rose out of it as 7 years of life. The process of creation was continuous and every 7 years a new cycle came into existence in the underworld.

In light of this, we can see that the epic describes a new 7-year cycle coming into existence. An analysis of the theme reveals it as a capsule description of the formation of the 7-year cycle beyond the underworld and the structure of its formation. The structure is a calendar of days personified as gods of the Moon and Sun who combine in a uniform movement in which life and time are created. The picture must be viewed against a background of Sumerian mythology which is implicit in the context. The relevant mythology relates to the cult of the Divine King. Enkidu is the Moon or, more precisely, he is the Moon which takes form beyond the universe and comes into being to rise on earth in the person of the king.

Gilgamesh traveled the path made by Enlil and Ninlil when they begot the four Moons and created the lunar cycle. To recapitulate, Enlil had been banished to the underworld for raping Ninlil and, as he made his way there, Ninlil followed him. At each of three stages as Enlil traversed the underworld, he disguised himself and, when Ninlil appeared, he raped her. The reason for this seemingly outrageous behavior was to ensure that the offspring of the first rape, which would be the Moon God Nanna, would be born in the upper life region of the underworld after their return. Ninlil duly gave birth to three Moon brothers in the underworld and Nanna was born as planned.

In formulating the planetary cycle, the theologians made Saturn the first Moon brother. The second Moon brother became the new Moon. He was born at the point of death where the road changes and becomes the road to life. His place of birth made him the planetary Moon emerging from death with Mercury carrying the Sun. They assigned the third Moon brother the position of the planetary Mars, as the Moon coming with Mercury and the Sun into the life region of the underworld.

Nanna, who was born as the full Moon, was given the planetary form of Jupiter. He was the antithesis of his planetary new Moon brother. He, too, was paired with Mercury carrying the Sun; but, whereas in the constitution of the new Moon, Mercury was the evening star bringing the Sun to the Moon's death, in the full Moon, Mercury was the morning star bringing the Sun to the fullness of the Moon as life.

The summer of life that came on earth was the divinity of the full Moon which formed in the underworld. The end of the summer brings the harvest

and, in the lunar theology of the planetary cycle, the harvest was reaped in the death of the Moon. The final stage of the cycle was Venus as the Earth Mother and Death Goddess. Ishtar revealed herself as the harvest when she called on Anu to send the Heavenly Bull. Anu was reluctant, fearing that the Bull might destroy the life which had formed, but Ishtar assured him that she had stored food for men and animals for seven years, so he sent the Bull. In the metaphor of vegetation, the first six gods of the planetary cycle formed the life cycle of the grain crop from planting to maturity. The last three — Mercury, Jupiter, and Venus — constituted the full Moon as the ripened grain and the harvest.

In the epic, the creation of the seven years is metaphorically described as the formation of the diurnal motion of the Moon into a cosmic being or world-man personified as Enkidu. The planetary gods formed the days and life of the seven years. In the mythologies of peoples who adopted the Great Goddess religion, the gods had to die in order to come into existence and, when they had formed themselves as seven years of life, they combined as a cosmic being. This being was imagined as a world-man who died in sacrifice and so brought the gods into being as seven years of earthly life. Thus, the world-man formed at the threshold between nonexistence and existence.

Enkidu's formation as the world-man began when he met Ishtar who came as the harlot sent by Gilgamesh and he copulated with her for six days and seven nights. To understand the conduct of Enkidu and Ishtar, we must first consider the tenets of the planetary doctrine. In the planetary doctrine of creation, life was formed by the joint motion of the Sun and Moon. The manifest motion of the Sun was its cycle from sunrise to sunset as the daytime. The manifest motion of the Moon was its cycle from Moonrise to Moonset as the night. The two formed the full cycle of the day; but their motions were not uniform in the visible sky. The planetary doctrine conformed the two motions by combining them in the invisible region of life creation outside of the world on earth. In the combining, the

Sun was held to be the life spirit of the Moon and the Moon, being the body of the spirit, was held to be the vehicle of the Sun's motion; but the moving spirit of their combined motion was the Moon spirit Mercury.

The Moon in its divinity was the staple of life and was mortal. To the ancients, life was associated with daylight and night with death and returning life. The Moon's motion was measured in days and, since the planetary gods constituted the changing phases of the Moon, they were identified with the days. Since they were aspects of the Moon, they were counted as Moons. The cycle of the planetary gods was part of the process of creation of yearly life.

In creation, life appears first and movement follows. Life was created as the divinity of the Moon and and a planetary god began the cycle. His life was day. When the planetary god died, the day changed to night and the Moon spirit started on its underworld journey of death to renew its life in the planetary god of the succeeding day. In its journey, it cast off its dead Moon body and put on the body of the next planetary god. At dawn, life formed in the new body and the god rose as the Moon of the next day.

Thus the Moon spirit moved from one planetary god to the next, and its changes created the life and movement of the Moon as the planetary cycle. The Moons of the planetary gods were the stages of life and, paradoxically, the nights were the days. The seven stages of the cycle equaled the seven stages of the original creation and the days of their creation formed the length of the created life into periods of months and the year.

Since, in the planetary theology, there were four Moons in the full lunar cycle, or month, and the succession of the seven planetary gods constituted a cycle in itself, each Moon was constituted by a succession and there were four cycles of succession in a full cycle, or 28 days. The 28 days were counted as the length of the lunar month. Thus, the formulators of the planetary doctrine translated the measure of the Moon's daily movement from degrees of celestial arc to the length of the planetary day, and by combining the light of the Sun's daily course with the night course of the

Moon, they made 13 the number of months in the year. This changed the length of the lunar year from 354-plus days to 364. The lunar year was consequently approximately equal to the solar year and combined the motion of the two bodies into a year of life.

Now we return to the epic and the conduct of Enkidu and Ishtar. When Enkidu came out of the steppe, he was the unformed new Moon emerging in the region of death. Ishtar was the Moon spirit Venus whose consort was the Sun. In the cycle of the Moon, she was reborn at new Moon as a spirit form of the new Moon. Ishtar was polyandrous, and the Sun God and the planetary gods were part of her. Her conduct with Enkidu brought him into the same relationship with her and, as they copulated, Enkidu was constituted as the days of the Moon's planetary cycle. The planetary gods were formed as new Moons in the process.

The nature of the planetary gods as full Moons in the daylight and as new Moons at night was twofold; as the one, they were created life, as the other, they were time as days. In the metaphor of the epic, days were the life of the Moon and nights the days of its creation. This explains why Enkidu and Ishtar continued copulating on the seventh night but stopped during the seventh day. Venus was the seventh planetary god — on her day, the life of the Moon was complete and the Moon returned to its death state as the new Moon to begin a new cycle of life. Their copulation at night formed Enkidu as the days of the Moon's motion; but because Enkidu's life as the Moon was complete on the sixth day, they stopped copulating on the seventh.

The steppe in the metaphor was the death state of the Moon and, in his liaison with Ishtar, Enkidu was created as the new Moon. But he was the new Moon not yet risen. He rose and formed into the full Moon in the stages of the planetary gods in the course of his adventures which followed. Most of those adventures have already been related, so let us review them in the light of additional details.

Before meeting Ishtar, Enkidu had run and lived with gazelles. When he separated from her, he went back to them, but they rejected him. The metaphor connotes return to the steppe, the region of death; hence, Saturn descending to death.

Enkidu returned to Ishtar who dressed him in some of her clothes and took him to civilization. There he was given food and drink. The drink made him merry. Intoxication was a literary figure for divine inspiration; the metaphor is the incarnation of Enkidu as the Sun.

Ishtar then took Enkidu to Erech. Traveling with Ishtar and wearing her dress, Enkidu was the planetary Moon.

Erech represented the gateway to the life state of the lunar cycle; their arrival signified their entry into the planetary stage of Mars.

In Erech, they met Gilgamesh on his way to his wedding (the epic does not identify the bride). Enkidu barred his way, then the two wrestled and Gilgamesh was the victor. The victory united Enkidu to Gilgamesh and, since Enkidu was already Ishtar's consort, the wrestling match proved to be the wedding ceremony.* The planetary god of the metaphor is Mercury.

Enkidu then went with Gilgamesh to the cedar forest where they killed Huwawa. In this adventure, Enkidu formed as the full Moon of Jupiter.

The seventh adventure was the meeting with Ishtar who brought the life of the Moon to completion and, by bringing down the Heavenly Bull, sent Enkidu to his lunar death.

Thus, the planetary gods formed in Enkidu as the life stages of the Moon. In the theology of divinity, the part is equal to the whole; therefore, each god who had been created as a new Moon formed as a full Moon and, together in their cycles, they constituted the life which would come into existence through the medium of the world-man.

Enkidu's death as the Moon was the sacrifice of the Heavenly Bull. When the bull died, Ishtar (who in the full Moon was the Moon Goddess) was transformed into Ereshkigal, the Death Goddess and Earth Mother, and

*Jacobsen makes Enkidu the victor; either way, the match united the two as one.

Enkidu as the Heavenly Bull became her consort in death.* But, although Enkidu was sacrificed and descended to the death region, life continued within him and he lived for 13 days, including the day of his immolation. On the day of the sacrifice, he held the bull while it died and the following 12 days he was deathly ill. Then he died. In the metaphor of the epic, as he holds the dying bull, and then in his illness, he is half-dead and half-alive, a state which describes him as a new Moon. In this death and life image, Gilgamesh hurled the thigh bone of the Heavenly Bull at Ishtar and metaphorically mated with her; for in the metaphor he was the life spirit of Enkidu as the dead bull.

When Enkidu died, Gilgamesh was grief stricken and ran about the steppe for 7 days and nights. Then he buried Enkidu and set out to find Utnapishtim. The steppe in the epic represented the region of death, and Gilgamesh was the seven planetary gods. The succession of the days and nights and the movement of Gilgamesh, and his going out on the steppe at the death of Enkidu denote the cyclical movement of the Moon. The significance of the 13 days of Enkidu's illness will appear in the next chapter.

*Sumerian mythology describes the Heavenly Bull as the consort of Ereshkigal (See: Jacobsen, *The Treasures of Darkness*, p. 96); she appears in the epic as Siduri, the innkeeper at the edge of the Abyss.

CHAPTER 12

Gilgamesh and the Planetary Calendar

ca. 2600 through 1750 B.C.

A new cycle of world life came into existence at Enkidu's death. His Moon figure metaphorically represented the earth. In the cosmology of the Great Goddess, the Moon was the life form of the earth and the manifestation of the life cycles of the goddess and her consort. The divinity of the Moon was the life which the earth produced. The Moon in death was the death of vegetation and earthly life, identified as the Death Goddess and Earth Mother.

The account in the epic of the formation of Enkidu into a world-man describes the creation of the Moon into seven years of world life. The action proceeds in the region of nonexistence. The story which follows the death of Enkidu describes the resurrection of his spirit Gilgamesh as the new Moon in the spirit world beneath the earth. The action is the formation of Gilgamesh into 7 years of life which would come on earth above. Mystically, the scene is the womb of the Death Goddess and Earth Mother.

The mystery of the death of Enkidu and his resurrection as Gilgamesh follows the doctrine of the hunters. When the hunters killed their animal-god, the god did not die, but journeyed to the god world where its body was renewed and where it gathered new food animals. Then the god returned to the hunting grounds on earth, bringing the animals with him. The god did not leave his body immediately after the kill; the hunters ate him in a communion meal and the body, or its head and pelt, were given a place of honor at the meal. The god was believed to consume his own flesh where it remained because the god was still alive in all his body parts. Nor did the god depart after the meal, but remained in the head and bones for varying lengths of time before leaving for the god world.

In the epic, the sacrifice was the killing of the Heavenly Bull, which was the animal form of the Moon and Enkidu in his aspect as the full Moon. But like the animal-god of the hunters, Enkidu did not die and Gilgamesh as his life spirit remained with him. After 12 days following the day on which the Heavenly Bull was killed, Gilgamesh left the body of Enkidu and ran about the steppe for 7 days and nights. The steppe was symbolically the underworld region of death and Gilgamesh's movements on it and his journey to Utnapishtim's correspond to the animal-god's journey to the god world.

The place where Utnapishtim lived in the Abyss is a mythical version of the animal-god world. The loaves which Utnapishtim's wife baked while Gilgamesh slept are its mystic version of the food animals which the animal-god gathered. Gilgamesh's return journey to Erech brought seven years of life to the world above, just as the animal-god's return brought a new supply of game to the hunting grounds.

The gods constituting Enkidu reveal the structure of the calendar. When Shamash charged both Gilgamesh and Enkidu with carrying the Sun, he made the Moon's yearly cycles the length of the Sun year. In its course as the year, the Moon moved in two cycles: one was its course as the month, and the other was the Sun's course as the year.

The Moon's course as the month was the course of the planetary gods forming as full Moons during the daylight half of each day. Each planetary god died as a full Moon at nightfall and, during the night, the Moon spirit formed as the new Moon body of the next planetary god.

The Moon's course as the year was the movement of the Moon spirit as he formed each new Moon during the night. The successions of the planetary gods as full Moons of the month cycle created the life of the days, and the Moon spirit as the new Moons of the year cycle formed the life into the days of the year.

The two movements were distinct. The progression of the planetary gods created life, the progression of the Moon spirit created time. Four Moons constituted the full Moon cycle and the planetary gods moved each Moon in seven stages. In the formation of the calendar, therefore, the stages of life were counted as the planetary god in series of seven. In the progression of time, the Moon moved as 13 new Moons and the stages of time were counted in series of 13 days.

Now while the two movements were distinct, they were nevertheless combined in the creation of the year. In the calendrical construction, they were coupled to form units of creation with each series repeating until the year was complete. Thus, the calendrical count was as follows (the new Moons are denoted by numbers):

Saturn	1
Sun	2
Moon	3
Mars	4
Mercury	5
Jupiter	6
Venus	7
Saturn	8
Sun	9
Moon	10
Mars	11
Mercury	12
Jupiter	**13**
Venus	1
Saturn	2
Sun	3
etc.	*etc.*
Mercury	11
Jupiter	12
Venus	**13**

There is, to be sure, no calendrical record of this count, but it is a corollary to the creation of Enkidu as a world-man. Enkidu was the Moon and its cyclical movements with the Sun. His cyclical life side was formed by the planetary gods and his death side by Gilgamesh and his 13 days of half-life as the new Moon. When he died, he came into being as the 7-year cycle of life.

As we have seen, the new Moons which formed each night in the planetary cycle were counted as days; therefore, the 4 Moons of the month cycle multiplied the new Moons and made the 28 days of the month. The days of the month and the days of the year were the same; therefore, the days of the month had to be counted with the 13 new Moons, thus making the calendrical count of the year of creation 7–13–28. The 28-day count combined the life created by the seven planetary gods with the days of the month and year cycles and formed the length of the year as 364 days.*

The gods who formed the life of the seven years came into being through the death of Enkidu. When he died, the theme of the epic changed to Gilgamesh's journey through the underworld; which brings us to a consideration of the calendrical implications of that theme.

To that end, we should consider the nature of Gilgamesh's journey. He traveled when it was summer in the underworld. He was the Moon spirit leaving the body of the dead Moon. He carried the Sun which made him the conjunction of the Moon with the Sun and, therefore, a new Moon. The new Moon did not spring fully formed from the dead Moon and, when Gilgamesh left the body of Enkidu, he ran about the steppe for 7 days and nights. During that time, he was a bodiless spirit and in his running he formed the cyclical motion of the Moon. Bodiless, his being as a new

*Modern calendars still combine the count of the planetary gods and days of the month, e.g., Sunday - 1, Monday - 2, Tuesday (Mars) - 3, Wednesday (Mercury) - 4, Thursday (Jupiter) - 5, Friday (Venus) - 6, Saturday (Saturn) - 7. The 7 days make the week and the 4 weeks of February make that month 28 days. The English names for the days of the week are the Anglo-Saxon names of the planetary gods.

Moon was inchoate. From this and his subsequent action, clearly he was the new Moon in formation.

Gilgamesh acquired a new Moon body in his adventure on the shores of the Abyss. The gods who had formed in Enkidu as a world-man came into existence at his death. They included Ishtar in all her aspects as the Moon Goddess, and Enkidu himself transformed into the Heavenly Bull. When the Heavenly Bull died, Ishtar in her full Moon aspect was transformed into the Death Goddess and Earth Mother whom the Sumerians called Ereshkigal. Enkidu, who had been Ishtar's consort in life, became her consort in death as the Heavenly Bull.

If we refer again to the myth of Inanna's visit to Ereshkigal, we will see how the new Moon formed as the body of Gilgamesh. (Bear in mind that Inanna was the Sumerian name of Ishtar.) Ereshkigal was Inanna's Death Goddess aspect. In the myth, when she died and was transformed into Ereshkigal, Inanna came to life again as a new Moon Goddess. Thus, in her meeting with Ereshkigal, Inanna was Ereshkigal in death and the new Moon in Ereshkigal's womb. Inanna was not single in the womb; she had a twin brother, the Sun Utu, who came to life with her and became her consort.

Siduri is actually Ereshkigal in the epic. Her calling and the location of the inn which she kept identifies her as the Goddess of Death. The location was the shore of the waters of death and life, and the rooms of the inn were lodging places for the dead. Gilgamesh came to her place of death as Inanna had come to Ereshkigal — in his union with Ishtar, the two were one and he was as much Ishtar as Gilgamesh.

Mythological descriptions are seemingly inconsistent because they describe the gods in different circumstances and are composed at different times. Ereshkigal appears single in the Inanna myth, but in fact, her consort of death was the god Nergal. Ereshkigal's relation to Inanna makes it clear that she was the dead Moon; Nergal, therefore, was perforce the male half of the dead Moon.

Mythology records that the Heavenly Bull was Ereshkigal's consort, which makes it certain that the Heavenly Bull was an alias for Nergal. Enkidu, who had been created as the body of Gilgamesh, came into existence as the consort of Ereshkigal in death. He came as the Heavenly Bull, alias Nergal. The new Moon was half-death, half-life — half-female and half-male. Siduri and the Heavenly Bull formed as the death half of Gilgamesh's new Moon body.

Ishtar, who was both Moon and Moon spirit, became the female side of the life half. The male side was constituted by Urshanabi. The nature of Urshanabi and his action attest his identity. Urshanabi was part of Utnapishtim. Utnapishtim was the immortality of the new Moon, and the role of Urshanabi in the formation of Gilgamesh as a Moon was the same as that of Enkidu in the creation. Further, Gilgamesh punted Urshanabi's boat across the waters of death. Only the Sun could make the crossing and Gilgamesh gave both the Sun and Moon their motion. Urshanabi, as the Moon, rode in the ferry boat with the Sun.

Urshanabi's character as Gilgamesh's bodily form as the new Moon is implicit in the mythology of the epic. The Sun God Shamash had made Enkidu a carrier of the Sun equally with Gilgamesh. When the gods came into existence through his death, a god came into being as the life form of Enkidu to carry the Sun. In the account of the epic, the only one who could perform that function is Urshanabi.

Here we should note the theological nature of the new Moon. It was the source of cyclical motion in which the Moon rose from death and became full and died. It was like a seed which contains the growth, maturity, and harvest of a plant. In the theology of the Great Goddess religion, the life of the earth was contained in the body of the Moon. The mythology of the formation of the Moon was the metaphysics of creation. In the mythology, the spirit formed a body as the larva forms a cocoon, develops its life form within, and emerges in the fullness of life.

When Gilgamesh embarked on the waters of death, he had formed the inchoate Moon in the body shell of the new Moon. The next stage of formation was the creation of the life cycle of the Moon within the body. It began with Gilgamesh's sleep at Utnapishtim's. The sleep was the mortal sleep of death. Utnapishtim's immortality made him the source of life and he caused Gilgamesh to sleep six days and seven nights, and formed him into the source of the Moon's monthly life.

Utnapishtim's wife was the female part of his new Moon immortality which included all things that had provided his livelihood in the golden age before the flood. The seven loaves of bread which Utnapishtim's wife baked must, therefore, have represented the fruits of the soil which the seven created years would bring. Thus, the loaves formed him into the life source of the years.

The six gods of the planetary cycle constituted the life of the Moon and in his next adventures Gilgamesh formed as those six gods. The epic metaphorically describes his formation as a departure from Utnapishtim. It starts when Urshanabi takes him to the bath. He is then still wearing the skins which mark him as the dead Moon and the planetary god Saturn. When he casts off the skins, be becomes the planetary Sun; and when he puts on the new garment which Utnapishtim provides for him, he becomes the planetary Moon. Urshanabi's boat is docked in the waters of life and as Gilgamesh and Urshanabi shove off, they leave the shores of death and Gilgamesh changes into the planetary form of Mars. Next, when he stops at the pool to bathe, the serpent steals the magic plant. The serpent represents his immortal part, while he, having entered the region of life, constitutes his own mortal part. In the part-immortal, part-mortal state he is Mercury. In the end, he comes to Erech and when he takes Urshanabi up on the walls and shows him the Temple of Ishtar and the surrounding orchards and city within them, he is the planetary Jupiter.

Thus the narrative ends with Gilgamesh and Urshanabi viewing Erech from its walls. If we refer again to the myth of Inanna's visit to Ereshkigal, we realize that implicit in this ending is the transformation of Gilgamesh into the seventh planetary god, the goddess Venus. In the myth, Inanna returns from the underworld of death and finds her consort, Dumuzi, lording it as the sovereign of Heaven. She fixes the eye of death on him and orders the demons which accompany her to carry him to Ereshkigal as her replacement in the palace of death. When the demons seize him, he tries to escape and calls on the Sun, Utu, to help him. Utu changes him into a snake and the demons seize him and carry him to Ereshkigal. Gilgamesh is the transfiguration of Dumuzi — in the theology of Divine Kingship, there is no difference between them.

The return of Inanna, the transformation of Dumuzi, and his abduction by the demons explains the metamorphosis of Gilgamesh into Ishtar. Inanna was Queen of Heaven; but she was also the earth and the plants and fruit of the earth. Dumuzi as the sovereign of Heaven was the full Moon; Gilgamesh with Urshanabi as Jupiter was the full Moon. Erech, with its orchards and Temple of Ishtar, was Ishtar herself.* The epic records that all that Gilgamesh achieved by his journey was to show Erech to Urshanabi from the height of the walls. Thus, Gilgamesh vanished in the presence of Ishtar, as Dumuzi had vanished in the clutches of the demons.

Here we must remember that the Moon was a single body constituted as both god and goddess and that, as a divinity, the Moon could appear in either sex. In the Inanna myth, the sex of the Moon God Dumuzi changed to that of the Moon Goddess Inanna; in the epic, Gilgamesh in his full Moon body was changed into Ishtar as the planetary goddess Venus.

The planetary goddess Venus was a goddess of death. The incident in the epic in which the earth-lion steals the magic plant is a version of the transformation of Dumuzi into a snake. The earth-lion is the immortal part of Gilgamesh, the part that becomes the full Moon is his mortal part.

Gilgamesh and Urshanabi surveying Erech from the walls constituted a world-man figure of the new Moon composed of the Sun and Moon Gods as the days of the year of earthly life. The world-man was a cosmic figure

Cf., Horus as Egypt.

of the Moon cycle formed as the phases of the Moon. His planetary nature enables us to reconstruct his constitution. The gods Saturn, Sun, and Moon composed the lower parts of his body; Mars, Mercury, and Jupiter composed the upper parts. These six gods constituted the waxing life side of his cyclical being; Ishtar, the planetary goddess Venus, constituted his waning death side.

The world-man figure of Gilgamesh was formed as the season of summer in the death constellations of the zodiac in four stages. First, as the inchoate Moon in the death stage of Virgo; next as the new Moon in Scorpio; then the life side of his body formed in Aquarius; and his death side formed in Pisces. The stages, translated into the plant life of summer, were the growing and harvest stages from germinant seed to the new seed in the withering stalk.

The four stages were the four Moons of the Moon cycle. The first three were the Moons which Enlil and Ninlil had created in the death region of the underworld as the Moon in the process of formation. The fourth Moon was created in the life region of the underworld and was the fully formed Moon at the point of beginning life. In the doctrine of sacrifice, death was the entrance to life and the goddess of death and life was Ishtar. The fourth Moon was the Moon God united with the Moon Goddess. In the metaphor of the epic, the walls of Erech and the temple and orchards which they surrounded represented Gilgamesh with Urshanabi and Ishtar in union as the full Moon.

Let us now examine the calendrical nature of the world-man image of Gilgamesh. The gods who composed him were the gods of the Moon in motion with the Sun. They moved in the year cycle of the Sun and the month cycle of the Moon. They were gods in being in the underworld; therefore, their movements formed the underworld creation years. The gods of the year cycle were the 13 new Moons and the 7 new Moons of the planetary cycle which formed during the evening and morning of each day. The 13 new Moons of the year cycle and the 7 planetary new Moons moved

together in repeating series of 13 and 7 until the completion of a quarter-year of 91 days (13 x 7 = 91). Then they repeated their cyclical movements to make the year 364 days.

The gods of the month cycle were the gods of the planetary cycle who formed as full Moons during the daylight half of the day and the gods of the 28 days. On the twenty-eighth day of each month, they joined the Sun as a new Moon that would form the days of the succeeding month. The new Moon joined the cyclical movement of the 13 and 7 gods of the year cycle, making the day count 13–7–28 and bringing the year to conclusion at the end of the thirteenth month.

When Gilgamesh died as the world-man and so brought life on earth as an incarnation of the king, his immortal Mercury-Sun spirit continued along the path of the zodiac in the underworld. Its course was through Taurus, Gemini, Leo, and the first stage of Virgo. Following it, he brought his mortal Moon body into the underworld of death in the constellations of the second stage of Virgo, Scorpio, Aquarius, and Pisces, where the underworld creation year ended.

In Babylon, Marduk was the god of life, or the year Sun as we may call him. His life span was 360 days and when he died, there was a 5-day period during which the Moon Gods rose and came on earth as a new Marduk. Presumably the change in the length of the year from 364 days was a Babylonian reformation of the planetary calendar; but in any case, early in the second millennium B.C., the Babylonians defined a new zodiac of 12 constellations which marked the Moon's annual course with the Sun. The Babylonians had inherited their mathematics from the Sumerians and thought of the circumference of a circle as having 360 degrees. They divided the zodiac into twelve 30-degree arcs and evidently counted each degree as a day. The circle of the zodiac is the annual course of the Sun as a year on earth and, therefore, the Babylonians made the god's life as the year 360 days which they divided into twelve 30-day months.

The additional five days of the actual year were considered days of

during the year that had ended, and which would be the life of the year that was beginning. The ceremony signified that the new Marduk rose on earth on that day and lodged in the person of the king. Each year Marduk died and the king's divinity left him at the end of 360 days; his death coincided with the end of the underworld summer when the creation of the new year of life was complete. This was marked by sacrifice of the Moon bull on the evening of the fifth day. There were five days between the fifth and eleventh day, and during those five days there was no god to give life to Babylon. The city was filled with tumult and all across the land there was death and desolation; it was a time comparable to the days in Egypt between the death of Horus and the coming of a new Horus to the throne. On the eleventh day, a new Marduk was lodged in the King, and Babylon had returned to life.

The *Akitu* ceremonies as they have been recorded in detail are the performances of the later Babylonian period; but the *Akitu* festival was celebrated in Sumerian times. The Sumerian seal **[Figure 7]**, dated circa

Figure 7. Sumerian seal depicting the ascension of Dumuzi.

2200 B.C., depicts the ascension of Dumuzi as the incarnation of the king and his union with the goddess. The central figure is a god rising from the underworld. The figure has been identified as the Sun God Utu; but the identification can only be partly correct. The figure must be Nabu, or Ninurta as the Sumerians called him, the Moon spirit Mercury carrying the Sun. This will be evident from the following consideration:

In the Sumerian myth describing Enki organizing world order, Utu is described as a bull that has a lapis lazuli beard and that roars like a lion. The beard marks him as a god of vegetation and the bull associates him with the Moon. His roar is his Sun nature as a lion. The Sun by itself could not move; it was the life spirit of the Moon combined with the Moon spirit Mercury which moved the Sun and Moon together. Mercury gave Utu his vegetal and lunar appearance.

In the seal, Utu or rather Ninurta-Nabu is pictured in the center of the mountain in the underworld which covered the Abyss. The mountain is abstractly portrayed as two towers rising from the same foundation. The god is between the towers. The other figures show that he is rising in resurrection from death. The seal pictures the Moon spirit descending as a bird with a large beak, an eagle or hawk, with a snake in its talons lighting on the hand of a god who stands to the right of center with his foot on the side of the mountain. The bird is Dumuzi as a Sun-bird which Utu is changing into the Mercury Moon-serpent, Ninurta-Nabu.

The god is Enki in the midst of the waters of the Abyss. Fish are swimming in the waters and represent Enki regenerating the substance of new life which Ninurta-Nabu will bring on his return to earth. His two-faced servant, Isimud, is beside him and symbolizes the descent and return of the god spirit.

The bird with the serpent and the gods are in profile turned toward the left. The rendering shows that the action is toward the center and Ninurta-Nabu as the rising Sun God, and indicates the course of creation in the underworld.

Ishtar in the Land of Death

The Sun God also is in profile turned toward the left. Above him and standing on the mountaintop toward which he is rising is the goddess Inanna with a tree for her insignia as vegetation and life. Beside her is another god with a lion as his sign. The lion was the animal form of the Sun in its underworld journey and the god-kings of the Near East adopted it as a symbol of their divine incarnation, compounding it with an eagle or hawk as a griffin or with a human head and body as a sphinx. The Egyptian pharaohs even had the sphinx heads carved as portraits of themselves. The lion properly marks Ninurta-Nabu rising as Dumuzi to incarnate the person of the King of Sumer.

This identification is confirmed by the composition of the figures on the seal. Ninurta was a hunter, and the god holds a bow in his left hand which identifies him as a hunter. He and Inanna are facing towards the front, giving them equal status and, as gods of life on earth, relatively superior importance over the gods of creation. The equality with Inanna accorded the god identifies him as her consort; but her position shows that she is the life which is coming with the Sun God as a new year on earth. Utu, or Ninurta rather, is rising toward the mountaintop where Inanna stands. The direction of his ascent, Inanna's position on the mountaintop in relation to Enki in the Abyss, and the tree which is her symbol of created life on earth in relation to the fish which are Enki's sign of life in creation in the underworld, all mark the goddess as created life. In the mythical imagery, the two would become united as consorts and Ninurta as the Moon spirit Mercury would have become the planetary form of the full Moon.

Ninurta is actually the god Dumuzi who was worshiped by different names in different parts of southwest Asia. Dumuzi, like Gilgamesh, was part mortal and part immortal. He came on earth as a mortal in the spring in the person of the king and was married in ritual to the goddess. His earthly union corresponded to an underworld union in which his immortal being was married to Ishtar transformed into the Death Goddess and Earth Mother. The death marriage marked the beginning of the winter half of the

year in the underworld and the imprisonment of the god in the Abyss of Death. At the end of the death winter, summer began in the underworld and the god was released to put on a new mortal form as the consort of Ishtar who changed back to her being as goddess of earth life.

In Babylonian times, Dumuzi was known mostly as Tammuz. In the eastern Mediterranean, he was called Adonis by the Greeks. Adonis spent one-half of the year in the underworld as consort of Persephone, the Greek goddess of death and equivalent of Ereshkigal. He spent the other half as consort of Aphrodite, the Greek form of Ishtar. Persephone was the Moon in its death state and Aphrodite, in her Asian aspect of Ishtar, life forming as a new Moon in the underworld summer. Like Dumuzi, Adonis came on earth incarnate in the king and his coming brought the life of the new year.

Frazer describes the marriage celebration at Alexandria as follows:

> "At Alexandria images of Aphrodite and Adonis are displayed as two couches... The marriage of the lovers was celebrated on one day and on the morrow women attired as mourners with streaming hair and bared breasts, bore the image of the dead Adonis to the sea and committed it to the waves... (but) they sang that the lost one would come back again."

The rites portray Adonis' death marriage to Aphrodite in which she is transformed into Persephone. The sea was symbolic of the waters of the Abyss to which Adonis and Persephone would descend for the half-year of the underworld winter. The marriage was celebrated at the beginning of the new year of life when the mortal Adonis came on earth incarnate in the king. It was his mortal Adonis who was the "lost one" of whom the mourners sang.

Attis was the name by which Dumuzi was known in Phrygia. His rites were celebrated in the spring when life returns to the earth. In Phrygia, Ishtar was known as Cybele, and in the Attis cult, the god's divinity lodged in the high priest who was called Attis. Attis was a beautiful youth. The hermaphrodite, Agdistis, offspring of Zeus and the Earth, loved Attis passionately. When Agdistis discovered that Attis was planning to marry the king's daughter, he became furiously jealous and struck Attis with frenzy. In the frenzy, Attis emasculated himself under a pine tree and died. Attis was Cybele's carnal lover and, lamenting wildly, Cybele bore the pine tree into her cave and, with the remorseful Agdistis, asked Zeus to preserve Attis' body from waste and decay. Zeus granted the prayer and permitted Attis' hair to grow and life to remain in his phallus. Attis' growing hair symbolized growing vegetation and the resurrection of Attis and Cybele as the grain growing in the fields. Attis' phallus was the sign of his union with Cybele.

The rituals of the cult were fraught with intense religious fervor. The celebration of Attis' death began with a procession of his worshipers who carried a pine tree which was the god's idol. As they marched, drums and cymbals stirred them to a frenzy until they slashed themselves with knives and spattered their blood on the pine tree as they identified themselves with Attis' sacrifice. So great was their excitement, that many made the identification absolute by repeating Attis' act of self destruction. One or another of the frenzied worshipers would break from the line, castrate himself and throw the severed genitals through the open door of a house along the way. The open door was the sign of the cave into which Cybele had carried Attis as a pine tree. The worshiper's identification with Attis also identified him with Cybele and thereafter he wore a woman's dress to signify his union with the goddess. The owner of the house singled out by the worshiper had to provide him with that dress.

The devotees of Attis who emasculated themselves and threw their severed genitals into houses as they passed in procession reveal the meaning of the myth of Attis. Attis and Cybele personified the male and female nature of the full Moon. The houses represented Cybele's lunar aspect as the Earth Goddess and the action of the devotees signified her death union with Attis and transfiguration into the Death Goddess and Earth Mother. The pine tree represented the pine tree which Cybele carried into her cave; it formed the pathway through which the united pair descended to the Abyss where Cybele kept Attis bound for the winter half-year in the underworld. Agdistis personified Attis and Cybele united as one. Attis would be released to form as a new Moon during the underworld summer when it was winter on earth; his godhead would incarnate the high priest when spring returned on earth.

CHAPTER 15

The Five Stages of Creation

ca. 3000 B.C. through 1500 A.D.

The religion of the Great Goddess with its cult of the Divine King and the planetary doctrine was carried eastward to Mesoamerica along with the two Suns, the world-man, and the calendar. The land connection between southwest Asia and middle America through which the Sumero-Babylonian culture was carried to America was across the steppes to northern India and beyond to China or southeast Asia. We can trace the movement by the theme of the creation myth which, with regional variations was common to the Indo-European peoples whose origins were on the steppes, and which is found in fragmentary form in the mythology of ancient China. There the track disappears in the waters which separate the continents of Asia and America; but the theme reappears clearly in Mesoamerican mythology.

There are gaps in the Sumero-Babylonian record describing the religion and its practices; but the mythology of the peoples who adopted it as it passed eastward fills in details which confirm the relation of the Mesoamerican religion to it. We will, therefore, look first at the creation myth and then consider the mythology of some of the peoples who carried the religion across Asia.

The Sumero-Babylonian creation myth which we considered in Chapter 8 describes six stages of creation which preceded the coming into being of the existing world. These stages constituted a dynastic succession of cosmic rulers of the universe: Apsu and Tiamat, Mummu, Lamu and Lahamu, Anshar and Kishar, An (Anu) and Ninhursag, Enlil and Ninlil. The created world came into being as the seventh stage.

In the Indo-European creation myths, which were derived from the Sumero-Babylonian, there are four rather than six stages preceding the final creation of the existing world, with rulers in a dynastic succession who were cosmic counterparts of the rulers in the third, fourth, fifth, and sixth stages of the Sumero-Babylonian creation. It is probable, although there is no evidence to support it, that the Sumero-Babylonian creation was divided into seven stages at a later time when the planetary cycle was adopted. This can be deduced from the fact that the first three stages readily merge as one in which Anshar and Kishar, as the frame of the universe, are the darkness covering the primordial waters constituted by Apsu and Tiamat, in which life in the form of Mummu and the copulating serpents Lamu and Lahamu appeared spontaneously. Such a stage would be comparable to the first stage of the Egyptian creation in which Khepri (Atum) appeared in the form of a serpent on a primeval hill which rose from the waters and had intercourse with himself. As in the Indo-European myths, the Egyptian creation was divided into five stages of which the last was the stage in which the world of Egypt was formed.

In following the eastward course of the Sumero-Babylonian culture, we should start with the Hittites. The Hittites were Indo-European peoples who overran and settled on lands occupied by Hurrians in northern Syria around the middle of the second millennium B.C. The Hurrian culture was Babylonian and the Hittites adopted it. Their creation myth, therefore, which was written in the Hittite language, reflects the early Babylonian and precedent Sumerian cultures.

The cosmic dynasty begins with Alalu, a Sumerian god, who corresponded to Anshar and Kishar, for he seems to have been both celestial and terrestrial; next was Anu, the same god as the Babylonian Sky God; and then Kumarbi the Earth God, corresponding to Ea. Each reigned for nine years and each was overthrown by his successor. When Anu dethroned Alalu, Alalu went down into the earth. Kumarbi was sometimes equated in Hittite mythology with Enlil; but in the creation myth, his part corresponds to that of Ea, and Enlil was a Storm God who in the Hurro-Hittite mythology was Teshub. Kumarbi was the offspring of Anu and, when he dethroned Anu, he bit off and swallowed Anu's genitals; as a result, he became pregnant and gave birth to Teshub.

In the Sumero-Babylonian creation myth, the universe was formed as the world of life through the death of the serpent Tiamat. This image of the transformation of the serpent into the life of the universe goes back to the phallic concept of the spirit of the sacrificed animal-god traveling through the underworld, bringing new life on earth. This phallic image, which was illustrated by the Trickster myths, evolved into the image of a serpent. The serpent theme in the Hurro-Hittite myth reveals the earlier image of a phallus which, like the images of Hermes, was rendered as a stone column. In the myth, it follows the succession of Kumarbi by Teshub as the ruler of the universe.

Kumarbi determined to raise up a rival to Teshub and had intercourse with a rock which consequently gave birth to a stone monster named Ullikumi, which grew as a giant pillar in the sea from the shoulder of Ubelluri, who held the sea and earth on his back. Ullikumi challenged Teshub to a combat which Teshub finally won when Ullikumi was cut from Ubelluri's shoulder and his strength failed. The text describing the end has been lost and Teshub's victory is presumed; but the theme is of the creation myth and, not only Teshub's victory, but the release of the gods into created life may be presumed.

Mesopotamian influence spread onto the steppes where the Greeks formed their early culture. The theme of their creation myth is the same as that of the Hurro-Hittite myth and confirms the presumption. The first god in the Greek dynasty was Hypsistos; the next Uranus, the sky, who begot Cronus the Earth God and Rhea his Earth Goddess spouse. The Storm God, son of Cronus and Rhea, was Zeus. Cronus seized the throne from Uranus by castrating him. Zeus succeeded Cronus when he waged a fierce 10-year war against him and, after defeating him, made himself king; but

before Zeus became finally established, he was attacked by and had to defeat Typhon.

Typhon introduces the serpent theme of the final stage of creation. Typhon was the offspring of Cronus, and from the thighs downward he was coiled serpents and his arms had serpent heads instead of hands, fire flashed from his eyes, flaming rocks hurtled from his mouth and he had other monstrous qualities. The battle was terrible and although Typhon at first overpowered Zeus, Zeus finally prevailed. With the defeat of Typhon, the Olympian god-world was firmly established and the gods were free to perform their tasks in the created universe.

The Typhon myth has become separated from the Olympian creation story, but combined with the dynastic succession, it parallels the Hurro-Hittite myth so exactly that it must originally have been a part of it. In this creation theme, the dynastic succession shows the progressive formation of the universe as the arena of life and follows the pattern of Trickster materializing as the source of sustenance for mankind. Potential life is generated spontaneously in the dark of nothingness which forms as the celestial and terrestrial frame of the universe, the night sky and the earth. Potential life develops into life and the night sky is transformed into the living sky, the sky with its cosmic luminaries. Generative power develops in the living sky; and, in the next stage, the sky is embodied in earth form and the generative power is transferred physically to the earth embodiment. This transfer was constituted by the castrations of Anu and Uranus. In the creation of the universe, the earth form was both male and female and, in this dual combination, the forms of life were created. In the fourth stage, which evolved as air and motion, the life form of the universe was completed as the world of life, which was then brought into being as the final fifth stage by the gods.

The Hittites and the Greeks were Aryan peoples whose background culture was shaped by the Sumerian civilization. Their ethnic relatives were the Indo-Aryans whose Vedic religion had a corresponding creation story.

Unfortunately, the Indo-Aryan mythology has not been preserved in coherent form and it has had to be reconstructed from the *Rig Veda* and other allied Vedic texts. The *Rig Veda* is a collection of hymns and the mythology has been gleaned from their content and reconstructed, but because of the nature of the record, there are gaps and missing details. There were four Indo-Aryan gods who are comparable to the dynastic gods of the Greek; the Hurro-Hittite and Babylonian creation myths and the Sumero-Akkadian or early Babylonian influences in Vedic mythology are so apparent that it may be presumed that they constituted a dynastic succession.

The first god was Dyaus who was called *Dyaus Pitar* which means Sky Father. His spouse was Prithivi whose name identifies her with the earth. The two were usually thought of as paired together as the progenitor couple — in that aspect, they were known as Dyavaprithivi. Dyaus was the night sky and together, like the Babylonian couple Anshar and Kishar, Dyavaprithivi constituted the celestial and terrestrial halves of the universe. The sky was the god Varuna, his consort Varunani; the Earth God was the Fire God Agni whose consort was Agnayi; and the Storm God Indra, with the consort Indrani. The consorts were of little importance.

The manner in which the dynasty fits into the creation picture does not appear, but when the sky and earth were joined together, Indra apparently was born miraculously from the side of Mother Earth. Shortly after birth, he drank soma — the juice squeezed from the soma plant, which was held to have divine properties. Soma was identified with the Moon and with vegetation. The drink caused Indra to swell to such huge proportions that he split the sky and earth apart, and filled the space between them. The shape of the universe thus came into existence.

At the time when Indra separated the sky and earth, beings were thought to exist called Asuras, a name which means something like "living power" and who therefore represented potential life. One of the Asuras was a great serpent named Vritra, whose mother was Danu, the personification of restraint. Danu perhaps represented the mortal bondage of life to the

Death Goddess and Earth Mother. The image of Danu as restraint is surely a development of the concept of Tiamat who spawned the gods and then sought to prevent their coming into being by destroying them. The Asuras were divided into two groups: the Asuras in one group were led by Vritra and were called Danavas from the name of Danu, Vritra's mother, while those in the other group were called Aditya because they were the offspring of Aditi. Aditi was described as "sky, air, earth, mother, father, son, all gods and the five tribes, whatever has been born and whatever will be born and, in particular, sky and earth and mother of all." Aditi thus appears as the source of life and a form of Dyavaprithivi. The Aditya, therefore, represented the forces of life, and their leader was Varuna.

The Adityas and the Danavas were battling with each other and the Adityas, who were being worsted, asked Indra to be their leader. Indra consented, as Marduk had consented in the Babylonian creation story, with the stipulation that he be made king of the gods. Indra slew Vritra with a lightning bolt, called a vajra, cleaving him and splitting the mountain on which he lay with the strike, whereupon the cosmic waters gushed forth pregnant with the embryo Sun and lowing like cattle. Thus the forces of life were released into the realm of Indra.

The cosmic waters contained in Vritra were the Indo-Aryan version of the waters contained in Tiamat and the sea from which Ullikumi grew. When the Sun was born of the waters, the Moon was already on the scene because it was formed of the soma which Indra left in the cup from which he drank and, according to one myth, part of Vritra's body which was severed in the encounter with Indra became the Moon.

At this point, the elements of the universe had been formed, but they had not yet come into existence. Sacrifice, which was necessary for the creation of life, was also necessary to bring the world of life into being and maintain it as a living system. The gods, therefore, met to perform the archetypal sacrifice. The gods themselves were the universe and in performing the rite they had, perforce, to sacrifice themselves. In their

constitution as the universe, the gods formed themselves into an anthropomorphic cosmos, or world-man, and built a fire for their own sacrifice. As a world-man, they were called Purusha, and when they died in the fire their body parts rose from the flames and became parts of the universe. The gods comprising Purusha thus came into existence as the created world.

The universe which was constituted by the creator gods before the sacrifice was a preworld of forms in which no life existed. Life came into being from this state of nonexistence which was the state of death. Doctrine held that life was created from the death of sacrifice, and when the gods sacrificed themselves, they created themselves as the world of life. But they did not cease to function as creator gods, for all living things must return to the death state from which they came — if the gods who were the pre-world had transformed themselves into the living world, the universe would have quickly come to an end.

The creation of the life world divided the universe into an underworld of death and creation, and the life world which ended periodically. The creator gods proceeded to establish order in these two worlds. They called the underworld Asat and the life world Sat, and they placed a horizontal plane between Sat and Asat; they made a path through the sky for the Sun and placed cosmic waters in the sky to provide rain; then they spoke the names of the creatures and things which were to be in the world of life, and the creatures and things came into being; finally, they created man to perform sacrifices and to keep the life which had been created moving harmoniously in its established order.

This concept of two worlds of the universe was the Sumero-Babylonian concept in which life on earth ended periodically, but during its course, new life was being created and when life on earth ended, the new life began. The sacrifice of the gods as Purusha was the Indo-Aryan version of Enlil's self-sacrifice, metaphorically described as the Flood.

The established order in the Indo-Aryan doctrine was called *rita*. Rita had its precedent in the Sumerian *me's* which were laws established by the creator gods which kept the features and functions of created life moving in harmonious order. The Egyptians had a similar concept which they called *maat*, and at later times the Greeks transformed it into the law of fate which they called *moira*.

The doctrines of creation which were carried into the steppes and adopted by the Aryan nomadic peoples had been formulated by the end of the third millennium and incorporated into the Sumerian religion. The doctrines as they were restated in the Vedic culture were probably carried to China, although the ancient Chinese mythology as it is presently known, has left only a fragmentary record to attest it. The fragment is a myth which describes the creation of the universe from the body parts of a cosmic man. One of the details of the myth describes the universe in its original state as an egg. This is an image which was found in the Pelasgian creation myth of the peoples who lived in Palestine and southwest Asia and migrated to Greece sometime about 3500 B.C.; it also appears in the mythology of Castor and Pollux, who were Indo-Aryan Asvins. In combination with the cosmic man, it suggests a relationship with Mesopotamian and Indo-Aryan heritage.

The doctrine of creation and the Mesoamerican religion was the same as the Vedic doctrines, and the Nahuatlan and Indo-Aryan myth and related rites are parallel. The four kings of the Eurasian cosmic dynasties have their counterparts in the four Suns of the Nahuatlan creation and, just as each king represented a stage in the universe's creation, each Sun represented a corresponding stage. The following shows the comparable stages:

Babylonian	**Hurro-Hittite**	**Greek**	**Vedic**	**Nahuatlan**
Anshar-Kishar	Alalu	Hypsistos	Dyavaprithivi	Tezcatlipoca
Anu	Anu	Uranus	Varuna	Quetzalcoatl
Ea	Kumarbi	Cronus	Agni	Tlaloc
Marduk	Teshub	Zeus	Indra	Chalchiuhlicue

The Five Stages of Creation

The Nahuatlan creation myth has already been told; let us now see how it compares with the Indo-Aryan myth. Tezcatlipoca was the night sky and Lord of the Earth. Thus, he combined the celestial and terrestrial worlds to constitute the frame of the universe where nothing existed and where life first formed. Further, as the Above and Below, he was Ometeotl and so, like Dyavaprithivi, he was the progenitor couple. The era of Tezcatlipoca's Sun ended when Quetzalcoatl struck him with his staff, and Tezcatlipoca fell into the water and became a jaguar. The jaguar was the fire of the earth Sun. The combination of fire and water signified the creation of Quetzalcoatl's Sun which was the living or blue sky. The jaguar as the Sun fire was the life spirit of the sky and it infused the sky through Quetzalcoatl's staff. Tezcatlipoca's descent to earth at the end was like Alalu's.

Quetzalcoatl's Sun was brought to an end when the jaguar struck him down with his paw. Here the jaguar was Tezcatlipoca as the earth jaguar, Tepeyolotl, and the end came with a violent wind which uprooted the trees. The wind was the sky descending into the earth and the uprooted trees were the route of its passage. The living sky of Quetzalcoatl was now combined with the earth and the combination created Tlaloc's Sun which followed.

Generative power developed in Quetzalcoatl's sky, and was transmitted to Tlaloc's Sun when the men of Quetzalcoatl's Sun turned into monkeys. The monkey was a symbol of sex — monkeys lived in trees and when the trees were uprooted, they were carried down to the earth. The monkeys signified the transmission of the procreative power of the Sky God to his earth embodiment; the account of their creation and descent to earth was a euphemism for the castration theme of the Hurro-Hittite and Greek creation myths.

Tlaloc in his earth form was the Fire God and, hence, was dual in sex. His Sun was an era of procreation of life, which took form in the next Sun of the Earth Mother represented by Chalchiuhlicue, who was Tlaloc's spouse. The fiery rain which ended Tlaloc's Sun was the flood-and-fire

symbol of creation and signified the transmission of the created forms of the Sun of Chalchiuhlicue. The men of Tlaloc's era who did not perish were transformed into birds as symbols of life which would be created in the Sun which followed.

Chalchiuhlicue's Sun corresponds to the province of the Storm God in the Eurasian creation myths. The substitution of an Earth Goddess for the Storm God is merely a change of emphasis from the life-giving properties of the atmosphere to those of the soil cover of the earth's surface. The theme of the Storm God killing the serpent and releasing life in the fourth era is apparently missing; but it was implicit in the waters which ended Chalchiuhlicue's Sun and from which the god forms of Nanauatzin and Tecuciztecatl emerged and became the Sun and Moon. Nanauatzin was the scabby god who came into existence as the serpent Xolotl. His scabbiness was the dead skin which he was casting off as he took on new life form. The men who did not die when the Sun ended were transformed into fish, signifying the bodily forms of the Sun as vegetation which still had to be brought into being.

The waters of Chalchiuhlicue's creation are comparable to the cosmic waters which flowed from the mountain Earth Mother beneath the body of the dead serpent Vritra; and whereas those cosmic waters carried lowing cattle, Chalchiuhlicue's flood carried fish as the Nahuatlan equivalent.

When the flood came at the end of Chalchiuhlicue's Sun, the work of creation was not complete but it was at the same point as that in the Vedic creation at which the Storm God Indra had cut open Vritra's body and the mountain beneath, and the cosmic waters were flowing from the opening — further action was required. Here the Mexican Storm God comes onto the scene in the person of the Wind God Ehecatl and the myth continues with the theme of the Vedic creation. The gods assembled and decreed an original sacrifice. A great fire was burning for a holocaust and Tecuciztecatl and Nanauatzin came forward, the first to become the Moon and the second, the Sun. The two were sacrificed in the fire and when Nanauatzin, who rose first, and Tecuciztecatl were both in the sky, all the gods were sacrificed, rose, and came together again. Ehecatl, who had killed them all, started the Sun and Moon moving in their orbits. Thus, the gods and the life world came into existence in an act of original sacrifice just as the gods and their life world had been brought into existence by their sacrifice in the being of Purusha in the Indo-Aryan creation. And here the parallel continues, for the motion of the Sun and Moon established the harmonious order of life. This was the motion and the order which the Indo-Aryans called rita, and which in the Nahuatlan culture was called ollin.

In the Vedic religious system, sacrifice was necessary to maintain rita. Rites which were performed for this purpose were adopted into the post-Vedic period and the manner of their performance was prescribed by the Brahmanas. The principal rite was a Soma sacrifice in which the sacrifice and the sacrificer were identified with Purusha. This rite was an adaptation on an earthly scale of the original sacrifice in which the parts of Purusha's body became the life world. An altar was built in five layers to contain the sacrificial fire, the five layers representing the universe and its provinces. Now there were five gods which constituted the universe and its separate provinces: Dyavaprithivi who was the frame of celestial and terrestrial space, Varuna the sky, Agni the earth, Indra the atmosphere, and Soma. Soma's province was the fifth stage in which, in Asat, the forms of life became complete and ready to be brought into existence. All together, these gods constituted Purusha and when Purusha was sacrificed and came into being as the life world, Soma constituted that part of him which was life in being, and the other gods were the regions of the created universe. The altar was an altar of sacrifice, which was an act of creation of life from life through death, therefore it represented Purusha as life, and as death, and as renewed life. With its fire, the altar was Agni and, so, Purusha and Agni were one.

The Brahmanas explain the metaphysics of the sacrifice in terms of mystic identification of the sacrificer with an ascetic ideal of immortal serenity which was achieved by communion with Purusha in the death state prior to the creation of the universe. To enter this communion, the process of creation had to be reversed and the ritual as prescribed by the Brahmanas required the sacrifice of Soma as the life aspect of Purusha. In this aspect, Purusha was the life world of the universe and was called Prajapati, the Lord of Creatures. Soma was the Moon and the incarnation of the Sun.

The sacrifice was a holocaust. In the material form in which Soma was sacrificed as Purusha, he was ghee — clarified butter which was melted and poured on the sacred fire. Ghee was made from cow's milk and also from buffalo milk, in which case it was not so highly regarded. Cattle were animal forms of Soma in his earthly being and ghee must have been regarded as a refined abstract of his divine being. Horses were sacrificed when the ritual required blood; the nomadic peoples of the steppes quite generally substituted the horse for the bull as the animal form of the Moon as the Sun's earth incarnation. In the principal Soma sacrifice, a gold image of Purusha was laid on a gold plate which represented the Sun and which was placed beneath the first layer of the altar.

In the sacrifice, the sacred fire was within the altar and the flames consumed the parts of Purusha in the inverse order of their creation — Soma, Indra, Agni, and Varuna — until all were absorbed in the death being of Purusha as Dyavaprithivi. Theologically, the sacrificer in his identity with Purusha had left the life state of Prajapati and entered the divine state of preexistence which was the source from which life came.

Now, while the Brahmanas prescribed the sacrifice as an escape from life and a means by which the sacrificer could enter into communion with the creator gods in the world of death, the peoples of the Vedic period must have regarded it as a means of creating life on earth. Purusha was "whatever hath been and whatever shall be." From the death state of Dyavaprithivi, Purusha first came into being and, as the source of life, his body parts formed as the life world of the universe anew. For the Indo-Aryans, the divinities of the Sun and Moon combined as the life forms

which sustained mankind and which ended periodically. Without new life, the living world would end. But during the course of the life of each period of time on earth, a new Sun and Moon were created in the underworld as the earthly life to come; this Sun and Moon were combined and brought into existence by sacrifice, just as the life world had been given existence in the original creation.

If the Soma sacrifice were to be regarded as a ritual of creation and projected backward into the Vedic time, the sacrifice would have been a state function. We would see the gold image of Purusha on the gold plate as the image of Soma constituted as the Sun and Moon combined as one, and the altar as the world of life completely formed in the underworld of nonexistence and constituted by the creator gods in their aspects as the elements of the universe. We would then see the flames of the holocaust subsiding and the pre-world coming into existence as a new life world with Soma moving as the cycle of life. Since Purusha was the past, the present, and the future, he was time and the sacrifice when held annually would have renewed rita for a year.

Now if we turn to the *Codex Fejérváry-Mayer** we will find this same concept of the universe as a cosmic man and his sacrifice as a renewal of ollin and time. Just as sacrifice was necessary to maintain rita in Vedic India, it was necessary in pre-Columbian Mexico for the maintenance of ollin. The cosmic man who was sacrificed was Tezcatlipoca. The sacrifice and creation is pictured on page 1 of the codex. Tezcatlipoca, like Soma, was the Moon incarnation of the Sun and the Lord of Vegetation; but he was also the Fire God and as such was Ometeotl, the universe. The universe was, like the Indo-Aryan universe, divided into a nonworld of creation and a world of created life limited in duration. The codex pictures the life world as the Sun and Moon combined as the nine Lords of the Night and moving in a year cycle of life. The codex shows their creation from the different parts of Tezcatlipoca's body [Figure 15].

*A Mixtec codex containing a pictograph representing a calendar.

When we compare the Eurasian doctrines of creation and the Soma sacrifice with the Nahuatlan creation and the Tezcatlipoca sacrifice which created the Lords of the Night, we see that, despite the differences in the details of the mythologies and the rites, some details relate to basic doctrinal concepts and are the same. Thus, in the Hurro-Hittite and Greek creation myths, which were closely related to the Vedic, the succession was by violence and this was also the case in the Nahuatlan succession. In the Vedic myth, before the gods came into existence, the Moon appeared on the scene of creation before the Sun — he was Vritra from whose body the Sun proceeded; in the Nahuatlan myth, when the gods consulted among each other and asked, "Who will be the Sun?" Tecuciztecatl, the Moon, stepped forward and volunteered. Only afterwards did the gods single out Nanauatzin and appoint him to be the Sun. The transformation of Nanauatzin into the Sun was a disguised version of Indra slaying Vritra: the fire-serpent was the Sun-bearer in the underworld and when Nanauatzin appeared, he was brought by the fire-serpent which perforce served as Nanauatzin's body. In the sacrifice, the fire-serpent died and was transformed into the plumed serpent as the Sun-bearer in the sky. In the process, Nanauatzin became the Sun. In the comparable action of the Vedic myth, the fire of Indra's lightning released the Sun from the body of the serpent Vritra.

The Vedic gods talked together and named the things they wished to create which thereupon came into being; the Nahuatlan gods were described as talking over the problem of creation and selecting the two Suns and their discussion had the same effect. Both cases record the doctrine of the word as the source of creation, which was part of the earlier Sumerian religion. That it was part of the Mesoamerican religion is attested by the *Popul Vuh** which related that "then came the word," and after the gods spoke the names of the things which they wished to create — thereupon the things came into existence.

**Popul Vuh*, the sacred book of the Quiché Maya.

The Five Stages of Creation

In the Indo-Aryan mythology, the universe was created as the Fire God Agni, and the different Vedic gods were all part of Agni. The Indo-Aryans were essentially patriarchal and while the Vedic religion was a form of the religion of the Great Goddess, the Indo-Aryans transferred the emphasis of worship to the goddess' consort and made their gods the chief objects of divinity. Thus, while the goddess held her own as Aditi, the feminine form of the Supreme God as the universe was otherwise largely obscured. Before the Indo-Aryans overran northern India, however, the Great Goddess had been carried from Mesopotamia to the Indus Valley, a part of India which came under Indo-Aryan domination, and, while the goddess lost her importance in the religion of the ruling castes, she continued to be worshiped outside the priestly circles. In the Hindu religion which developed directly from the Vedic, her worship revived generally and Aditi became Kali, or Durga as she was called. Kali was the female side of Agni as the universe and her appearance shows her to have had a character much the same as that of the feminine side of the Fire God Ometeotl.

In the Hindu religion, Agni as the god-universe evolved into Brahman who combined in his being the chief gods: Brahma, Vishnu, and Siva, and all the other gods as well. Kali, or Durga, is the female or Earth Mother side of Brahman. Mythology shows her relation to the Fire God Agni. A demon who had acquired Brahman's power by means of yoga and had taken the form of a gigantic buffalo, threatened the cosmic order.

Brahma and the other gods were helpless against him and, together with Vishnu and Siva, they breathed out their full forces as fires which formed into a single flame that grew and condensed and took the form of the goddess Kali. Kali rose and, gathering all the forces which she had received from the other gods, destroyed the demon buffalo. Kali restored their powers to the gods and preserved the cosmic order. In Hindu theology, the divine powers of the Supreme God, when at rest, are in Brahman and, when in action, are in Kali as the creator and preserver of life.

By virtue of her creation, Kali is a Fire God, as was Coatlicue. In their iconography, where Coatlicue wears a skirt of braided serpents, Kali wears garlands of cobras; where Coatlicue wears a necklace of hearts and severed hands and a skull pendant, Kali is pictured lolling her tongue and holding a severed head which she grasps by its hair; and where Coatlicue's hands and feet are monster claws, Kali is accompanied by a ferocious lion, while her Mongolian counterparts wear necklaces of skulls and have feline fangs for teeth.

The Mesoamerican creation myth looks like the Eurasian version, with Eurasian gods taking the names and places of the local gods.

CHAPTER 16

Jason

Second Millennium B.C.

During the first half of the second millennium B.C., the Indo-Europeans adopted the Great Goddess religion with its Divine King cult and the doctrine that life was created in cycles of new world existence by the Moon, Mercury, and the Sun moving together in the underworld. The Greek myth of Jason and the Argonauts is but one example. The myth recounts the adventure of a company of Greek heroes who set out under Jason to secure the ghost of Phryxus and the Golden Fleece of a sacrificed ram. The Golden Fleece came from a ram endowed with reason and speech. The ram, which could move through the air, had been created by the god Hermes. The Golden Fleece had come into the possession of King Aeëtes of Colchis at the eastern end of the Black Sea when the ram arrived there carrying a Grecian king, Phryxus, on its back. Phryxus sacrificed the ram. King Aeëtes kept the fleece, suspended from a tree in a grove sacred to Ares, guarded by an indestructible serpent-dragon.

Jason commissioned the building of a ship, the *Argo*, with an oracular prow provided by the goddess Athene. Jason gathered the kings of Greece to sail with him; they are called the Argonauts. Setting sail from Greece in the *Argo*, the Argonauts reached Colchis sailing along the southern shore of the Black Sea. Aeëtes agreed to relinquish the fleece to Jason if he could yoke a pair of fire-breathing bulls with brazen hoofs and plough and sow a field with dragon's teeth. Jason succeeded in the task with the help of Medea, Aeëtes' daughter, who had fallen in love with him.

Medea was an Earth Moon Goddess with magical powers. When Jason promised to marry her for her help, she gave him a lotion which made him proof against the fire of the bulls so that he was able to get close enough to harness them, and thus perform his task. Aeëtes, however, refused to give up the fleece to Jason. Again with the help of Medea, who first soothed and then magically put the dragon to sleep, Jason secured the fleece. Taking Medea along, Jason made a getaway with Aeëtes in hot pursuit.

They now followed the north coast of the Black Sea, moving, according to the myth, counter to the direction of the Sun. They had with them, in addition to Medea, Medea's younger brother, Apsyrtus. When they came to the mouth of the Danube, Aeëtes was pressing them closely. To gain distance, Medea killed Apsyrtus and cut off the members of his body one at a time, throwing them into the water as she did so. Aeëtes was delayed by having to stop and retrieve each member separately and the Argonauts were able to continue their escape.

The Argonauts had been voyaging through the north — to get them to the west, the mythographers took them over a route which carried the ship up rivers and across mountains, and brought them vaguely to the northern end of the Adriatic Sea or the west coast of Italy, to where Circe lived. While staying with Circe, who was Medea's aunt, Jason and Medea were married and mated under the covering of the fleece.

The *Argo* then completed its voyage by traveling south where a great wave washed it inland onto the desert of Libya; with the help of supernatural powers, the *Argo* returned to the Mediterranean and crossing the sea regained the shores of Greece. Jason went with Medea to Corinth, where the throne was vacant. Medea happened to be heiress to the succession, so Jason as her husband was duly proclaimed king.

Jason and Medea had seven sons and daughters. After a time, Jason decided to divorce Medea and marry Glauce, the daughter of the King of Thebes. Medea pretended to agree to the arrangement, although she was against it, and sent Glauce a long white robe and a golden crown which, when Glauce put them on, burst into flames and destroyed Glauce and all the assembled guests and everyone in the palace, except Jason who jumped

out of a window and escaped. Medea, for her part, fled in a chariot drawn by winged serpents which the Sun, Helius, her grandfather, had loaned her. Jason and Medea returned to Colchis.

The theme of the myth is the doctrine of the Divine King, the theme of the *Epic of Gilgamesh.* The myth describes the creation of 7 years of life in the underworld. The region through which Jason made his voyage is the underworld; the actual places named are their projections into the world beneath the real world. The Black Sea forms the waters of the Abyss of Death with Colchis at its center; Corinth, where Jason rules with Medea, is in the life region of the underworld. The action proceeds as the four Moon stages in which the planetary gods of the 7 years formed as a new Moon.

Phryxus represents the pre-world in which the 7 years were created. He is a version of Enkidu, whose death brought the planetary gods into existence. His ram was created by Hermes (Mercury) at the request of Hera who, in the days of Jason, was a Moon Goddess. His ram was the Moon, its Golden Fleece the Sun. Phryxus himself was Mercury as the spirit form of the Moon and the divinity of the king.

In the first stage, the life spirit appears as the inchoate Moon in the death state of creation. This is the stage in which Gilgamesh ran about the steppe grieving for the dead Enkidu. In the myth, this stage is described as the building of the *Argo* and the gathering of the Argonauts. Athene helps in the building of the *Argo* by fitting an oracular beam in the prow. She appears as the Death Goddess — her presence places the shipbuilding in the underworld region of death, and her action marks Jason as the Mercury Moon spirit.

The Moon of the second stage is the creation of lunar motion and the beginning of life in the new Moon. This is the stage of Gilgamesh's sleep in the house of Utnapishtim, and of Jason's voyage to Colchis. Jason travels along the south coast of the Black Sea — south was the direction of death. Athene was also a Moon Goddess and the *Argo*, which she endowed with an oracular prow, is a metaphorical description of Jason's body as the Moon. The movement of the *Argo* through the waters of the Abyss constitutes the cyclical motion of the Moon.

The Moon of the third stage is the creation of life as the waxing phases of the Moon. This is the stage in which Gilgamesh journeyed to Erech changing from one planetary god to the next until he arrived as Jupiter. Since he was the consort of Ishtar, she traveled with him, although this is not specifically stated in the epic. In the Greek myth, Jason forms as the first four planetary gods at Colchis before departing for Corinth. King Aeëtes is a Greek version of Utnapishtim, and Ishtar has been changed into Medea as the Moon Goddess in the planetary form of Venus.

Jason becomes Saturn when he comes ashore at Colchis. The fleece and the serpent-dragon guarding it represent the planetary Sun and Moon, and the fire-breathing bulls represent Mars. When Jason harnesses the bulls and ploughs and sows the field, he becomes the Mars bull as the Moon. The planetary gods are the changing Moon bodies of the Moon-serpent which is Mercury's bodily form as the carrier of the Sun. When Jason overcomes the serpent-dragon and takes the fleece off the tree of life, he becomes the planetary incarnation of the Sun and Moon. Thus, when he is ready to sail in the *Argo*, he has passed through the changes of Saturn, Sun, and Moon.

The tree of life from which he takes the Golden Fleece has symbolism as the waters of life on which Gilgamesh embarked when he left Utnapishtim. Jason leaves as Mars taking Medea and Apsyrtus with him. In the symbolism of mythology, a child represented the corporeal spirit of the Moon — the sacrifice of Apsyrtus described a puberty rite of passage in which the child becomes a man. When Apsyrtus is killed, he is thrown piecemeal into the waters; the corresponding episode in the epic is Gilgamesh's descent to the bottom of the sea to pick the magic plant and his reemergence cast up alive on land.

The Moon of the third stage becomes full when Jason mates with Medea under the fleece. Their union is their marriage and they become

Jupiter and Venus as the full Moon.

This is the point in the cycle at which Venus succeeds Jupiter and brings death to the Moon. When the Moon dies, Venus is transformed into the Death Goddess and Earth Mother. This is the fourth stage in which the Moon rises from death, bringing the new year of life on earth. This is the stage of Gilgamesh-Dumuzi's death union with Geshtinanna and his resurrection as the king-consort of Ishtar and ruler of Sumer. The *Argo's* descent to death is the wave that washed the ship onto land in Libya, leaving it stranded on a lifeless desert. The salt lake to which the Argonauts drag the ship across the sand symbolized the waters of the Abyss where Gilgamesh-Dumuzi spent half the year as consort of Geshtinanna in death.

When Medea marries Jason, she is the goddess of the full Moon; when the *Argo* comes to rest on the lifeless desert, she has changed to the Death Goddess and Earth Mother, and Jason and Medea have become the new Moon. Medea's death nature is dominant in the desert, and her Earth Mother nature becomes dominant in Corinth. There she bears seven sons and seven daughters who represent seven Moons which rise successively as the Moon Goddess and her king-consort bringing 7 years of life on earth.

Jason in Corinth is not part of the story of the Argonauts. Jason coming to Colchis is the spirit of the deceased Divine King of Corinth. The myth established the divinity of his dynasty. The Argonauts who accompanied him were kings in their own cities and their inclusion similarly gave their thrones claims to divinity. Certainly the myth had other purposes, too, such as recording trading rights in ports along the Black Sea; but the main theme of the myth adheres to the planetary doctrine and identifies Jason with the divine powers of life creation and, in the Divine King doctrine, these powers operated in 7-year cycles.

CHAPTER 17

Cernunnos

Second Millennium B.C. through First Millennium A.D.

The elements of the planetary calendar are implicit in the Jason myth; they are explicit in the mythology of the Celtic God Cernunnos. Cernunnos was a Supreme Being who was time and the universe, and who was imagined as a world-man. In this image, he was the consort of the Earth Goddess, and the planetary gods formed the parts of his body.

The Celts were one of the Indo-European peoples whose religion was formed on the doctrines of the Great Goddess and the cult of the Divine King and planetary gods. We know them as a fusion of pastoralists and farmers. The farmers were peoples living in the region of Europe north of the Alps; presumably their farming culture had its origin in the Neolithic, but there is evidence that it was recast with Indo-European traditions brought from the southern Russian steppes around the beginning of the second millennium B.C. The pastoralists were one of the successive waves of warrior-herdsmen who came out of the steppes of eastern Europe and western Asia and settled as overlords over the Bronze Age farming peoples of central and northern Europe. In this fusion, they formed the Hallstatt culture. By the fifth century B.C., they had moved into western Europe and were penetrating into Britain whence, eventually, they crossed over to Ireland. In this phase, the culture is known as La Tène.

The Celtic culture survived longest in Ireland where no foreign invaders arrived until the Vikings in the ninth century A.D. Consequently, Irish tradition had provided a record of the Celtic institution of Divine Kingship, which is supplemented by the historical records of the Romans who

conquered Gaul and Britain in the closing years of the last century B.C. and in the early years of the Christian era. According to Irish tradition, when a new king was chosen, men who had the qualifications for the office were brought before the Stone of Fal, a stone phallus, which cried out when the future king touched it.

The queen was the Earth Goddess and constituted the land and sovereignty of Ireland. A myth describes how she first appeared to the king-to-be as an old hag and asked him to have intercourse with her. When he did, she turned into a beautiful woman and the union made him king. Kingship was conferred by the marriage ceremonies which included coitus with the queen, a rite which transferred sovereignty and divine authority. At one time, the queen seems to have been represented by a white mare; in his inaugural ceremonies, the king mated with the mare which was sacrificed afterwards and eaten by the king and people in communion.

Cernunnos was represented sitting cross-legged, tailor fashion, in a position called *accroupi.* He had antlers or horns on his head and an accentuated phallus. He was shown holding a ram-headed serpent as a scepter and, quite often, one or more torques and a heavy sack or purse. He was originally the earth and had a consort who was also horned and sat *accroupi.* He was a creator and nourisher of mankind and animals and, with his consort, was a god of springs, rivers, and fountains. Furthermore, he was a god of death and the night; but he was also god of life who raised the dead.

Cernunnos was sometimes depicted with three heads, sometimes as a triumvirate, and sometimes as one or another of his god aspects. The Romans who conquered Gaul in the last century B.C., in their descriptions of the Celts and their religion, identified the three forms of Cernunnos with their own gods: Mars, Jupiter, and Mercury. The Celtic names for Mars and Jupiter were Teutates and Taranis. There seems not to have been a common native name for Mercury in Gaul, although Ross identifies him as Erriapus; but in Ireland he was the god Lugh. Cernunnos' three godheads, therefore, corresponded to the three planetary gods of the life stages of the Moon and Sun cycle.

Cernunnos' cyclical nature was symbolized by the ram-serpent. The ram-serpent was a sign of the planetary cycle; the ram represented the Moon. The serpent represented the Mercury Moon spirit, the Divine King, and tanist of the kingship doctrine. Cernunnos' three heads, his function as creator and nourisher of life, and his earth nature and province of death constituted him as the lord of the universe.

In considering Cernunnos, we should note that Cernunnos was not necessarily that god's name, but that it was a descriptive designation for the god who was worshiped throughout the Celtic world under presumably different names. Cernunnos means the "horned god," he was of ancient origin. By the Roman period, in Gaul the distinction between the three god forms had begun to blend in Mercury. The Remi, a tribe in Gaul, regarded the heads of Cernunnos as a triple form of Mercury, whom they represented as wearing a crown of leaves. In Ireland, Mercury, as Lugh, was the "divine prototype of human kingship." The Celts regarded Cernunnos as their common ancestor.

In ancient Ireland, the year began with the Feast of Samhuin, or Samhain, which was held on November first. Fires were extinguished and new fires kindled from a sacred fire which was lit on the eve of the feast. This new year, however, like the Sumerian new year, began in the otherworld and was a creation year which would have its earth counterpart in the second half of the year, the real spring and summer. The evidence for this is as follows:

The Celtic year was divided into halves, winter beginning November first and summer beginning May first. The year division has no relation to the seasons in Europe, and the date which became November first was originally the date on which the Pleiades came to the meridian at midnight. The association of the Pleiades with the new year conformed with the Sumero-Babylonian belief in a creation year, which began at the start of the real winter. The famous kings of Ireland all died on the Feast of Samhuin. On that day, or rather on the evening before, the entrance to the otherworld was open and the dead could return to the living world and the living could pass to the otherworld, the way led through a cave known as Cruachan. When the kings died, they entered the otherworld through the cave. When the famous king Conn "of the Hundred Battles" passed through the cave, instead of finding a world of death, he found a world very much alive in which Lugh (Mercury) occupied the throne as consort of the Earth Goddess.

The feast which began the true summer was held May first and was called Beltain. At the midpoints between Samhuin and Beltain, on February first and August first, there were feasts called Imborg and Lughnasad. The Imborg feast theoretically celebrated the time of nursing ewes. The theme of this feast and the time of its celebration did not relate particularly to the land economy of the Celtic territories and the date is early for lambing. Neither did it relate to the winter solstice or the spring equinox. The feast, therefore, must have celebrated a date fixed by a tradition inherited from the past.

European folk customs, which were inherited from pagan antecedents, included fire celebrations at the beginning of Lent, which, therefore, corresponded so closely to the Imborg that they must have been changed to the Lenten date as a result of Christianization. The significance of these fire ceremonies, which were also held at other times during the year, changed; they were centered around bonfires which were thought to keep pests from destroying crops and to give fertility to the younger women and men who jumped over them. They were performed originally to promote the growth of crops and they continued to be performed for the same purpose. The pagan fires had been invocations of the workings of their gods, but the teachers of Christianity made Cernunnos the Devil and the other gods his witch associates. The Christians made the Devil and his witches the destroyers of crops, changed the fires into means of destroying the witches, and so turned the pagan rituals against the gods which they had served — altogether changing the meaning of the fires. Therefore, interpretation of the original meaning of some of the Imborg ceremonies is difficult; but one of them was rolling a fire-wheel down a hill. This clearly would seem to symbolize the sun's descent toward the south in its daily course through the sky as it changes its annual course after the summer solstice. This was, therefore, a summer harvest celebration as is shown by the fact that similar ceremonies were performed in the middle of the true summer.

The Earth Goddess who presided over the Feast of Imborg had the Roman name Minerva and the Christian name Saint Brighid. Let us call her Minerva-Brighid. She had three forms. She was an Irish form of Cernunnos' spouse who, like Cernunnos, had three heads and who was Cernunnos' feminine counterpart. Each head, therefore, represented the same stage of the planetary cycle as that represented by the corresponding head of her husband; she was the Celtic Earth Goddess corresponding to Venus.

When summer began in the otherworld, Minerva-Brighid was goddess of reviving vegetation. As the summer progressed and the crops ripened, she became goddess of harvest. Cernunnos and his spouse were the nourishers of men and animals and, at this time, they performed that function by bringing forth the abundance of the earth in the harvest and increasing the otherworld crops and animal stock; in this aspect, the goddess was feasted on Imborg as the ewe nursing lambs. The Imborg, being in winter, quite obviously celebrated the otherworld summer, surely with the purpose of ensuring a harvest in the otherworld in order that an equally abundant harvest would follow on earth.

There is an Irish myth about Samhuin which is a word-portrait of Cernunnos that confirms this interpretation. The Cave of Cruachan was in Connacht where the Divine King and Queen were Aillil and the Earth Goddess Medhbh. On the eve of Samhuin, two men had been hanged and Aillil and Medhbh offered a prize to anyone who could put a withe around the foot of one of them. Nera made the attempt and succeeded in putting the withe around the foot of one of the dead men hanging on the gallows when the dead man told him how to do it. The dead man complained of being thirsty and Nera took him on his back and carried him to a house where there was water; then he returned him, and hung him on the gallows again.

While Nera was doing this, a host from the otherworld attacked the castle of Aillil and Medhbh, put it to the torch and cut off the heads of the entire court. Nera, returning to claim his prize, found the castle in flames and the bodies with severed heads, and the host retreating through the Cave of Cruachan. He followed them into the otherworld where he married a woman living there.

Nera learned from his new wife that the destruction of the castle was a vision of what would happen on the eve of the next Samhuin if the armies of Aillil and Medhbh did not first attack and overcome the otherworld host. Nera then returned to Aillil and Medhbh to warn them and took with him the fruits of summer — "wild garlic and primrose and golden fern" — as proof that he came from the otherworld and told the truth. He found the court seated around the cauldron as he had left it when he went to fasten the withe on the hanging corpse. When the next Samhuin came, the king's warriors invaded the otherworld and brought back the three great treasures of Ireland. Nera, however, remained with his wife in the otherworld.

In looking at the myth as a portrait of Cernunnos, we must keep in mind his nature as god of death and creator of life, nourisher of mankind and animals and god of fertility, whose consort was his female counterpart. We must also remember that he was originally the earth and that he had antlers or horns. His triple being as Mercury, Mars, and Jupiter, or rather their Celtic equivalents, gave him an underworld life nature to supplement his nature as death and creator of life from death.

The myth describes the first three Moon stages in the formation of Cernunnos as the new Moon world-man. The fourth stage in which he dies and the life which he has created comes on earth as the rising Moon Saturn in the time of Beltain. In the myth, Nera is Mercury. The castle of Aillil and Medhbh is in the underworld region of death in a location comparable to the Grove of Mars at Colchis. The stages are portrayed metaphorically. Things and events are described as they appeared in the real world of life; thus Aillil's castle is pictured as his real castle in Connacht with the court in residence, and the summer and winter are pictured symbolically as seasons on earth. When Nera returns with the fruits of summer, it is the winter season on earth which began on Samhuin.

One of the two men hanging on the gallows represents the dead Moon. Nera is his life spirit which has departed from the dead body. They are the first stage — the death stage of the Moon in which the Moon spirit Mercury forms as the inchoate Moon.

The other body represents the new Moon in which motion and beginning life take form. He is the one who instructed Nera on how to fasten the withe and who called for a drink of water; with Nera, he is the second stage.

The withe is a symbol of vegetation springing from the earth in the revival of life in the spring. Although the tree from which it was cut is not identified, it was probably a willow shoot; willows growing on the banks of streams were symbolic of the creation of new life. To complete the symbolism, the foot denotes movement in the earth and the withe wrapped around the foot denotes germination. The water which Nera gives the man to drink symbolizes the waters of creation and the beginning of life.

In the third Moon stage, life formed in the new Moon as the first six of the seven planetary gods. Before analyzing the metaphor of the myth, we should consider the symbolism of the gallows. Gallows were formed by two uprights and a cross-piece from which criminals were suspended by the neck. The sign of the Roman god of beginning, Janus, was a gallows without a noose. Janus was the source and origin of life. The gallows in the myth are the sign of the death-life nature of Cernunnos as the creator of life.

Nera's formation as the six gods begins when he carries the dead man to the house where there was water. The image of a house and water signifies the island of life in the waters of the Abyss. Like the Grove of Mars at Colchis on the waters of the sea, it is a place where life begins. Nera then is Saturn of the planetary cycle of seven.

Nera as Mercury is the Sun-bearer. When he carries the dead man back to the gallows, he is the Moon spirit moving the lifeless Moon. He is then the planetary Sun.

The Moon spirit was a serpent. When Nera hangs the corpse back on the gallows, the symbolism is of the serpent casting its dead skin and renewing its Moon body. Nera then is the planetary Moon.

The fire burning the castle is the holocaust of creation. The otherworld beyond the Cave of Cruachan is the underworld of life. The host which Nera sees in his vision retreating through the cave is the life force of the new Moon returning after vanquishing the force of death which blocks the entrance. The warning which he brings back to Aillil is eternal death if he does not overcome that force on the eve of Samhuin. When the next Samhuin came, Aillil conquered death and proved himself to be the planetary Moon.

When Nera follows the retreating host, he is the planetary god Mars. Nera himself is Mercury. By his marriage, he became Jupiter as the full Moon, and the life of the underworld summer symbolized by the fruits which he gathers in the otherworld. Thus the myth describes the six planetary god stages which formed the life of the Moon: Saturn, Sun, Moon, Mars, Mercury, and Jupiter.

Cernunnos is not specifically identified with the Sun in Ireland, but his cycle as vegetation is the annual cycle of the Sun. Mercury, who appears as Nera, was the Sun God of the underworld; the fire ceremonies of the four feasts of Samhuin, Imborg, Beltain, and Lughnasad are feasts of agriculture and husbandry which mark the Sun's yearly course and show the association. The association is confirmed by the fact that Beltain, the May

Day feast, received its name from the Sun God Belgenus. A carved stela from Rheims shows Cernunnos flanked by Mercury on one side and the Sun God Apollo on the other; and at Samhuin in Ireland, fires were extinguished and new fires kindled from a sacred fire.

The three-headed image of Cernunnos seated *accroupi* represents his creation and life nature as a world-man. His legs folded beneath him signify the cessation of motion and the death and returning life phases of the Moon. The account in the myth of the two men hanging on the gallows explains the symbolism of his legs. In the myth, the first man hanging represents one leg as the dead Moon. The withe which Nera fastens to the foot of the other symbolizes life; the foot represents movement; hence the beginning of life. But the life which begins in the dead man is transferred to Nera when he carries the lifeless body to the house where there was water and then hangs him back on the gallows. Nera becomes the Moon and enters the otherworld of life, thus the motion symbolized by Cernunnos' legs begins in Nera rather than in the dead man who is left hanging. Nera represents Cernunnos' other leg.

The house to which Nera carried the dead man for water is the house of the new Moon where its life begins. The withe which Nera ties on his foot represents the embryo body of the new Moon — Nera, shouldering the dead man as he leaves the house, puts on the embryo body as a man puts on a cloak.

The action describes the renewal of life which, in the metaphors of the earliest mythology, was given a phallic image. In the symbolism of the figure of Cernunnos, it is denoted by his exaggerated phallus.

The symbolism is in the tradition of the mythology of creation which began with Trickster who was called First Born in the Winnebago creation cycle. In Eurasia, it formed as the early image of Mercury whose idols were phalli, called by his Greek name, Hermes. The mythological tradition evolved the Egyptian god of beginning, Atum, who rose from the primeval waters and formed into life as a serpent.

Cernunnos' three heads signify the life cycle of the Moon as the underworld summer. His Mars head represents the Moon entering the underworld region of life as the spring and, with one leg, constitutes Cernunnos' life side. His middle head as Mercury is the Moon combined with the Sun moving in the year cycles of created life. His Jupiter head is the full Moon which brings the harvest that ends the summer. His Jupiter head represents the Moon beginning its descent to enter the underworld region of death and so with the other leg, constitutes Cernunnos' death side. The two legs of Cernunnos as the dead Moon hanging on the gallows and the new Moon coming to life, and Nera as the planetary Moon entering through the Cave of Cruachan as Mars and changing to Jupiter by taking a bride in the otherworld, are mythological developments of the four Moons begotten by Enlil and Ninlil on their circuit of the underworld.

Cernunnos' spouse was his female counterpart. Her bodily form duplicated his; their marital relation made them one.

Aillil and Medhbh are part of Cernunnos' two sides. In real life, they are the King and Queen of Connacht; but because they are the Divine King and the Earth Goddess, they can appear as part of Cernunnos whom the King incarnates and whose consort Medhbh incarnates. In her divinity, Medhbh is the land of Ireland which is made fertile by her cohabitation with Aillil. On Samhuin, the Dagda, who was an Irish aspect of Cernunnos, mates with one of her Earth Goddess counterparts who takes the form of a life-giving river, in a procreating act of life creation.

There are two events described in the myth that show the year which began on Samhuin was a creation year bringing a true year into being on Beltain. First, there is Nera's return bringing plants from the otherworld to warn Aillil; the plants prove that it was summer there. At the same time, Nera found the court just as he had left it, seated around a cauldron; since he left when winter began, this meant that it was still winter. The second is Aillil's defeat of the host barring the entrance to the otherworld. Aillil's army constituted the life-giving power of Cernunnos; the host which he defeated was Cernunnos' death forces. The victory released the powers of creation. The fact that the engagement was fought on the eve of Samhuin shows that new life began in the otherworld when winter was beginning on earth and life there was dead.

The image of Cernunnos coupled with the myths and the feasts shows that the year which began on Samhuin was a creation year which would be followed by a true year. The creation year was formed by cumulating 7-day planetary weeks, making the length of the year 13 months. Although the Celts have left no record of their day count, in western Europe the planetary week bears the imprint of the Celtic feasts and the 13-month year survived in Europe as a religious tradition until the Middle Ages. The survival attests the ancient pre-Christian calendar, and, coupled with the planetary Moon constitution of Cernunnos as a world-man and the creation year, shows the ancient Sumero-Babylonian heritage.

CHAPTER 18

Hercules and the Nine Planetary Gods

ca. 2000 through 1000 B.C.

The length of the cycle of created life described in the Jason myth was 7 years, but the Indo-European peoples generally seem to have adopted a cycle of 9 years. The labors of Hercules describe the formation of 9 years of new world existence constituted by nine planetary gods. The nine gods were the seven, with Saturn changed into a triple god formed by the dying quarter Moon, the deceased Moon, and the reviving new Moon.

Hercules was son of Zeus. The myths which tell about him come from the Greeks, but they were originally composed in the Mycenaean period, if not before, and they describe a god similar to the Syrian and Phrygian Adonis and Attis and with the character of Gilgamesh. The myths relate him to the religion of the Great Goddess rather than the religion of Classic Greece.

In considering Hercules, we must bear in mind that the Olympian religion was not the same as that of the early Greeks whose religion was the Great Goddess. When the later Greeks added Hercules to their Olympian pantheon, he ceased to be a god of creation of life on earth; but served as a porter on Olympus who, each day, opened Heaven's gates to let the Sun and Moon begin their courses.

Hercules was a figure in the underworld of creation. He was the elder of twins and, consequently, apparently destined to become the archetype Divine King, and his brother, Iphicles, the tanist-to-be. But in the mythology of Hercules, Iphicles' tanist nature was transferred to Hercules when two serpents crawled into the nursery. Although Hercules was still an infant, he seized a serpent in each hand and strangled it while Iphicles screamed in terror.

Hercules married Deianeira. Deianeira was a local name for the goddess whom the Babylonians called Ishtar. There are many myths about Hercules and different myths describe the same episodes with local variances. In the Hercules mythology, the goddess was particularly known as Deianeira. In wooing her, he wrestled and defeated the river god, Achelous, who came at him first as a bull-headed man and, when Hercules threw him on his back, turned into a speckled serpent. Then, when Hercules seized him, Achelous turned into a bull and charged; but Hercules took him by the horns and hurled him into the ground. Achelous' transformations revealed him as the three aspects of the Moon cycle which were characterized in the *Epic of Gilgamesh* as Enkidu in the composite life state of Mars-Mercury-Jupiter; Gilgamesh as the Moon-serpent, Mercury; and Enkidu as the Heavenly Bull.

Like Gilgamesh, Hercules was part-mortal and part-immortal. Hercules' combat with Achelous corresponded to Gilgamesh's wrestling match with Enkidu. By defeating Achelous, Hercules acquired his threefold planetary nature. He became the creator of the cycle of Moon years in the underworld by performing twelve labors in the service of Eurystheus, the Divine King of Mycenae.

The labors of Hercules are fabulous but, in their succession as individual actions, are quite meaningless in the idiom of modern expression. However, to the peoples of ancient times, whose religious images were formed in the doctrine of the planetary cycle, Hercules was the triple Moon God Achelous whose labors were the cycles of the Moon moving in the creation of life. The serpent in his nature was the Moon-serpent Mercury with the Sun. His first two labors make this evident.

The first two labors were to kill the Nemaean Lion and the Lernaean Hydra. The lion was the animal form of the Sun — after Hercules killed it, he wore the skin continually. The hydra was a monstrous dog with nine

serpent heads. In Indo-European mythology, Mercury was identified with both the serpent and the dog; thus, when Hercules killed the lion and the hydra, he became Mercury as the Sun-bearer. Of the hydra's nine heads, one was immortal and the heads represented the years of life which would form in the course of Hercules' labors.

His labors identified Hercules with the planetary cycle. Thus he was the motion of the Moon forming the years. He formed each year as the planetary god; but, while he moved as the orthodox seven planetary gods, he formed them into a cycle of nine. The nine represented a change in the length of the completed cycle which, in the Indo-European creation, was changed from 7 to 9 years. In the change, the planetary god of the first year became the Sun, and Saturn was made into a triple god and placed at the end of the cycle. In his first two labors, Hercules formed the first year of the cycle as the planetary Sun.

The next two labors were to bring the Cerynaean Hind and the Erymanthean Boar to Eurystheus at Mycenae. The hind was the animal form of the Moon Goddess Artemis and the boar was an animal form of Ares, the Greek name for Mars. The metaphor of these labors describes the formation of the second and third years as the planetary gods, Moon and Mars.

The first two labors reveal the serpent nature which Hercules acquired from Achelous, the third and fourth each reveal his nature as the new and first-quarter Moons which he similarly acquired. This is evident from the setting of the myths. In the metaphor of the myths, Mycenae was on the border between the regions of nonexistence and existence. The walls of the city formed the borderline. The completion of each task necessarily involved a change of locations and, since Mycenae was in existence, the places where the hind and the boar were to be found were outside the realm of existence. The antithetical locations metaphorically describe the two fabulous animals as the new Moon in death and the full Moon on the verge of life. Hercules as Mercury in the planetary cycle was the motion of the

Moon and when he brought the hind and then the boar to Mycenae, he changed each from a new Moon into a full Moon. In the metaphor, the full Moon is the year of life constituted as a planetary god.

The fifth and sixth labors were to clean the stables of King Augeias and to disperse the birds which flocked in the Stymphalian swamp. Augeias' flocks and herds were so numerous that their dung, which had accumulated for years, covered the valleys in such deep layers that the fields could no longer be ploughed or sown with grain, and the stench spread pestilence over the land. Hercules turned the courses of the rivers, Alpheus and Peneius, so that they flowed through the stables and fields and washed them clean. The Stymphalian birds killed the human and animal life in the countryside surrounding the swamp in which they lived. Hercules killed a multitude of birds and drove the rest away.

Here we can see an abstract version of Gilgamesh diving to the bottom of the waters of life and, after recovering the old-man-becomes-young plant, being cast upon the shore of the sea transformed from Mars into Mercury. In the Indo-European creation myth, when Indra killed the Moon-serpent, Vritra, waters flowed from his body and the embryo Sun was in the waters. Like the waters flowing from Vritra, the waters of Alpheus and Peneius brought life to the land. In the epic, the magic plant was the regenerative power of the Moon contained in the life-giving power of the Sun.

When Gilgamesh was washed upon the shore with the magic plant, he brought the life of the Sun and Moon to the land. The dispersal of the Stymphalian birds symbolized this same imagery. The birds were fish-eating marsh birds, and fish were symbolic of the Sun in an embryo Moon body. The birds rising and flying in the sky were associated with the rising Sun. Their death-dealing nature represented the mortality of life which the Sun brought on Earth. The death which followed the full Moon and the dispersal connoted the coming of life. In these two labors, Hercules was Mercury and he formed the fourth year.

The next god in the cycle is Jupiter. Hercules' seventh task was to bring Eurystheus the Cretan Bull, which he did. The Cretan Bull has been identified by scholars as Zeus (Jupiter) in the form in which he carried Europa across the sea to Crete. But the identity cannot be proven, since no one knows when Zeus swam her across and, when he came ashore, he transformed himself into a bird and ravished her. Certainly, however, the animal form of the full Moon was a bull, its planetary form was Jupiter, and the Mediterranean Sea separates Crete from Mycenae. To bring the bull to Eurystheus, Hercules had to cross the waters which symbolized the creation of life and, hence, the formation of the new Moon into the full Moon. In his seventh labor, Hercules formed the fifth year into the planetary god, Jupiter.

Hercules' next task was to bring the flesh-eating Mares of Diomedes to Eurystheus. The Greeks incorporated the Asian Ishtar into their classical religion in different forms. One of these was the mother-daughter pair, Demeter and Persephone. Demeter's animal form was a mare and, while the Moon Goddess as Artemis was a hind, she had different aspects and one of them was a mare. The Mares of Diomedes, therefore, fit into the planetary sequence as Venus. Their lethal appetite for flesh confirms this identity, for Venus in her aspect as the Moon Goddess brought about the death of Enkidu as the Heavenly Bull.

Venus had two sides, one of life and one of death. In life she was the female side of the full Moon and, when Hercules brought the death-dealing mares to Eurystheus, he made the year of Jupiter complete. In death, Venus was the Death Goddess, and the creation of the sixth year was only half finished. Hercules finished it when Eurystheus next sent Hercules to secure the girdle of Queen Hippolyte.

The taking of the girdle was a euphemism for ravishing her. After he ravished her, Hercules killed the queen. The relation of the labors to the planetary cycle makes this ninth labor a version of the rape of Ishtar by Gilgamesh when he and Enkidu killed the Heavenly Bull.

As a sequel to the Mares of Diomedes, Hippolyte is a substitute for Persephone, the Greek Ishtar transformed into Ereshkigal. Persephone was the Moon, but she was particularly the Queen of the underworld region of death. When Hercules took Hippolyte's girdle, he formed a union which was theologically the same as Gilgamesh's with Ishtar when he killed the Heavenly Bull. By taking Hippolyte's girdle, Hercules consummated the task he had begun in his eighth labor and formed the sixth year into the planetary goddess, Venus.

Because he was the Moon's motion with the Sun and, hence, the life which would animate the planetary gods as years, Hercules formed each of the gods as an aspect of himself. Consequently, when he formed the planetary Moon and Venus in the third and eighth labors, he changed his sex. When he ravished Hippolyte, he became her consort in which relation the two were one god. In their union, Hercules and Hippolyte constituted the death state of the planetary Venus. In that death state, Hercules performed his next three labors. He formed the life of the Moon, completed the creation of the 9-year cycle, and brought it out of the outer world of nonexistence to the gate of the underworld of the world in being.

Hercules' task in the tenth labor was to bring Geryon's cattle to Eurystheus. Geryon had three heads and bodies joined at the waist and had powerful wings. He pastured his herd on Erytheia, the island of death in the midst of the western ocean beyond the entrance from the Mediterranean Sea. Hercules made his way to Erytheia with the aid of the Sun, Helius, who accompanied him. He quickly dispatched the herdsmen and the dog and, taking a position on Geryon's flank, he shot an arrow through the three bodies and killed him. When the goddess, Hera, appeared to aid Geryon, Hercules wounded her with an arrow and she left the field. Hercules then herded the cattle together and began the drive back to Mycenae.

In its cycle as the new Moon, the Moon had three forms — one as it disappeared from the sky, one in its passage across the boundary between life and death, and one as it began its return to the sky. Erytheia was the death point in the Moon's cyclical journey and Geryon was the Moon's inanimate body. When Hercules shot Geryon, the two became one and Geryon lodged in Hercules' body. The crossing to Erytheia was a passage to death, Erytheia itself was the seat of death, and the crossing back to the mainland was a return to life.

In the planetary cycle, Geryon was Saturn which was constituted as a triple god: the dying, dead, and reviving Moon. The constitution of the dead Moon was like that of the Death Goddess and Earth Mother in whom a new generation of life formed. When Hercules took possession of Geryon's cattle, he became Saturn as the dead Moon. He began his return to Mycenae by crossing over the water to the mainland in Spain in his aspect as the reviving Moon and the third form of Saturn.

When Hercules killed Geryon and took possession of his cattle, he completed the formation of the nine-god planetary cycle and accomplished the purpose of his tenth labor. His planetary transformations on his route back to Mycenae, therefore, were not planetary or time additions to the cycle. In the theology of the myth, they recorded the Moon life which was contained in Geryon.

Hercules' Moon character would not have been complete if a Moon Goddess had not been a part of him. This part was filled by Hera. While in the planetary cycle, Venus was the female aspect of the Moon, and the myth puts Hera in her place. In ancient Greece, before the Olympian mythology had crystallized, Hera was a Moon Goddess, and was therefore a proper substitute for Venus. In the planetary cycle, Venus was coupled with each planetary god, just as Mercury was part of each one. In the cycle, Venus came to life through death. The arrow which struck Hera was a sign of sacrifice which united her to Geryon in his death from Hercules' arrow. The wounded Hera was Hera returning to life as a part of the reviving new Moon, and as Hercules made his way back to Mycenae, she accompanied him.

Hercules had crossed to Erytheia with the Sun, Helius, and when he landed in Spain, he came to the Kingdom of Chrysaor. Chrysaor had been born together with the Moon horse, Pegasus, from the body of the Moon Goddess, Medusa, when Perseus decapitated her in the death region of the underworld. He carried a golden falchion and symbolized life as the crescent Moon springing from winter death. He represented the planetary stage of new Moon.

As he continued his journey, Hercules made a detour through Italy where he fought many battles. In Italy, Hercules was the planetary Mars, a god of war.

Hercules' chariot mares were Hera, herself, as the Moon Goddess moving with him as Mercury in the planetary cycle. When he left Italy, he went to Scythia, traveling in his own planetary form as Mercury. In Scythia, Hera sent a gadfly which attacked and stampeded the cattle. The myth relates that while Hercules was searching for them, his mares were stolen by a figure who was half-woman, half-serpent tails. When Hercules found that she had them, she refused to give them to him until he lay with her in the cave.

The serpent-tailed woman was, of course, Hera who had transformed herself and, after Hercules had complied with her demand, she reappeared as the mares.

The anatomical features of the serpent-woman identify her as the Asian goddess in her full Moon aspect. The place at which she appeared was the point in the planetary cycle at which Mercury became Jupiter as the full Moon; Hercules' union with the serpent-tailed woman was the sacred marriage which transformed him into Jupiter.

In the final stage, Hercules delivered the cattle to Eurystheus who sacrificed them to Hera. The cattle, in the symbolism of the myth, represent earthly life and the fullness of the Moon. When Eurystheus sacrificed them, the cycle of the Moon was complete and the nine planetary gods were ready to come on earth as the days and life of the year.

Hercules and the Nine Planetary Gods

The life which has formed as the full Moon and which was contained in the nine planetary gods was constituted by the seven planetary gods. These seven had come into being as gods of the days of the Moon's cycle as the changing planetary forms of Hercules during the journey of his tenth labor. These forms fell into order as he made his way to Erytheia and began his return to Mycenae. He came to the shore of the western ocean as Saturn and crossed to Erytheia as the planetary Sun. On Erytheia, he formed as the Moon and, after returning to the mainland, he changed into Mars, then Mercury, and then Jupiter.

The seventh god was Venus. While Venus was the seventh god, she was also, like Mercury with the Sun, united in turn to each of the planetary gods of who preceded her. They were gods of the Moon's life cycle, but in the seventh place Venus was a goddess of death and the full Moon waning to the end of its cycle. In the myth, Venus is called Hera, Geryon's cattle are animal forms of the Moon; when they are delivered to Eurystheus in Mycenae, their delivery denotes the fullness of the Moon. Their sacrifice is the Moon's death and Hera's planetary death as Venus, likewise Hercules' death as a planetary god. The cattle are the Moon and, being the Moon, they are the planetary Venus in the goddess person of Hera; Hercules and Hera became one by virtue of their union in the cave. The sacrifice made the sacrificed god and sacrificer one and, when Eurystheus sacrifices the cattle, he united himself to Hercules and Hera. In the union, Hercules becomes the planetary Venus and completes the cycle of the seven gods.

The seven gods constituted life on earth and the divinity of the Moon; but the Moon moved in cycles of life and death and they had combined in Hercules as its life cycle in the course of its death cycle. In the death state of that cycle, Moon life formed in Hercules as the four quarters of the Moon: Chrysaor, new; Mars, first; Jupiter, full; Venus, last.

Hercules had entered the Moon's death state when he formed the sixth year as the planetary Venus, and had continued in that state when he crossed to Erytheia and shot Geryon. He had then been transformed into the three

Saturns and he had continued in the death state while he completed his tenth labor and performed his eleventh and twelfth. In these three labors, he formed the seventh, eighth, and ninth years and created a 9-year cycle of life on earth.

In the eleventh labor, Hercules brought three golden apples to Mycenae from the Garden of the Hesperides. The Hesperides were the three daughters of Atlas. Their garden was in the farthest west where the Sun set in the western ocean. The apples grew on a tree guarded by a hundred-headed snake named Ladon which coiled around the trunk. Hercules killed Ladon with an arrow and obtained the apples.

The symbolism of the apples has been debated, but it is clear within the context of the creation of the planetary cycle. The garden is in the region of death beyond the boundaries of the created world; Ladon is the Moon-serpent appearing in the waters of creation; and the tree is the tree of life. Ladon as the Moon-serpent is the new Moon forming as life in process of creation; he and the tree of life are one. The new Moon forms the full Moon which as life coming on earth is symbolized by the fruit of the tree. In the planetary cycle the gods Mars, Mercury, and Jupiter constitute that life. In the myth they are represented by the three apples — golden because they are Suns, and fruit because they symbolize earthly life metaphorically constituted by the Moon. The three Hesperides are Venus as the consort of the three gods.

In the metaphor of the myth, the Garden of the Hesperides denotes the life on earth created as the seven planetary gods in the nine-god planetary cycle. The eleventh labor is a mystic abstraction portraying the second planetary Saturn.

In his twelfth labor, Hercules brought Cerberus, the dog of Hades that kept the souls of the dead from leaving the underworld, to Mycenae. Cerberus had three heads with manes of serpents. His anatomical features identify him with the death image of the Moon; Graves identifies him with the Moon as Hecate, one of her early aspects as the Death Goddess, and the

three heads with the three seasons which formed the ancient year: spring, summer and winter. In his dog form, he was the dog star Sirius, which at one time marked the beginning of the new year, the temporal realm of the Moon's image as the Death Goddess-Earth Mother in its cycle as time. Cerberus' three heads relate him to the three Saturns. When Hercules brought him to Mycenae, he came as the third planetary Saturn, thus completing the creation of the 9-year cycle of the nine planetary gods.

The mythology of Hercules was part of the Divine King mythology. In the context of the Divine King, the planetary gods, which constituted the substance of earthly life, Moon, Mars, and Jupiter, constituted the godhead of the Divine King. The new Moon was the life spirit of the full Moon and the godhead of the tanist king. When Hercules brought Cerberus to Mycenae, he came as the lunar tanist. He was the third Saturn as the Moon returning to life. But in the theology of kingship, the Divine King was the incarnation of the tanist and, had to die in order to become reincarnate.

With Cerberus at Mycenae, Hercules had become the multiple being of the nine planetary gods. He had thus become a period of created life on earth in the image of a world-man and had brought himself to the sacrifice which would be necessary to bring him into being as nine new years of life in the medium of the king.

Here we should consider for a moment the nine planetary gods. They were the original seven with Saturn reconstituted and moved from the first place to the last place in the cycle. The change of Saturn's position and his reconstitution into three phases of the new Moon change the cycle into one beginning with life and ending with new life. Where the movement of the gods as seven was part of the process of creation, their movement as nine was the product of creation. As nine, they were a cycle of created life. When Hercules died as the world-man and came into being, he came as the divinity of the nine planetary gods.

Hercules had to perform his own sacrifice, and his doing so should have been counted as a thirteenth labor, but it was not part of his service for

Eurystheus and its relationship to the other labors became lost in the development of the classic Greek religion. Although the labors are recounted in Greek mythology, they are not relevant to its classic Olympian form. They were retained by the Greeks because the Greek hegemony included peoples of the popular Great Goddess faith and they felt it necessary to adopt Hercules into the Olympian pantheon. In the process, the coming into being of Hercules as the 9-year cycle was separated and rewritten as an independent myth. The myth describes the adoption of Hercules into the Olympian family, but it clearly belongs to the planetary cycle of creation. It is the myth of Hercules and Nessus.

Hercules, traveling with Deianeira, came to the River Evenus where a centaur, Nessus, offered to carry Deianeira across while Hercules swam. Hercules accepted the offer, threw his club and bow across, and plunging into the water, swam to the other side. Climbing out on the bank, he turned and saw that Nessus had thrown Deianeira on the ground and was at the point of ravishing her. Hercules picked up his bow and shot Nessus. Nessus fell to the ground ejaculating and died.

The theme of the *Epic of Gilgamesh* is clear in the Herculean version of the myth. Gilgamesh, traveling with Enkidu and Ishtar as his consort, has been changed into Hercules traveling with Deianeira. The Heavenly Bull appears as Nessus. When the Heavenly Bull died, Ishtar was transformed into the Earth Goddess, Ereshkigal. In the metaphor of the Herculean version, when Nessus dies, Deianeira becomes the Earth Goddess and the union of Nessus and Deianeira is consummated. Nessus and Hercules constitute the Moon as the world-man and, when Hercules climbs out on the opposite bank of the river having left Nessus and Deianeira, he is the spirit of the dead Moon, while Nessus as Hercules is the full Moon. The sacrifice of the Heavenly Bull and the rape of Ishtar have been reconstructed as the death of Nessus and rape of Deianeira.

When he shot Nessus, Hercules died as a world-man and the gods which formed within him came into being as gods of the underworld creation years. This is evident from the subsequent action — Hercules fought a duel with Ares (Mars) which he won with the aid of Athene; he married a Moon Goddess; and he joined the circle of Greek gods on Mt. Olympus.

We will follow his action in more detail in the following chapter and see how it describes him changing from one planetary god to the next and finally ascending on earth as the godhead of the king. Here we will see how his action brought the nine planetary gods into being as nine new years of life.

The account of Hercules' labors metaphorically describes Hercules as the Moon moving through its cycles. The prologue is his wrestling match with Achelous which forecast his role as the changing stages of the Moon. The myth places Mycenae on the border between existence and nonexistence because it describes Hercules forming as a world-man outside the gate, and the Moons which Hercules brings to Mycenae in the animal forms are the life which formed as the 9-year cycle.

The metaphor of Hercules' labors is formed on the nature of the planetary cycle in which the planetary gods are full Moons as life and the planetary Moon spirit Mercury is the maker of life as time and the new Moon. The province of the full Moon is the daytime of life and the province of the new Moon is the night of death and revival. Thus, Mycenae is the place of the full Moon, and the places to which Hercules goes in performing his labors are places of death where the new Moon forms.

Erytheia and the Garden of the Hesperides are specifically located in the region of death and, while the significance of each location where Hercules goes to perform his other tasks is not descriptively specified, it is certain that they, too, represented places of mythical death. In Mycenae, Hercules is the full Moon. Each time when he departs from Mycenae, he enters the region of death transformed into the new Moon. He is then the serpent Moon spirit but when he returns to Mycenae, he returns as the full Moon. The death of Nessus made Hercules a new Moon so that in the course of his labors and death, he formed as the new Moon 13 times. These 13 new Moons were his year track on which he carried the Sun.

Thus Hercules returning from each of his labors was the planetary god which he had created as a year of life and, when he formed as a world-man and came into being, he came into being in the underworld as the nine planetary gods who thereupon began forming the nine underworld creation years. The nature of the nine gods makes it evident that they formed the years in 9-day cycles. As we have seen, they were the same gods as the seven who were the days of creation, but they moved in a different order and Saturn had three bodies instead of one. In the changed order, the planetary Sun came first and Saturn came at the end. Each was a Moon which, as we have seen, moved through a complete lunar cycle in the course of a day.

In creating the nine planetary gods as years, Hercules moved in 7-day cycles. This is evident in the tenth labor and in the planetary nature of the creation. The 7 days formed a quarter-month making the months 28 days; Hercules formed as a new Moon 13 times and the new Moons formed the months. Therefore, the days in a year numbered 364 (13 x 28), one day less than the actual year which was counted as 365 days. Therefore, after 9 years, 9 days remained before the new 9 years of life could begin. When Hercules died as a world-man, he was dead for 9 days. There is nothing in the mythology of Hercules to show this; but the period of the Indo-European world-man's death is recorded in the mythology of the Germanic Odin.

The Germans were Indo-European peoples and, like the Celts, they derived their religion from the Indo-European culture of the steppes as it had formed in the Mycenaean times by the middle of the second millennium B.C. They adopted the 7-day planetary week as a unit of their calendar. In their planetary calendar, Odin was Mercury. Odin sacrificed himself by hanging on Yggdrasil, the tree of life which supported the universe. He hung for 9 days and then revived, renewed in youth. His self-sacrifice,

though not the immolation, is comparable to Hercules'.

The metaphor of myth is abstract and complex, and the mythology of Odin and his death records the creation of a 9-year cycle of world existence. Odin had a bosom friend, a giant named Mimir who lived in a spring which watered the roots of Yggdrasil and which contained the knowledge of the past and future.

The metaphor clearly fixes Mimir's home between nonexistence and existence, between death and the world of life. Mimir was blind and Odin gave him one of his eyes for a drink from the spring. Odin had come to Mimir's spring in the state of death and nonexistence when he hanged himself and, when he drank the water, knowledge of the future gave him consciousness and brought him into being.

Odin had the power of changing himself into the different animal forms of the planetary gods and, before he gave Mimir an eye, his two eyes were the morning and evening stars of Mercury. Thus with Frigg, the Germanic Venus who was his wife, in his miraculous changes he constituted the cycle of the seven planetary gods. When he gave one of his eyes to Mimir, he made Mimir his double as the evening star form of Mercury in the underworld.

Odin's eye made Mimir the three planetary gods of Saturn, and, therefore, the new Moon. Odin for his part retained his being as the planetary gods of life, Sun, Moon, Mars, Mercury, and Jupiter which, with Frigg as Venus, made him a full Moon. In consequence, combined with Mimir, Odin constituted a world-man — in that form he hanged himself.

The mythology of Odin does not record the planetary gods, but he must have come into existence as the nine gods because there is no way of relating the seven gods to the 9 days of death except as part of the nine-god cycle. We do not know that the mythology of Odin was composed as early as Mycenaean times, but the planetary theme proves that it was derived from the same religious beliefs as those in which the Hercules mythology had its origin.

Hercules' death was calendrical. The new 9-year cycle could not begin in the created world until the Sun came to an end of a 365-day year cycle and the new cycle of creation and the 9 years of created life could begin at the same time. Now, if we look closely at the nine gods — Sun, Moon, Mars, Mercury, Jupiter, Venus, and the three Saturns — we see that they are the Sun and Moon combined in a common motion.

We recall that the planetary cycle was a construct of the Sumero-Babylonian sacred calendar, and that the Sun was a bodiless spirit that was moved through its course by the planet Mercury. In forming their later Olympian mythology, the Greeks retained the concept of a lunar planetary power moving the Sun.

The Sun, Helius, rode in a chariot drawn by white horses and driven by the god, Apollo. Horses were animal forms of the Moon. Mercury also gave the Moon its motion. Therefore, the progression of the nine gods was certainly based on the Sumero-Babylonian theology and described the Sun and Moon moving together on a single course.

Now, since the planetary gods were days and, since there was no way in which the gods could move evenly together month by month, the nine-god progression must have followed the track of the Sun. But, because the Sun year was counted as 365 days, the gods could not end their march at the Sun year end. Thus they perforce had to halt at the end of 360 days, the closest number to 365 divisible by 9.

The planetary year was the life year of the Babylonians from whom the Indo-Europeans derived their religious culture, and it was the life year of the Egyptians. The nine gods dictated the 360 days and it must, therefore, have been the life cycle created by Hercules.

The five days which followed were days when life on earth was theologically dead. We shall see again in the next chapter that when the year had formed in the underworld, the planetary gods combined in Hercules as a world-man who died and so brought them as life on earth. The 5 days of death would, therefore, have been days when the world-man was dead. In

the combination of the gods, the world-man was the Moon. After 5 days, he would come to life on earth to begin a new series of 9-day cycles and complete a new 360-day year.

CHAPTER 19

Hercules, the Indo-European Godhead of the King

ca. 2000 through 1000 B.C.

The 9 years which Hercules created by his labors formed in the underworld as the godhead of the King of Mycenae. In those times, the cult of Hercules as the godhead of the king was not limited to Mycenae, but was widespread. He was the Indo-European equivalent of Sumero-Babylonian Dumuzi, or Tammuz; the Canaanites worshiped him as the consort of Astarte (Ishtar) and called him Melkarth.

The cult of Hercules was carried onto the steppes in the religion of the Great Goddess, where it was adopted by nomadic herdsmen. Among these were the Scythians, who appeared around 1700 B.C. when the steppes were in a ferment of farmers moving westward and nomads moving eastward looking for new pastures.

These nomadic tribes all spoke a common language and their art, which reflected Mesopotamian mythological concepts and ways of life, was the same. Accordingly, it has been thought that they, or at least a majority, were linked by a common racial tie. The tribes which came to be known generally as Scythians became the most important of those living on the steppes.

The Scythians occupied the region extending from north of the Black Sea in southern Russia to the Altai mountain district in central Asia. Their culture reached its peak in the region north of the Black Sea between the early seventh and late sixth centuries B.C. Other peoples, notably the Celts and the Teutons or Germans, migrated westward into Europe where they carried the cult of the Great Goddess and her consort.

Hercules became the ancestor of the Scythians in the course of his tenth labor, when he mated with the serpent-woman and begot Scythes. This was in the time of the creation of the Scythian world. When that world came into existence, Scythes became the king. As the offspring of Hercules and the Goddess, Scythes was divine. We know from the funerary rites and the burials of Scythian kings that his successors were held to be god-kings.

In the funeral rites and burials, the body of the dead king was embalmed, placed on a wagon, and carried in procession through the tribes over which he had ruled. When the procession passed, the men of the tribes cut off a piece of their ears; cut their hair short; and slashed their arms, stabbed their hands with arrows, and made cuts in their foreheads and noses in a symbolic ritual of self-immolation. The king's body was finally carried to an elaborate tomb constructed of logs on a burial ground high on a sacred mountain.

There the king was interred with a concubine or a second wife who was strangled. Other servitors were sacrificed and the tomb was covered with a mound of earth. In the final rites, a large number of warriors and horses were sacrificed.

The Scythians held Hercules to be their ancestor and presumably their kings inherited their divinity from him through Scythes. The mythology of Hercules which we considered in Chapter 18 described the creation of the world as a repeating process.

As we saw in the account of Hercules' labors, life came into existence in 9-year cycles in which the years formed as gods in an intermediate underworld. The year-gods combined in multiple forms as Hercules, who was nine gods in one and who had a double being: one in the underworld where he was formed, and one on earth where he became the godhead of the king. This intermediate world was a god-and-spirit otherworld or underworld which was part of the world in being and which was divided into a life-part above and a death-part below.

Hercules, the Indo-European Godhead of the King

The myths which we considered were related to the labors of Hercules in the outer void, where life and time formed before coming into being. Other myths describe the action of Hercules in the underworld part of the created world, and these myths show the formation of the divinity of kings. Let us now return to the mythology of Hercules and consider it in relation to the Scythian gods.

The Scythians called the Great Goddess in her death and Earth Mother aspect Tabiti, and Artimpasa in her life aspect. She appeared in the myth about Hercules and Nessus as Deianeira. In the myths that describe Hercules in the created underworld, she also appears with other names, which makes the record confusing. In our consideration of the myths, therefore, we will identify the aspect in which the goddess appears in the different names.

Hercules had created 9 years of life by his labors. He had created them as the planetary gods. They were gathered in the death state of the Moon in the underworld. They were the gods of the life cycle of the Moon and the stages of its joint motion with the Sun. In their nature as stages, they were a cycle of days. Hercules was the god of motion, the Moon spirit Mercury, and the Sun-bearer. He came into being when he crossed the Evenus River and shot Nessus. At that point, he had entered the death region of the underworld of the created world of life. His divinity contained the planetary gods and his function was to form them into a series of 9 years of life and to come on earth each year as the godhead of the king.

There are three myths which metaphorically describe Hercules forming the planetary gods into the year cycles of life and incarnating the king. In considering them, we must bear in mind the nature of the Sun and Moon divinities. The Sun, the animating fire of life was immortal — the Moon, on the other hand, the nature of the substance of life was mortal. Mercury had a double nature. As motion, he was bodiless and indestructible; being the motion of the Sun and so united with it, he was immortal. But as a planet, he was a body spirit of the Moon and so he was mortal. In his aspect as Mercury, therefore, Hercules was part-mortal and part-immortal, like Gilgamesh.

We must also bear in mind that when the Moon died, it came to life again as a new Moon. The new Moon rose out of the death state of the old Moon. Consequently, Hercules in his planetary form had to die in order to begin a new life as the godhead of the king.

The elements of life formed a trinity: the Sun, which constituted the life principal; the Moon, which constituted the content of the life being; and Mercury, the divine spirit of life. When Hercules stood on the far bank of the Evenus River and watched Nessus die, he was constituted as the three planetary gods: Sun, Moon, and Mercury. He began his work, therefore, by transforming his planetary godhead into Mars.

The myth describes this transformation as a duel between Hercules and Ares. Ares was the Greek name for Mars. Hercules defeated Ares, and so became Mars in the planetary cycle. The translation of the divinity of the defeated to the victor was, of course, part of the doctrine of sacrifice. The myth is as follows:

A king, Cycnus, had angered the Sun God called Apollo by carrying off cattle which were being driven for sacrifice to Apollo. Cycnus was Ares' son. He enticed men who entered his domain to fight duels on chariots; he always won, then beheaded the loser and hung the head on a skull rack at the temple of his father. Apollo induced Hercules to fight Cycnus; Hercules won, and killed him. In the duel, Cycnus had been supported by Ares, who then dueled with Hercules. In this fight, Athene rode in the chariot with Hercules and gave him victory by deflecting Ares' spear thrust. Her action enabled Hercules to wound Ares as the chariots came abreast of each other. In the myth, the planetary goddess Venus appeared as Athene.

The next god in the planetary cycle was Mercury. Hercules himself was Mercury. This is shown by the chariot duel in which he defeated Ares. The planetary goddess Venus was a part of each of the planetary gods and

the multiple aspects of the Moon, as was Mercury. Horses were animal forms of the Moon and symbols of its motion, while wheels were symbols of the Sun's motion. Hercules driving off the field victorious with Athene, was Mercury, the Sun-bearer and Moon spirit.

The next planetary god was Jupiter, and Hercules' transformation into Jupiter is recorded in the second myth. According to the myth, Hercules led an army against Eurytus, the Divine King of Oechalia. In the battle which ensued, Hercules killed Eurytus and his sons and was about to seize his daughter, Iole, when she jumped off the castle wall, for the purpose of killing herself to avoid capture.

But Iole was wearing full skirts which spread out as she fell and acted as a parachute so that she landed alive. Hercules captured her, married her, and sent her off to live with Deianeira.

Iole was none other than the planetary Venus in her life aspect as the full Moon, while Deianeira was Venus' aspect as the Death Goddess. Hercules' marriage to Iole was a sacred marriage by which he succeeded to Eurytus' divinity as king and became Jupiter in the planetary cycle.

In the third myth, Hercules formed successively into the stages of Venus and the three Saturns. These were the stages in which new life formed in death. The scene changes to a mountain summit where the gods had their life beings — while in the life part of the underworld, it was in the midst of the death region.

This seeming paradox is consistent with the nature of the underworld when it is considered that the Great Goddess was the earth and that she was the mother of life. The life region was her womb. The life which formed within her formed in the image of all things on her surface. One of her images was a mountain, from the summit of which the winds and rain came — the two elements which represented the breath and fertility of life. So in the imagery of the ancient religion, beneath the inert soil and rock of the mountain, there was another mountain on which the gods lived and directed the affairs of men.

The myth thus describes the apotheosis of Hercules. After he had killed Eurytus and taken possession of Oechalia, Hercules celebrated by offering 12 bulls to Zeus. In order to perform the ceremonies, he had Deianeira send him the ceremonial garments. But before she sent them, she treated them with a mixture of Nessus' blood and seed which had spilled on the earth as he lay dying from Hercules' arrow. Nessus had told her that if she would collect the mixture and rub it into a piece of Hercules' clothing, after he had worn the garment on which she rubbed it, he would thereafter be faithful to her. She had believed Nessus and because Hercules was notoriously faithless, she had followed his instructions.

She had rubbed the mixture into the shirt which Hercules wore next to his skin. Nessus' blood contained the poison of the Lernaean Hydra, which Hercules had killed in his second labor for Eurystheus. Thus, when Hercules had killed the 12 bulls, the poison began burning into his flesh. Hercules tried to rip off the shirt, but his flesh tore off with the strips, leaving his bones bare and the remaining flesh burned more fiercely.

In the agony of the fire, Hercules raged over the fields and mountains tearing at his shirt, but to no avail. Finally, he called Hyllus, his son by Deianeira, and together they made a pyre on a mountaintop. When all was ready, Hercules lay on the pyre, his agony gone. Although others had come to his death, none would light the pyre until Poeas, a shepherd passing by with his son, Philoctetes, directed Philoctetes to do so.

When the flames began to consume Hercules, Zeus destroyed Hercules' mortal form with a thunderbolt, and brought him to the summit of Olympus in a chariot drawn by four horses. Athene greeted him on his arrival and introduced him to the other gods. Deianeira, in remorse, killed herself on their marriage bed and descended to Tartarus where Hercules' mortal spirit joined her in death. Tartarus was a death division of the underworld between the life division and the world of life on earth.

The story of the sacrifice of the bulls and the apotheosis of Hercules describe his transformation into the planetary Venus and then into the first

Saturn. Venus followed Jupiter in the planetary sequence. She was the spouse of Jupiter in her aspect of the full Moon, but she was a Death Goddess who brought the Moon to its death, and so she began the death side of the planetary cycle. Deianeira, as Venus, brought Hercules to death. Deianeira was Hercules' spouse and when he sent Iole to live with her the two became one. In the planetary cycle, Jupiter was the life spirit of the full Moon. When Hercules became Jupiter and sent Iole to live with Deianeira, his relation to Iole and Deianeira made him the planetary Venus.

Venus and the three Saturns were the gods of the death and returning life-side of the Moon cycle. The first Saturn was a god of ending and beginning. The transformation of Hercules into the first Saturn began when he put on his ceremonial garment for the sacrifice. In each of his transformations, Hercules was a division of time. His cyclical state as the first Saturn continued until he died on his pyre and ascended to the company of gods on Olympus.

In the metaphor of the myth, the poison burning in Hercules' flesh, and the agony in which he ripped strips of flesh from his bones is a version of the symbolism of a serpent sloughing its dead scales as it moves off in the new skin covering its body. Hercules' death on the pyre completes the metaphor describing his transformation into the first Saturn.

The year formed by the nine planetary gods was 360 days divided into 12 months of 30 days each. The 12 bulls represented the 12 months and their sacrifice signified the death of the gods at the end of their year cycle. Hercules' action following the sacrifices describes his role as the first Saturn leaving the life cycle of the year, and his own death in the fire of his pyre describes his transformation into the second Saturn.

The second Saturn was a god of the new Moon forming in the death state of the old Moon. He was a god of continuing life, but also a god of death. Like the Sumerian Gilgamesh, he was part-mortal. As in the case of Gilgamesh, whose mortal part returned to the mortal state while his immortal part went on to the god world, Hercules' mortal part left his pyre to go to Tartarus, the death region of the mortal underworld, while his immortal part ascended to the place of the gods.

The mythical description of Hercules' action as a god forming the life which each new year brought on earth is abstract and is centered on the Moon as the divinity of life's substance. Beginning with his arrival at the seat of the gods, Hercules' welcome by Athene denotes his planetary nature. Athene had taken Venus' place as the planetary goddess. He had come to Olympus as the dying and dead Moon, and was reborn on Olympus. Hera, who in the Greek pantheon was Zeus' wife, adopted him as her son.

Because Hercules' planetary nature gave him the divinity of the Moon, the ceremony describes his rebirth as a divine aspect of the new Moon. Hera went to bed, pretending to be in labor, with Hercules under her skirt. Hercules then appeared from Hera's skirt in a newborn state of immortal life. Hera then married him to her daughter Hebe, who was the goddess of youth. In an earlier age, she had been the Hittite Earth Mother — in either case, she was a goddess of new life and a suitable bride for the newborn Hercules. Hercules was then made porter at the gate of the god world on Olympus.

One of the Olympian deities was the goddess Artemis, who was the Moon. Artemis was the goddess of the hunt and every morning she left to follow the chase. When Artemis returned every evening, Hercules was at his post by the gate and he received the game which she had killed. Hercules skinned and cleaned the game, eating the portions he liked.

In interpreting this part of the myth, we must recall the sacrifice doctrine of the ancient hunters. Artemis hunted with bow and arrow; her kill was sacrifice. The game was part of her own divinity and, when Hercules ate, he did so in communion with her. The hunter doctrine further held that the animal-god killed and eaten would return to life as a new animal-god. In the communion, therefore, the game which was dead, and yet was new life, became a part of Hercules and made him the second Saturn.

Hercules, the Indo-European Godhead of the King

The third Saturn was the new Moon returning to the sky. We must keep in mind that the Moon was a manifestation of the divine nature of the year cycle of domestic animal and plant life and that the Moon's divinity was the succession of the nine planetary gods who came on earth incarnate in the king. Hercules was the latter-day Gilgamesh; in the fire which consumed his pyre, his mortal and immortal parts separated, and his mortal part went to reside in Tartarus.

Tartarus was the realm of Hades, a brother of Zeus, and lord of death. It was not a geographical location, but the earth into which all life returned. The gods of the underworld had different aspects, but they were part of the realm of death. Deianeira, who retired to Tartarus when the poison of the hydra killed Hercules, was the Earth Mother in death.

In this same imagery, when the Moon disappeared after the last quarter, it was dead and had merged with the Earth. But there was life in the death of the Earth; Iole was the life part of Deianeira, she contained the life that had been created by the Moon Goddess' hunt, and Hercules in Tartarus was still the planetary Mercury who gave motion to bring the life back to the world above. The myth describes him as stalking through the congregation of souls of the dead carrying his bow drawn and an arrow fitted to the string. The description denotes motion and the bow signifies resurrection.

Hyllus was the resurrection of Hercules. He was the offspring of Hercules and Deianeira, and another bond identified him with Hercules. When he and Hercules were building the pyre, Hercules made him swear an oath by which he bound himself to marry Iole and, after his father's death, he made Iole his wife. Iole was surely the planetary Venus by another name. Her descent when she jumped from the castle wall metaphorically describes her as the evening star, and her marriage to Hyllus identifies her with a new generation and the morning star.

Hyllus' inheritance made him the nine planetary gods and his union with Iole gave him her nature as vegetation and animal life. Thus his divinity was the year cycle of life on earth. Hercules had died as a world-

man whose constitution was all the gods of life on earth. He came to life in Hyllus as the godhead of the king.

The mythology of Hercules relates to the peoples who worshiped him as a god — specifically, the Scythians, who looked upon Hercules as their progenitor. The first Scythian king was Scythes whom Hercules begot on the serpent-tailed woman in the course of his tenth labor. In that labor, Hera had appeared as the serpent-tailed woman whose cave dwelling and serpent characteristics identified her with the Earth Mother-Moon Goddess. She was the goddess whom the Scythians called Tabiti in her death and earth aspect, and Artimpasa in her life and Moon aspect.

The myth does not specifically associate Hyllus with Divine Kingship, but the introduction of Poeas and Philoctetes into the scene of Hercules on his pyre must have been for the purpose of identifying him with that doctrine. Poeas is described as a shepherd — a description which identifies him with the divinity of the Moon and, hence, the divinity of Hercules. Further, because Philoctetes lighted the fire which consumed the pyre, Hera sent a serpent which bit Philoctetes and caused his death. In the theology of the Divine Kingship, when the king died, he was succeeded by his tanist who inherited the king's armor and married his consort. Since Hera, in the myth, is a Moon Goddess, the serpent was a Moon-serpent and the animal form of Mercury. Thus Philoctetes is identified with Hercules and, since a new Divine King succeeded the tanist, Poeas must have been an alter ego for Hercules, Philoctetes an alter ego for Hyllus, and the serpent the generations of Hercules as the god-king.

Let us now follow the passage of the Great Goddess with her planetary gods and their cyclical movement as time eastward, and go on to India.

CHAPTER 20

Agni

ca. 2000 B.C. until after 1000 A.D.

In the eastward diffusion, the planetary doctrine was carried to India by Indo-Aryans, who appeared in northwest India about 1500 B.C. Their god of the universe was Agni, who was time and movement, and whose principal form was fire. The other gods were all parts of Agni.

Agni was Varuna in the evening, Mitra in the morning, Savitir (the Sun) crossing the sky, and Indra as he illuminated the atmosphere. Varuna in the fullness of his being was the sky, but in a lesser form he was the Moon; Mitra was Mercury; thus, Agni was Mitra as the movement of the Moon combined with the Sun. Indra was the god who, in the original creation, formed the life region of the universe and set the Moon and Sun in motion by killing the Moon-serpent Vritra — thus forming the life of the world. Varuna and Mitra are said to have brought the day — meaning that they brought the time of life — and this was the meaning when it was said that Agni was Indra when he illuminated the atmosphere.

One of Agni's important qualities was that he brought himself to sacrifice. When the world was created, the gods which formed the life on earth came into being through sacrifice. Sacrifice was necessary to maintain rita, which was the ordered motion of the Moon and Sun as the days of life brought by Agni, as Varuna and Mitra.

Consequently, when Agni brought himself to sacrifice, he came as Varuna and Mitra with the Sun. When he sacrificed himself, he formed into a world-man and died in his own flames. When he rose out of the fire in life, he rose as the gods who had died in it.

Agni's movement as Varuna and Mitra was in Mitra's shining car — shining as we may well conjecture, because his car was Savitir and his movement was the succession of the seven lunar planetary gods. The Sun was both male and female. The male Sun had three names, each of which denoted a different aspect: Surya, the actual solar element; Savitir, the active power of the Sun; and Vishnu, the Sun's motion as a year. Varuna was a creator god and with Savitir and moving with Mitra in the creation of days, the three created a cycle of life which would come into being when Agni sacrificed himself.

In his image as a world-man, Agni was pictured with three heads, three legs, seven arms, seven rays, and riding on a ram. His seven arms and rays were the seven planetary gods, the arms being their Moon bodies, and the rays their Moon spirit united to the Sun. Earlier, in the story of Jason, we saw the Divine King Phryxus coming in death to Colchis riding on a ram. Phryxus in death was the Moon spirit Mercury and the ram was the Moon. The symbolism of the ram in the image of Agni thus shows him as Varuna and Mitra bringing himself to sacrifice. Agni mounted on his ram has the same symbolic meaning as Cernunnos' ram-serpent scepter. Agni was fire; as fire, he was the Sun. The ram was the spirit Moon; carrying Agni, it was the Sun-bearer, hence, the planetary god Mercury. The ram and Agni were like the ram in the myth of Jason. When the ram with the Golden Fleece was sacrificed, it turned into the serpent form of the new Moon spirit. The ram with the Golden Fleece and the ram-serpent scepter were variant symbols of the motion of the Moon and Sun united as one. Thus the ram-serpent identifies Agni with Cernunnos and his three heads with the three heads of Cernunnos — the planetary gods Mars, Mercury, and Jupiter.

In the planetary doctrine, the motion of the Moon created the life which came on earth. The Moon spirit Mercury carrying the Sun formed the stages of the Moon cycle as the planetary gods. The life stages of the cycle were completed as the full Moon by the gods Mars, Mercury, and Jupiter.

The completion reveals the symbolism of Agni's three legs. Legs denote motion. As the opposite of the heads, they are Saturn, Sun, and Moon as the planetary gods who formed as the new Moon.

Agni is the composite form of the gods of the planetary cycle, combined as a world-man whose destiny is death. His ride is the combining of the gods as he brings himself to sacrifice along the Moon's path through the sky. His form as the world-man becomes complete when the last of the planetary gods, Venus, joins the combination. Venus is the death which follows the full Moon. She is Agni's destiny as the world-man.

In their image as the world-man, Venus was represented in Cernunnos by his spouse who was his feminine counterpart, and in Hercules by the three Hesperides. The Indo-Europeans were nomadic stockmen and the elements of the sky, more than the fertility of the earth, determined their lives. Consequently, the Earth Goddess' consort tended to become predominate and displace her as the supreme divinity of the universe, and the goddess faded into the shadows of mythology. The Venus figure in Agni was his shadowy spouse Agnayi.

While Agni was represented pictorially as a composite form of the planetary gods, as the Creator-Maker, he was the Fire God and the holocaust which brought the gods into existence as a cycle of world life. His pictorial image is fixed, but in motion it is formed by the planetary gods moving as the days as though marked on a calendar. Features of this calendrical image which do not appear on his portrait as a world-man are recorded in god-lists which have come down to us from the later Hindu period.

The first is a list of 28 gods who were gods of a cycle of 28 days. This is a Hindu revision of an earlier list of Vedic day gods, because all but two have Vedic names. They appear as gods of 28 stars or combinations of stars which constitute a lunar zodiac. There are comparable zodiacs in ancient Chinese and Arabic astronomy, and the three have so many similar features that all scholars agree that they must have had a common origin; but when or where is not definitely known. The star groups or asterisms of these zodiacs are generally termed lunar mansions or stations.

In the Hindu lunar zodiac, the lunar mansions are called *nakshatras*. Its antiquity is attested by the first sign which is the Pleiades and by the fact that Vedic gods preside over the *nakshatras*. A list of 28 appears in the *Atharaveda* which dates it as far back as 1000 B.C. although some scholars will not accept a date earlier than 800 B.C. Nevertheless, the lunar zodiac must have been established at an earlier date.

The comparable system in China, called the *hsiu*, was being developed in the Shang period, 14th century B.C. Since the Indian and Chinese zodiacs had a common origin, the Hindu zodiac in its originating form would have been brought to India at as early a date, and probably earlier. Almost certainly, although not surely proven, the lunar zodiac was a construct of Sumerian and early Babylonian priest-astronomers. The Indo-Aryans who brought the Vedic culture into India evolved their culture from the Sumero-Babylonian in common with other Indo-European peoples, notably the early Greeks. The lunar zodiac with its 28 stations marked the diurnal course of the Moon in its monthly cycle. It was a function of the planetary calendar which, as we have seen, was invented by the Sumerians, modified by the Babylonians, and adopted by the Greeks of the Mycenaean period.

When the 28 lunar mansions were originally defined, the Moon was imagined to determine the position of the Sun in the underworld. Since the course of the Moon's month cycle was the circle of the heavens, the lunar zodiac would also have marked the Moon's course with the Sun as a year of creation, and so it became the Moon's path in the course of a planetary year. The year cycle was divided into quadrants determined by the equinoxes and the solstices, and each quadrant was divided into seven sectors. The year was 364 days and, since the 28 mansions were thus the stations of the year, the division made each quarter 91 days and the sectors 13 days.

In this division, there should be 13 days between each of the lunar mansions. The spaces occupied by the lunar mansions are not equal, however, in the forms in which the zodiacs are known. There are several possible explanations for this. If, as is quite certain, the zodiac was originally established by the stars which marked the Moon's daily progress around the earth, the stars would necessarily have been equidistant. When the stars were made the marks of the Moon's progress through the year, they would naturally have continued to be regarded as marking equal stages. Indeed, there is an ancient tradition according to which 27 of the lunar mansions were wives of King Soma, the Moon, who was required to divide his time equally among them. The other mansion, we may presume, was his house of death as the new Moon.

The inequality, however, may have been determined by the relative positions of the lunar mansions and not by the time between the passage across the meridian of the marker star in one lunar mansion and the marker star in the next. The Moon's path in the underworld was imaginary, and it could be delayed or its rate of progress changed by incidents occuring in the underworld, as happened to Gilgamesh on his journey along the path. The astronomer-priests who established the zodiac may have disregarded the time of the star passages and defined the lunar mansions as stations in time, separated by lesser or greater intervals in space, which conformed to the mythology of the Moon's path through the underworld.

Inequalities in the divisions of the lunar mansions may also have resulted from later changes in their stellar structures, or from the observation that in actuality the Moon does not move uniformly through the stars. At the time of the autumnal equinox, when the Moon is nearly full, for instance, the Harvest Moon rises for several nights at about the same time, as does the next month's Hunter's Moon. The astronomer-priests could have used such variations as license for varying the time passages of the lunar mansions.

The generally accepted theory for the division of the sky into 28 asterisms is that the length of the sidereal month, i.e., the period of the

Moon's revolution around the earth from one star to the same star, is approximately 27-1/3 (27.3216+) days. The synodic month, i.e., the time from full moon to full moon, is approximately 29-1/2 (29.53+) days. Needham, who has made a careful study of *nakshatras* in his work on the *Science and Civilization of China*, considers that the division was a compromise between the two periods.* Surely, however, the division was made to coincide with the 28 days of the planetary month.

Since the *nakshatras* marked the diurnal progress of the Moon in its circle through the sky and, since the stars through which it moves are the same as the stars on the Sun's path in its annual circuit, the zodiac could be used to tell the Sun's position. Thus, Leopold de Saussure wrote that the lunar zodiac was invented for the purpose of establishing the position of the Sun in its monthly course. This is apparently confirmed by the fact that the equinoxes and solstices were the orientation points of the zodiac. However, if that had been the sole purpose of inventing the zodiac, the Moon would have been eliminated from it at its inception because the motions of the Moon and Sun have no time relation.

Ancient Babylonian star-maps, referable to the second millennium B.C., divide the heavens into three roads, one through the northern sky, one around the equatorial belt, and one through the stars in the south. The stars of the northern road are the stars of Enlil, those on the equator are the stars of An, and those in the south are the stars of Ea. The first sign of the zodiac formed by the lunar mansions was the Pleiades which, in the second millennium, were close to the point where the ecliptic crosses the equator into the north, whence it returns to the equator on the opposite side of the sky and crosses into the south.

The mythology of the stars identifies the *nakshatras* as milestones along the Moon's road through the underworld and, when the full Moon crossed into the north under the sign of the Pleiades, the summer began in the underworld and the winter began in the northern latitudes on earth.

*Joseph Needham, *Science and Civilization in China*, Vol. III, pg. 239.

Returning to the equator and entering the south, the road of the *nakshatras* passed through the stars of Ea and led to the Abyss and the waters of death and life where Ea lodged. There the road turned northward toward the underworld of life.

The name of the *nakshatra* which marked that turning point is Abhijit; it was formed by stars in Lyra with the bright star Vega. Vega was the star which presided at the victory of the Adityas over the Danavas when Indra cut the Moon-serpent Vritra in two, and the waters of creation gushed out carrying the embryo Sun. Its position is apparently anomalous because Lyra is in the north among the stars of Enlil, but the anomaly is explained by the fact that Enlil performed a comparable function in the Sumerian creation by killing the serpent Tiamat and bringing the world into existence between the two halves of her body. South was the region of death, north the region of life. On the path of the Moon, Lyra was the point at which the new Moon formed in the death of the old Moon. Its position in the north signified the beginning of a new year.

The two *nakshatras* in the south which followed Abhijit confirm this explanation. The planetary life stages formed in the underworld summer were Mars, Mercury, and Jupiter. They were on the northern half of the road. The road south of the equator leading to the Abyss began in the planetary stage of Venus as the dying Moon. Following the road, upon coming to the waters of the Abyss, the Moon died. The opposition of Vega in the stars of Enlil to the *nakshatras* in the stars of Ea, symbolically described the life of the new Moon contained in the death state of the Moon. Abhijit, therefore, signaled the turnaround of the Moon in death. The next two *nakshatras* were in Aquila (the Eagle) and the Dolphin. The former is the Sun-bird, the latter the fish embryo body of the life of the Sun; together they signify the Moon's creation of a new year of life.

Abhijit on the opposite side of the equator from the Abyss explains another anomaly; it was one of the 28 *nakshatras*, but the arcs between them were only 27. The concept of the Moon traveling the road of the *nakshatras* evolved in the planetary doctrine described in the *Epic of Gilgamesh*; the road ended on the brink of the waters of death and the epic describes the crossing of the waters as the way where only the Sun could go. Gilgamesh crossed with the Sun and threw his punting poles into the water after each thrust. In the symbolism of the Deer Cult, which was incorporated in the epic, the poles were the pathway to the underworld and the return to life through death, and this symbolism of the poles was translated into the symbolism of the serpent as the Sun-bearer. The punting poles which propelled Gilgamesh across the waters of death symbolized the end of the Moon's road and, when he cast them away, he was the metaphorical serpent sloughing its dead skin. There was no way across the waters for the dead Moon, only its serpent-spirit as the power of regeneration could cross with the Sun. Consequently in the epic, Gilgamesh buries Enkidu before setting out to find Utnapishtim. The missing arc in the road of the *nakshatras* was the section blocked by the waters of death.

Abhijit is very significant because it relates the *nakshatras* to the Indo-Aryan doctrine of creation and to the planetary cycle of the Moon.

Thus, the rising and setting stars in the lunar mansions marked the movement of the Moon and Sun in the creation by the gods of the planetary cycle which would come as life on earth. The Hercules myth showed that this life was created as the nine planetary gods and the evidence which confirms this and relates it to Agni is a list of nine planetary gods from the book *India* written in 1030 A.D. by Alberuni. The date when Alberuni published his list does not invalidate its antiquity, since gods of the Hindu religion are very ancient and many go back to the Vedic religion from which Hinduism evolved. When we examine the list, we find that although it contains two planetary gods not among those created by Hercules, the Alberuni list must have been derived from the nine planetary gods of Hercules.

The following are the nine planets and their divine identities:

Sun	Agni
Moon	Vyana
Mars	Kalmasha
Mercury	Vishnu
Jupiter	Venus with the name of Sukra
Venus	Devi with the name of Gauri
Saturn	Prajapati
Rahu	Ganesa
Ketu	Visvakarman

The first seven are the gods of the seven planets of the lunar creation cycle, starting with the Sun and ending with Saturn. The last two are gods of the invisible planets, Rahu and Ketu. According to the legend which accounts for these planets, Rahu was a serpent that caused eclipses by eating the Sun and Moon. He offended Vishnu who cut off his head and tail. The head became Rahu and was identified with the ascending node; the tail became Ketu and the descending node. The node is the point at which the Moon's path around the earth crosses the ecliptic; when the crossing is toward the north, the node is known as the ascending node, and when the crossing is toward the south, the node is called the descending node.

On its face, the Alberuni list shows gods which are not the same as the nine planetary gods of the Hercules cycle. Vishnu takes the place of Mercury, and Rahu and Ketu take the places of the dead Moon and the reviving Moon Saturns. We shall see that these gods were the same as the gods whom they replaced.

In the Vedic pantheon, Vishnu was a Sun God who was particularly identified by his triple stride which Clerke interprets as the "track of the Sun."* He was thus associated with the Sun's motion and was kindred to

*Agnes Mary Clerke, "Zodiac" in *Encyclopedia Britannica*, 11th Ed., Vol. 28, pg. 996.

the Greek Apollo. As the motion of the Sun, he was identified with the Indo-Aryan Mercury who was known as Mitra and was a natural substitute, even if the substitution had been made in the Vedic period. We shall see when we have considered the natures of Rahu and Ketu that they were the same as the two Saturns of Hercules' creation; Rahu as the Moon in death, and Ketu as the reviving new Moon. They were proper substitutes for the two Saturns and do not constitute a change in the Indo-European doctrine of the nine planetary gods.

The nine planetary gods thus go back to Vedic times and, when we examine the list of the *nakshatra* gods, we find that all but one were Vedic gods. The exception is Brahma, who was the Hindu creator god. Significantly, he was the god of Abhijit and his place in that *nakshatra* shows the adaptation of the planetary cycle doctrine to the Hindu religion.

The Indo-Aryans who established the Vedic religion were Indo-Europeans who adhered to the planetary doctrine. The Vedic character of the planetary and *nakshatra* gods relate them to the multifeatured Agni on his ram bringing himself to sacrifice. In this image, Agni is the Sun carried by Mercury, moving as the Moon in repeating successions of the seven planetary gods, and forming a cycle of 9 years of creation ending in death as a world-man. The *nakshatras* formed a cosmic calendar which marked the road on which he traveled, and his motion was the planet Mercury.

When the planetary gods combined to form the body of a world-man, they combined as Venus and the three Saturns. If we consider the natures of the last three gods on the Alberuni list — Prajapati, Ganesa, and Visvakarman whose planetary forms were Saturn, Rahu, and Ketu — we will see that they are the same as the orthodox three Saturns. Prajapati was the god form of the Hindi Saturn. In the rites prescribed by the Brahmanas, he was sacrificed as the world-man Purusha in his life aspect as Soma, the Moon. Purusha came into being as the new Moon and the source of life on earth; thus he was identical with the three Saturns.

Now, although Rahu and Ketu substituted for the last two Saturns on

the Hindu list, the substitution did not change the character of the planetary gods or of Agni as their combined form. To be sure, Agni was imagined in human shape with multiple features, while Rahu and Ketu were imagined as the head and tail of the Moon-serpent. The god who was Rahu and the reason for Vishnu's anger identify Rahu's head as the Hindu descendant of the sacrificed and dead Moon Saturn. Rahu was the Moon spirit which left the Moon's body when it died and he ate the Sun because as a spirit he was the life spirit which dwells in the head, and the Sun, being life, was the Moon's power of regeneration. The god who was Rahu was Ganesa whose usual shape was an elephant and who was the god of beginning, who cleared the way of earthly life. The way of earthly life was the path of the Moon.

The tail of the serpent follows the head as death follows life. When Vishnu cut off Rahu's tail, the tail died; but serpents and the Moon cast off their dead bodies and appear as new life. That Rahu and Ketu were invisible was logical because they were in the death state in which the new Moon formed. Ketu was a god of sacrifice who was called Visvakarman and who was the architect of heaven and earth. Heaven and earth were the lands of resurrection of life. Clearly Ketu was a Hindu variant of the reviving Moon Saturn.

Let us now turn to the cosmic calendar of the *nakshatras* and see how Vishnu moving as the planetary gods formed the 9-year cycle of the nine planetary gods, and came into being through death as a world-man.

The Alberuni list attests the planetary doctrine and the 28 *nakshatras* relate precisely to the planetary cycle of creation. They form the path of the Moon moving the Sun along the circuit of the stars; but in its daily movement, the Moon completes the circuit in a month which, in the planetary doctrine was counted as 28 days. Vishnu was Mercury as one of the planetary Moons, but he was more particularly the Moon spirit united to the Sun. The *nakshatras* were a concomitant of the planetary doctrine and although the mythological record is missing, on the basis of Agni with his

planetary features riding his ram and the mythologies of Gilgamesh and Hercules, we may consider that Vishnu was imagined as carrying the Sun and Moon along the road of the *nakshatras* and that he moved as the seven planetary gods.

Now, as we have seen, the seven gods were the Moon bodies of Mercury with the Sun. Each day at evening, the planetary Moon died and Mercury, departing from the dead Moon body, renewed life in the succeeding god. During the change, Mercury held the Sun disembodied and the day which its light created reconstituted the planetary god as a day. As the gods succeeded each other and formed the movement of the Moon, the hours of daylight created time as life and the hours of night formed time as days. Thus, when we look at the night sky and think of Vishnu traveling as a Moon from one *nakshatra* to the next, we can see him disappearing as he enters his *nakshatra* mansion and reappearing as a new Moon the next morning.

The image of the Moon moving with the Sun in the creation of life had its beginning with the Sumerian myth of Enlil and Ninlil traveling through the underworld and creating the four Moons which formed the full cycle of the Moon. The 4 Moons multiplied the cycle of the 7 gods and made the full cycle 28 days, and the days came to be counted in the stars as 28 stations or lunar mansions which were defined as the *nakshatras*.

We have no description in mythology of Vishnu traveling along the path of the stars, but the image of Agni mounted on his ram identifies him with Vishnu so we can construct a picture of his journey which we will describe as a mythological event.

Agni, as we have noted, was described in the *Vedas* as Varuna in the evening, Mitra in the morning, Savitir crossing the sky, Indra as he illuminated the atmosphere, and Varuna as he rode in Mitra's shining car. These transformations were the transformations of the Moon spirit Mercury as he formed the cycle of the planetary gods. At evening in the planetary cycle, Mercury's planetary Moon body died and he was left bodiless as the

spirit of the new Moon. This was the state of the night sky and the cosmic nature of Varuna in the evening. In the morning, Mercury rose as a morning star bringing the Sun and forming his life body as a planetary Moon; the planetary Moon moved the Sun across the sky, creating and giving the breath of life to the forms of the earth. This was the nature of Agni as Mitra, Savitir, and Indra; riding in Mitra's shining car, he was the Moon spirit moving the Moon and Sun on the star-road of the zodiac. In the planetary doctrine, Vishnu was Mitra. Vishnu on the road of the *nakshatras* traveled as Agni.

On his journey, Vishnu moved the Moon and Sun along two time tracks. He began his journey as all gods, Visvedevah, in the nineteenth *nakshatra* and, moving by day as the Moon, he crossed the arc of death and came to Abhijit on the evening of the new Moon. On the second day, he followed the arc which led to the twenty-first *nakshatra* and, proceeding in this manner he returned to Visvedevah on the evening of the twenty-eighth day.

Vishnu, moving as the Moon, followed this course 13 times; but when he moved as the Sun, he only moved during the night as a new Moon. A day was created each night, and each night he moved the Sun along the year track one day. The *nakshatras* were 13 days apart and every thirteenth evening, he moved the Sun toward a new *nakshatra*. When he came to the twenty-eighth, the two tracks ended and Vishnu had formed a lunar year. His combined movements on the 2 tracks formed as 28 days and 13 nights made the year 364 days.

Vishnu began his journey under the sign of the Pleiades and moving as the seven planetary gods, each as a day, he formed the gods into the 9-year cycle of earthly life. In the last stages of their creation, he combined all the gods into his person and formed as a world-man in the image of Agni. When the cycle was complete, Vishnu brought the 9 years into existence through sacrifice. Agni's world-man image shows that the nine planetary gods were part of him.

Here we must keep in mind the distinction between the seven and the nine planetary gods. The seven were gods of the creation of life, the nine were gods of created life. When Vishnu moved as the seven gods, his movement created the nine gods who would come into being as the Moon moving the Sun in a cycle of 9 years of world existence. Each day he formed the life of one of the nine planetary gods. In his movement as the seven planetary gods, he created the year as 364 days; but 364 is not a multiple of 9, and at the end of the year he had formed the nine-god cycle 40 times plus 4 gods of another cycle (364 ÷ 9 = 40 + 4). Because of the mathematical relation of 7 (planetary gods) to 9 (planetary gods) and 364 as days of the year, Vishnu had to continue his journey of creation of 3,276 days in order to complete the formulation of full nine-god cycles: 9 x 364 = 3,276 (7 x 468).

Vishnu's combined movements as the seven planetary gods on the month track of the Moon and as the 13 forms of Mercury as the bodiless spirit of the new Moon on the year track of the Sun formed each of the 9 years as one of the planetary gods, each as a Moon with the year as its cycle of motion. His movement as the 3,276 days formed the nine gods into a great 9-year Moon cycle. In this great Moon cycle, the gods of the first 5 years constituted the waxing life phases of the Moon. The god of the first year was the Moon spirit Mercury combining with the Sun; the second was the new Moon; the third, fourth, and fifth were the gods of the waxing phases: Mars, Mercury, and Jupiter. The last four constituted the waning death phases in which the gods combined as a new Moon constituted as a world-man. The four were Venus and the three aspects of Saturn who are counted in the Alberuni list as Venus, Saturn, Rahu, and Ketu. In the sacrifice that brought the 9 years into existence, the world-man died and rose again as Ketu.*

*The four stages in the Gilgamesh creation cycle were: Enkidu's life as a gazelle; civilizing Enkidu; meeting Enkidu and Gilgamesh and the death of Huwawa; and the sacrifice of the Heavenly Bull.

Agni

The 364-day year meant that Vishnu's journey ended 9 days before Agni appeared in the Pleiades to signal the beginning of a new year of creation. During those 9 days, Agni was dead, as Odin had been dead hanging from the branch of Yggdrasil. This appears in the gods of the stars of the last four *nakshatras* which end the road in the sky. The gods and their stars were: Indra as Jyestha, Nirrti as Mula, Apah as Purvaasada, and Visvedevah as Utarasadha.

Indra killed the Moon-serpent Vritra and signified the planetary stage of Venus; Nirrti was death and signified the planetary state of the dying Moon Saturn; Apah was the Water Goddess, signifying the waters of death and the stage of the dead Moon Saturn; and Visvedevah was all gods, signifying the resurrection of the world-man as the reviving Moon Saturn. Here Vishnu as Visvedevah brought the gods back to Brahma in Abhijit; Abhijit was the *nakshatra* of the twentieth day.

Counting the day of Vishnu's arrival, there were nine *nakshatras* which marked the days of death. At the sign of the Pleiades, Vishnu rose as 9 new years of world existence and a new cycle of creation began on the road of the stars.

The life of each of the 9 years which Vishnu brought into existence was 360 days. This is evidenced by a mythical phase of Vishnu's nature. Vishnu as Mercury in the nine-god cycle was the god which rose each new year incarnate in the ruler. In the mythology of the *Vedas*, Vishnu is described as owning 90 steeds which he set in motion like a revolving wheel. The 90 steeds had 4 names.

Keith considers that their motion was the wheel of the Sun as the year divided into four quarters.* Mythographers used metaphors and symbolism in composing myths; therefore, Keith's interpretation is surely correct (except to note that the horses were Moon horses pulling Vishnu with the Sun). Therefore, a certain conclusion is that at the time of the *Vedas*, the year of created life was the Babylonian year of 360 days.

*A.B. Keith, *Indian Mythology Myths of All Races*, Vol. 6, pg. 29.

The last 5 days of the Babylonian year were counted as days when the god of life was dead and life had left the land. During those days, the god of the new year rose on earth. They were days of creation and were part of the underworld creation year of 365 days which began under the sign of the Pleiades. This means that Vishnu came to life in the underworld as the 9 planetary gods and that the 9-year cycle which he brought was constituted by creation years which came on earth as 360 days of life.

On reviewing the *nakshatras*, we must necessarily conclude that they were calendrical manifestations of the days of creation. In the calendar of the gods, there were four time divisions of days formed in series of 28, 13, 9, and 364. The 28 days were months subdivided into four 7-day series. The 13 days were divisions of the years of life creation; and the 364 days were the planetary years.

The days in the divisions were the same; but, like the days of present-day calendars, their relation to the divisions were distinguished by the way in which the divisions were designated. In each division, a different god ruled each day. In the Hindu period, the 28 *nakshatras* each had a name and a god who ruled it, and in earlier time this was certainly true. The nine planetary gods each had a name so that the days in the divisions were distinguishable; but the numerical calendar sequences must have been used for convenience in relating the divisions to the passage of time. The calendar of days of creation would have been divided into series of 7, 28, and 364. The numerical relation would have made the cycle 3,276 days.

We must also conclude that the basis of the astronomical calendar of the *nakshatras* was astrology. The nine planetary gods formed the years of life in 360 days which could be related to the cycle of the zodiac and enable the astronomer-priests to translate the past and future of creation to the present. The Babylonians developed astrology to a very high degree and probably they were the innovators of the nine-god cycle with its 9 years of life. Similarly, the Babylonians were probably the first to define the 28 star groups which formed the *nakshatras*.

CHAPTER 21

China

1750 through 221 B.C.

The doctrine of the Great Goddess and the Divine King could not have been carried directly from the Asian steppes to America, but was first carried to China. Our lack of knowledge of Chinese prehistory obscures details of its practice in ancient China, but rites performed by the kings of early dynasties link China to ancient Mesoamerica. Hercules was the ancestor of the Scythians and his cult naturally evolved into ancestor worship. Chinese sources which describe the religious practices of tribes, such as the Huns and Wy-huan, which lived east of the Altai and which revered their deceased sovereigns as gods, indicate these tribes had the same culture as the Scythians and their burial rites were essentially the same.

The tribes to the east of the Altai were in direct contact with China and, through them, the Scythian form of the cult was carried to that land. In the Shang period (18th to 14th century B.C.), the king and his queen were worshiped — they were buried in tombs with divine honors in a manner comparable to the burials at Ur in Sumer and the later burials of the Scythian kings.

In this period, an elaborate system of ancestor worship had evolved and three of the deceased queens came to supplant the Great Goddess as the Fertility Goddess. But underlying the ancestor worship was the old doctrine of the Divine King and the death union with the Earth Mother. This appears from a rite performed by the emperor in the time of the Chou Dynasty (1027 – 221 B.C.) which followed the Shang. When a severe drought threatened the people's welfare, the emperor prayed that the sins of the people would descend upon his head; then he cut off his front hair and fastened it onto the head of a black bull which was sacrificed.

In this rite, the bull was clearly the king's alter ego. When the king fastened his hair locks on the bull's head, he transferred his own divinity to the bull. A black bull was chosen because black was symbolic of the underworld and, in the sacrifice, the bull would descend and unite with the Earth Mother and their union would bring rain. Here the doctrine of creation through sacrifice had been extended to the preservation of life by ending the drought.

The ceremonies were performed as a scapegoat sacrifice and were essentially the same as the sacrifice described in *Leviticus*, when Aaron placed his hands on the head of a goat, confessed the sins of the Children of Israel and so transferred the sins to the goat, then sent him into the wilderness. Both rites must have had a common origin. Aaron, the priest, was the Israelite successor to the Divine King and the scapegoat sacrifice was a ritual which evolved in the cult of the Great Goddess and her divine consort.

The scapegoat sacrifice grew out of the belief that sacrifice was necessary to maintain the harmonious movement of the established order of created life which the Sumerians called *me's*, the Egyptians called *maat*, and the Indo-Aryans called *rita*, because the cycles of life had to be continually recreated. Failure to perform sacrifice broke the rhythm of recreation and was sin. In time, sin was extended to include in its meaning failure to observe the injunctions of religion by the people as a whole. Droughts and other calamities, therefore, were believed to be the result of the sins of the people, and a special sacrifice was required to reestablish the continuity of ordered life. This required bringing the people into communion with the gods which created the cycle. In the ancient religion, these were the Great Goddess and her god consort in the underworld.

In early times, when the god was sacrificed, all members of the community had to be present and take part. The god was their kinsman and

the people ate the body of the god in a communion with the sacrificed god who joined with them by consuming himself. All the people and the god were one; but when the people resumed their day-to-day tasks, they lost their immediate identity with the god. The people, therefore, in their relation to their god had two states: one sacred, the other profane. The profane state was mortal. So it was believed that as long as the people maintained their sacred identity with the god by performing the sacrifices and observing the holy ordinances, the life of the community would continue in well-being. When the public welfare was in peril, it was held to be the result of the people having lost their sacred relations through sin. Consequently, sin was the mortal state of man.

In the Deer Cult doctrine of sacrifice, the hunters believed that the body of the god was mortal. The sacrifice was necessary to release the god spirit from its body so that it could return in a new body, bringing a renewal of life. In the Chou rite, the people, collectively, were the god and their profanity was his mortal body. The person of the king represented the body politic and the king, therefore, should be sacrificed as the bodily being of the people; but the king was their life being and the animal-god was their being in death, because it was in animal shape that his spirit descended in union with the Earth Mother. The people were kindred to their god and together they formed a holy nation. Therefore, the fiction was established whereby the sins of the people were transferred by prayer to the body of the king and the king, in turn, transferred them to the animal-god. In the sacrifice, the king represented both the god and the people and, when the animal-god died, all were brought into communion with his divinity. In their atonement, their profanity was purged and their sacred state restored. Thus, the regular cycle of life was believed to be reestablished.

A change in the sacrifice rites which was brought about by the higher level of civilization that came with agriculture and consequent urbanization is apparent in the scapegoat rites. In the doctrine as it was established by the hunters, the atonement was constituted by the communion meal in which all members of the community participated together with the sacrificed god. When the god was a human, the cannibalistic nature of the meal made it abhorrent and, when animal substitutes were killed, the increase in the size of the communities made the communion meal impractical — so it came to be limited or abandoned. The atonement then was provided through the medium of the priest (king) and the ritual of the sacrifice.

In Mesoamerica, also, there was the "holy nation" concept which was the basis of the scapegoat sacrifices of Eurasia. The Spanish chronicler, Tomas Lopez Medel, describes a scapegoat sacrifice performed by the Quiché Mayas of Guatemala in the sixteenth century. According to his account, whenever many sins were known to exist and the gods were angry, the people of a whole town took an old decrepit woman to a crossroads outside of their village where all shouted at her in unison, each proclaiming his own sins by his shouts. When the main confessions had been made, a priest killed the poor wretch by hitting her on the head with a stone; then the people made her tomb by piling stones over the dead body and so left her, believing that they and the town had been purified of all sin.

This rite of the Guatemala Indians had the same essential elements as the sacrifice by the Chou emperor and as that of the scapegoat described in *Leviticus*. In each, the animal or person sacrificed represented a god — in the ancient Near East, the goat was an alternate for the bull and, in the Hebrew rite, it still retained divine sanctity for the purposes of the sacrifice. In the Guatemalan sacrifice, the old woman represented the Earth Goddess. In each, an intermediary transferred the sins of the people to the sacrifice: in the Chou sacrifice, the intermediary was the Divine King; in *Leviticus*, he was the priest Aaron, who was the representative of God; and in the instance of the Quiché Maya Indians, he was again a priest. In each case, the sins of the people were transferred physically to the god being sacrificed: the Chou emperor by fastening his hair on the head of the bull, Aaron by placing his hands on the head of the goat, and the Indian priest by means of the stone with which he struck the old woman. The stone, incidentally, probably represented the goddess herself in her death aspect so that, in all cases, the communication between the sacrificer and the victim was through the hand.

The scapegoat sacrifice was related to the sacrifice of children in times of peril. The children represented the spirit of the new life begotten in the union of the sacrificed god and the Earth Mother and, so, the creation and preservation of life. Children were regularly sacrificed in ancient Mexico. For example, in the Aztec feast of Atlcoualco, which was held during the first month and which meant "want of water," children were sacrificed to Tlaloc, the Rain God. Atlcaualo was a month which fell during the dry season and the sacrifices were believed to ensure the rains which would come in the spring. For an Asian instance, the Semites of Phoenicia sacrificed children to Baal in times of peril.

The precision of the parallel between the rites of the Quiché Mayan scapegoat sacrifice and those of the Chou emperor and the Children of Israel prove that the ceremony of the Quiché Maya followed a very ancient tradition in Mesoamerica. The time of the sacrifice described in *Leviticus* was the early part of the thirteenth century B.C., and it also attests to an established tradition. It is safe, therefore, to associate the scapegoat sacrifice with the religious practices in China at least as early as the Shang dynasty when kings were held to be gods. The China link, therefore, had been forged by the middle of the second millennium.

INTERLUDE

On Two Sides of the Ocean

Our study has brought us onto the Asian and American shores of the Pacific Ocean. When we stand on either shore, we see two religious cultures each with the same fundamental features. In each, creation was through death by sacrifice. In each, the original creation was in five stages. In each, it was by a progenitor couple which was constituted as a single god. In each, it was through the death of all gods who, in their resurrection, created the world by words. In each, the world that was created was formed in a world of nonexistence and was constituted by an underworld where life came into being annually, and a world of life above.

We see, too, in both instances, a divine presence in the movement of time manifest in a trinity of the Sun, the Moon, and the Evening and Morning Star. The star was the manifestation of the divine power which moved the Sun and Moon; its motion was regularly recreated and its movement created the life on earth. Sacrifice maintained the joint motion which was created by repeating successions of nine gods, each of which was a day. The successions ceased periodically at the end of every 360 days. The 360 days constituted a year, and in the calendar of life, time ceased until the solar year came to an end; then the gods began moving again. In life's calendar, time was created in continuous cycles.

We have seen that in the early years in Asia, the gods of the days were numbered seven and that later their number was increased to nine. We will find as we pursue this study, that in America, while the Lords of the Days were 9 and 360-day years were formed in 9-day divisions, there were also 7

gods who formed cycles of 7 days. We will find, too, that in America, as in Asia, people kept track of these cycles by a calendrical system which was the one we found in our studies of Hercules and Agni.

In America, too, as in Asia, the ruler was held to be the incarnation of a Solar Moon and the medium through which life came on earth. Nor was the ruler the sole source of life, he was a fertility god who consummated a union with the Earth Goddess or her earthly representative, which fertilized the forms of earthly life.

Much of the symbolism of the two cultures was the same. For instances: Amerind, the plumed serpent, was simply a composite form of the Asian serpent Sun-bearer and the eagle form of the Sun; deer took the place of cattle or sheep as body forms of the Moon; and the Moon's embryo form was represented by fish. In both cultures, the Solar Moon and the divine ruler were represented by animal or composite animal-and-human images; the left hand or arm signified life, while the right was a death sign; images of the Earth Mother were formed with skull headdresses and serpent skirts; the heads of men killed in sacrifices were hung on skull racks; reeds growing in water were a symbol of returning life; the serpent casting its skin was a symbol of life regeneration; and rare stone such as lapis lazuli, jade, or turquoise was manifestation of the divine nature of the earth.

In our study of the Indo-European development of the Great Goddess religion, we found the concept of the creator gods forming as a World-Man, who died and revived to become the living world. While this did not appear in the Aztec sacrifice ceremonies which we have described, it was recorded in the *Codex Fejérváry-Mayer* as an important part of Mesoamerican metaphysical thought. As we pursue our study, we will find many cultural traits which show their origin in the religion of the Great Goddess.

Interlude

Let us now look back to early America and see how the doctrines of the Great Goddess formed the structure of Mesoamerican civilization. We will begin with the Classic Period in the seventh century A.D., and then go back to the Olmec, beginning around the middle of the second millennium B.C. — not very long after the Great Goddess had come to the shores of the Pacific Ocean.

PART III

CHAPTER 22

Palenque: The Divine King

ca. 600 through 800 A.D.

In Mesoamerica, governments were theocratic; affairs of state were affairs of religion and the rulers were god-kings. There were two chiefs at the head of the Aztec government — the *tlatoani* was the civil chief, and the *Cihuacoatl* or "Snake Woman" was the military chief who, despite his title, was a man.

Additionally, the terms civil and military are somewhat misleading. A theocratic government is founded on a religious order and its administration requires its officers to perform both civil and religious duties; as we have seen, warfare itself was a religious rite. The *tlatoani* had military duties and the Snake Woman had religious functions and was honored as the high priest of the Aztecs. Both were thought to be divine incarnations, although the quality of their divinity varied, as did the extent to which they exercised their divine functions.

The *tlatoani* was the incarnation of the Fifth Sun, which brought the new year of life on earth. In the Feast of Toxcatl, he was portrayed as the image of Huitzilopochtli, which was raised on the serpent bench and rose as the transformation of the Moon and the Morning Star.

The Snake Woman or Cihuacoatl was the incarnation of the Venus god as the Sun-bearer in the underworld united to the Earth Mother in her death and new life aspect as the Moon. He was portrayed in Ochpaniztli as the priest dressed in the Earth Mother Toci's skin. The action of the drama was the creation of the Sun of the new year of life which would come on earth. The priest was the protagonist. In the ritual, the Morning Star (Venus) rises and merges into the Sun. In the last act, the priest also merges into the Sun, which is represented by the *tlatoani*.

The Flowering War was a ritual of creation and was one of the acts of the drama. In keeping with the military nature of his divinity, the Snake Woman wore armor with a golden breastplate on which a woman's breasts were fashioned. The Snake Woman in armor exemplifies the significance of Tezcatlipoca's marriage to the quadruple goddess. The divinity of the *tlatoani* was the plant life which supported the people, consequently he was the more venerated of the two.

The *tlatoani* was the Mesoamerican counterpart of the Eurasian Divine King, the Cihuacoatl was the counterpart of the tanist. His form was the tanist as the spirit Moon-serpent united with the Earth Goddess. Thus, in the mythical mysticism of theology, he was like Gilgamesh as the serpent-lion and consort of Ishtar in the death region of the underworld, and like Attis united with Cybele as the hermaphrodite Agdistis. When the Cihuacoatl was transformed into the *tlatoani*, his union with the Earth Goddess became part of the constitution of the *tlatoani* and formed his consort relation to the goddess.

The Mayan city-states, which preceded the Aztecs, had governments similar in form to the Aztec. The co-rulers were the *halach uinic* and the high priest who bore the title Rattlesnake Tobacco — or Rattlesnake Deer — corresponded to the Snake Woman. The *halach uinic* was so sacred that no one was allowed to speak to him without a cloth held before his face. The Mayans identified their rulers with their Supreme God Itzam Na and modeled their portraits in stucco or carved them on stone pillars known as steles.

The rulers were thus shown holding ceremonial bars or manikin scepters as insignia of the god, and wearing headdresses adorned with Itzam Na masks. Sometimes the Maya set images of their king on shields within cosmic frames which represented Itzam Na as the Supreme God and universe.

Palenque: The Divine King

In general, the steles were erected every 20 years of 360 days, a period designated on the Mayan calendar as a katun. While it used to be thought that the steles were idols, many scholars no longer accept that interpretation, but their divine insignia identify them as gods. Their function as idols comports with their periodic erection. The Maya believed that the life of their nation lasted 260 years, after which it was continually renewed for like periods. The 260 years contained 13 katuns. In the renewed cycle, events which occurred during a particular katun in the preceding cycles were repeated during the corresponding katun. The repetition, however, was general and the course of events were subject to divine influences. As idols, the steles brought the ancestral gods into being on earth where they could better direct their influences, and modify the events in each katun for the public welfare.

This idolizing of deceased rulers has been recorded by the early Spanish writers. At the time of the Spanish conquest, the Maya deified their rulers after death, and their ashes were encased in pottery or wood and set up with idols of other gods.

The divine nature of Maya rulers is clearly recorded in four temples of Palenque. The ruler of that city from 615 to 683 A.D. was named Pacal. The temples portray Itzam Na, the Mayan Supreme God, in the guise of Pacal creating life as each new year Sun in the person of his dynastic successor on the throne. Like the Aztec Supreme God who was the Fifth Sun and Sun of Movement, he was the process of creation and the created life of the earth. His Sun nature was merged in the Moon. The Moon's motion gave the Sun its movement and the motive power was the Moon spirit Venus. Venus was a Moon-serpent and carried the Sun.

Pacal was buried in a sarcophagus in a crypt beneath a great pyramid which formed the base of the Temple of the Inscriptions, one of the four temples. When his corpse was placed in the sarcophagus, a jade mask was placed over his face and jade and other rich objects were laid by his body. Jade and the symbolic objects contained the divinity of maize and the riches of the living earth in transition from death to a new life. The dead Pacal, like the new Moon, was the power of regeneration.

The Maya built their temples as structural idols of Itzam Na, and the four temples represented Itzam Na creating himself on earth as the new year Sun in the person of the ruler. The stages of creation are portrayed by reliefs in each of four temples which represent Itzam Na in a dual form as Pacal and his son, Chan Bahlum, the title of his dynastic successor. Pacal's godhead was the Moon spirit as Venus and Chan Bahlum's was the Moon.

The first three stages are pictured in three temples which are set at the points of a triangle. The base of the triangle is a line running southeast-northwest and the apex is at the northeast angle. The Temple of the Foliated Cross is at the southeast angle, the Temple of the Cross at the apex, and the Temple of the Sun at the northwest. The baseline continues northwest from the Temple of the Sun across the Otulum River to the Temple of the Inscriptions. The process of creation begins in the southeast, at the Temple of the Foliated Cross, and proceeds along the side of the triangle to the Temple of the Cross and the Temple of the Sun, and then continues along the prolongation of the baseline to the Temple of the Inscriptions where the final stage of creation is portrayed.

In considering the four temples, we should note that Chan Bahlum is not the actual name of Pacal's son and successor on the throne. His name is not known and the name by which he is designated here describes the glyph which identifies him in the reliefs. The glyph means "snake-jaguar" and it is significant that, in his human form, Tezcatlipoca, whose animal form was a jaguar, had one foot which was generally formed as a mirror, but sometimes it was formed as a serpent.

In the relief in the Temple of the Foliated Cross [**Figure 8**], the figure of Pacal is on the right and that of Chan Bahlum is on the left. They are facing each other and there is a considerable difference in their sizes. Pacal is the smaller because he is the life spirit and the motion of Chan Bahlum and, since he dwells within him on earth, he is smaller. Between the two is

Figure 8. Temple of the Foliated Cross, Palenque.

a maize tree growing out of a skeleton head. A moan bird is perched at the top with his tail to the right and his head to the left. There are death masks in the maize leaves which form the branches of the tree, and Pacal stands on a maize plant covering a conch shell with a death mask of the Maize God in the leaves. There is a tiny god figure in the conch shell — Bolon Dz'acab, or God K as he is known. His miniature size shows him to be a divine spirit. We will see him portrayed in the Temple of the Inscriptions as an infant with a leg formed as a serpent and as the scepter held by the ruler of Palenque which has his image at the top and the staff shaped to represent a serpent. Scholars have identified him as the Mayan equivalent of Tezcatlipoca who, we may recall in the Feast of Toxcatl, became one with Ixteucale. In that feast, Tezcatlipoca was the godhead of the Moon and Ixteucale was the godhead of Venus, and the two were sacrificed and rose united as the Sun, Huitzilopochtli. The ascension was portrayed by the raising of the serpent-bench to the top of the pyramid, and by dancing the serpent dance. God K, therefore, is Iztam Na's immortal spirit constituted by the combined divinity of the Moon and Sun as the life vegetation.

In the Palenque reliefs, he appears in two forms. One with a device curving upward and ending in what appears to be a leaf-shaped object on his headdress, and the other with a flare on his forehead. In the first, he is known as the Jester God and is associated with Chan Bahlum; in the other, he is known as the Flare God and is associated with Pacal. The leaf-shaped object on the headdress of the Jester God is a *le* which signifies a dynastic line of ancestors.

The skeleton head from which the maize tree grows is the skeletal or earth Itzam Na in his form as the giver of life in death. This potential life is indicated by the kan cross at the base of the tree where it rises from the top of Itzam Na's skull. The moan bird has a fleshless jaw. Thompson identifies it as an owl, a symbol of night; its fleshless jaw is a sign of death. The symbolism of all the figures in the relief is clearly of death. In their series, the reliefs show Itzam Na's act of creation. The tablet in the Temple of the Foliated Cross portrays the death state in which life is generated. In Maya symbolism, the hand was a sign of sacrifice. Bolon Dz'acab was the spirit image of Chan Bahlum's divinity as the Moon; held in life form on Chan Bahlum's hand, he signifies his sacrifice and resurrection.*

The relief in the Temple of the Cross [**Figure 9**] shows Pacal on the left and Chan Bahlum on the right, and the moan bird is turned toward the right. In the symbolism of the reliefs, the right side represents mortality, the left side represents creation. The divinity of Pacal as the life spirit was the planet Venus which we saw, in our consideration of the Nahuatlan religion in Seler's account of the voyage of the planet Venus through the underworld, died as Xolotl (the Evening Star) and revived as Quetzalcoatl (the Morning Star). In the Temple of the Foliated Cross, Pacal is portrayed on the right in his divine nature as the Evening Star. In the Temple of the Cross, where he is shown on the left side of the tablet, his divinity is that of the Morning Star.

On the other side, the Jester God lying as though dead on the outstretched arms of Chan Bahlum, shows that in his Moon nature, Chan Bahlum is in the state of death and transition to becoming the new Moon. The reversal of the positions of Pacal and Chan Bahlum means that the tablet depicts the beginning of a new year of life. This meaning will be confirmed when we consider the tomb of Pacal a little later and observe the lighting effect of the Sun on the Temple of the Cross when setting at the time of the winter solstice in the beginning of a new year. It is shown by the symbolism of the tablet itself.

New symbols are present in the details of the relief. The kin sign of the Sun replaces the kan cross on the forehead of the skeletal Itzam Na at the bottom center. Apparently combined with the kin sign and forming the base

*In the myth of Quetzalcoatl of Tollan, Titlacauan (Tezcatlipoca) made the Sun God Huitzilopochtli, in miniature form, dance in his hand; afterward, Huitzilopochtli caused the people to sacrifice Titlacauan by stoning him and subsequently Titlacauan came again to life.

Figure 9. Temple of the Cross, Palenque.

of the trunk of the maize tree is a group of three symbols which, in their essential features consist of a St. Andrew's cross in a cartouche, a leaf, and a shell with three dots. In his discussion of Mayan iconography, Kubler calls the combination of these three symbols the "triadic sign." Scholars have not settled on the meaning of the triadic sign. The shell is a symbol for the earth and for birth. The St. Andrew's cross stands for the fire-serpent, which gives the Fifth Sun its movement, and for its motion as Venus carrying the Sun. In the Nahuatlan creation myth, the Suns were set in motion by the sacrifice of all the gods. In this relief, there are bone symbols of death affixed to the shell symbol and to the St. Andrew's cross as though the Fifth Sun's birth and movement began in death. Since the relief portrays the point in the cycle when the motion of the Solar Moon as the Fifth Sun in the underworld starts, and since the triadic sign is placed where the maize tree emerges from the death side of Itzam Na to become his life side and where the kin sign shows that the Sun begins its course, we may interpret the triadic sign in the context of the temples as a sign for the beginning of the Fifth Sun's movement.

The leaves which branched with death heads from the maize tree in the Foliated Cross relief have a new conformation which resemble abstract serpent heads. Because they are abstract, they cannot be interpreted with certainty, but they seem to be forming as maize tassels and rows of grain which serve as teeth for the serpent form of Venus bearing the Sun with new life for the earth.

The Temple of the Cross portrays the second stage.

The Sun Temple tablet [**Figure 10**] portrays the third stage. It shows the life of the Moon as a succession of gods. The gods constitute the life which will come with the new year on earth and which lodges in Pacal and Chan Bahlum who combine to form the godhead of the ruler. Pacal forms the cycle and in the process becomes first one god and then the next until he combines with Chan Bahlum as the full Moon and stands on the left, with Chan Bahlum on the right facing him. Each is pictured standing on the back

Figure 10. Temple of the Sun, Palenque.

of a god. The god supporting Chan Bahlum is bent double, bowed to the earth. The one supporting Pacal is kneeling as though rising. Each has a *bil* in his headdress which was the symbol for maize, and the *bil* and other signs on the bodies of the figures show that they are God C, who was a Moon incarnation of the Sun.

In the center, between Pacal and Chan Bahlum, is a jaguar mask with serpent features on crossed standards with feathers and sacrificial knife blades at their tips. The standards rest on a band with a skeletal jaguar mask in the center and with serpent heads at each end. A maize symbol forms the headdress of the skeletal mask. The band is supported by two addorsed gods who are seated tailor fashion. The god on the right is the Sun God. Thompson has identified the one on the left as 7-Jaguar. In the relief, the two appear to be the same god in different dress.

The jaguar mask in the center above is the face of Itzam Na as the full Moon and the year of life which has formed in the underworld; and the mask in the center of the band beneath is his face as the new Moon and the origin and course of life. The band is cosmogonic; it represents the night sky as the void of death with the life of the vanished Moon immanent in the head of the skeletal Itzam Na and its motion in the heads of the Venus serpents. There it marks the two states of creation, the one being the death state where the gods of the Moon and Sun combine as the new Moon and begin forming as the cycle of yearly life, and the other is the life state where they mature as the full Moon and the life cycle becomes complete before coming into being.

Pacal's Moon incarnation as Chan Bahlum is mortal. When he comes from the Temple of the Cross to the Temple of the Sun, he is in the underworld state of death and begins the formation of the cycle of life. He is pictured as the prostrate God C who, bowed down to the earth under the feet of Chan Bahlum, represents the Moon in death. The next two stages of the cycle are symbolized by the positions of the Sun God and 7-Jaguar. Back to back, they are at the turning point from death to life. The Sun God holds the skeletal jaw of Itzam Na with his right hand, 7-Jaguar holds it with his left hand. The skeleton face and the *bil* headdress show that Itzam Na is, at once, a god of death and new life. The symbolism of the hands is the same as the symbolism of the action in the drama of Tlacaxipeualiztli when the right-handed warrior bound to the stone died and was translated by the sacrifice into the life being of the left-handed warrior who overcame him; the flow of life through death was through the right hand into the left.

In the symbolism of the relief, the skeletal Itzam Na is generating new life in the Moon which has died. The Moon appears as the Sun God on the right because it has vanished in death leaving Venus as the Sun God holding the Sun; but in the relief, the Sun God is dead because the Moon which is its body is dead. The Moon returning to life is represented as 7-Jaguar who was the night sky of the underworld region of death which enveloped the Sun and which formed from the void as the body of the Moon.

At this point, we should digress briefly to consider the nature of the Sun God as he is represented in the Sun Temple tablet. It was believed that men had been fashioned from maize which was of the divinity of the Moon; hence, the Moon was usually represented in human form and, since the Venus and Sun elements were incarnate in the Moon, the human form also represented the Sun. While our practical concept of the Sun makes the image of the Sun contained in the Moon seem unnatural, it was mystically real to the Mesoamerican ancients. The Moon embodying the Sun is pictured in the codices with solar symbols on its rim, and the creation myth describes the transformation of the Sun into the bodily form of the Moon, imagined as a rabbit.

The Fifth Sun, however, was ollin or movement and, hence, its image was variable. Maize and other forms of life which the Sun brought on earth were believed to be transubstantiated forms of the Moon's divinity and, consequently, the Sun, bringing a year of life on earth, was represented as a Sun-bird with the serpent body of the Moon spirit and with plumage symbolizing its divine lunar nature as maize.

When the Fifth Sun was thought of as the universe, the night sky was its underworld region where its movement as the cosmic trio — Moon-Venus-Sun — created life on earth. While the Fifth Sun as ollin was invisible, its movement was apparent as the changing face of the night sky, visible as the rising and setting of the stars and Moon. The Moon, which embodied Venus and the Sun in its cycles of life, death, and new life, and which was the governor of time, and consequently the creation of life, was seen as the manifestation of the work of creation. By its nature, therefore, the Moon was the sign of the night sky in its movement as the Fifth Sun, and the night sky and the Moon were synonymous as manifestations of the Fifth Sun in the underworld.

In the creation myth, when Tezcatlipoca, the Moon as the night sky and the first Sun, was overwhelmed by Quetzalcoatl, he died as the Moon and reappeared as a jaguar. This was his animal form as the Moon body of the Sun in the death region of the underworld. After the world was created as the Fifth Sun, Tezcatlipoca's life cycle as the Moon was formed by its changing phases and, when he died and disappeared from the sky, his Venus-spirit with the Sun was left without a body and his sky image was the moonless night. His spirit was his motion and the passage of the stars across the heavens revealed his spirit's movement carrying the Sun. The stars were the spots on the Sun's jaguar pelt and the starry firmament was the Moon body of the Sun in the underworld in its animal form as a jaguar. In the Sun Temple tablet, the cloak worn by 7-Jaguar represents Venus with the Sun in the night sky of the vanished Moon, and the Moon reviving as life forming in the underworld.

This concept of the dead Sun and its revival is illustrated in the *Codex Borbonicus*. The dead Sun is represented as a human corpse with a Sun disk [**Figure 11**]. The corpse is set in the open jaws of the earth monster and wrapped as a mummy bound by ropes. Venus is pictured opposite the dead Sun as Xolotl in his dog image. The two figures are facing each other with their backs against a square frame formed by a border of straight and

Figure 11. The Dead Sun.

wavy lines interspersed with volutes. The border represents the underworld and the flood and fire of the Fifth Sun's creation.

The dead Sun on the left and Xolotl on the right and their relative positions show that they are in the state of death. Symbols herald the return of life. An arrow passing through the mouth of the Sun's corpse and entering the throat signifies sacrifice and denotes the Sun's incipient resurrection which is also indicated by the Sun disk which appears to be emerging from the death jaws of the earth monster. The sign of Xolotl's coming reincarnation as the life spirit of the new Sun is his tongue which is extended and forms into a water lily at the end with a thigh bone in the flower cup. The tongue is synonymous with speech. In the creation, the gods spoke among themselves and chose two of their number to be created as the Sun. The creation proceeded from their speech, although it required further action for completion. (In the Quiché Maya creation myth, the act of creation was the spoken word.) The water lily was the symbol of vegetation which the earth would bring forth and the thigh bone was the symbol of procreation.

Where the tablet in the Sun Temple pictures only the Moon form of the Sun in the death state and leaves Venus as the Moon spirit and the Sun implicit in the Sun God's death image, the *Codex Borbonicus* pictures Venus and the Sun disembodied by the Sun God's death. In *Borbonicus,* the space around the dead Sun and Xolotl is filled with signs of creation of life and these, with the border framing the composition, take the place of the skeletal Itzam Na in the Sun Temple tablet.

The dog is a proper animal form of Venus as the corporeal spirit of the dead Moon, and the Sun wrapped as a mummy's bundle is a realistic representation of the dead Moon as the body of the Sun. The symbolism of Xolotl's tongue and the Sun disk rising from the clutches of the earth monster show them to be the new Moon forming in the death of the old Moon; and their right and left positions equate them to Pacal and Chan Bahlum in the Temple of the Foliated Cross. That symbolism coupled with the fact that they face in opposite directions likewise equates them to the addorsed figures of the Sun God and the 7-Jaguar in the Sun Temple tablet.

Thus Pacal as 7-Jaguar becomes the new Moon and then moves on to become his next god image as the kneeling and rising God C. As that god, his rising posture shows him entering the life state where, in his own being as Pacal, he combines with Chan Bahlum as the full Moon — thus bringing to completion the life of the year which will come on earth. Pacal, in this state, being the life spirit, is on the left and Chan Bahlum, being mortal, is on the right. The jaguar mask with its symbols of abundance of life takes the place of the skull of the skeleton Itzam Na.

CHAPTER 23

Palenque: The Ascension

ca. 600 through 800 A.D.

The Temple of the Sun shows Pacal and Chan Bahlum forming as the full Moon at the point from which it descends in death and becomes the new Moon. The last stage in the creation is the death and resurrection of Pacal and Chan Bahlum as the godhead of the ruler of Palenque. It is portrayed in the Temple of the Inscriptions. In the corresponding stage of Toxcatl, Tezcatlipoca's hair is cut, he is married to the four Moon Goddesses, he is sacrificed with Ixteucale, and the two become the Sun Huitzilopochtli.

The Temple of the Inscriptions is on the other side of the Otulum River from the Temple of the Sun, and the sequence of the temples gives symbolic significance to the river. In the creation mythology of Mesoamerica, the source of creation was in the universal waters which were before the world came into being. In the rituals which portrayed the creation of the Sun and Moon, these waters were represented by physical settings. In Toxcatl, on each of the last days before his sacrifice and ascension, Tezcatlipoca crossed to different places on a lagoon which represented these waters. The river, like the lagoon, represented the primordial waters.

Pacal's tomb is under the center of the pyramid on which the Temple of the Inscriptions is built. The temple pyramid is another form of the tree of life — the way of ascent out of the underworld. This concept is shown by the ritual of the Feast of Ochpaniztli in which Centeotl ascended the sacred mountain Ixtacihuatl. The pyramid was a replica of the mountain and the temple constituted the godhead at the top.

Pacal's skeleton is on its back in the sarcophagus, painted with red

cinnabar, and his portrait in a cosmic frame representing Itzam Na as the universe is carved on the cover. He wears a net garment of the Sun around his waist and a shell pectoral, symbolic of genesis of life, and is represented as though on the threshold between death and life [**Figures 12a, 12b**]. The symbolism of the portrait is complex. The figure of Pacal is half-lying in the open fangs of a skeleton serpent. Beneath is the mask of the skeleton Itzam Na in the back fangs of the serpent. The mask is an abstraction of bones with a headdress composed of symbols of returning life. Kubler refers to it as a skeletal long-nosed head which, in the portrait, is associated with death and rebirth. At the top, supporting the figure of Pacal, is a triadic sign in which the cartouche is open and an elongated oval with four dots on each side takes the place of the St. Andrew's cross [Figure 12b].

The triadic sign, as we have seen, signifies the beginning. The tomb of Pacal is the root of the tree of life. Only the lower part of its trunk is shown in Figure 12b, but it is shown growing from the head of the skeletal Itzam Na in the way that the maize tree is growing from the triadic sign which forms the headdress of the skeleton Itzam Na in the tablet of the Temple of the Cross. The St. Andrew's cross was a sign of the Fifth Sun's movement in the creation of life, and the Temple of the Cross was a stage of creation. The Temple of the Inscriptions constitutes the last stage in which the new year of life has been created and in which it comes on earth as Pacal embodied as Chan Bahlum.

The created year was the combined movement of the Sun and Moon as days of life. The days of life were constituted by the Lords of the Night. They were the embodied Pacal as the movement of the Fifth Sun and, in their life forms, they were the Sun and four new and four full Moons. In the cartouche in the figure, the oval represents the Sun and the eight dots represent the Moons.

In the Temple of the Cross, the tree represents the process of life creation which was the movement of the Fifth Sun as Venus. In the carving on the cover of the sarcophagus, the tree represents created life coming on

Figure 12a. Sarcophagus cover, Temple of the Inscriptions, Palenque.

earth as the movement of the nine lords. The triadic sign signifies that the Lords of the Night have been formed in the underworld as the days of the new year; between the fangs of death, it signifies the resurrection of Pacal as the Lords of Night and the beginning of a year on earth.

Figure 12b. Detail of sarcophagus cover, Temple of the Inscriptions.

Palenque: The Ascension

The position of Pacal completes the symbolism. The serpent's jaws are open and Pacal's head and hands are outside; the tree of life grows from between the parted fangs. The branches of the tree, covered with stylized maize grains, form a cross. A serpent head at the end of each arm holds a Bolon Dz'acab in its jaws. Between the frame of the figure and the branches of the maize tree are sun shields, and under the serpent head of the left branch is a flower symbol with the St. Andrew's cross of Venus in its center. These all signify the flow of life. The Bolon Dz'acab in the mouth of the serpent head on the left is the Flare God — the one in the mouth of the serpent on the right is the Jester God. The Flare God was the spirit form of the Venus Sun-bearer, Pacal, and the Jester God was the corporeal spirit of his mortal Moon form, Chan Bahlum. The maize serpents, therefore, represent the life which proceeds from the skeletal Itzam Na. The maize serpents' relative left and right positions, which are the same as those of Pacal and Chan Bahlum in the Temple of the Cross, show that they have come into life from death.

There are two other symbols to note: the moan bird (which faces left) and the position of Pacal on the cover (in which he faces left). Both relate him to the death side of the skeletal Itzam Na. The dead Pacal inside the sarcophagus is the body of the Moon. He, too, has signs of life; the jade mask over his face and the cinnabar on his bones mark him as a god of returning life. We will consider the significance of these two aspects of Pacal later.

From the Aztec rituals of Toxcatl, we know that the godhead of the ruler was renewed each year. That this was also true of the Maya is shown by murals in a temple at Bonampak. Reliefs on piers of the temple at the summit of the pyramid above the tomb portray the sacrifice of Pacal and Chan Bahlum and their resurrection as the godhead of the ruler for the coming year. The reliefs are on four piers in a row on the northeast front of the temple. Each, executed in stucco on the front side, portrays a figure in the center of a cosmic frame which represents Itzam Na as the universe.

The figures are men and each is shown in a frontal position standing on the skeletal head of Itzam Na. The heads of the two on the right of an observer facing the temple are in profile and face toward the left, and the heads of the two on the left are likewise in profile but face right [**Figures 13 and 14**].

Each man in the piers holds a composite infant child and serpent formed in such a way that the serpent is an extension of the child's foot. The two figures on the right wear men's attire and hold the infant part of the body in the left arm with the right arm extended so as to hold the head of the serpent in the right hand pointing to the right. One of the figures on the left is dressed in men's clothes [Figure 13], but the one nearest the center wears a woman's dress [Figure 14]. These two figures hold the serpent-footed infant in the same manner except that the child body part is in the right arm and the serpent head is held by the left hand pointed toward the left. The piers divide the northeast face of the temple evenly so that the heads of the two sets of figures are turned toward the center, and the serpent heads are similarly pointing toward the center.

The infant is an alternate for the miniature figure as a means of representing a god-spirit, and the compound image of the infant and serpent represents the Moon spirit. The features of the infants' heads have been destroyed, but Merle Robertson has shown that the features originally were those of Bolon Dz'acab.* Bolon Dz'acab was God K, who has been identified as a Mayan version of Tezcatlipoca; the human foot on each infant has six toes, a deformity peculiar to Chan Bahlum, which mark the infants as Moon spirits and as the godhead of the ruler. The relation of the Temple of the Inscriptions to the other three temples makes it clear that the two figures are Pacal and Chan Bahlum. This is confirmed by the headdress of the right-hand figure on the death side, which contains the jaguar-serpent emblem of Chan Bahlum.

The rituals of the Aztec Tititl Feast and a pictograph in the Mixtec *Codex Vindobonensis* enable us to interpret the iconography of the piers.

**Tercera Mesa Redonda de Palenque*, Vol. IV, pg. 131.

Palenque: The Ascension

Figure 13. Pier b – Pacal.

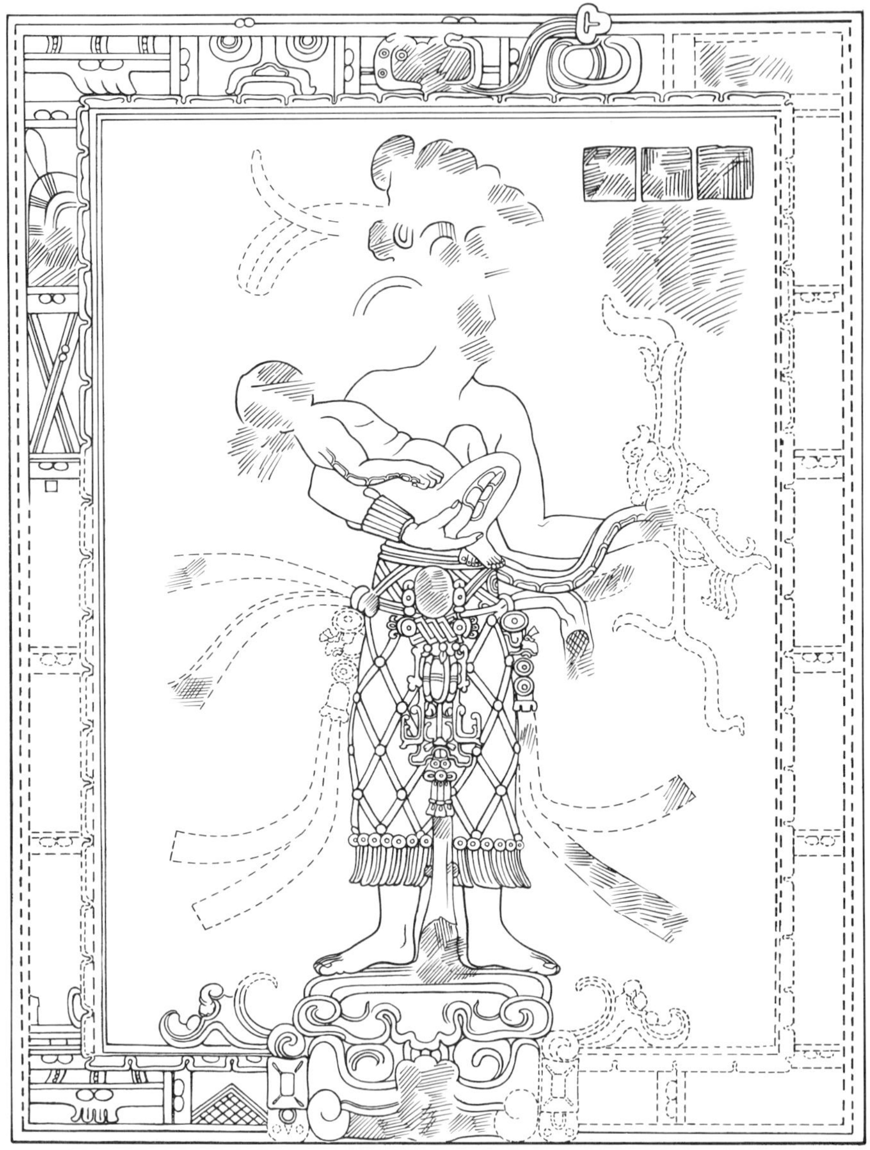

Figure 14. Pier c – Chan Bahlum.

The codex pictures a tree of life growing out of a severed head with its tongue protruding [**Figure 15**].

A god stands in profile on each side of the tree facing toward it. Both are painted black to show that the tree is growing in the underworld. A small naked ithyphallic figure painted red is rising from the cleft of the branches at the top and moving upward toward a naked female figure comparable in size.

Students call the tree the Birth Tree of Apoala. It pictures the sacrifice from which the Mixtec rulers came on earth. A sign above the god on the right of the tree identifies him as 7-Rain and a sign similarly placed on the left gives the name of the other god as 7-Eagle. The names do not properly identify the gods. From their attire, they appear to be two forms of the same god. The codex is genealogical and shows their descent from the Mother and Father of the Gods, Lady and Lord 1-Deer.

The head from which the tree of life grows is a woman's head with long hair and bangs which symbolize vegetation. Furst identifies the head as that of the goddess 9-Reed.* A blue tubular earplug shows that the goddess was half-male. The severed head and the symbolism of the hair mark her as the Earth or Moon Goddess. As such, she is the Mixtec counterpart of the Nahuatlan Toci, or Illamatecuhtli as she was also called.

7-Rain is pictured elsewhere in the codex wearing the regalia of Xipe and is recognized generally as the Mixtec equivalent of that god. Xipe particularly was a god of sacrifice and of the death/revival of maize. He was the fire-serpent that died and rose from the underworld, transformed into the quetzal serpent, bringing the Sun and maize to the earth above.

7-Rain's identity as Xipe and 9-Reed's severed head denote a sacrifice. A line of arrows descending through the right side of the tree symbolizes the immolation, and a line of circles on the left side symbolizes the resurrection. The circles are jade signs. Jade was believed to contain the divinity of maize in its latent state in the earth; in contrast to the line of arrows, the jade

*J.L. Furst, *Codex Vindobonensis Mexicanus*, Vol. I, pg. 136.

Figure 15. The Birth Tree of Apoala, *Codex Vindobonensis*.

signs are ascending because they represent life coming into being from death.

The death and life symbolism of the arrows and jade signs is supplemented by the actions of 7-Rain and 7-Eagle. 7-Rain holds an instrument with a cutting blade in his right hand, which he is driving into the death side of the tree trunk. 7-Eagle drives an instrument with jaguar claws at the ends, which he holds in his left hand, into the life side of the trunk. The jaguar claws are the sign of the rising Sun, Tlachlitonatiuh.

Students of the codex have not identified 7-Eagle with one of the gods of the Nahuatlan pantheon, but surely he is Xipe in resurrection. On another page of the codex, he is pictured as 7-Rain's companion. Both wear the same dress and the number in their names links them together. Xipe in resurrection rose with the Sun which had the animal form of an eagle; warriors sacrificed in Xipe's feast were called eagle men. The symbol for rain in 7-Rain's name is the face of Tlaloc. In the theology of Tlaloc, when the rainy season ended, Tlaloc became Quetzalcoatl; when Xipe rose with the Sun, he was transformed into Quetzalcoatl and, in some parts of Mexico, Quetzalcoatl was manifest as rain. The positions of the two figures on the right and left of the tree facing each other signify the descending and ascending movement which, in itself, identifies them as the same god. Thus, 7-Eagle is 7-Rain returning to life from death.

As Quetzalcoatl, Xipe and Tlaloc are both identified with the Sun — 9-Reed also had a Sun identity. She is pictured in the codex kneeling in the center of the Sun disc. In Nahuatlan theology, the Sun traversing the sky was united with Quetzalcoatl in the morning, and to Tlazolteotl when it descended in the west. Tlazolteotl is the name for the Death Goddess and Earth Mother who is pictured in the codex as 9-Reed. She also was named Illamatecuhtli. In the Feast of Tititl, a woman was consecrated as Illamatecuhtli and sacrificed. For the consecration, she was dressed in a white robe on which strips of a sacrificed warrior's skin had been sewn. In the immolation ceremony, her head was cut off and a priest, carrying her severed head, danced backwards.

In the Nahuatlan form of Mesoamerican religion, the Moon — which was both male and female — waxed in its male form, and changed to its female form when it became full and waned. The sacrifice of Tititl portrays the Moon as Illamatecuhtli coming in death to its new Moon state. Warriors were sacrificed as the god Xipe and when the sacrificed woman was dressed as Illamatecuhtli and thereby made the goddess, the warrior skins formed her male nature as the fire-serpent Venus in the guise of Xipe. When the goddess was beheaded, she became the new Moon with her divinity lodged in the severed head.

In the action of the ceremony, dancing symbolized returning life and, when the priest took the head and danced, the spirit of the goddess left the head and lodged in the priest. The priest thus became the fire-serpent transformed into the quetzal-serpent as Xipe combined with the Moon spirit Illamatecuhtli. The backward direction of his dance signified his ascension because it symbolized opposition to Illamatecuhtli's coming in death.

Now, when we consider the Tree of Apoala pictured in *Codex Vindobonensis* in the light of Tititl, it is apparent that 7-Rain and 7-Eagle are Mixtec identifications of the ruling lord with the Moon and Moon spirit Venus (Xipe-Quetzalcoatl) as the Fifth Sun. This appears from the figures emerging from the fork in the branches at the top of the tree. 7-Rain is the god descending as the male aspect of 9-Reed in death. 9-Reed's severed head is the dead Moon with the life of the new Moon lodged within; 7-Eagle is the Moon spirit returning to life embodied as the new Moon. The continuing action is portrayed by the naked male figure rising from the fork of the tree to embrace the naked lady figure. They are combining in spirit form as the godhead of the ruler.

The nature of 9-Reed as the Moon Goddess and of Xipe, who was a god of life returning in the spring, prove that the picture of the Apoala Tree represents the annual reincarnation of the rulers of a Mixtec dynasty. The dynastic rulers are pictured in subsequent pages of the codex. They include

Lord 1-Flower and Lady 13-Flower and the Lord 5-Wind. 1-Flower and 13-Flower established the Mixtec dynasty of Apoala through the marriage of their daughter 8-Alligator to 5-Wind, who became king with the name Descending Rain Deity.

This consideration brings us back to the Temple of the Inscriptions. The pyramid and the temple over the tomb of Pacal correspond to the tree of life growing from the head of 9-Reed in the codex, and the path of descent and resurrection through the center passes between the two sets of piers or columns on which the figures holding the serpent-footed infant are modeled. The two figures on the right facing the center represent the descending death side of the path and equate 7-Rain driving the death blade into the tree. The serpent-footed infant represents the Moon as the divinity of maize, and the serpent represents the Moon spirit and vehicle of the Sun.

Each of the two figures on the right holds the serpent head in the right hand pointing toward the path of descent. The right hand was the symbol of sacrificial death; the action gives the serpent the symbolism of 7-Rain thrusting the cutting blade into the tree. The two figures on the left equate 7-Eagle on the left of the tree driving the jaguar claw into the trunk. 7-Eagle holds the jaguar claw in his left hand, signifying the transmission of the Sun divinity to the god rising and coming to life. The serpent-footed infant has the symbolism of the jaguar claw and the two figures hold the serpent heads in their left hands with the heads pointing toward the center. The symbolism is the same as that of 7-Eagle on the left. The infants in descent represent the spirit leaving the body and changing into the Moon-serpent in death and, in their ascent, the serpents represent the Moon spirit changing its shape and giving life to the rising Moon.

The symbolism of the serpent-footed infants supplements the serpent heads on the right and left sides of the tree of life carved on the sarcophagus cover. The serpent was the animal form of the life of Moon spirit manifest as the planet Venus. The Bolon Dz'acab in the mouth of the serpent head on the right is the Jester God and, as in the Temple of the Cross where he is

depicted prone on the outstretched arms of Chan Bahlum, signifies mortality and death and, therefore, the Evening Star descending with the Sun. On the other hand, the Bolon Dz'acab in the serpent's mouth on the left is the Flare God, who was identified with Pacal and the Morning Star rising with the Sun. Thus, the carving of Pacal on the sarcophagus cover pictures him as the divine spirit rising to incarnate the ruler as the medium through which life would come to earth.

Carvings on the sides of the sarcophagus show that Pacal's divine nature was dynastic and that it was both female and male, just as the head of 9-Reed showed a female-male root. The carvings are portraits of Zak-Kuk, the mother of Pacal, and Lady Kan Ik (his grandmother). Other carvings show the male side of the dynasty. This female ancestry explains the woman's dress which Chan Bahlum wears in the ascension. The dress marks Chan Bahlum as both Moon God and Goddess ascending as the dynastic offspring of Pacal and Zak-Kuk. This bisexed image accords with Tezcatlipoca's resurrection transformed into Huitzilopochtli in Toxcatl. The union was pantomimed by the girls in the popcorn dance when they leaped to embrace Huitzilopochtli.

The relation of Zak-Kuk and his ancestors to Pacal is an apparent diversion from the theme of the first three temples; actually they show the divinity of Pacal and Chan Bahlum as god aspects of Itzam Na. The four temples portray the Fifth Sun culminating in the formation of life in the underworld as Pacal and Chan Bahlum. In the theology of creation, the Fifth Sun was the world in existence manifest as the annual and Calendar Round cycles. The Fifth Sun was the product of the four Suns of creation, and the ancestral images of Pacal in the tomb show that Pacal and Chan Bahlum are the dynastic product of creation by four ancestor Suns who ruled Palenque in earlier times. Their names have been recorded in the archaeological archives of Palenque. They are Chaacal I, Kan-Xul I, Pacal I, and Chan Bahlum I. Like the rulers in the Mixtec dynasty, the lineage of Pacal stems from a god like 9-Wind who was an aspect of Quetzalcoatl.

CHAPTER 24

Palenque: Pacal

ca. 600 through 800 A.D.

The dynastic divinity of the rulers of Palenque recalls the divine nature of the early kings of Egypt. We considered the Egyptian theology of kingship in the chapter on the Divine King; we should review it here.

The first king of Egypt was Osiris. When Osiris died, he became the god of death and growing grain and the founder of the divine dynasty of Egypt. He lodged in the underworld and there consummated his marriage to the goddess Isis. The offspring of their union was the god Horus, who became the king. Osiris was the Moon with solar attributes; in the underworld of death, he was the new Moon. Isis was his sister-wife — the relation made her the Death and Mother Goddess as the female side of the new Moon. Horus, like Osiris in life, became the Moon; when he died, he became Osiris, and a new Horus rose from the new Moon union of Osiris and Isis.

Horus was two gods in one. As one he was the Moon, as the other he was the morning star. In his double animal form, he was two serpents which, like Horus, were one and which were called the *zet*-serpent manifest in the king as the uraeus. The uraeus was a serpent-shaped crown which the king wore over his forehead.

As one serpent, the *zet*-serpent was the Moon spirit, as the deceased Osiris and Horus as the Moon was his incarnation; as the other serpent, he was the morning star and the carrier of the Sun. When Horus died, his Moon being was transferred into the *zet*-serpent as the Moon spirit which descended to the underworld and merged into Osiris. His being as the morning star was transformed into the *zet*-serpent as Seth. Seth was the tanist king who ruled during the interregnum that followed the king's death. Seth took the uraeus from the dead Horus and descended with Horus in order to carry the Sun through the underworld across the waters of death.

In the underworld, a new Horus formed in the union of Osiris and Isis and as a child began ascending to Egypt. His child body was a lifeless Moon. The child Horus met and overpowered a serpent on the way to Egypt. The serpent was the *zet*-serpent which lodged in the body of Horus and gave it life as the Moon. Seth also returned to Egypt where he resumed his human form. In Egypt, the new Horus overpowered Seth and took the uraeus from him. Horus as the living god was the life of Egypt and, when the new Horus had the uraeus, he put it on his head and the divinity of Seth as the morning star merged in his Moon divinity. At the same time, he put the uraeus on the dead king's head. The dead king had become Osiris and, by his act in placing the uraeus on his own and then on the dead king's head, he united himself to Osiris and became the Moon and Sun moving together in annual cycles of grain and vegetation. The identity of Chan Bahlum as the Moon and Pacal as Venus to Horus and Seth is obvious. The descent of Chan Bahlum and Pacal in death to the tomb of the deceased Pacal and resurrection as the life form of Chan Bahlum follows the theology of the succession of Egyptian kings. Apparent differences disappear when examined closely. Chan Bahlum rises in union with the Moon Goddess, while the goddess is not specifically mentioned in the Egyptian succession as united with Horus. But Horus embodied Osiris and part of him as the Moon; hence, the union was implicit in the nature of Horus.

Let us consider the similarities which become apparent when we consider the iconography of the Temple of the Inscriptions. The figures on the sides of the sarcophagus identify Pacal with a dynastic succession. Osiris was the lord of a dynastic succession which began with Atum (the bisexed creator god of the beginning), and continued with Shu (a Sky God of life), and Tefnut (his goddess counterpart), then Geb (the earth and representative of former kings), and his Queen Nut (the sky). Osiris was the son of Geb and Nut. Because the figures carved on the sarcophagus are dynastic progenitors of Pacal, their identity as an integral part of the sarcophagus identify them with the dynastic divinity of Pacal. Pacal's lineal antecedents, like those of Isis, were his mother and grandmother. The creator god from whom the dynasty issued is carved on the cover as the skeletal or earth Itzam Na and the root of the tree of life with the triadic sign of beginning at its base. Itzam Na was bisexed — he is comparable to Atum as the source of dynastic divinity.

In considering the dynastic nature of Pacal and Chan Bahlum, we should recall that when Horus came on earth he brought new life to Egypt in the form of grain, the divinity of the life nature of Osiris.

The jade mask on the face of Pacal lying in the sarcophagus symbolized dormant maize. The life nature of Pacal is represented by the open serpent jaws out of which his life spirit is pictured rising with the tree of life and the serpent with symbolic maize teeth.

In Egyptian theology, the divinity of Osiris was transmitted to the sovereigns as his dynastic successors through the *zet*-serpent or uraeus which was worn on the king's forehead. The Jester God is fixed in the hairdresses of Pacal's dynastic ancestors and in that of Chan Bahlum who was his dynastic successor. The name sign of Chan Bahlum is serpent-jaguar; the nine figures on the walls of Pacal's tomb chamber who are thought to be the nine Lords of the Night, all wear the image of the Jester God in their headdresses. They also carry the royal scepter fashioned with the Flare God at the top with the staff forming his leg and foot as a serpent.

What is more, the image of Pacal on the sarcophagus cover is carved with the Flare God in his headdress. The Flare God, by his alphabetical name God K, had been identified with the Nahuatlan god Tezcatlipoca, one of whose legs was at times a serpent. One of the nine figures on the wall of the tomb chamber portrays the Jester God wearing the headdress of the Flare God. The Flare God, therefore, is comparable to the Egyptian uraeus.

Not only does the Flare God conform to the uraeus symbolism, but the skeletal serpent jaws in which Pacal is pictured on the cover connect him mystically with the deceased Pacal in his tomb.

We should further note at this point that Tezcatlipoca was the Moon and that, consequently, the divinity imparted to the dynasty of Pacal was lunar; and that Pacal, like Osiris, was the Moon in one of his god aspects.

The ritual in which Horus unites himself to Osiris by the double crowning of himself and the deceased king with the uraeus has its counterpart in the structure of the Temple of the Inscriptions. Robertson describes a sycoduct, a conduit for spirit communication, which begins at the figure of Chan Bahlum united to Zak-Kuk as his goddess-half on the pier of ascent and leads to the stairs descending to the tomb beneath. The duct follows the contours of the steps and turns into the tomb chamber where it is joined to an opening in the sarcophagus. She likens it to a "twisting, turning serpent which winds its way to the crypt below, and the umbilical cord connecting the generations."*

In the doctrine of Divine Kingship, the life of each year was created in the underworld before beginning on earth. The process of creation was the motion of the Moon moving the Sun in its cycle of a year and forming the cycle of life in the image of the king. At the end of the year, when the process of creation was complete, the Moon died with the Sun as in sacrifice and rose on earth as the godhead of the king in real life. The resurrection was the regenerating power of the Moon constituted by the union of the Moon God and Goddess in death; and the godhead rising on earth was the offspring of the union. The creation of the king as the life of each year was a succession of kings in a dynasty of the death-and-life-god as the new Moon in the underworld. When kings were no longer sacrificed, the doctrine of dynastic succession was extended to the dynastic succession of earthly rulers. When the first king and founder of a dynasty died, the new theology made him the life-giving god of the new Moon and

***Tercera Mesa Redonda de Palenque*, pg. 136.

his descendents the gods of the waxing Moon as kings on earth. The change did not alter the nature of kings as gods of annual life; nor did it change the doctrine of annual creation of the kings of the underworld.

The nature of the Divine King as the annual cycle of vegetation and animal life and the cyclical divinity of the dynasty were part of the orthodox doctrine of kingship. In its Sumerian form, Utnapishtim had been king in a golden age and was the ancestor of Gilgamesh-Dumuzi. His death-life nature was metaphorically described as the waters of death and life which lapped at the sides of his house in the Abyss.

In its Indo-European form, the Divine King was exemplified by Hercules whose death-life nature was constituted by his double-being as an archer in Tartarus and porter on Olympus. Hercules was the progenitor of the Scythian kings.

The serpent-footed infants depicted with Pacal and Chan Bahlum on the piers of the Temple of the Inscriptions express the theological transformations of the human forms of the Divine King into the spirit Moon-serpent when the Moon dies in the underworld; and at the same time, they express the transformation of the serpent into human form in the resurrection of the Moon as the king. In Sumero-Babylonian mythology, Dumuzi was transformed into a serpent when he died; in the New Year Festival at Babylon, the transformation of the serpent into human shape was enacted in ritual when two puppets were sacrificed.

One puppet held a scorpion in his right hand and the other held a serpent in his left hand. The puppets were idols of the Moon God and were beheaded. The serpent in the left hand of the sacrificed puppet then appeared as the god Nabu (Mercury) who, by marital union with Ishtar, was transformed into the god-king Marduk.

In the Hercules myth, the child Philoctetes as the Moon spirit of Hercules was transformed by death into a serpent sent by Hera in her aspect as the Death and Earth Mother-Moon Goddess; and Philoctetes came to life as Hercules' son Hyllus who rose as the Moon king on earth.

The concept of the serpent-footed human infant was adopted into the Biblical creation story. In the theology of the divine dynasty, the serpent was the medium for the transmission of life from one generation to the next. When the compilers of the *Book of Genesis* described the expulsion of Adam and Eve from Eden, they quoted the Lord as cursing the serpent saying, "And I will put enmity between thee and the woman; and between thy seed and her seed; it shall bruise thy head and thou shalt bruise thy heel." In the eyes of the Lord, as the compilers wrote it down, child-bearing was sorrowful, wherefore the relation between Eve and the serpent was one of enmity. God's curse was an adaptation of that theology to the then-new religion of Judaism.

The right and left which symbolized the descent and ascent of Pacal and Chan Bahlum were, likewise, a symbolic feature of the Divine King imagery. The symbolism is clear in the decapitation of the puppets in the Babylonian New Year ceremony. It is implicit in the mythology of Hercules' infancy, which describes Hercules in his cradle strangling two serpents at once, one with each hand. The serpents were Moon-serpents sent by Hera in her role as Death and Earth Mother-Moon Goddess. The metaphor pictures the infant Hercules changing into the Moon-serpent, and changing back to human form, and so describes his nature as the Mercury-Moon spirit.

CHAPTER 25

Palenque: Chan Bahlum

ca. 600 through 800 A.D.

On the walls of the tomb chamber of Pacal, there are reliefs of nine figures. Archaeologists believe that they represent the nine Lords of the Night — the natures of Pacal and Chan Bahlum certainly confirm this likelihood. The nine Lords in combination are the Moon moving the Sun in the underworld in the formation of the days and life of the year; on earth, they are the days of life which constitute the divinity of the Fifth Sun.

The first lord was *Xiutecuhtli*, the Fire God whose fire was that of the Sun.* Paired as a Moon spirit and a Moon, the next eight:

Itztli, whose bodily shape was a sacrificial knife which marked him as death and resurrection, hence, a spirit form of the Moon in its death state.

Tonatiuh Piltzintecuhtli, the Sun rising in its Moon body.

Centeotl, the Maize God and, hence, the divinity of the full Moon.

Mictlantecuhtli, a god of death and resurrection, who was represented in physical form as a skeleton with fleshed hands and feet. His fleshed hands and feet, combined with his death image marks, make him as the immortal spirit of the Moon.

Chalchiuhlicue, the Creator Goddess who completed the cycle of creation which came into being as life on earth.

Tlazolteotl, the Death Goddess and Earth Mother. In her death image, she is a spirit form of the Moon; in her Earth Mother image, she is a goddess of resurrection.

*The nine Lords of the Night are identified herein by their Aztec names.

Tepeyolotl, the Heart of the Mountain. The mountain was the bodily part of the Moon as the living earth. In death, it was stone; in life, soil and vegetation. Its summit represented the sky and the home of the gods of life; its base, the rock matrix and the inert state of death. The heart was the source of the mountain's life as the Moon.

Tlaloc, the mountain animated by Tepeyolotl — life formed on his flanks and rain clouds on his summit.

The Lords of the Night were gods of time. They moved as Moons of the four quarters, first from new Moon to full Moon; then through the waning quarters from full Moon to new Moon; and finally ending the cycle as the new Moon Tepeyolotl forming and returning to the full state of Tlaloc.

The Lords of the Night are essentially identical to the nine planetary gods of the Eurasian planetary cycle. This becomes obvious when the Lords of the Night and the nine planetary gods are matched. The planetary cycle began with the Sun, the Lords of the Night with the Fire God whose fire was the Sun.

We should remember that the first god of the Indo-Aryan cycle was the Fire God, Agni. The other eight were Moon, Mars, Mercury, Jupiter, Venus, and the three Saturns. When they are matched to the Lords of the Night, the order of Mercury and Venus in relation to their planetary forms as full Moon changes; but the nature of the cycle is substantially the same:

	Lords of the Night	**Planetary Gods**
First Quarter	Itztli	Moon (in new phase)
	Piltzintecuhtli	Mars (returning with Sun of Spring)
Full	Centeotl	Jupiter
	Mictlantecuhtli	Mercury (as immortal Moon God)

Third Quarter	Chalchiuhlicue	Venus (as the ending and beginning of a Moon cycle)
	Tlazolteotl	Saturn (as generation of life)
New	Tepeyolotl	Saturn (deceased Moon containing the seed of life)
	Tlaloc	Saturn (as reviving Moon)

There is an apparent variance which is without substance. In the regular order of the nine planetary gods, Mercury precedes Jupiter, while in the Lords of the Night, Mictlantecuhtli follows Centeotl. Similarly, Venus precedes Saturn, whereas in the order of the Lords of the Night, Tlazolteotl follows Chalchiuhlicue. The change in the order of the Lords of the Night does not change the Moon's motion, it only changes the points at which the Moon begins waning and dies. Also, in the succession of the Lords of the Night, the seventh lord is female while in the planetary cycle, the seventh god is male. Since the Moon was both female and male, the variance is purely one of sexual emphasis.

The identity of the two cycles is confirmed by the nature of the planetary gods and the Lords of the Night as 9-day cycles. Both formed the length of the year of life on earth, making it 360 days. In the Eurasian planetary doctrine and in the doctrines of Mesoamerica, each year of life was created in the underworld. In both doctrines, the cycles created the year in the underworld.

The identities of the Lords of the Night and the nine planetary gods link the four temples of Palenque to the planetary doctrine of creation and, when we view the temples in light of that doctrine, we can see that they are stages in the formation of Pacal and Chan Bahlum into the image of a Moon world-man. To see how they combine to form the Lords of the Night into a single being as a world-man, we must stop and consider the world-man in relation to the nine Eurasian planetary gods.

First, we note that the first six of the Eurasian nine gods formed the life stages of the Moon's cycle, the sixth stage was that of Venus, whose stage in the cycle brought the Moon to its death. To return to the life stages of the cycle, when the Moon died, the gods had to form as a new Moon. The generation of the new Moon began in the death stage of Venus and proceeded to completion in the following three stages of Saturn.

Now let us go back in theory to the theologians who constructed the cycle of the nine Eurasian planetary gods. They began with the seven planetary gods whose cycle was the joint movement of the Moon and Sun in the creation of life and they saw life as the same movement proceeding in the opposite direction. Creation began in death; life ended in death. The theologians saw that when the Moon as a living body died, a new body formed in its lifeless body. In the cycle of creation, this was the Moon of the first god, Saturn, who in the seven-god cycle, represented life forming in death. His mythical image was a serpent casting off the scales of its dead skin. The serpent was Mercury, the carrier of the Sun; the Sun was the animating fire of life; and the serpent emerging from its dead scales was the Moon emerging from death in a new Moon body. At the moment that preceded his leaving the skeletal form, the serpent was neither in death nor in being, he was merely an abstract form as a process of change; for that moment, the Sun was a bodiless spirit at the point of animating new life. Therefore, to change the planetary cycle from one of creation to one of life, the theologians made the Sun the first of the nine planetary gods.

Thus, in the reconstruction of the theory, the first five gods — Sun, Moon, Mars, Mercury, and Jupiter — formed the life stages of the cycle. Mercury and Jupiter formed as the full Moon which is changed by death into the new Moon. The theologians saw that the Moon of each month grew from the new Moon which formed in the death of the full Moon. In their theology, the life of the Moon was constituted by the five planetary gods which formed the life stages of the cycle. The theologians pictured them as forming in the death stages of the cycle as a new Moon.

Palenque: Chan Bahlum

There were four stages of death, each constituted as a planetary god. The god of the first stage was Venus. In lunar theology, the disappearance of the waning Moon and the reappearance of the new Moon was associated with the Moon's earth aspect as the Death Goddess and the Earth Mother. Venus was a planetary form of the Moon. Since she disappeared as the Evening Star in death and reappeared in the Morning Star as new life, she was made the first god of the death stages.

In the creation cycle, Saturn was the death state in which the new Moon formed. In order to make the seven gods into nine, the theologians divided that state into three phases: first, the emergence of life; second, the stage in which life forms were created as the divinity of the Moon; and third, the revival and ascension of the Moon divinity to become incarnate in the ruler over the land on earth.

The planet Saturn was thus conceived of as a triple Moon body and each body was counted as a separate planetary god. Venus and the three Saturns were, thus, gods of transition which moved the Sun and Moon through the death stages of the Moon cycle and renewed the progression of the planetary gods. The progression created the days of the year. In the transition, the gods formed as one and came into being through a single death.

Now, when we turn to the four temples at Palenque and study the reliefs within them, we see that they represent the stages of Chalchiuhlicue, Tlazolteotl, Tepeyolotl, and Tlaloc who, like the last four planetary gods, combined to form a world-man who was equally a woman. In the relation of those four to the planetary gods, Chalchiuhlicue takes the place of Venus, and Tlazolteotl takes the place of the first Saturn. The change is not inconsistent with the theology of the world-man, however, because Chalchiuhlicue was the flood of death which contained earthly life and the gods who rose from the flood died in sacrifice to become the Sun and Moon. Tlazolteotl as goddess of death and childbirth equates Saturn as the ending and beginning.

The first of the four temples is the Temple of the Foliated Cross [Figure 8]. The relief within portrays the death state of the Moon. In the lower right-hand corner, it pictures the Moon's life spirit as Bolon Dz'acab in the opening of a conch shell. The shell is a symbol for the earth and birth and the symbolism of the relief is life forming in death. The stage is that of Chalchiuhlicue, the counterpart of Venus, as the ending and beginning of a life cycle.

The nature of the next temple, the Temple of the Cross, is best described by the phenomena of light cast by the sun setting at the winter solstice as it has been described by Linda Schele.* At the time of the winter solstice, the light of the setting sun falls on the face of the temple. The relief on the back wall of the sanctuary pictures Pacal and Chan Bahlum [Figure 9]. The front of the sanctuary is open to the outside. Figures are carved on each of the panels which form the jambs on either side of the opening, which is on the front of the temple. The figure on the jamb on the right is of a person entering the sanctuary, called God L. The figure on the opposite jamb is Chan Bahlum dressed in the regalia and holding the god sign of the ruler of Palenque. God L is shown wearing a jaguar skin and holding a pipe in his mouth. Flames appear to issue from the pipe, his shoulders are bent, and his face is old and wrinkled. His markings are those of the dead Moon God and he is pictured in the Temple of the Sun as the dead Sun God.

Here we should recall that the relief in the sanctuary shows Pacal standing on the head of the skeleton Itzam Na on the left, and Chan Bahlum on the right. Between them a tree of life grows from a much larger skull of the skeleton Itzam Na. The palms of Chan Bahlum's hands are open before him and a Bolon Dz'acab lies prone on its back on the open palms.

According to Schele's description, the sunlight falls on the front of the temple, lighting the interior of the sanctuary. The structure of the temple is such that as the sun sets, a shadow gradually covers the front until the

*"Palenque: The House of the Dying Sun," *Native American Astronomy*, pp. 43 *ff.*

interior is dark and only the figure of God L is in the light. Then, as the sun continues to sink, the shadow descends along the body of God L until the last rays fall on his feet.

The light moving down the body of God L presents a moving picture which enables us to see the temple as the stage in which the days of the year that have been created in the underworld form in Chan Bahlum as the new Moon. The Moon as the god of a year just ending, is dead and appears on the jamb of the temple as God L. Pacal the Moon spirit and Sun-bearer, is the force moving the Sun which is without motive power of its own. Chan Bahlum opposite is the Moon and the god of a year about to begin. Now, if we think of the Birth Tree of Apoala pictured in the *Codex Vindobonensis* [Figure 15], we see that God L on the right jamb and Chan Bahlum on the left jamb are like 7-Rain and 7-Eagle. The tablet in the sanctuary takes the place of 9-Reed's severed head and the tree of life growing from the skull of the skeleton Itzam Na takes the place of the Tree of Apoala.

The tablet shows Chan Bahlum on the right of the tree of life with his arms held out straight before him, cushioning the little body of Bolon Dz'acab lying in death. Pacal is on the left standing on a skeleton head of Itzam Na. In this image, the light moving down God L is Pacal leaving the body of the dead Moon, God L. Departing through the foot, he enters the sanctuary where a new Moon body forms as Chan Bahlum and where Pacal, as the beginning of life, transforms it into the image of the ruler of Palenque on the threshold of life.

The time is the winter solstice, when the Sun begins it return from the season of death. It is the point of the beginning of new life; but life forms in a body and Chan Bahlum as the Moon is without life, which is indicated by the prone position of the Bolon Dz'acab on his arms, the bone symbols on the triadic sign, and the composition of the tablet which shows that the tree of life is locked in the underworld of death. The manifestation of Pacal as the light of the Sun returning from death was his movement as time and days of the year.

In the Temple of the Cross, Pacal as the Moon spirit of life and motion formed in Chan Bahlum as the new Moon and the beginning of life. It is Tlazolteotl's stage. Tlazolteotl was the Death Goddess of renewal of life in death and corresponds to Saturn as generation of life.

The third temple is the Temple of the Sun. The tablet within the sanctuary shows the formation of the stages of the Moon cycle, each stage as a god [Figure 10]. There are seven gods, counting Itzam Na. The seven correspond to the seven-god planetary cycle. The first is God C. He is pictured prostrate on his knees. The position is one of submission to death; but it is death with the resurrection because he is pictured again as the fourth god rising toward life. In the prostrate position, he corresponds to the Saturn who is the first god in the planetary cycle of seven.

The second god is the Sun God represented in the body of the dead Moon as God L, the second of the seven planetary gods was the Sun. The third is God L coming to life as the Moon, 7-Jaguar. He corresponds to the planetary Moon as the third god in the planetary cycle.

The fourth is God C again. In this position, he is rising to life. God C was a god of vegetation and in the fourth place he corresponds to the fourth planetary god, Mars, bringing new life from death in the underworld. The fifth and sixth are Pacal and Chan Bahlum, who correspond to Mercury and Jupiter, the fifth and sixth gods of the planetary cycle. The seventh god in the planetary cycle was Venus. In the Great Goddess religion, as it was established by the Sumerians, her planetary manifestation as Venus was identified with all of the stages of the Moon. The skeletal and jaguar masks of Itzam Na represent the beginning and culmination of the Moon's cycle; accordingly, Itzam Na corresponds to Venus as a Moon Goddess and forms the gods portrayed on the tablet in the sanctuary as a succession of seven.

The stage of the Temple of the Sun is Tepeyolotl's. In the metaphor of mythology, the Moon in its death state in the underworld was a mountain; the heart represented the divinity of the Moon as the life of vegetation; Tepeyolotl as the "Heart of the Mountain" represents the life which formed as the full Moon and his stage corresponds to the stage of Saturn in his aspect as the Moon in its death stage containing the seed of life.

The fourth temple is the Temple of the Inscriptions, which is the stage of Tlaloc, who corresponds in the temple series to the stage of Saturn as the reviving Moon. Tlaloc was worshiped as a mountain, he was the Rain God who fertilized the fields. In his mountain image, he was the soil on the mountainside coming to life in the maize planted by the people. The temple contains the tomb of Pacal and, with the tomb, constituted an idol which united the people with their gods. This divine relation was the completion of the divinity of the four temples.

When we consider the Temple of the Inscriptions in light of the Birth Tree of Apoala, we see an Amerind version of the Egyptian theology of Divine Kingship. Like the king of Egypt (Horus), the ruler of Palenque (Chan Bahlum) is by virtue of his office the son of the death lord of the underworld. Just as Horus in death became Osiris, the death lord, Chan Bahlum in death becomes the deceased god-king Pacal. Like the new Horus who rises from death to become the king of Egypt, a new Chan Bahlum rises from the tomb of Pacal to become the new godhead of the Palenque ruler.

We also see that the symbolism of the Temple of the Inscriptions reflects the symbolism of the New Year Festival in ancient Babylon. The king of Babylon was the godhead of the lord of plant and domestic animal life, whose life span was 360 days, at the end of which time his godhead died and descended to the underworld and, when the new year began, rose to reincarnate the king. In the Babylonian ceremonies, the king was sacrificed symbolically and the reincarnation was enacted in drama, while in the Temple of the Inscriptions it is represented pictorially.

The Palenque ruler wore an image of the serpent-footed God K in his headdress which, we may be sure, gave him his divine nature. This piece of his regalia is closely comparable to the uraeus which the Egyptian king wore fastened on his forehead and which was fashioned in the image of a snake. The scepter fashioned with the body of God K, and his serpent leg and foot symbolically was the same as the ram-serpent scepter held by the Celtic god Cernunnos. In this regard, the serpent-footed God K recalls the image of the Sumero-Babylonian god Dumuzi who, while hiding in a sheep fold, was transformed into a serpent. One of Dumuzi's animal shapes was a sheep.

An especially striking feature of the four temples that relates them to the Great Goddess religion is the assemblage of the gods in the Temples of the Sun and Cross. In the Sun Temple, with Itzam Na represented in his skeletal form with serpent heads at either end of a cosmogonic band, and in his jaguar mask between the figures of Pacal and Chan Bahlum, there are seven god figures. These seven gods correspond to the seven planetary gods of the Eurasian lunar cycle. When these are considered in relation to the nine figures portrayed on the walls of the tomb chamber in the Temple of the Inscriptions, it seems clear that the seven must represent the diurnal motion of the Moon through its quarterly phases, and that the nine must be the Lords of the Night who were gods of the days of the year.

This conclusion surely explains the reason why the Temple of the Cross was built so that, at the time of the winter solstice, the rays of the setting sun would illuminate the sanctuary in a particular way. In Mesoamerican religion, the succession of days in monthly cycles of 28 and in yearly cycles of 360 were divine and were recorded by a sacred calendar. We will see in the next chapter how the Mesoamerican calendar conforms to the planetary god calendar of the Great Goddess religion and that it includes the 7-day and 9-day combinations.

One of the most significant features of the temples is the assemblage of the gods in the tomb-chamber of Pacal. The images on its walls and the sarcophagus are idols. Idols are seats intended to receive the gods which the idols portray. The relation of the days of the calendrical year tell us that they are gods of the year's creation. The temples portray death and hence, the underworld. The gods themselves take their places in their figures when the time to create the new year comes. Then they come together in death and they are united in death as one with the deceased Pacal.

The gods whose images are on the walls of the chamber and the sides of the sarcophagus are not the only gods who are one with Pacal in death. The two piers on the death side of the temple above show the Palenque ruler Chan Bahlum and his spirit, God K, descending to the tomb. The gods who became one with the deceased Pacal were the nine Lords of the Night, the dynastic ancestors of Pacal, and Chan Bahlum with God K, the dual godhead ruler of Palenque whose divine life had come to an end on the evening of the day 360 of the year on earth.

In Chapter 15, we recounted the Nahuatlan creation myth which described the gathering of the gods at the time of creation. The place of their assembly was not described, but it had to have been the void of the universe in which the terrestrial world came into existence. The carvings on the temple and the sarcophagus, and on the tablets in the sanctuaries of the temples which have been described, center on the image of Itzam Na, the Mayan god of the universe. The death region where Pacal reigned in his sarcophagus was the death side of Itzam Na. The gods which assembled in the tomb chamber of Pacal were like the gods of the creation myth. In the myth, the creation of the Sun and Moon proceeded from the sacrifice of all the gods. In their common death, the gods created life as the movement of the Sun and Moon.

The tomb chamber of Pacal portrays a common death. The sarcophagus cover shows Pacal coming to life and rising amid the Sun and Moon signs. The Moon signs are implicit in the triadic sign, the tree of life, and the serpent symbolism; the Sun signs are carved as sun shields and as Pacal's raiment. The piers above the left show him translated into Chan Bahlum and rising from the pyramid to the temple above, incarnate as God K, the nine Lords of the Night, and his dynastic heritage through Lady Zak-Kuk. The symbolism describes the reincarnation of the ruler as Chan Bahlum bringing the days of a new life year of vegetation to Palenque.

In our consideration of the Nahuatlan creation myth, we saw that it was fundamentally like the Indo-European or Indo-Aryan creation myths. We saw that in the Indo-Aryan form of mythological imagery, when the gods united in death, they formed a human shape as a cosmic or world-man being who rose from death to become gods of the days and substance of life. We also saw that the same imagery was illustrated in the *Codex Fejérváry-Mayer* which pictured the Lords of the Night and the sacred calendrical order of time springing from the dead body parts of the Moon, Tezcatlipoca, and the flames of the Fire God, Xiutecuhtli.

In the ceremonies of the Soma sacrifice, as they were described in the Brahmanas, an image of Prajapati as the world-man was sacrificed in the flame of the Fire God, Agni. Prajapati was the life form of Soma, the Moon, and the planetary god Saturn and the ceremonies were performed to reenact the original sacrifice.

Now, let us turn our attention back to the Temple of the Inscriptions and the dead body of Pacal in the sarcophagus in the tomb chamber. The divine nature of Pacal was constituted by God K, as we saw, and God K was a Mayan counterpart of Tezcatlipoca. Pacal, then, was an identity of the Moon and, in his sarcophagus united as one with the gods who gathered in his tomb chamber, he was like Prajapati, the Indo-Aryan Saturn and world-man.

Prajapati's resurrection was in the flames of Agni, but Agni was not just fire, he was all the gods in one, and Itzam Na, the Mayan Supreme God and the universe itself, by virtue of his complete divinity, must be accounted as all the gods. On the sarcophagus cover, Pacal is rising from the image of Itzam Na. The idols carved and painted in the tomb chamber and on the piers of the Temple of the Inscriptions show Pacal in the image of the world-man. They show the nature of the divinity of the Palenque ruler and that it was the same as the divinity of the god-kings of the Great Goddess religion.

The divinity of the god-kings has been confused in modern minds with the concept of gods as rulers of destiny and the powers of nature. In

attributing divinity to the rulers of ancient America, we must be aware that — like the rulers of ancient Eurasia — they were gods only as the media through which the true gods gave life to the people.

CHAPTER 26

The Calendar of the Sun of Movement and the *Codex Fejérváry-Mayer*

In Mesoamerican doctrine, as in the planetary doctrine, the duration of the world was finite and the life of the universe was continually recreated in cycles. As the days of each period of world life passed on earth, the days of a new cycle were being created; when the period of world life ended, the new cycle began on earth. As in the planetary doctrine, there were three spheres of time in each period of world existence. The first was beyond the horizon of the universe where nothing existed and the new worlds were created. The second and third were in the created world of life on earth.

Time and life were created as gods and, when the creation of each period was complete, the gods came into existence in the underworld as a cycle of creation years. As each creation year came to an end, the gods came on earth as a year of life. The cycles of creation and created life were two Calendar Rounds of 18,980 days (approximately 52 years), totaling 37,960 days.

The Mesoamerican calendar was the calendar of the Sun of Movement, based on the Eurasian planetary doctrine. According to that doctrine, the process of creation was the movement of the gods of the Sun and Moon combined as the Moon. In their combination, they formed the different phases of the Moon. The gods of the waxing phases formed its life as the full Moon, but when the Moon passed the full stage, it died and the spirit gods of the Moon's life and motion formed the death phases.

Daytime was associated with life, night with death. In the theology of creation, each day was counted as a cycle of the Moon in which the Moon

waxed during the daytime and died at night. The divinity of the Moon formed as the substance of life, consequently the diurnal motion of the Moon through the month created life. The Moon's motion carrying the Sun along its course through the year created time. This distinction is a corollary to the doctrinal relation between daytime as the life-half of the Moon cycle and night as the death-half. In the life-half, the Moon waxed full, forming at night as the new Moon. Death terminated the life-half of the cycle; thus, the new Moon was the measure of the length of life created as each full Moon.

The work of creation was divine — each full Moon that formed during the daytime was a god and each new Moon that formed during the nights of the year cycle was a god. The gods of the daylight were the seven planetary gods, and the gods of the nighttime were the 13 new Moon aspects of the planetary Moon spirit Mercury. The daylight successions of the seven planetary gods as full Moons formed the life of the Moon. The nightly successions of the 13 new Moons formed the life cycle of the Moon as a year. Since time was measured in days, the new Moons which created the full Moons, although they were periods of night, were counted as days. The product of the creation was a cycle of years constituted by 9 life years of the Moon.

In the planetary calendar, the daytime change of each planetary god to the next was counted with the nightly changing of the 13 new Moons from one to the next. In the double count, the new Moons as days and the planetary gods as the day-to-day progression of life were combined as a single unit of time [the first columns in **Figure 16**]. The column of numbers 1 to 13 denotes the 13 new Moons, and the column of names denotes the planetary gods.

The counts of the new Moons and the planetary gods were each repeated until the thirteenth new Moon and the seventh god were counted together. This occurred on the ninety-first day. The 91 days constituted a quarter year which was 364 days in length.

1	Saturn	1	Alligator
2	Sun	2	Wind
3	Moon	3	House
4	Mars	4	Lizard
5	Mercury	5	Snake
6	Jupiter	6	Death
7	*Venus*	7	Deer
8	Saturn	8	Rabbit
9	Sun	9	Water
10	Moon	10	Dog
11	Mars	11	Monkey
12	Mercury	12	Grass
13	Jupiter	**13**	Reed
1	*Venus*	1	Jaguar
2	Saturn	2	Eagle
3	Sun	3	Vulture
4	Moon	4	Ollin
5	Mars	5	Flint Knife
6	Mercury	6	Rain
7	Jupiter	7	*Flower*
8	*Venus*	8	Alligator
9	Saturn	9	Wind
10	Sun	10	House
11	Moon	11	Lizard
12	Mars	12	Snake
13	Mercury	**13**	Death
1	Jupiter	1	Deer
2	*Venus*	2	Rabbit
3	Saturn	3	Water
...	...	...	...
13	*Venus*	**13**	*Flower*

Figure 16. The Sumerian planetary calendar (reconstructed) on the left, compared with the Mesoamerican sacred calendar on the right.

The full cycle of the Moon had been created as four Moons, each of which was created as one of its quarter phases. The four, combined in succession, constituted the Moon's motion.

The planetary gods were the stages of the Moon's life cycle. They were distinct from the days as time. They had the quality of time only when joined to the 13 new Moons. As the life of the days, they could be the Moon's motion in its 91-day cycle as the quarter year, or its monthly motion as the 4 Moons. When the planetary gods moved in the month cycle as the 4 Moons, their succession made them the life of the 28 days and, in the year cycle, they were joined to the 13 new Moons as 28 days of the month. Thus, the 13 new Moons and the day-to-day progression of the planetary gods was formed as repeating series of 13-7-28.

The Mesoamerican calendar had the same combined count of 13 new Moon gods and gods formed as days of the month. However, the time factors were different. The days of the month were 20 instead of 28, and the seven planetary gods who were also gods of the 28 days, were not counted separately as part of the calendar. Without the 7-god count, the 13 new Moon gods and the gods of the days, counted as 20, were combined as single time units. The 13 new Moon gods were the Lords of the Day, as we have already noted, while the days were designated by names [as shown on the right in Figure 16]. The names of the days were not the same as the names of the Lords of the Day. The combination of repeating series of 13 and 20 made the year 260 days. The Nahuatlan name for the combined count was *tonalpohualli*, which means "count of the days."

Although the number of days was 20, some of the days were constituted by two gods. David H. Kelley has shown that the gods of the 20 days numbered 27 or 28.* Although three are not certainly identified, day count tables in the *Dresden Codex* show that the count was 28, not 27.

Here, if we turn back to the chapter on Agni, we will find that the gods of the 28 days were related to the gods of the planetary cycle. Vedic

*Moran and Kelley, *The Alphabet and the Ancient Calendar Signs*, Daily Press, 1969.

mythology does not specifically describe Vishnu's journey on the road of the *nakshatras*, but his journey is implicit in their stars which formed the Moon's path through the sky and Vishnu's character as Mercury which was its motion. When Vishnu traveled the *nakshatra* road, he moved in two cycles — one which passed through the 28 *nakshatras* in 28 days and which he repeated 13 times, and the other in which he took 364 days to complete the cycle. In the one, he traveled as the seven planetary gods, his movement was the monthly cycle of the Moon; in each *nakshatra* a god took form as a stage in the cycle. In the other, he was the bodiless Moon spirit Mercury carrying the Sun and it took him 13 days to go from one *nakshatra* to the next. In this cycle, his course was the annual course of the Sun which he could not follow in his more rapid motion as the Moon. Being a spirit with a nonexistent Moon body, he was the Moon in its new phase of death and the direction of his course was the Moon's retrograde motion from new Moon to new Moon.

In this course as the new Moon, Vishnu had 13 forms, one for each day of his route between the *nakshatras*. As he moved around the circle of the *nakshatras*, he coupled his new Moon form as a day with the *nakshatra* stage of the month. When, therefore, he came to the end of the cycle at the completion of the year, each of the 28 days was coupled with each of his 13 forms as a new Moon.

When the cycles of the *nakshatras* are translated into calendrical form, they record a year divided into 13 months of 28 days each, and the days are counted as two combined series — one of 13 representing the new Moon phases of Vishnu with the Sun and one as the Moon's 28-day stages of the month. Each series repeats: the 13 new Moon series 28 times, and the 28 Moon stages 13 times, making the Moon year 364 days.

In the *tonalpohualli*, the 13 number gods were Tezcatlipoca's bodiless spirit as new Moons moving in 13-day stages. As the Moon spirit, he was Venus and the carrier of the Sun and his movement as the 13 Lords of the Day equates the movement of Vishnu as the bodiless Moon spirit Mercury carrying the Sun along its course as the year. In the planetary doctrine, the movement of the Moon spirit as a succession of new Moons formed the days; in the *tonalpohualli*, the succession of the 13 Lords of the Day created the days which formed the 20-day months.

Vishnu's journey with the Sun was divided into twenty-eight 13-day stages and he formed the year as 364 days. The *tonalpohualli* divided Tezcatlipoca's movement as the 13 Lords of the Day into twenty 13-day stages. The year was thus formed as 260 days. The 364-day year of Vishnu's creation was a Moon year stage in a 9-year Sun cycle of 3,285 days (9 x 365). The 260-day year of the *tonalpohualli* was a Moon year stage in a 52-year Sun cycle of 18,980 days. This 52-year cycle is called a Calendar Round; it was, however, a stage in a greater cycle constituted as two Calendar Rounds of 104 years of 37,960 days.

The *Codex Fejérváry-Mayer* is a calendar of the days of creation in pictograph form, including pictures of gods and rituals, and undecipherable text. Page 1 of the codex portrays the *tonalpohualli* [**Figure 17**]. The days are represented by day signs and dots in a border forming the outline of a formée cross combined with a design commonly known in our culture as a St. Andrew's cross.

The arms of the formée cross are four trapezoids around a center square. The arms of the St. Andrew's cross are between the sides of the trapezoids and are formed as mule shoe loops. The formée cross is a variant of the kan cross which generally symbolized maize and vegetation, and was associated with the Sun. The St. Andrew's cross was a sign of Venus' motion carrying the Sun.

The day signs and dots total 260 days. They are arranged in series of 13, each day sign being followed by 12 dots. They are read counterclockwise beginning in the lower right corner of the top trapezoid which represents the east. The trapezoid on the left represents the north; that on the bottom, the west; and on the right, the south. The count follows the direction of Vishnu's journey through the *nakshatras*.

The Calendar of the Sun of Movement

Figure 17. Calendar page, *Codex Fejérváry-Mayer*.

The first day is 1-Alligator. Following the day signs and dots counterclockwise, the count reaches day 260 on the day 13-Flower, the dot preceding the day sign for 1-Alligator. The count does not end there, but is repeated 73 times to complete the 18,980 days of the Calendar Round.

The Calendar Round, 52 years, was counted in 365-day solar years and was divided into four 13-year cycles, one in each direction; the days of the calendar years were counted as 360. Thus, the days in the 13-year cycles numbered 4,745, while the days in the calendar count numbered only 4,680, leaving 65 days to even the count. When counting the 260-day cycle on the codex, the count is repeated 18 times to complete the 13 calendar years of the quarter cycle, and then is continued for 65 days, ending on the day 13-Snake and completing the count through the east arm of the kan cross and the loop of the St. Andrew's cross. The count then begins the north 13-year cycle on the day 1-Death at the base of the first side of the trapezoidal arm of the kan cross.

The first lord of the fifth 13-day series in the east governs the 65 days. He is the day 1-Reed, pictured in the codex as a bird in a circle in the bend of the St. Andrew's loop. In the continuation of the count, at the end of the second eighteen 260-day cycles, the ending and beginning of the count shifts 65 days through the five 13-day series in the north arms of the two crosses. As before, the first lord of the fifth 13-day series governs the 65 days. In the west and south, the count shifts in the same manner at the end of eighteen 260-day cycles and the governing day lord is similarly marked by a bird in a circle in the bend of the St. Andrew's loop. In the north, the day is 1-Flint Knife; in the west, 1-House; and in the south, 1-Rabbit.

The Lords of the Night were counted with the days of the *tonalpohualli*. They are not pictured on the calendar page of the codex, although they are pictured on the three pages following the calendar page. Their number, 9, is not evenly contained in 260; consequently, two lords were counted as gods of the first day, as in the Zapotec calendar, or as gods of the last day, as in the Aztec calendar ($260 \div 9 = 28$ with a remainder of 8).

The Calendar of the Sun of Movement

We have noted that Vishnu had two motions in his circuit of the *nakshatras*, the second was the 28 stages of the month cycle of the Moon which he repeated 13 times. The last page of the codex pictures Tezcatlipoca moving as the 20 days of the Moon's month cycle and repeating the cycle 13 times [**Figure 18**]. The movement is shown by the day signs and dots surrounding the figure of Tezcatlipoca. The register of the days is divided into the four quarters of direction. The count begins in the north with the day Flint Knife, which is pictured issuing from Tezcatlipoca's navel, and continues for 5 days in each quarter before repeating. The 20-day count is as follows:

NORTH:	Flint Knife	Wind	Rain	Flower	Alligator
WEST:	Eagle	Ollin	Reed	Jaguar	Vulture
SOUTH:	Grass	Monkey	Dog	Water	Rabbit
EAST:	Deer	Death	Snake	Lizard	House

This last page of the codex records the creation of the life of the 52 Calendar Round years. The days of life in each year were, however, 360 days which made the cycle of life complete at the end of 18,720 days, i.e., seventy-two 260-day cycles (72 x 260 = 52 x 360 = 18,720). Since the Calendar Round was 18,960 days and life was the divinity of the Moon, the last 260 days were days of death during which the new Moon formed. This was the time when the gods combined as a world-man and a study of the symbolism of the pictograph reveals Tezcatlipoca as the figure of world-man.

In this consideration, it is necessary to keep in mind that the days were god aspects of Tezcatlipoca as the Moon. In his pictograph image, Tezcatlipoca's mirror foot is on Vulture, his right foot on Ollin, House governs the days of the right side of his body, and Rabbit the days of his left side. The 4 days are gods of the new Moon forming as a world-man.

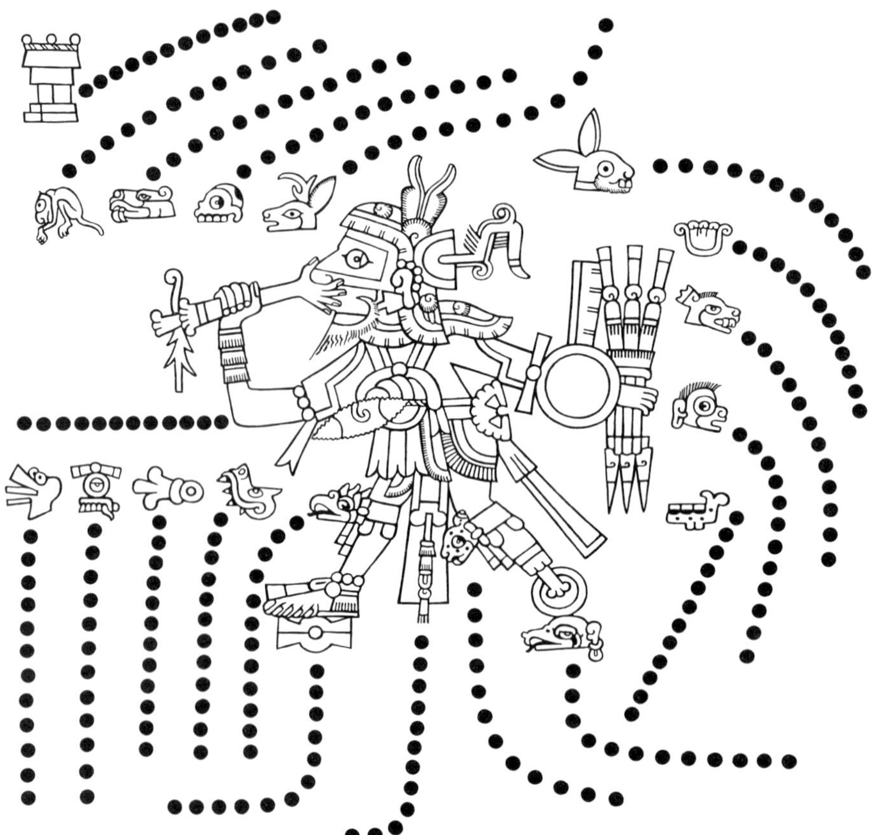

Figure 18. Tezcatlipoca, *Codex Fejérváry-Mayer*.

Vulture is the goddess Itzpapalotl, whose name means Obsidian Butterfly. Her name describes her function. Obsidian was the mirror stone of the dead Moon as the earth; it was the stone that formed Tezcatlipoca's foot. The mirror signified the generation of life, because life was the inverse of death, and the butterfly was the life which emerged from the cocoon of lunar death.

In her divine nature, Itzpapalotl was the death state of the earth nurturing the seed; she was the inchoate Moon in the first stage of formation of the new Moon as a world-man.

Ollin was two gods, Tonatiuh and Xolotl. Tonatiuh was the Sun, Xolotl was the Venus Moon spirit as the Evening Star which carried the Sun through the underworld of death. The divine nature of Ollin constitutes it as the new Moon in its formation as a world-man.

House, also, was two gods, Tepeyolotl and Tlaloc, the Heart of the Mountain and the Mountain, respectively. Together they constitute the life and body of the Moon and their joint nature in the death image of Tezcatlipoca is that of the life generation within the new Moon, which was the third stage in the formation of the world-man.

The right side of the world-man was life, his left side was death.* Rabbit on the left side is the goddess Mayuel. As the Moon, she was particularly the maguey goddess. Maguey was a staple of Mesoamerican life and its divinity was the same, although not as necessary to life, as that of maize.

In her divinity, therefore, she was the full Moon; but when the Moon was full, it returned to the earth in death and in the mythology of Mayuel, the Venus Moon spirit Quetzalcoatl seduced her and led her off to the underworld.

The myth reflects Gilgamesh's rape of Ishtar when he killed the Heavenly Bull and led Ishtar to the underworld where she was transformed

*This is his mirror image. From the standpoint of the viewer, the left side is life and the right side is death, which accords with the symbolism of the Tree of Apoala.

into the Death Goddess and Earth Mother.**

Vulture, Ollin, House, and Rabbit mark the formation of Tezcatlipoca as a world-man. As a world-man, he was all the gods of the solar Moon cycle and the pictograph on the last page of the *Codex Fejérváry-Mayer* shows him as the gods of the *tonalpohualli.* Among these the god of the day Reed in conjunction with Vulture and Ollin, and Tezcatlipoca's head in conjunction with House and Rabbit, portray him as the life cycle of the Moon and complete his world-man image.

Reed forms his loin cloth. His godhead is at once Tezcatlipoca and Itztlacoliuhqui. The latter was the death aspect of the Maize God Centeotl. Centeotl died each year with the winter frosts, but always revived in the spring. In death, therefore, he contained the genesis of life. The loin cloth symbolizes the phallus as the agent of generation. Reeds grow in the margins of lakes and streams and were symbolic of life emerging from the waters of creation.

In the lunar theology, the Sun gave the Moon life. In the symbolism of the figure of Tezcatlipoca, Itztlacoliuhqui had the nature of God L. God L was the Sun incarnate in the body of the dead Moon. Vulture, Reed, and Ollin are the Mesoamerican counterparts of the Eurasian Saturn, Sun, and Moon in the planetary god cycle of seven.

The life spirit was believed to have its seat in the head. The Moon's life spirit, being the Sun, was united to the Moon's moving spirit. The Moon's motion changed the Moon's form as it crossed the sky in its monthly cycle and Tezcatlipoca's head, therefore, represented its waxing life forms. In the planetary doctrine, the world-man had three heads which represented Mars, Mercury, and Jupiter as these forms. House, Tezcatlipoca's head, and Rabbit were Tezcatlipoca's calendrical counterparts in the codex figure.

**In her death aspect, Mayuel was the Moon spirit and the goddess of intoxication; intoxication was the possession of her divine spirit inspired by pulque, the fermented juice of maguey. In her death aspect, she was also identified with the Mother Goddess and was pictured with 400 breasts as the mother of new life.

The Calendar of the Sun of Movement

The sacrifice and resurrection of the gods in the body of Tezcatlipoca is symbolized by the arrows, which he is holding with the points downward, and the thigh bone in his right hand. Blood flows from one end of the bone, and a hand at the other end grasps Tezcatlipoca's head by the nose. The thigh bone symbolizes procreation of life and the blood, life; the hand symbolizes sacrifice and its corollary resurrection; the nose is the conduit of breath which animates the life spirit in the head.

These two movements of Tezcatlipoca as they are pictured by the *tonalpohualli* on page 1 of the codex, and the 20 days of the Moon cycle on the last page, register the days of the Calendar Round. The codex also shows a third day count which combined the two Calendar Rounds into the full cycle of 37,960 days. This was the Venus-Sun count in which the days were formed by Venus as the moving spirit of the Moon and the carrier of the Sun. Venus, of course, was the star spirit form of Tezcatlipoca and the stellar motion combined the time cycles of the Moon and Sun into a single cycle of days. The time span was determined by the cyclical appearances of Venus as the Morning Star on the same date after its disappearance in conjunction with the Sun.

The time between such conjunctions is 8 years which were counted as 2,920 days; actually during that period, Venus appears as the Morning Star 5 times at approximately 584-day intervals; but its appearances are at different times of the year. The 52-year period of the Calendar Round is not a multiple of the 8-year Venus-Sun cycle which was distinct from it. The cycle formed by the Venus-Sun cycles with the 260-day Moon years and the actual 365-day years was a grand cycle of 37,960 days or 104 years. In the calendar, therefore, the *tonalpohualli* did not end with one Calendar Round, but continued until the full cycle of 37,960 days was completed.

The day count of the Venus-Sun cycle in the codex is shown by the day signs between the loops of the St. Andrew's cross and the trapezoids of the formée cross. The arrangement shows that the days were counted concurrently with the days of the *tonalpohualli* but not in the same sequence. The count begins at the center in the "V" between the north trapezoid on the left, and the loop of the St. Andrew's cross in the northeast corner, and proceeds counterclockwise around the center outward in a spiral [**Figure 19**].

The count begins on the day Alligator in the east and, following the spirals through the four directions, reaches day 2,920 at Rabbit after 146 months of 20 days each. In the continuation of the count, thirteen 2,920-day cycles bring the 37,960-day cycle to completion. Each of the days in the Alligator series begins a 2,920-day cycle, thus the 5 days in the series — Alligator, Reed, Snake, Ollin (Motion), and Water — mark the appearance of Venus as a Morning Star.

The calendrical sections of the *Codex Fejérváry-Mayer* thus record the daily motion of the Sun in the creation of the year constituting the Calendar Rounds; the motion of the Moon in the creation of life as the days of the months; and the motion of the Morning Star in the creation of the 37,960-day cycle of world existence.

The days of the three cycles were gods of the combined motions of the Moon and Sun. When the days of the motions ended on the completion of the 37,960-day cycle, all the gods came into existence in the underworld as a succession of creation years. The succession constituted the second sphere of time. It was a sphere of life and in life, the calendar shows that the gods changed the order of their formation.

In the calendar, the 18,720 days of life are divided into 52 years, each 360 days in length; and the 260 days in which they formed as a world-man are divided into 52 periods of 5 days of nonlife. Each 365-day year is divided into 18 months of 20 days with the 5 days of nonlife added as an anomalous month at the end. The gods of the 20-day Moon cycle formed the 18 months. The calendar counted them as days, but they were divine stages of the Moon in its movement with the Sun in the formation of the life of the years. They were, therefore, stages of life as distinguished from periods of time.

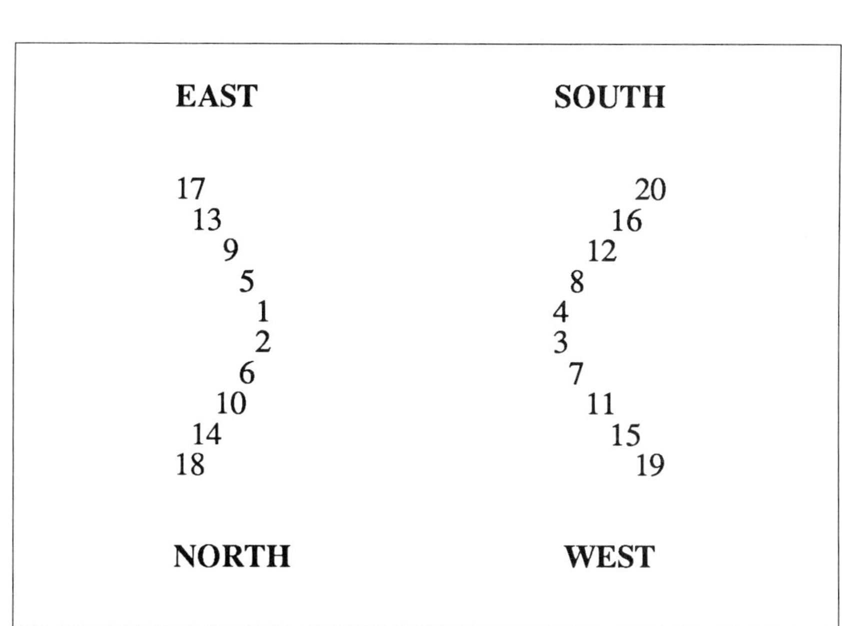

Reading from the inside outwards, the days are as follows:

NORTH		EAST		SOUTH		WEST	
Tiger-Jaguar	2	Alligator	1	Flower	4	Deer	3
Death	6	Reed	5	Grass	8	Rain	7
Flint Knife	10	Serpent	9	Lizard	12	Monkey	11
Dog	14	Motion	13	Vulture	16	House	15
Wind	18	Water	17	Rabbit	20	Eagle	19

Figure 19. Arrangement of days of the Venus cycle in *Codex Fejérváry*.

The Lords of the Night formed the days of the underworld creation years as divisions of time. During the first 360 days of each year, they formed the god days of the Moon and Sun into a world-man who rose through death bringing the years of life on earth. The nine Lords are not shown on the calendar pages of the codex in their 360-day course, although they are pictured individually on the second, third, and fourth pages. Page 1 pictures their formation and ascension as a world-man during the last 5 days of the year.

In their combining as the world-man, as it is shown on the calendar, they are pictured in the trapezoidal arms of the kan cross, which in itself was a symbol of life. In the sequence of the formation as the new Moon, the Moon lords are paired as gods of the new and full Moons. To signify the death state, they are counted in inverse order beginning with Tepeyolotl and Tlaloc in the north arm of the cross. The count follows with Tlazolteotl and Chalchiuhlicue in the west arm at the bottom, then Centeotl and Mictlantecuhtli in the south, and Itztli and Piltzintecuhtli in the east, at the top of the calendar.

The body of the world-man is pictured as severed members of Tezcatlipoca to signify sacrificial death. The Sun lord, Xiutecuhtli, is pictured in the center of the square. The severed parts of Tezcatlipoca's body are shown in the corners of the pictograph between the third leg of each trapezoid and the first leg of each loop as the ends of double wavelike lines which lead from the body of Xiutecuhtli in the center. They represent streams of blood flowing from the Fire God and vivifying the body members of Tezcatlipoca.

The symbolism of the pictures of the four pairs of lords shows them as the four stages in the formation of the new Moon. In Palenque, the four stages were constituted by the four Lords of the Night — Chalchiuhlicue, Tlazolteotl, Tepeyolotl and Tlaloc — represented by the four temples. In the Palenque temples, the god forms of the new and full Moons were constituted by Pacal as the Venus Moon spirit and Chan Bahlum. In the codex, the lords themselves are the gods of the new and full Moon. Each pair is pictured standing on opposite sides of a tree of life, facing it, in the way that Pacal and Chan Bahlum stand. Except in the instance of Centeotl and Mictlantecuhtli, the Moon spirit lord is on the right and the full Moon lord is on the left. They are thus in the symbolic positions of Pacal and Chan Bahlum in the Temple of the Foliated Cross, signifying the death state of the new Moon.

The lords of the first day, Tepeyolotl and Tlaloc, form Tezcatlipoca's mirror foot. The mirror is a sign of the creation of life in the underworld and the foot signifies movement. The tree between them is a *mexolotl*; it grows from a thigh bone in a bowl. The *mexolotl* was the form into which the Venus Moon spirit Xolotl transformed himself when the Fifth Sun was created in the sacrifice of the gods. The thigh bone signifies the generation of life. The symbolism, therefore, shows Tepeyolotl and Tlaloc as the inchoate Moon, which is represented by the Temple of the Foliated Cross at Palenque.

The lords of the second day, Chalchiuhlicue and Tlazolteotl, form the body of Tezcatlipoca, indicated by his ribs. The leaves on the tree of life are dead, but the bird in the fork is a hummingbird, which is the sign of life returning in the spring. Chalchiuhlicue was goddess of the waters of creation and Tlazolteotl, although a goddess of death, was the goddess of childbirth and, therefore, of returning life. The symbolism shows the two lords as the death and life sides of the new Moon. In Palenque, the compound of death and life which was the new Moon was represented by the Temple of the Cross.

The lords of the third day, Mictlantecuhtli and Centeotl, are on the left and right, corresponding to the positions of Pacal and Chan Bahlum in the Temple of the Sun. The left is the side of ascension; Centeotl was the Maize God and his position represents the waxing Moon. The symbolism is supplemented by the bird, a yellow macaw, in the fork of the tree and by the trunk of the blossoming tree. The yellow macaw symbolizes ripened maize

and the trunk of the tree, which is studded with sacrificial knives, signifies resurrection. The two lords form as Tezcatlipoca's head, which is the lodging place of the life spirit; they represent the waxing new Moon which in Palenque was represented by the Temple of the Sun.

The lords of the fourth day, Piltzintecuhtli and Itztli, are again in the positions denoting death — in this case, the death of the full Moon. The lords form Tezcatlipoca's arms and hands, indicated by the hand at the end of the blood stream. The hand was a sign of sacrifice and the tree with the bird in the fork represents the resurrection. The tree is turquoise and stems from the Sun which rises from the pyramid of a temple. The Sun ruled the sky, the realm of life, from which he took the title "Turquoise Prince"; the bird in the tree is a quetzal, the bird of maize; and the pyramid represents the mountain which is the Moon's form as the earth. Piltzintecuhtli himself was the rising Sun.

Xiutecuhtli in the center is the source of Tezcatlipoca's resurrection. He is the lord of the fifth day and his counterpart in Palenque is the deceased Pacal. Piltzintecuhtli and Itztli on the platform of the pyramid and Xiutecuhtli in the center giving life to Tezcatlipoca correspond to the stage of creation represented by the Temple of the Inscriptions.

The third time sphere was the year of life which the nine Lords of the Night brought on earth. It was 360 days in length and the time count was the succession of the nine lords who resumed their regular single file.

The calendar made no correction for a leap year. None was necessary. It was not an instrument by which people arranged their daily lives, it was a sacred document which revealed the working of the gods. Only the days of creation of life were included on the calendar; historical events were recorded as days of the 360-day year and dated by reference to the days of creation. Historical time was counted as the passing of the 360-day years as though the last 5 days of the 365-day year were not a part of time. The building of the Temple of the Cross at Palenque to record the sunset on the winter solstice and New Fire Ceremony fixing the beginning of the

Calendar Round on the appearance of the Pleiades proves that the cycle of life was adjusted to the seasons. The extra day in leap year was never created, it was a nonday which had no calendrical significance. On the calendar, the creation begins on the day 1-Alligator; but the days of the Calendar Round years as they were counted on earth were only 360. They came into being in the resurrection of Tezcatlipoca as a world-man on the first day of the year governed by 1-Rabbit. Consequently, historical Calendar Round days are not necessarily the same as the *tonalpohualli* days.

CHAPTER 27

The Mesoamerican Reformation of the Planetary Calendar

Intrinsic and related evidence prove that the Mesoamerican calendar was originally the same as the Eurasian and that it was reformed by the Amerind astrologer-priests. When we compare the two calendars, we see that the real difference between the two is in the day and year counts on the creation time spheres. In the Amerind calendar, the 260-day cycle takes the place of the 364-day year, and the created cycle of world existence is 37,960 days (104 years), in contrast to the Eurasian 3,285 days (9 years). But the years constituted by the days of the creation cycles are the same 365-day years and the life which is contained in each year is 360 days. In each case, the years come into existence as underworld creation years in which 360 days of life are followed by 5 days devoid of life.

The 260-day cycle was formed by 20-day months and, in the created time spheres, the months of the 360 days of life were counted as 20 days, making their number 18. The Eurasian year was formed by 28-day months and the length of the months of the 360-day year must have been changed, because 360 cannot be divided into 28-day months. Although there is no clear evidence as to what was the length of the months, almost certainly it was 30 days. Whatever the variance in the length of the months, the 260-day cycle makes it immaterial; the identity of the creation section of the two calendars is proven by the 9-day count of the Lords of the Night, which was the same as the 9-day count of the nine planetary gods. In each calendar, at the end of 360 days, the eight gods of the Moon cycle formed as pairs and brought the god of the Sun on earth during the 5 days of nonlife. In each calendar, the new year began on earth at the end of the 5 days and its duration was 360 days.

There is no trace of the day count of the seven planetary gods in the calendar itself, but astrologer-priests used the calendar for divination. The Maya codices contain tables of day counts which are part of the Eurasian form of the planetary calendar. One of the counts is for 819 days. The time units are 7, 9, and 13. The 819-day count could not, however, have been a complete cycle. The Mesoamerican calendar was divided into quarters with each quarter assigned to a cardinal direction; 819 was one-fourth of 3,276 — the number of days of life created by the seven planetary gods of the Hercules and Agni-Vishnu calendrical mythology. The full count was, therefore, the 9-year cycle of the seven planetary gods in the Indo-European calendar. The months in this cycle were counted as 28 days.

The identity of the full count with the Indo-European planetary year is confirmed by the divinatory tables in the *Dresden Codex* of the Mayas. These tables are based on day counts of 7, 28, and 364. To make 28 relevant to 364, it must be combined with a factor of 13, the cycle of days which in combination with the lunar month cycle, formed the Eurasian year and 260-day *tonalpohualli.**

The names of the gods of the 7-day series are not known. Thompson designates them as the Lords of the Earth. They are, doubtless, the same as the six gods of the Moon cycle carved on the tablet in the Temple of the Sun at Palenque, combined with the skeletal or earth Itzam Na.

In any case, the 28-day gods of the Eurasian month were aspects of the seven planetary gods, and we saw in the last chapter that the gods of the 20 days were actually 28 in number. That they were the same gods as the 28

*The *Paris Codex* contains a tabulation based on 364-day years constituted by thirteen 28-day months; it groups the years into a series of 5 totaling 1,820 days, thereby conforming them to the seven 260-day periods of the Maya calendar. (See A.F. Aveni, *Skywatchers of Ancient Mexico*, pp. 201f.) We can conclude from the *Paris Codex* and *Dresden Codex* that the Mayas retained the original Eurasian calendar for divinatory purposes and conformed their divinations to the reformed calendar.

planetary gods is evident when they are compared to the Hindu list of the gods of the *nakshatras* or lunar mansions. (The *nakshatra* gods were the 28 planetary gods.) Gods were days and when the gods were listed, either by day name or god name, the list shows that the names of more than half of the 20 days were the same as those of the 28 planetary gods [**Figure 20**].

One very significant thing about the comparison is that the order of the Mesoamerican days follows the order of the Hindu list.

Now, when we consider the aberrant count of the Lords of the Night with the *tonalpohualli*, it becomes clear that in its original form, the day counts of the Mesoamerican calendar were the same as the day counts of the Eurasian calendar. Mathematics prove that the nine planetary gods counted with the seven planetary gods and the 13 aspects of Mercury as the new Moon in the creation cycle of world life determined its 9-year length. The creation year was 364 days and the lowest number of days which could contain cycles of 7, 9, 13, and 364 is 3,276 — making a complete cycle of 9 years. The number 3,276 left 9 days before the end of nine 365-day years for the death and revival of the Sun and Moon gods and their coming with life on earth. In the Mesoamerican calendar, the Venus-Sun count determined the 37,960-day (104-year) length of the cycle of world life.

The count of the Lords of the Night with the *tonalpohualli* was superfluous and the merging of two days to conform them to the first or last day of the *tonalpohualli* was an arbitrary device for including the count. The Lords of the Night came into existence as days of the created cycle of life and, therefore, it must have been considered that they were a necessary part of the process of creation.

Thus it is obvious that the Mesoamerican calendar in the form in which it has come down to us was a reformation of the Eurasian. Why was it reformed? One reason, certainly, was because the visibility of Venus in its appearance after conjunction made it a more useful measure of time. In Mesoamerica, astrology became one of the principal branches of religion and the calendar was the principle means for its practice.

No.	Lunar Mansion	God	No.	Day Name	God
2	Deer	Prajapati with animal form of deer	7	Mazatl (Deer)	
3	Stag's Head (Moon Symbol)	Soma – Rabbit in Moon, Intoxication	8	Tochtli (Rabbit)	Mayuel – goddess of the Moon, Intoxication
4	Andra (Moist)		9	Atl (Water)	
6	Flower		11		Xochipilli (Flower as symbol of life, Sun and vegetation
11		Savitir – Sun	14	Oceotl (Jaguar) Earth Sun	
15		Mitra – Mover of the Sun	17	Ollin (Sun's movement)	Xolotl – mover of Sun in underworld, Tlachlitonatiuh – Rising Sun
17		Nirrti (decease)	18	Flint Knife (instrument of sacrificial death)	

Figure 20. Lunar mansions and/or comparable associated Aztec day names and/or associated gods in sequential order. [Reconstructed from Moran and Kelley, *The Alphabet and the Ancient Calendar Signs.*]

Mesoamerican Reformation of the Planetary Calendar

No.	Lunar Mansion	God	No.	Day Name	God
18		Apah – the Water Goddess	19	Quiauitl (Rain)	
22		The Vasus (Earth gods)	1	Cipactli – monster Earth God	Tomacatecuhtli – god of life
23		Varuna – Sky and Creator God, maker of life	2	Ehecatl (Wind), animating god of creation	
25		Ahi Budnya (Serpent of the deeps, the Vedic mythical image of the source of life on the mountain)	3	Calli (House)	Tlazolteotl – Earth Mother with serpent attributes, with Tepeyolotl, Heart of the Mountain
27	Asvini	Asvins – Twin gods of the sea with serpents entwining earth jars as symbols	5	Coatl (Serpent Twin)	Chalchiuhlicue – goddess of waters, Earth Goddess with snake symbols
28		Yama (Death)	6	Miquiztli (Death)	Tezcatlipoca – Moon-Earth God of death and new life, with Tecuciztecatl, Moon God

NOTE: Number indicates place in sequence, such that the sequential order is in terms of the Vedic days.

The basis of the reform was obviously the substitution of Venus for Mercury as the Sun-bearer. The change was not, however, a complete innovation. In the planetary cycle, Mercury and Venus were consorts and they traveled as one. The Venus-Sun cycle of 2,920 days not only made the 9-day count of the Lords of the Night superfluous, but it abrogated the 364-day year as the unit of the combined motions of the Moon and Sun. The elimination of those time counts necessitated a reconstruction of the month count of the solar year to provide for the 360-day year. The calendric reformers resolved the problem by making the months 20 days and their number 18, there was no need to change the addition of 5 uncounted days at the end of the year.

There is no obvious basis for the adoption of the 20-day month; but when we consider the divine nature of the calendar, we can account for it. The motions of the Moon and Venus with the Sun were ruled by the gods. There were four gods who governed each quarter of the Moon cycle. Venus as a god changed its identity as it moved in its cycle; in its motion through the 2,920 days, it formed a conjunction with the Sun five times, thus changing its identity five times, and could be counted as five gods. The changing phases of the Moon and Venus therefore could be factored as 4 and 5 and, since motion multiplied the factors, the motion of the two bodies could be counted in terms of 20.

CHAPTER 28

The Olmec Supreme God

14th through 4th Century B.C.

We have reached the point at which our study has disclosed that the Mesoamerican religious culture has an identity very similar to that of the Great Goddess religion of Eurasia. We have found the Great Goddess religion in the cultures of the Classic and Postclassic periods of Mesoamerican civilization, spanning the centuries from the beginning of the Christian era to the destruction following the Spanish conquest of Mexico. Let us now turn back to the Preclassic and the Olmecs, to see how the religion of the Great Goddess began in Mesoamerica.

The physical nature of the Supreme God of the Olmecs proves him to be the ancestor of the Nahuatlan Sun of Movement, the Supreme God Ometeotl. The Sun of Movement was the Fifth Sun. The first Sun was Tezcatlipoca who fell into the waters of creation and was transformed into a jaguar, whereupon he ate the giants who inhabited the preworld. When he ate the giants, he became half-jaguar and half-human. The second Sun then rose as the serpent Quetzalcoatl. Tezcatlipoca was the inchoate Moon and Quetzalcoatl was the Moon spirit of life and motion. The third and fourth Suns formed their life body as the Moon. When the creation was complete, the Sun of Movement had come into existence. The third Sun, Tlaloc, was constituted as a mountain and the fourth Sun, Chalchiuhlicue, was constituted as his earth consort. Together, they formed the features of the Fifth Sun as the Moon incarnation of the true Sun.

The idols of the Olmec God represent him as half-jaguar, half-human, and as the embodiment of the serpent Moon spirit, which is indicated by a serpent tongue. They portray him as a mountain, and as a goddess in union with a mountain, and as jade and serpentine stone, which is the Heart of the Mountain and appears in living form as the food plants which grow on the mountainsides. The shield which represents the Mayan Supreme God as the universe is a symbolic copy of a court in the pyramid complex at La Venta. The court represents the Olmec Supreme God. In the same La Venta complex, a sarcophagus identifies the ruler with the Olmec God. The solar Moon God Pacal-Chan Bahlum was on the direct line of descent from the Olmec God to Tezcatlipoca.

When we trace his ancestry, we find that he was a cultural descendant of Hercules and Gilgamesh. This is apparent in his physical nature. In tropical Mesoamerica where there are no lions, the jaguar took the place of the Eurasian lion as the king of beasts and the animal form of the divine ruler. The compound human-jaguar idols of the god thus identify him with the Divine King incarnations of the consort of the Great Goddess. In the Old World, the animal form of the Sun, as in Mesoamerica, was feline and, where they abounded, it was the lion or the panther. Dress imputed divinity and, when Hercules killed the Nemaean lion and put on its skin, the Sun became a part of him. In his labors, he was a Moon God combined with the Sun; but, while he assumed different animal shapes of the Moon, his proper Moon shape was human and it was in his human shape that he came on earth as the Divine King Eurystheus bringing a succession of 9 years of life.

Gilgamesh was represented in combination with a lion and, in the art of the ancient Near East, the god-kings were represented crushing lion cubs in their arms or killing lions from chariots with arrows shot from bows. In the symbolism of the art, the killing infused the divinity of the Sun into the person of the king who, as king, was a Moon God giving life on earth. Egypt provided the clearest image of the composite lion and human form in the sphinxes, which were carved with lion bodies and portrait heads of the kings. The kings were life forms of the Moon Osiris and, at the same time, incarnations of the Sun. As gods, their function was to give life to Egypt.

The Olmec Supreme God

The World-Man Image of the Jaguar God

A little statue of the Olmec Supreme God from Las Limas shows him as the waxing Moon form of a world-man and, therefore, as the Mesoamerican Sun of Movement. The statue is of a human figure seated tailor fashion holding an infant child in his arms which are resting on his lap [**Figure 21**]. The infant is dead. The top of the infant's head is shaped to form a jaguar fang and the lower lip curves in a feline snarl; a band around its forehead is marked with a kan cross over each eye and there is a St. Andrew's cross on the chest and another beneath it on the stomach. A god's head with jaguar features is incised on each knee and shoulder of the seated figure of the Supreme God and there is incising on its face which marks the god as half-jaguar. The line of the headdress where it rests on the god's forehead forms an ogee curve.

The heads on the knees and shoulders are in profile; those on the shoulders are turned inward and those on the knees are turned upward so that, were the figure in a standing position, they too would be facing inward. The head on the god's left knee is the Death God's; the one on the right knee is the the head of Xipe as the fire-serpent Xolotl and on the right shoulder it is Xipe risen and become the quetzal-serpent, Quetzalcoatl; and lastly, the one on the left shoulder is the Moon God which the Aztecs called Tezcatlipoca.

A word should be said here in explanation of this identification of the gods on the Las Limas statue. All have the cleft head of the Jaguar God and (except for the Death head) the jaguar fang. In *America's First Civilization*, Michael Coe identifies the face on the right shoulder by the band curving through the eye which is diagnostic of Xipe in the art of the Zapotecs. He hesitatingly identifies the face on the right knee as Quetzalcoatl's by the St. Andrew's cross in the eye and the squared nose of the Wind God; but these marks of identification apply equally to Xolotl who was Quetzalcoatl's twin in the death region and who was the jaguar fire-serpent.

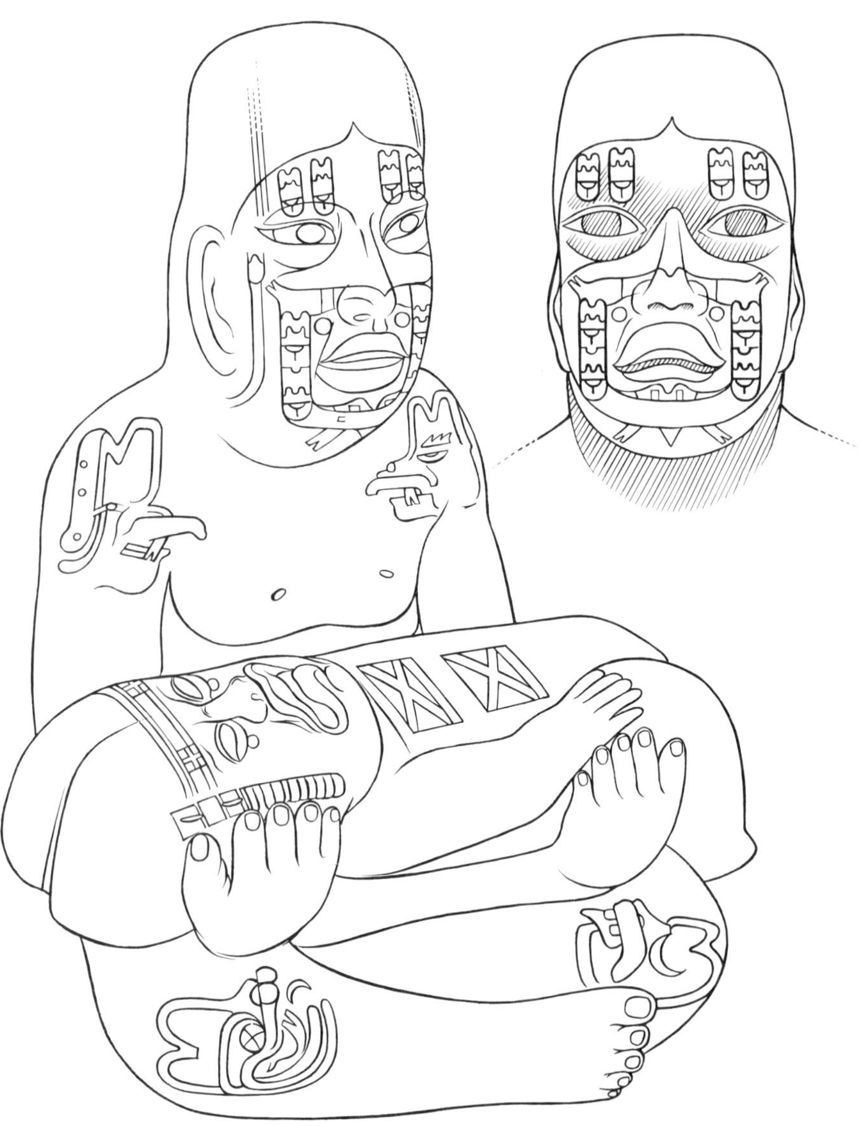

Figure 21. Las Limas idol, Museum of Anthropology, Jalapa, Mexico.

The Olmec Supreme God

The position of the head on the right knee opposite the Death God makes it certain that it is Xolotl. The Las Limas concept of the Jaguar God makes his image that of the new Moon figure of a world-man. The Death God and the dead infant are the gods of the new Moon's death state. Xolotl, as the Evening Star fire-serpent, carried the Sun through the underworld region of death and rose transformed into Quetzalcoatl as the Morning Star.*

In the sacrifice of the Tlacaxipeualiztli, Xolotl and Quetzalcoatl were identified as two aspects of Xipe, the one carrying the Sun in its underworld form as a jaguar, and the second carrying it transformed into an eagle in the sky.

The gods on the right knee and on the shoulders of the Las Limas figure are the gods of the new Moon's life side. Xipe on the right shoulder reveals the identity of the god on the left shoulder. Coe identifies a flame brow [**Figure 22b**, *page 336*] which is shown over the eye of the left shoulder god as the insignia of the Fire God or the fire-serpent. The flame brow was the sign of the jaguar. As such, he was the same god as the Jaguar God Tezcatlipoca, who was the Fire God's life form as the Moon; the fire-serpent was equally the Evening and Morning Star and the animating spirit of Tezcatlipoca. The face on the left shoulder is Tezcatlipoca.

We can most easily identify the symbolism of the infant by recalling the Huichol myth of creation of the Sun which told how, as a limp boy, he was thrown in an oven but escaped and traveled underground through the earth to rise and become the Sun. The infant in the arms of the Las Limas god is limp and lifeless. The arms and hands of the Supreme Jaguar cradling the infant signify the revival of life through sacrifice. Thus, the infant is like the Huichol child in the oven, for the oven was the Huichol Fire God in whose flames the child died as a sacrifice.

*Xolotl and Quetzalcoatl as fire-serpents were identified with the planet Venus. In the Olmec period, the fire-serpents were identified with Mercury. The different planetary identity would not have changed their natures as gods.

The interpretation of the symbolism of the infant in arms requires substantiation. We have seen that the hand was a symbol signifying sacrifice and this symbolism extended to the arms. Xolotl shows this extension: Xolotl was sacrificed and returned to life as Quetzalcoatl; the codices picture his transformation as the skeleton god whose hands have flesh but whose arms are bones. The bones denote death, the hands life.

In the *Codex Magliabecchi*, a rite is described in which a youth impersonating Quetzalcoatl cut a piece of flesh from his arm and placed it in the vulva of a girl impersonator of the Earth Goddess. When the youth was consecrated as the god, his flesh was transubstantiated into maize and, in the symbolism of the rite, the flesh would be born by the Earth Goddess as a new Maize God. The cutting of the flesh from his arm was symbolic of death through sacrifice. An Olmec celt, known as the Humbolt Celt, which as a ceremonial ax represented the sacrificial knife and the Jaguar God as the creator of life, has incised on its blade a pair of arms and hands with the arms folded at the elbows, in a position comparable to the arms of the Las Limas god.

The Huichols regarded the Sun and maize as divinely synonymous. In Mesoamerica, where maize was regarded as the divine substance of the Moon and the Moon was held to be the bodily form of the Sun, the infant — like the limp Huichol boy — symbolized the embryo Sun or, more properly, the composite fire and Moon spirit of the Fifth Sun which would be created as the new year Sun in the underworld by the Supreme Jaguar.

The child as the symbol of the bodily life spirit was probably universal in ancient times. The sacred Maya book, the *Popul Vuh*, pictured the embryos of the Sun and Moon in the process of creation in the underworld as two boys, Hunahpu and Xbalanque, and primitive Amerind mythology features twin boys as beings of the spirit world. The symbolism survived and appeared in early Christian art in Byzantine mosaics which portrayed the death of the Virgin Mary and the arrival of her soul in heaven, her soul being represented as an infant in the arms of God.

As the infant in the Las Limas figure, his nature as the Moon spirit appears as the markings on his body. The jaguar fang shape of his head is the sign of his function as Sun-bearer and the kan cross over each eye in the band around his head show his Moon and maize nature. His identification with the Moon spirit is completed by the two St. Andrew's crosses on his chest and abdomen. These represent the fire-serpents that carried the Sun. He is the god spirit which was pictured as the serpent-footed infant in the Temple of the Inscriptions at Palenque.

That the Olmecs had the idea of the serpent as the Sun-bearer is proven by Monument 47 at San Lorenzo Tenochtitlan, a very early Olmec site. Monument 47 is a basalt stone human figure, seated tailor fashion and holding the head of a feathered serpent on its lap — much in the manner in which the Las Limas idol holds the infant. The serpent head is pointed forward, held between the palms with the left hand beneath and the right hand over it. The serpent has two bodies which separate behind the head and coil around the torso of the human figure, one to the left, and the other to the right. The human figure has been decapitated.

The two-bodied feathered serpent must be a prototype of Xolotl as the fire-serpent that carried the Sun through the underworld and was resurrected in death as Quetzalcoatl. Quetzalcoatl was the feathered serpent which, as the Morning Star, brought the Sun into the world above. The evidence for this is a fresco painting in the palace of Atetelco in Teotihuacan, which pictures a jaguar with a coyote behind traveling through the underworld. Both animals were forms of Xolotl who was described in the Aztec creation myth as having two bodies. In the fresco, they are represented in a frame formed by a feathered serpent with two entwined bodies, one with markings of a jaguar and the other with markings of a coyote.

The feathers on the head of the serpent in Monument 47 certainly identify him with the feathered serpent of later cultures, and the two bodies surely relate him to Xolotl. The decapitated body signifies sacrifice and the death state in Xolotl was resurrected as Quetzalcoatl and identifies the serpent as a fire-serpent and carrier of the Sun.

Although the Maya and the people of the later cultures identified the fire-serpent as the planet Venus, the Olmecs probably identified it with Mercury. Astronomical calculations (by David H. Kelley) based on the calendar show that Quetzalcoatl was sometimes identified with Mercury. As we have seen, Venus was a calendrical god and we will see evidence that the Olmecs used the Eurasian planetary calendar before its Mesoamerican reformation.

The Olmecs imagined the fire-serpent as the eye of the Sun, as did the Mayas and the peoples of the Nahuatlan culture. The Olmec God's jaguar aspect as the Sun was represented abstractly by the serrated or flame eyebrow which is the mark of the god incised on the left shoulder of the Las Limas figure. At Chalcatzingo in Morelos, a carving known as Relief I on the rock face of a mountain represents the Supreme Jaguar. We shall consider this carving in the next chapter, but we may note here that the flame brow over the eye denotes the god's solar nature, and that the god's eye has the sign of the St. Andrew's cross. A cave at Juxtlahuaca in Guerrero links the St. Andrew's cross directly to the fire-serpent. In the back recesses of the cave there is an Olmec painting of a crested serpent with a flame brow and an x-eye glyph on his head. The glyph must represent the jaguar as the Sun with its planet eye and, because of the setting deep in a cave, the picture must represent the serpent carrying the Sun through the earth. This reading of the meaning of the cave painting is confirmed by another monument from San Lorenzo, Monument 30, which is a fragmentary stela. On one side, a carving in low relief pictures a serpent with a jaguar head in profile. The eye of the head is a cartouche with a St. Andrew's cross. The St. Andrew's cross or x-sign was a sign for Venus in the later cultures. Venus was implicit in the fire-serpent as the Sun-bearer. The concept of the serpent as the eye of the Sun had its Eurasian precedent in Egypt where the uraeus, or *zet*-serpent, was called the Eye of Horus. Horus was a Sun God and the *zet*-serpent was the planet Moon spirit and Sun-bearer.

The Jaguar God in the Lineage of the World-Man

The Eurasian archetype of the Las Limas figure of the Olmec Jaguar God is the Celtic Cernunnos.* Cernunnos was represented sitting, as the Las Limas figure is sitting, with its legs folded beneath him tailor fashion. Like the Olmec God, he was part human, part animal. His animal part was a deer, symbolized by his horns. The deer was the spirit Moon body of the Sun. The jaguar part of the Olmec God was likewise the spirit body of the Sun. The human parts of both gods constituted their Moon divinity.

The figure of Cernunnos is his composite image as a world-man. His two legs folded beneath him represent his Moon being in death and in revival as the new Moon. Cernunnos was ithyphallic. His phallus symbolized the seed of life returning in the new Moon. Life was the fire of the Sun. The lower part of his body was constituted by the three planetary gods of death and returning life — Saturn, Sun, and Moon.

These gods whose images are incised on the left and right knees of the Las Limas idol likewise constitute the lower part of the god's body as the death and reviving state of the Moon. The dead infant on the god's lap has the symbolism of Cernunnos' phallus. A consideration of the figure of the infant makes this evident. The death state shows it to be the corporeal spirit of the dead Moon. Its jaguar features and the kan and St. Andrew's crosses on its head and body show it to be the life spirit of the Jaguar God and, hence, the seed which brings life to the godhead on the right knee. As in the planetary theology of Eurasia, life was the fire of the Sun; thus, the Jaguar God's legs and the child on his lap represent the three aspects of the solar Moon God constituted by the planetary Saturn, Sun, and Moon.

Cernunnos had three heads which form him as the triple godhead, Mars-Mercury-Jupiter. The Las Limas world-man also had three heads which correspond to the three heads of Cernunnos. One is the head of Xipe on his right shoulder. Mars was the planetary god who brought the Sun on its

*See Chapter 17.

return in the spring; Xipe as the Morning Star performed the same function. The third head of Cernunnos is Jupiter who was the planetary god of the full Moon; Tezcatlipoca was the corresponding Mesoamerican god. Cernunnos' middle head is Mercury, the god of the joint motion of the Sun and Moon. The middle head of the Las Limas world-man is the principal head of the idol with the composite human-double jaguar face of the Fifth Sun in movement.

In his world image, Cernunnos holds a scepter shaped as a composite ram-serpent. It is his sign as the cyclical motion of the Moon united to the Sun. The ram was an animal-god form of the Moon and the serpent was the Moon's moving spirit as the Sun-bearer. The symbolism of the ram-serpent is expressed in the figure of the Las Limas Jaguar God by the kan and St. Andrew's crosses on the infant.

In the chapter on Jason, we saw the deceased god-king Phryxus coming to Colchis (the land of death) riding on a phantom ram with golden fleece. Phryxus sacrificed the ram in Colchis where the god of the new Moon, Aeëtes, hung its fleece on a tree in the Grove of Mars and set a serpent-dragon to guard it. Phryxus, as king, was the Moon and in death was its corporeal spirit. The ram was the Moon spirit and its fleece was the Sun.

When Phryxus sacrificed the ram, the ram was transformed into the serpent-dragon, which was another form of the Moon spirit; and, when Jason overcame the serpent-dragon with the help of Medea and took possession of the fleece, the serpent-dragon lodged in Jason, who then became the third form of the Moon spirit. The tree on which Aeëtes hung the fleece was a tree of life in Mars' grove of death and — in the metaphor of the myth — the tree, the fleece, and the serpent-dragon constituted a composite image of the new Moon forming in the death of the old Moon.

In his world-man image, Cernunnos holds a scepter shaped as a composite ram-serpent. The story of Jason is a word picture of the gods forming as a world-man who was comparable to Cernunnos. Thus, by the

symbolism of Jason's story, we know the symbolism of the ram-serpent — it denotes the power of renewal of life through sacrifice.

The infant in the arms of the Las Limas idol has the symbolic meaning of the ram-serpent. We know that spirits were represented as little children. The serpent foot of each of the infants in the arms of the Moon gods, Pacal and Chan Bahlum, as they are pictured on the piers of the Temple of the Inscriptions at Palenque, show their natures as Moon spirits. The Las Limas infant unquestionably represents a Moon spirit that was like the winged ram in the story of Jason. The kan signs incised on its forehead are signs of the spirit's nature as vegetation, which has the cyclical life of the Moon, and the St. Andrew's crosses on its body are the spirit's nature as the fire-serpents. The fire-serpents were the Moon's cyclical spirit which moved the Moon in its combined course with the Sun to form its months into the year. The kan and St. Andrew's crosses symbolize life and movement forming in the dead body of the Moon represented by the lifeless infant in the arms of the Jaguar God, and the figure of the infant represents the god's reproductive power.

Where Cernunnos was a prototype for the Las Limas idol, the Las Limas idol in turn was a prototype for the images of the Mesoamerican gods of the Sun and Moon forming as a world-man. The painting of Tlaloc at Teotihuacan is such an image, and the calendrical image of Tezcatlipoca as the 20 days of the Moon cycle and the 13 Lords of the Day is another. Let us look first at the Tepantitla Tlaloc [Figure 4].

The Tepantitla Tlaloc, it will be recalled, was a fresco picturing a god wearing the mask of the Fire God and a goddess' dress. His headdress is a bird with rich and abundant feathers and he is seated on the waters of life creation. Two gods stand on either side of him — the Venus Moon spirit on the left, the Moon God on the right. Symbols denoting the subsistence and generation of life flow in streams from the hands of the two gods. The Las Limas idol of the Jaguar God as a world-man puts the Tepantitla painting in the light of the doctrine of the Great Goddess and makes it clear that it portrays Tlaloc as the Sun of Movement, the Fifth Sun.

The painting is in two panels. The second panel is painted beneath the waters on which the god is seated. It pictures a mountain; spirits in human form are dancing on the slopes, and other spirits as butterflies are flying overhead. A river flows from a spring on the side of the mountain. When the Moon died, it entered the underworld transformed into a mountain; the panel, therefore, pictures the dead Moon. The spirits represent the mountain coming to life as a new Moon. The source of life is the spring.

The two panels are separated by two entwined serpents with masks of Tlaloc between their coils. The serpents represent the Evening and Morning Stars of Venus as the Fifth Sun's movement.

The symbolism of the painting is the same as the symbolism of the Las Limas idol. The Death God on the left knee of the idol is portrayed in the fresco as the mountain, and Xolotl on the right knee, as the dancing spirits and butterflies. The river and the entwined serpents with the Tlaloc masks in their coils are abstractions of the symbolism of the infant in the arms of the idol. The arms denote resurrection; the river, returning life. The St. Andrew's crosses on the infant denote the life which is the divinity of the Moon. Tlaloc was a god of life which grew in the fields on the mountain; his masks have the symbolism of the kan crosses.

On the idol, the face of Xipe on the right shoulder is the Morning Star bringing the Sun with the annual maize crop. The face of the god on the left shoulder is the full Moon as the harvest and seed of the new year. The idol's head represents the god's being as the Sun, incarnate in the Moon, moving in the creation of life.

In the upper panel of the fresco, the god on the right hand of Tlaloc is the Morning Star; the stream carrying the jade symbols flowing from his hand represents the maize which the Morning Star brings with the Sun. The god on the left hand of Tlaloc is the Moon; the shells in the stream flowing from his hand represent the harvest and seed of the new crop. The head and

body of Tlaloc show him as the creator and giver of life.

Mesoamerican civilization followed two lines of development — one in the highlands of Mexico, the other in the Mayan lowlands. Teotihuacan is on the line through the Mexican highland. On the Mayan line, the world-man's image formed as the four temples of Palenque, as we have seen in Chapters 22 through 25. The gods that constituted the body of the Las Limas idol are the same as the ones constituting the new Moon in the Temple of the Sun [Figure 10]. In the Sun temple portrayal, the cosmogonic band supported on the shoulders of God L and 7-Jaguar takes the place of the Las Limas infant. The death state of the infant is denoted by the jaguar mask of the skeleton Itzam Na, the *bil* on the skeleton god's headdress, and the serpent heads at each end of the band have the symbolism of the kan and St. Andrew's crosses on the body of the infant.

A world-man image like that of the Las Limas Jaguar God is pictured in the *Codex Fejérváry-Mayer* at the end of his cultural descent. The gods that constitute the limbs of Tezcatlipoca are the gods which constitute the limbs of the Las Limas idol. Tezcatlipoca's loin cloth, formed by the day sign Reed, has the symbolism of the infant. Reeds growing on the margins of lakes and streams symbolized the emergence of life from the waters of creation. The day Reed was constituted as two gods — Tezcatlipoca and Itztlacoliuhqui — the one, the first Sun and lord of beginning; the second, the Maize God in the state of winter death. The divinity of both gods was the divinity of life locked in the inert seed kernel. Thus, the symbolism of the *Codex Fejérváry-Mayer* relates euphemistically to the ithyphallic image of Cernunnos. The world-man was constituted by the gods of the Moon's life and motion forming as a new Moon. They combined in four stages as the world in motion. The gods of the new Moon formed the third stage of the world-man's contained motion which ended when his Moon image was full. In the fourth stage, he died and rose in resurrection as the living Moon. In Palenque, his death and resurrection is in the Temple of the Inscriptions; in the idol, it is implicit in the incising on the face.

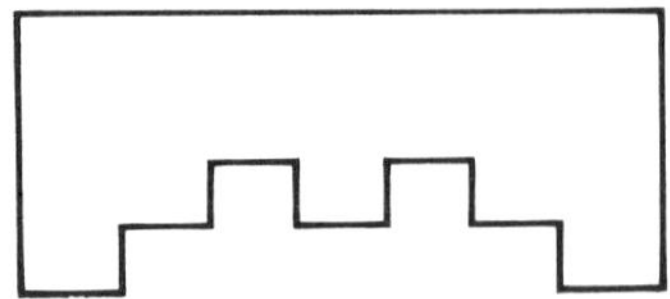

22a. Indented step motif.

22b. Flame brow.

22c. Face symbol
for the Jaguar God.

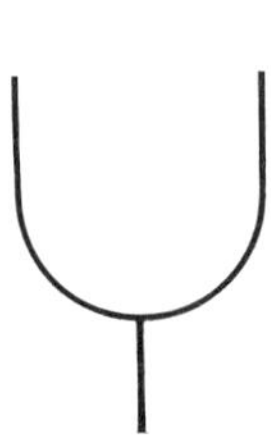

22d. Stem "u".

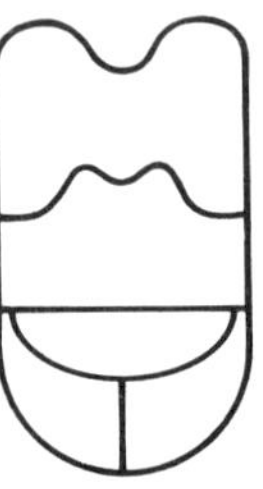

22e. Compound geometric
eye, cleft head, and u-symbol.

The Olmec Supreme God

The Coming on Earth of the Jaguar God

The configuration of the incising is symbolic. As it is recorded by Wicke in *Olmec: an Early Art Style of Pre-Columbian Mexico*, it portrays two faces of the Jaguar God. Two faces are in conformity with the concept of the two Suns which formed the Fifth Sun. To see the two faces, the abstract nature of Olmec art must be understood.

The Olmecs sometimes represented the Jaguar God by geometric figures in which two dots or circles represent the eyes and two beneath them the mouth, with a vertical bar in the center between them to represent the nose [**Figure 22c**].

In some instances, the eyes and mouth instead of being circles are represented by rectangular shapes with a step motif indenting the lower portion [**Figure 22a**].

Another sign which the Olmecs used in association with the Jaguar God was the u-symbol which could be upright, inverted, and could have a stem at the base [**Figure 22d**]. The cleft head, which is a feature of the four gods on the knees and shoulders of the idol, is a diagnostic sign of the Olmec Jaguar divinity.* These geometric figures in combination were signs of the god which could represent his facial features without being placed in symmetrical order.

In the configuration of the face, there are parallel twin signs over each eye of the human face, each of which is a compound geometric eye formed by the step motif, the cleft head at the top and the u-symbol at the bottom [**Figure 22e**]. The twin signs over each human eye are the eyes of the two jaguar faces. These same signs are incised on each cheek, one beneath the other. Their relation to the god's human mouth identifies them as the mouths of the two jaguar faces.

*Some students consider that the cleft head and flame brow identify the god with the alligator; others consider that the cleft head relates him to the serpent. In either case, the sign is derived from the cleft between ridges on the animal's head.

A number of examples of the doubling of eyes and mouths to represent two faces have been found on figurines at the Preclassic site of Tlatilco in present-day Mexico City. The Tlatilco figurines represent the Earth or Moon Goddess, but the sex of the Mesoamerican Supreme God was dual and the Olmec Supreme God was not different. The Tlatilco figurines are comparable.

Both jaguar faces on the Olmec idol's human face and the double faces on the Tlatilco figurines are turned forward and the symbolism, therefore, is not the same as the symbolism of the Janus heads which are common in the later iconography. The jaguar was the spirit Moon body of the Sun and, if we recall the Nahuatlan creation myth, we will remember that the Fifth Sun first came into being as two equal Suns and that one was incarnated as a rabbit and became the Moon. The first Sun which came into existence was Nanauatzin who was the Moon-serpent Venus. As the Moon-serpent, he was Xolotl in the regions of death and Quetzalcoatl in the regions of life. The second Sun was Tecuciztecatl, who became the Moon.

The Moon-serpent Venus was the Sun-bearer and, when Xolotl carried the Sun through the underworld, he took the shape of a jaguar. The Moon, which in the creation myth was called Tecuciztecatl, was properly Tezcatlipoca, who was the first Sun in the succession of four which preceded the creation of the Fifth Sun; his life spirit was the Venus-Sun spirit and, when he died, his departing spirit appeared in the waters as a jaguar. The two Suns which rose as equals from the flames of the Fire God were these two jaguars. But, when they appeared as two Suns in the sky, they remained motionless and the world was still nonexistent; only when Tecuciztecatl's Sun was transformed into the Moon and Venus-serpent, did Quetzalcoatl set them both in motion so that the world came into existence.* The myth is, of course, a metaphor and Quetzalcoatl set the Sun and Moon in motion by combining with each as the Morning Star. The union joined

*The myth names Ehecatl, the Wind God, as the god who set the Sun and Moon in motion, but Ehecatl and Xolotl-Quetzalcoatl were one and the same god.

the Sun and Moon into a single motion and formed them into the Fifth Sun as the Sun of Movement.

The two jaguar faces on the Olmec idol represent the two Suns — one is the Sun which in the creation myth rose as Nanauatzin, the other is the Sun which rose as the Moon. We saw them portrayed in the ritual drama of the Aztec feast of Toxcatl, one as Ixteucale who personified the Sun-bearer Venus, the other as Tezcatlipoca who personified the Moon. As Venus, Ixteucale was a serpent and, as the Moon, Tezcatlipoca was a jaguar. In the course of the drama, Tezcatlipoca as the Moon died and was transformed into the Moon-serpent spirit Venus. Thus, both were identical and as Moon-serpents they were the Venus god, Xolotl. Xolotl was as much a jaguar as a serpent and in the underworld of death and resurrection, Ixteucale and Tezcatlipoca were equal, and were like the two Suns in the creation before the rabbit formed Tecuciztecatl's body into the Moon.

The two gods as the Sun and Moon are portrayed as equals in the Temple of the Inscriptions at Palenque — as equals, they were one. When Pacal (as Venus) and Chan Bahlum (as the Moon) died in sacrifice, their spirits appeared as identical human infants which were transformed into serpents as they descended to the deceased Pacal as the Creator-Maker of life.

In the Aztec creation myth, when the two Suns were given motion by the Venus-serpent — one moved as the Sun and the other as the Moon, and their two motions formed the days and nights of the years. In the drama of Toxcatl, when Ixteucale and Tezcatlipoca had been sacrificed, both rose together united as one in the god form of the Sun, Huitzilopochtli.

In the Temple of the Inscriptions at Palenque, in the resurrection from death, the serpent-spirit forms of Pacal and Chan Bahlum returned to their human infant shapes, and to their bodily shapes as Pacal and Chan Bahlum, and rose on earth as one incarnate in the ruler.

The Olmec Jaguar God in his world aspect was manifest as a mountain. Within the mountain was the underworld path of the jaguar on which he

moved in the creation of life. The Olmecs pictured caves as the jaguar's mouth and the signs which denote the jaguar mouths on the human face of the idol are linked to form a "u" at the bottom with pendant jaguar fangs [**Figure 23**] on either side and a cleft inside the base of the "u." The top of the "u" is closed by fangs joined at the base over the end of the nose so that the "u" forms an outline of the opening of a jaguar-mouth cave around the human mouth. Thus the jaguar faces and the human face are formed as one and the combination gives it the character of the Olmec God: half-jaguar and half-human.

The cave symbolism denotes the coming of the god on earth. Caves were traditionally regarded as places of emergence in Mesoamerican religion. The Spanish chroniclers record that the Sun and Moon came out of a cave; Mendieta, describing the creation of the Fifth Sun at Teotihuacan, states that when the god who threw himself into the fire rose as the Sun, another god went into a cave and came out as the Moon.

The Aztec feast of Tlacaxipeualiztli celebrated the coming on earth of Xipe as the Morning Star, bringing the Sun with the maize of the spring planting. Xipe was called Xipe-Totec; he was Venus as the Evening Star in

Figure 23. Jaguar fang symbol.

the underworld and as the Morning Star on earth. He was the same two-fold god as Xolotl-Quetzalcoatl with a different name, and when he was not a serpent, he was a mountain. In the rituals of the feast, warriors were sacrificed as Xipe the Evening Star, and flayed. Actors, playing the part of Xipe the Morning Star, dressed in their skins. When they took off their skins at the end of the feast, the skins were placed in a cave near the pyramid of Xipe. The taking off of the skins symbolized the coming on earth of Xipe and the leaving of skins in the cave symbolized his emergence from the cave.

Figurines of Xipe dating from the early centuries A.D. have been found in a cave under the pyramid of the Sun at Teotihuacan. The tradition thus goes back to a time near the end of the Preclassic period and so puts it in a time relation to the Olmecs.

The compound jaguar and human face formed as a cave mouth represents the opening from the underworld inside the jaguar mountain. The jaguar fangs which form the top of the cave mouth and the cleft and pendant fangs on the curve of the "u" at the base of the opening unite the two jaguar Suns as one, and their images incised on the human face give them the Jaguar God's human shape. In their human transformation, they are like Ixteucale and Tezcatlipoca, and Pacal and Chan Bahlum, and their union at the cave mouth signifies their coming on earth bringing a new year of life.

This symbolism of the union and transformation of the two jaguar spirit forms is further signified by the ogee curve in the line of the headdress on the idol.

Carlo Gay, in discussing the ogee curve in the headdress of a god carved in relief at the top of the Cerro de la Canterra, states that the peak of the curve represents the button at the end of a rattlesnake's rattle.* The Cerro de la Canterra is a mountain. Reliefs carved on its face constitute it as a natural idol of the Jaguar God.

*See following Chapter 29.

In the abstract iconography of the Olmec and later Mesoamerican art, a curved line was sufficient to represent a serpent. An ogee curve properly represents twin serpents united at the ends of their tails with the ogee peak as the union. The Eurasian Mercury was not one serpent, but two; and the same is true of the Mesoamerican Venus. Venus was traditionally represented as two serpents with the ends of their tails twisted together to form them as one.

The Olmec God spirit, like Xolotl, was both jaguar and serpent. Tezcatlipoca, who had a jaguar image, had a foot which sometimes formed as a serpent; Chan Bahlum, by his sign and name, was a snake-jaguar. The mystic qualities of the Olmec God's descendants attest the ophidian qualities of his jaguar nature. The ogee curve on the Las Limas idol's headdress properly represents the union of two gods on their emergence from the underworld.

There is no sign of the female side of the Supreme Jaguar in his Las Limas image, unless it is abstractly represented as breasts by lines on the chest which are not recognizable as having that meaning. Cernunnos' female side is represented separately by a counterpart tricephalic image of his spouse. We shall see in the next chapter that the Supreme Jaguar did, in fact, have a female side and that quality of his nature may have been implicit in the little Las Limas statue.

In any case, its absence does not detract from the likeness of his world-man image to Cernunnos and the Eurasian planetary gods who formed themselves into the cosmic shape of a world-man.

CHAPTER 29

The Mountain God of Chalcatzingo

The Las Limas image of the Olmec God was a little statue, but there is another image of the god which is literally the size of a mountain. Outside the village of Chalcatzingo in Morelos, Mexico, is the mountain called Cerro de la Canterra, with features which give it the character of the Las Limas statue.

The Cerro de la Canterra rises abruptly from the floor of the valley and presents a steep rock face toward the northeast. Because of its orientation, the plane of the mountain face extends along a southeast-northwest axis. There are three groups of relief carvings on the mountain face; the reliefs have been numbered in accordance with the sequence of their discovery and consequently, the numbers do not necessarily relate to their most logical grouping [**Figure 24**].

Relief Number I is the most important in the first group, which is composed of five reliefs. They were carved on the northwest side of the mountain face about 100 feet above the base. Relief Number I is at the northwestern end.

Relief Number II dominates the second group which consists of four carvings on large detached boulders along the base of the mountain on the southeastern side.

There are only two reliefs in the third group, which is at the top center of the cliff. The two form a single composition, which was designated as Number X by Carlo Gay, who discovered them.

The mountain is a manifestation of the Jaguar God as the Fifth Sun — his movement in the creation of life is the succession of the reliefs. They

begin with Relief Number I, which shows the god in his human form seated in the opening of a cave carved as the mouth of a jaguar [**Figure 25**]. He wears the dress of a goddess and holds a ceremonial bar over his lap in the manner in which he holds the infant in Las Limas. The ceremonial bar is a symbolic substitute for the infant and the sign of the Moon spirit.

The jaguar mouth is carved as a cross section of the opening of a cave. Volutes spiral outside, and around it are rain and cloud symbols and plants. On the outline of the upper jaw is an oval cartouche combined with the maize shoot enclosing the eye of the jaguar. Over the eye is a flame brow [Figure 22b] and the x-sign of the fire-serpent is on the eye.

The seated figure in Relief Number I portrays the god's human nature and the cave mouth portrays his jaguar nature. The cloud and rain symbols show him to be the lord of the sky; the plants show him as the creator and

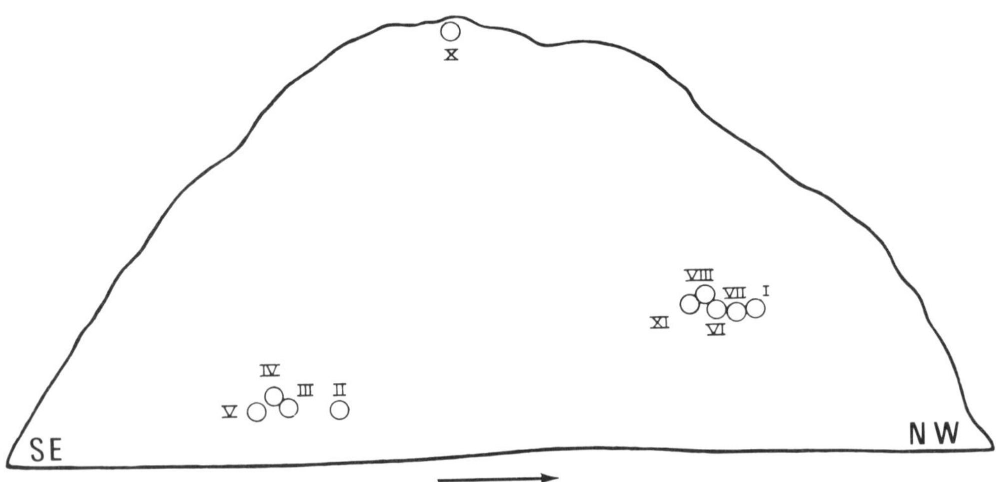

Figure 24. Outline of Cerro de la Canterra, a profile of the mountain [after Gay] showing the location of the reliefs, Morelos, Mexico.

The Mountain God of Chalcatzingo

Figure 25. Relief Number I, Cerro de la Canterra, Morelos, Mexico.

nourisher of life; and his seat in the jaguar mouth of the mountain shows his being as the earth. Thus, his province was the Fifth Sun.

In Eurasian and Mesoamerican theology, the Supreme God was the world of the universe. His divinity was the creation and passing of life and time constituted by the motion of the Moon and Sun. The Moon and Sun moved in cycles and, at the end of each cycle, a new cycle began. The cycles were divided into stages and the stages were gods. In motion, they were separate; but at the end and beginning of each cycle, the gods all came together and united as one.

The movement of the Moon and Sun then ceased and the state of the world was death. In this state, the Supreme God was formed as a cosmic being whose shape was the shape of man. New movement formed in the union of the gods as the potential that is contained in the death state of the Moon, until the world-man came to life and the gods returned to their stages of motion.

The Las Limas idol was made in the god's image as a world-man which could be recognized by comparative images of the Eurasian Cernunnos and the Tepantitla Tlaloc and calendrical Tezcatlipoca of Mesoamerica. The mountain image of the Chalcatzingo Jaguar God and the abstract character of the reliefs make it more difficult to recognize the god's world-man image. The formation of life and movement in the death state of the Maya Supreme God was portrayed in four temples at Palenque in a way that will enable us to identify the mountain as the world-man image of the Olmec Supreme God.

We should recall that in the Temple of the Foliated Cross, the gods formed in the world-man as the inchoate Moon. The gods were spirits with no Moon to give them life form. Then, in the Temple of the Cross, they gave the world-man the beginning of life and movement and formed him as the new Moon.

In the Temple of the Sun, all the gods of the Moon's life and motion gathered and formed the world-man as the waxing new Moon. In the

Temple of the Inscriptions, the world-man died and the Supreme God of the new Moon raised the gods from death and gave them life on earth.

Let us now consider the four reliefs which are associated with Relief Number I, in relation to the Temple of the Foliated Cross. Then let us separate for our consideration the relief on the boulder at the southeast end of the row of boulders from the other three reliefs associated with Relief Number II — we will consider this Relief Number V in relation to the Temple of the Cross. We may then consider the other reliefs in relation to the Temple of the Sun, leaving Relief Number X (at the top of the mountain) for consideration with the Temple of the Inscriptions.

We begin, then, with the four reliefs east of and behind Relief Number I. They extend along the face of the mountain toward the center and a point southeast of Relief Number I. Southeast is the compass point at which the Sun begins its return from winter death in the latitude of Chalcatzingo. Thus, the formation of the movement of the Fifth Sun proceeds toward a death point on the border of the beginning of new life.

The first relief is Number VII, which depicts an undefinable entity that Gay thinks could be a rabbit. A rabbit was the Mesoamerican animal form of the Moon in the Postclassic Period.

The next relief, Number VI, is a well-executed carving of a stem of a gourd vine. In the *Popul Vuh*, Hun Hunahpu — transformed into a calabash (i.e., a gourd) — begot the Sun and Moon. The fruit of the vine was a staple, and the relief surely symbolizes the divine nature of the Moon.

The third relief, Number VIII, is a mythical monster with, presumably, the body of a lizard curved to form a "u" [**Figure 26**]. The shape of the head is too eroded to be recognizable, but a bifurcated cubic double scroll projects upward where the head is and may be a part of it. There is a cloud symbol over the scroll with raindrop symbols beneath scroll branches.

In his discussion of this relief, Gay shows a Preclassic figure with eyes formed as rectangular spirals, much like the cubic scrolls in Relief Number VIII. He also shows a comparable figure in which the right angles of the

Figure 26. Relief Number VIII, Cerro de la Canterra, Morelos, Mexico.

spirals have been rounded. The eyes of the Maya Sun God appear to have evolved from such spirals — a reasonable interpretation is that they represent the eyes of the monster and that they are the rising and setting Suns in the coils of the Venus serpent.

In the mythical image of the world coming into existence, the earth emerged from the waters of creation as an amphibian or a reptile. Tezcatlipoca, as the new Moon, was the starry firmament. He was held bound to the earth by a crocodile which had seized him by the foot. His life spirit was the Sun-bearer Venus. The crocodile was Tezcatlipoca's form as the earth.

The Maya likewise imagined the divinity of the earth as a crocodile. They held that the Moon was a transubstantiated form of the earth, that the spirit form of the new Moon was the firmament of the stars, and that the Moon spirit was the Sun-bearer Venus.

The cloud symbols and the raindrops must represent the sky; the cubic scrolls, the Sun-bearing Moon spirit; and the reptilian body, the earth. The monster in Relief Number VIII is properly an abstract image of the Fifth Sun in its form as the invisible new Moon.

The fourth relief, Number XI, is very badly weathered and cannot be identified except to the extent that it represents a serpent. The serpent provided the motion of the Fifth Sun.

Now, if we study the relief in the Temple of the Foliated Cross [Figure 8], we find the same symbolic elements. The counterpart of the rabbit (VII) is the Jester God in the conch shell beneath the figure of Pacal.

The symbolism of the squash vine (VI) is pictured in the Foliated Cross as branching maize leaves with the death mask of the Maize God on one of the leaves. It is the plant stemming from the conch shell and Pacal stands on the leaf covering the face of the dead Maize God.

The symbolism of the monster (VIII) is contained in the cross which forms the center of the composition of the Temple of the Foliated Cross tablet. The skeleton mask at the base represents the earth Itzam Na. A

maize tree grows out of a kan cross which forms the headdress over Itzam Na's mask. The trunk of the maize tree forms a body for the head of the Sun God which is supported in the fork of the branches. A pectoral hangs beneath the head. A human face is carved on the pectoral and, because it is human, must represent the Moon. A moan bird is perched in the headdress — as we have seen, this owl represents the night sky.

The serpent carved in the last relief (XI) has it corresponding symbolism in the temple as the leaves which constitute the branches of the maize tree and which curve outward to represent the open jaws of two serpents with maize kernels for teeth.

The mountain, Cerro de la Canterra, on which the reliefs are carved, is the death image of the Moon. The reliefs portray the gods of the Jaguar mountain forming as the inchoate Moon.

The second group is likewise in series. The reliefs are carved on boulders at the foot of the cliff. The boulders separate them from the inert and lifeless mass of the stone cliff and place them on the life-giving soil of the surrounding earth. In themselves, the boulders are the potential movement which formed when they fell from the cliff and became contained at the base.

The first is Relief Number V, followed by Numbers IV, III, and II. By the position of these reliefs, we know that they are on the life side of the Mountain God, whereas the previously considered reliefs were on his death side. Relief Numbers V, IV, III, and II portray the movement of the Fifth Sun forming as a new year of life in the underworld.

The movement begins in the southeast and proceeds northwestward. Northwest is the compass point at which the Sun sets at the summer solstice. The direction point is the seasonal time of harvest and the movement is that portrayed by the gods on the right knee and the shoulders of the Las Limas idol.

The Temple of the Sun gives the clue to Relief Number V. In the Temple of the Sun, the gods formed as the new Moon; Relief Number V

The Mountain God of Chalcatzingo

[**Figure 27**] portrays a fabulous creature which is part-serpent and part-alligator. The ophidian part is marked by a St. Andrew's cross and its bifurcated tongue. The saurian nature makes it the "Earth Monster." Grove describes it as combining the traits of a *cipactli*, which was the mythical earth crocodile or alligator pictured in the codices and which lived in a huge lake or sea.* In Mesoamerican art, it represented the earth in which the tree of life was rooted. In the Mexican calendar, the first day was 1-Cipactli. Furthermore, in the *Codex Fejérváry-Mayer*, creation began on the day 1-Cipactli.

*David Grove, *American Antiquity*, Vol. 33, No. 4, 1968, p. 489.

Figure 27. Relief Number V, Cerro de la Canterra, Morelos, Mexico.

A trident sign [**Figure 28a**] on the body of the monster, just behind the eye and mouth, marks him as the beginning point of life. The sign closely resembles the stylized representations of a butterfly wing at Teotihuacan [**Figure 28b**]. The butterfly was a symbol of the Morning Star returning with the Sun from its Moon death in the underworld. Venus descending to the underworld as the Evening Star was a *tzitzimitl*, which became a butterfly. Warriors in death were believed to be one with Tlahuizcalpantecuhtli, the name of Quetzalcoatl as the Morning Star; the warriors died as *tzitzimimi* and so were changed into butterflies. The significance of the belief is this: the Evening Star was Xolotl who, in one of

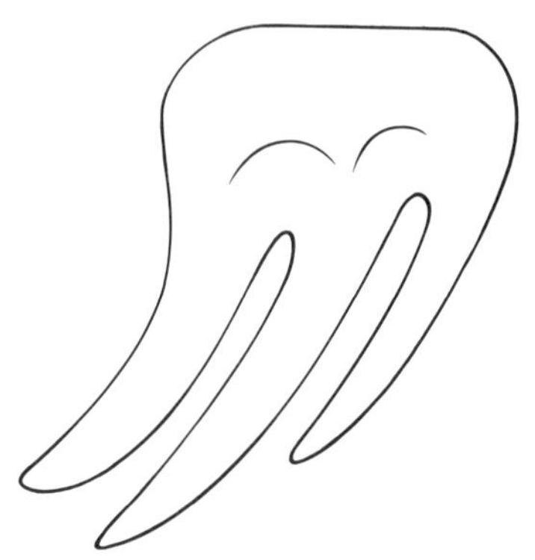

Figure 28a. Trident sign.

Figure 28b. Butterfly wing, Teotihuacan.

his representations, is a chrysalis; in death, Xolotl was transformed into Quetzalcoatl. The butterfly wing, therefore, is a symbol which describes the Moon in death as a cocoon from which the Venus Moon spirit emerges to lodge the Sun in the Moon of a new year. The trident, therefore, is a sign of a new Moon coming into existence.

A relief on the north temple of the great ball court at Chichen Itza corroborates this identification. The relief shows a tree of life rooted in the earth crocodile and butterflies in the branches.

The cipactli was the animal shape in which the Supreme God came into being as life on earth. The relief pictures him with a St. Andrew's cross on his body and a serpent tongue.

The tongue was an instrument of creation and the cipactli's tongue is extended — on it is a lifeless human body whose human shape marks it as the Moon.

The cipactli's tail is gathered to show movement, the nature of the tongue and the St. Andrew's cross signifies that the movement is the Moon spirit with the Sun. Relief Number V, like the Temple of the Cross, portrays the beginning of life and motion in the body of the new Moon.

The movement of the cipactli leads to the next relief, Number IV. This relief must be read with Numbers III and II. The Temple of the Sun is likewise the clue to all three. Relief Number IV is the only one in the group which does not face toward the northeast and the boulder on which it was carved has evidently moved.

In the boulder's present position, the four figures upon it — alternately jaguars and lifeless human bodies — are presented in seemingly impossible positions. However, when the picture is turned vertically, the two jaguars appear to be over the bodies [**Figure 29**]. The bodies are each the same as the body in the preceding relief. A cartouche with a St. Andrew's cross apparently represents the eye of each jaguar and there are (what are probably) plant symbols attached to the cartouche of the larger jaguar which is above the smaller one.

Figure 29. Relief Number IV, Cerro de la Canterra, Morelos, Mexico.

The Mountain God of Chalcatzingo

Relief Number III [**Figure 30**] is a jaguar with a branching plant stem.

In Relief Number II [**Figure 31**], there are five figures in a row. The two at the right end are addorsed. One of those two figures (facing right) is not too well defined, but it represents a fetal image of the Jaguar God, half-human, half-jaguar [**Figure 32**]. The other figure to the right is seated in a reclining position with his legs stretched before him. The other three figures (center and left of center) are in motion: the one at the left end of the line toward the left, the two in the center toward the right. The one moving toward the left holds a staff or maize stalk with leaves branching toward the front. He holds it raised before him. The other two hold paddle-shaped staves before them in the same way.

In the Temple of the Sun, the gods formed the world-man as the new Moon. The gods were: the prostrate God C, the Sun God, 7-Jaguar, the rising God C, Pacal, and Chan Bahlum. The first three formed as the stages of the new Moon and the last three formed as stages of the full Moon. The first God C was the dying or dead Moon, the Sun God was the invisible Moon spirit in the lifeless body of the Moon, and 7-Jaguar was the new Moon on the verge of life.

The body of 7-Jaguar was the same lifeless body as the Sun God's, but he wore the jaguar cape of the night sky as a sign of his revival. The Sun God and 7-Jaguar were united by the jaguar mask of the earth Itzam Na through which the spirit of the Sun God was transfused into the body of 7-Jaguar.

The kneeling and rising God C, Pacal, and Chan Bahlum were the stages of the full Moon.

If we now study Relief Numbers IV, III, and II, we will see that the jaguars with the lifeless human bodies in IV correspond to the first God C; the jaguar in III corresponds to the earth Itzam Na; the addorsed figures of the fetal Jaguar God, and the reclining figure in II correspond to the Sun God and 7-Jaguar; and the other three figures in II correspond to the rising God C, Pacal, and Chan Bahlum.

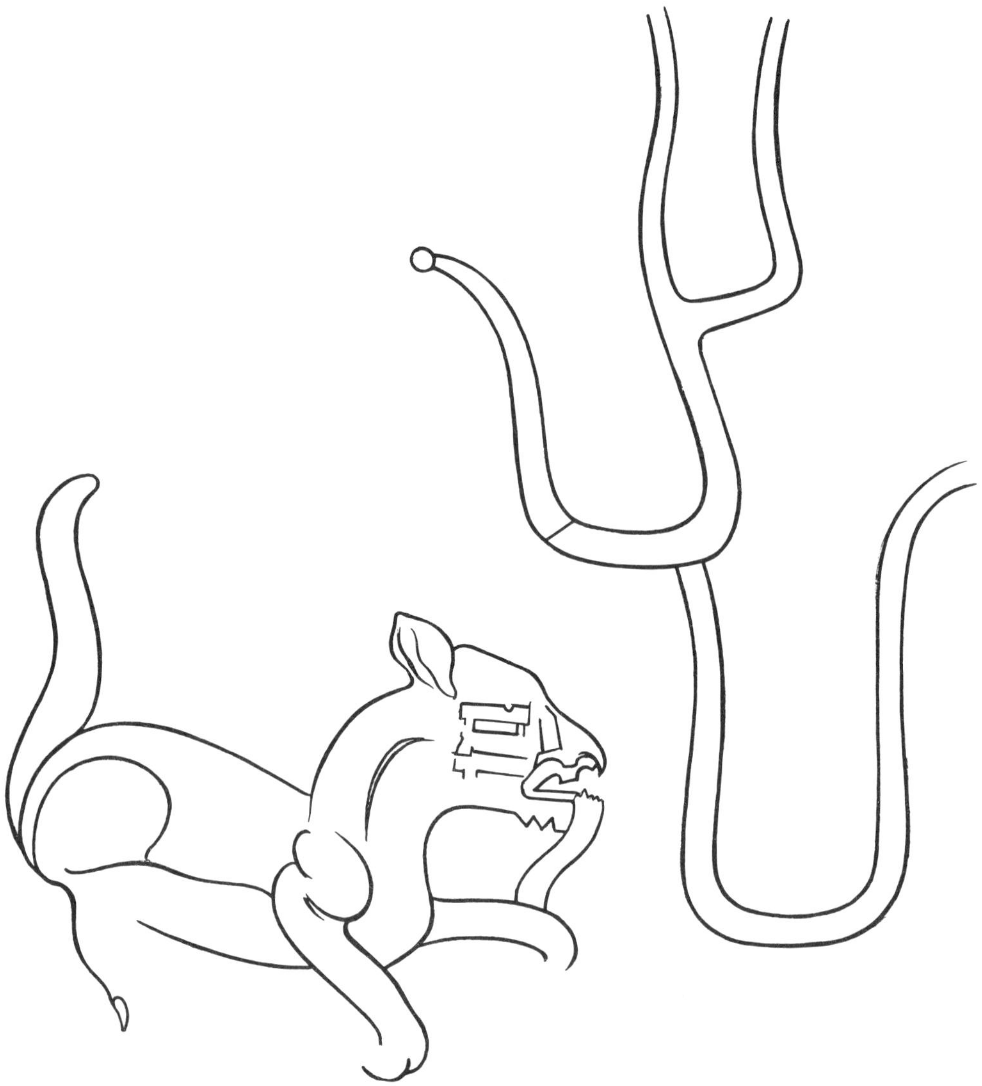

Figure 30. Relief Number III, Cerro de la Canterra, Morelos, Mexico.

Now back to Relief Number IV. The dead Moon could be represented as a human body or as the Moon spirit released from the body. The Moon's spirit had two forms of motion which made it a double spirit. As one, it was the spirit of the Moon's month cycle; as the other, it was the spirit of the Moon's year cycle. In the first, its life form was the full Moon; in the second, its life form was the new Moon.

In Relief Number IV, the two jaguars are the two forms of the Moon spirit. The St. Andrew's crosses in the cartouches, which form the eyes, properly symbolize their serpent natures as Sun-bearers, and their jaguar bodies identify them as the body spirits of the Moon.

Figure 31. Relief Number II, Cerro de la Canterra, Morelos, Mexico.

Figure 32. Jaguar God embryo, 4.75 inches in height, serpentine.

The Mountain God of Chalcatzingo

In Relief Number IV, the larger size of the top jaguar, the plant sign on the cartouche forming the eye, and the u-sign which forms his ear, mark him as the spirit of the Moon's month cycle and the full Moon. The bottom jaguar is the new Moon spirit, and the two lifeless human bodies are the full Moon and the new Moon which will embody them in life.

The jaguars are apparently attacking the human figures. The action represents the combining of the jaguar and human forms into the shape of the Olmec Jaguar God. It portrays the action of Tezcatlipoca who, when his being as the first Sun was destroyed, was transformed into a jaguar which devoured the giants who then inhabited the world.

Relief Number IV symbolizes the life which was immanent in the body of the dead Moon and has the same symbolic meaning as that of the prostrate God C with the *bil* sign of the Moon's divinity as vegetation in his headdress.

The succession of the gods changes in direction and order in Relief Number II. The change denotes the start of the life cycle of the Moon as the gods form its motion. The figures in Relief Number II proceed from Relief Number III, which is carved as a jaguar with a branching plant. If we first identify those figures in relation to the gods in the Temple of the Sun tablet, we will see how the Relief Number III jaguar corresponds to the earth Itzam Na.

The succession of the gods in Relief Number II begins on the right with two addorsed figures. There is a mask on the face of the fetal Jaguar God, and the headdress is marked with a St. Andrew's cross. The reclining figure against his back wears a pointed beard fastened to his chin, and his wrists are bound. He appears to be dead, but his phallus is in erection.

For the purpose of our consideration, we will designate the fetal Jaguar God as figure Number 1, and the reclining figure facing left as Number 2. Left signifies the life side of the Moon cycle, and right is the death side. The figures are the gods of the stages of the Moon's life cycle, as we shall see. Therefore, the next figure in the succession is the one at the end moving toward the left. We will designate him as Number 3, the first center figure on his right as Number 4, and the second center figure as Number 5.

All but the two addorsed figures wear dome-shaped helmets and masks. The helmets are decorated with identifying marks and each has an individual plumelike device on the front. The helmets of Numbers 3 and 5 are marked with St. Andrew's crosses. The headdress of the fetal Jaguar God and reclining figure are not distinguished, but show a device which is sickle-shaped and extends upward over the forehead of the reclining figure. The device and position of the two figures show that they are actually one.

The devices on the headdresses of the god on the left and the two in the center are symbolic abstractions of maize plants. The plume in the helmet of the figure on the left (Number 3) is the maize sprout; the one worn by the first center figure (Number 4) is a maize tassel and represents the grown plant in blossom; and the plume on the helmet of Number 5 has three pointed dots which spray from the base and which represent grains of maize. The plume properly represents ripened maize. The headdresses represent the jaguar mountain and that of Number 5 is decorated with jaguar fang and pendant brow symbols [**Figure 33**], thereby identifying the

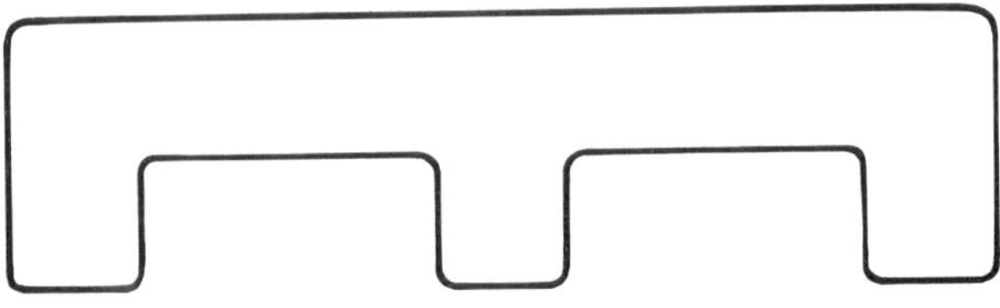

Figure 33. Pendant brow symbol.

figures as aspects of the Jaguar God. In his divinity as maize, the Jaguar God was the Moon; the three gods are the first-quarter, full, and third-quarter stages of the Moon.

Turning to the sickle-shaped device on the headdress which joins the jaguar dwarf and the reclining figure, we note that it is the shape of the crescent new Moon. Its Moon symbolism is supplemented by the beard of the reclining figure, which marks him as a god of vegetation. The St. Andrew's cross in the cartouche that fastens the device to the headdress is the sign of the Moon spirit as the Sun-bearer, and the jaguar is the animal form of the Moon spirit.

The death state of the reclining figure is indicated by the supine position of the body and by the rope binding the wrists. The rope has the symbolism of the rope that bound the warrior to the stone while the jaguar knight killed him in the sacrifice combat in the ritual of Tlacaxipeualiztli Feast. The fetal image of the Jaguar God is his Moon spirit aspect, and the union of the Jaguar with the reclining figure represents the transfusion of life to the dead body. The revival is signified by the phallic erection. The addorsed figures are the Sun and the new Moon.

Now, when we view the reliefs in relation to the tablet in the Temple of the Sun, we see that the two jaguars with the lifeless human bodies in Relief Number IV represent the stage of the new Moon represented by the prostrate God C. In Number II, the addorsed Moon spirit and the Moon God correspond to the Sun God and 7-Jaguar; the figure moving towards the left and carrying the maize stalk and the rising God C correspond; and the two gods in the center are antecedent forms of Pacal and Chan Bahlum.

Relief Number III is the jaguar with the branching plant. In the cyclical succession, the figures in Number II proceed from him, as the Sun God, 7-Jaguar, God C, Pacal, and Chan Bahlum proceed from the jaguar mask of the earth Itzam Na. Where the Relief Number III jaguar is associated with a branching plant, Itzam Na wears a *bil* in his headdress. The symbolism of the serpent heads at the ends of the cosmogonic band which supports Itzam

Na's mask is expressed by the St. Andrew's cross in the headdresses of the gods in Relief Number II. The crosses signify that the figures incarnate the serpent Moon spirit. The cross is missing on the left center figure which corresponds to Pacal. We may surmise that, like Pacal, the figure is the personification of the serpent spirit itself.

The serpent nature of the gods as incarnations of the Moon spirit and as the Moon spirit itself is signified by the masks on the two central figures and the fetal jaguar. While the animal shapes of the masks are obscure, Carlo Gay believes them to be stylized representations of serpent heads. The ophidian symbolism is consistent with the serpent nature of the Jaguar God.

When the Moon died, the Moon spirit began the Moon cycle as the new Moon and, as it moved through the cycle, its corporeal form was the Moon's changing body. The spirit, being incarnate, was the Moon itself and was represented in human form instead of in its animal spirit form.

The two gods in the center with the paddle staves constitute the full Moon. As the full Moon, they are at the turning points from life to death. Their counterparts in Palenque — Pacal and Chan Bahlum — go to their full Moon death as the world-man in the Temple of the Inscriptions. When they die, they are united to the Moon Goddess. In the succession of Chalcatzingo reliefs, Number X records the death of the Moon represented by the two gods; the union with the Moon Goddess is symbolized by the paddle staves which they are raising before them.

Let us consider the nature of the symbolism. Students identify the staves as war clubs, but war clubs are inconsistent with the context of the reliefs. The rituals of the Aztec Feast of Toxcatl and the reliefs in the temples of Palenque record the religious mythology of pre-Columbian culture which certainly dates back to the Olmec times. In the rituals of Toxcatl, the Moon and the planet Venus carrying the Sun were portrayed as the gods Tezcatlipoca and Ixteucale. When Tezcatlipoca was married to the Earth Goddess and sacrificed with Ixteucale on the pyramid, priests danced carrying staves. Each staff had a feather cup and ball at its base, and as they danced, the priests made circles with their staves and struck them on the ground. The action pantomimed the creation of the Sun as it was described in the myth of the birth of Huitzilopochtli, the Sun God.

To recall the myth: the Earth Goddess, Coatlicue, was sweeping out her temple when she found a feather ball. She picked it up and tucked it in the bosom of her dress, upon which, she gave birth to Huitzilopochtli. The feather ball was a mystical image for Tezcatlipoca as the solar Moon and the cup symbolized the earth. The myth is a metaphorical description of the union of Coatlicue with Tezcatlipoca and the consequent birth of the Sun.

In the imagery of the doctrine of the myth, the Morning Star and the Moon combined and were transformed into a serpent which rose from the earth transformed into the Sun. In the ceremonies of Toxcatl, Ixteucale was the Morning Star and Tezcatlipoca was the Moon. Their combining was performed in their sacrifices and their serpent transformation by the raising of the "serpent bench" to the top of the pyramid. Tezcatlipoca's marriage before his sacrifice portrayed his mythical union with Coatlicue.

A dance performed at the time of the sacrifices, called a "serpent dance," not only portrayed that union but the transformation of Ixteucale and Tezcatlipoca into a serpent and the bisexual nature of the Sun. The union was danced by the priests when they struck their feather-ball staves on the earth as they moved them in circles. The joint nature was danced by girls who were bedecked in garlands of maize tassels and leaped upward with their arms above their heads to simulate an embrace with Huitzilopochtli.

Before we return to a consideration of Relief Number II, we should note that this same theme is portrayed in the reliefs in the Temple of the Inscriptions at Palenque. Those reliefs portray the Morning Star immanent in the god-king Pacal, the Moon in the person of the ruler Chan Bahlum, the Earth Goddess in the ruler's mother and wife Zak-Kuk, and the serpent coming above from within the earth.

In this light we can view Relief Number II. The paddle ends of the staves are vulvate in shape and the staves themselves are phallic in shape. The figures holding them wear serpent masks; the two figures on the right (at the beginning of the sequence) are obviously phallic, and the following figures portray the sprouting, ripening, and harvesting of corn.

The economy was agricultural and the staple was maize. The religion could hardly have been other than that of the subsequent pre-Columbian cultures. We can, therefore, confidently conclude that the paddle-shaped staves are not war clubs, and that Relief Number II pictures the creation of the final process of time creation manifest as the Sun.

The end of the process was the coming on earth of the Sun bringing life. This end is recorded in the next Relief, Number X, which we will now examine.

Relief Number X [**Figure 34**], carved at the summit of the Cerro de la Canterra, pictures a face with goggle eyes and a headdress shaped to form an ogee curve with a peak at the center. Above the peak is a left hand with a jade bracelet on the wrist.

As we have seen earlier, jade was the earth substance which was believed to form into maize, and the hand was a sign of sacrifice. The hand, therefore, symbolizes the solar Moon rising out of the underworld bringing a sustaining crop of maize.

The line of the headdress across the forehead is the same as the line of the headdress across the forehead of the Las Limas idol. The line represents the two serpents that were represented as the eyes of the two jaguars in Relief Number IV.

In the Temple of the Inscriptions, Pacal and Chan Bahlum combined with the Moon Goddess and came on earth as one.

We may conclude that the ogee curve of the headdress on the face of the god at the top of the mountain symbolizes the release from the hand of death of the two gods with their paddle staves, combined with the Moon Goddess as one.

Figure 34. Relief Number X, Cerro de la Canterra, Morelos, Mexico.

The reliefs make it apparent that the Olmecs worshiped the Cerro de la Canterra as the mountain body of the Jaguar God coming on earth each year bringing new life to their fields.

The Great Goddess of southwest Asia was a mountain and her image was a conical stone. As Ereshkigal in Sumer, she was called "Lady of the Mountain." In Egypt, as Hathor, she was pictured as a mountain with a tomb in the center representing the underworld of the dead. As Sumerian Ninlil, her consort Enlil was a mountain who raped her and begot the four Moons of the Moon's cycle. In Syria, as Ishtar, she was raped by the mountain Pishaisha. In Palenque, the pyramids which supported the temples were iconic replicas of the god mountain. The Sumerians raised images of their Mountain Gods as ziggurats. The Egyptians built them as stone pyramids and Scythians made them as pyramids of brush.

CHAPTER 30

La Venta North: The Court of the Sepulcher

1100 through 400 B.C.

The Olmec center of La Venta constitutes the fullest expression of the Eurasian heritage. Built as a religious center on a small island in a swamp, the location symbolized the creation of the world. Mesoamerican doctrine held that the world came into existence when the earth appeared as reeds in primordial waters, and rose from the waters as a mound on which life formed as an earth monster. The earth monster generated the elements of the universe. La Venta was constructed as a workshop for the Olmec Supreme God where, as the Sun of Movement, he continually created cycles of time and life.

The god's seat in the center was constructed as a pyramid in the shape of a volcano. The pyramid was a replica of the god's mountain body and its volcano shape embodied the god's mountain body. The volcano shape also embodied the god's jaguar form as the life fire of the Fifth Sun. The pyramid faced north on an axis running 8° west of north. The area on the north side was the place where the god, in his movement as the Sun, created the cycles of life which he brought on earth. The axis of the pyramid formed the centerline of this area.

There is a rectangular court in front of the pyramid [**Figure 35**] which is enclosed by a long mound on each side and two platforms at the northeast and northwest corners. At the north end in the center, between the two mounds is a small mound which was once a platform mound. The two platforms formed the south entrance to a smaller oblong court, 188 feet across in the east-west direction and 135 feet across in the north-south

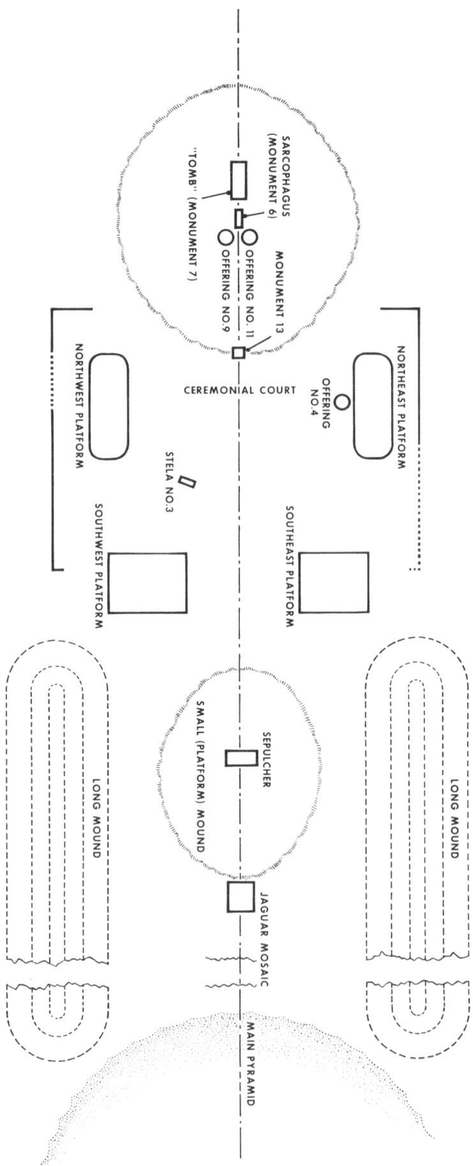

Figure 35. Plan of La Venta sepulcher and ceremonial courts.

direction. The two sides and end corners of this smaller ceremonial court were formed by a palisade of columnar basalt buried in the earth so that only the tops of the columns showed. A circular mound closed the court at the north end and there was a platform mound in the center. The corner and center mounds formed a quincunx, the sign of the Moon-serpent Sun-bearer.

Basalt is an igneous rock which is often found in columnar strata. The columns were brought from a considerable distance, the nearest place where they could have been quarried was approximately 75 miles away in the volcanic mountain on the coast. Some columns were almost 8 feet in length with diameters of 17 inches, so the labor of transportation was prodigious and, because it was performed, the columns must have had a very sacred character. The volcanic nature of the Jaguar God's being enables us to appreciate the significance of the palisade.

In the Supreme Jaguar's being as the universe, he was a mountain in which the interior was the underworld. The basalt columns were a part of his volcanic mountain being which the La Ventans set in the earth around the perimeter of the court in order to represent him in his mountain underworld. The columns were particularly appropriate for this purpose. Poles were traditionally set in the earth to constitute a path by which a god spirit could descend to or return from the underworld. The Supreme Jaguar as the earth and sky was the frame of the universe. The columns were set vertically and in contact with the ones on either side such that they not only formed a mountain wall, but provided passages through which the god could extend himself to fill the frame. The buried columns made the ceremonial court (as this court is called) an abstract idol of the Supreme Jaguar in his underworld aspect as the world mountain. Thus the columns reveal the symbolic character of the area north of the main pyramid.

The iconography of Itzam Na gives verification of this conception of the ceremonial court and the basalt columns. Itzam Na inherited the Supreme Jaguar's universe nature — the sign of his being as the universe was an

oblong shield framed by a border of contiguous oblong signs denoting his celestial and earth aspects such as the Sun, Venus, fire-serpents, and vegetation [Figures 13 and 14]. The shield has the same rectangular shape as the ceremonial court and the signs in the border were derived from the spirit godheads of the Supreme Jaguar, which lodged in the basalt piles and formed a cosmic frame around the court.

In the iconography of Itzam Na, the shield constituted a frame within which he was represented in his different aspects. The monuments in the ceremonial court are idols of the Supreme Jaguar in his different aspects. The monuments show that the shield and the ceremonial court each represented the universe in the same way; they differed only in size, material, style, and construction. The ceremonial court was a huge open-air temple in which the Supreme Jaguar lodged, just as the later Maya temples were the dwelling places and therefore the idols of Itzam Na.

The platforms and mounds served as stations in the combined movement of the Moon and Sun, and idols and offerings were buried at the stations as way places along the underworld road. They were first laid out and constructed with the pyramid circa 1100 B.C., and La Venta served as a religious center for some 700 years thereafter. During that time, the site was reconstructed three times; in the course of each reconstruction, new offerings and idols were buried. Many of the buried idols were figures in human or semihuman form, but a great number were in the form of celts which were arranged in different orders and numbers.

While a celt, as such, does not have the appearance of a god, if we consider the symbolic nature of a celt as signifying sacrifice and remember that the Jaguar God was immanent in the boulders at the base of the Cerro de la Canterra, it will be apparent that the celts were in fact idols. In all the Mesoamerican cultures, maize was divine. The Aztecs identified it with the Sun God Huitzilopochtli who was begotten by the Moon (Tezcatlipoca) and the Earth Mother-Moon Goddess (Coatlicue). Maize was the life which the Sun of each year brought on earth, the Fifth Sun in its aspect as the Maize

God, and the offspring to which the Earth Mother gave birth each year. The Earth Mother was Goddess of Death and the embryo Maize God in her womb was a stone. Certain rocks, mainly jadite and serpentine, because of their color, were believed to be embryonic maize, and the Olmecs carved them in the shape of fetuses of their human-Jaguar God.

The stone, at least in the form which identified it with the divinity of the Fifth Sun, became the lodging place of the god. In the shape of a celt, the stone was a sacrificial ax — the sign of resurrection and the coming of a new crop of maize on earth. The carved stone had the meaning to the Olmecs that the cross has in Christianity — but where the cross is a *symbol* of the Christian religion, the celt carved to form the image of the Jaguar was an *idol* to the Olmecs.

The features of the courts and buried idols in La Venta do not convey any meaning in themselves; but when we view the pyramid and its related features in the light of the Eurasian Great Goddess religion reflected backward in time by the later Mesoamerican cultures, their essential meaning becomes clear. In this light, the divinity tables of the Maya codices and the temples of Palenque are particularly revealing.

In the underworld setting of the stage at La Venta, on the centerline of the larger court immediately in front of the pyramid at its north end, a sepulcher containing 28 jade celts and 9 serpentine celts was buried in a mound. The contents included pottery, quite a number of beads, and other mortuary offerings. A stone mosaic forming a jaguar mask (shown in Chapter 31) was set in the floor of the court close to the mound on its south and pyramid side. The mosaic was also laid over the centerline.

The character of the celts as idols is the key to understanding the symbolism of this tomb. To the Mesoamerican ancients, the Moon was a manifestation of the Supreme Jaguar moving as time. In the underworld, his lunar motion created the life which came on earth. We know from our study of the Eurasian origin of the Mesoamerican calendar that the motion of the Moon was a combination of the 28 gods who formed its changing shape. In addition, the life which it created was formed by nine gods who were known as the Lords of the Night and who, in combination, were the Moon God Tezcatlipoca. The jaguar mask surely represented the Jaguar God as a creator, and celts as gods of his movement as time.

Except for possibly a few, there are no markings on the celts buried in the courts at La Venta to identify them as individual gods by name; but in Aztec times, the Lords of the Day were identified by numbers. The placement of the celts at La Venta generally would have permitted similar identification. The number of celts in a group, therefore, serves to identify the gods whose idols they were. The differentiation between the 28 and 9 celts enables us to say from their numbers that, when the Olmec builders of La Venta placed the jade and serpentine celts in a sepulcher, they counted the 28 as the gods of the month cycle of the solar Moon and the 9 as the gods of the days of life created by the motion of the solar Moon.

This identification is proven by the celts buried in the Ceremonial Court under the monument designated as Number 10.* In this monument, the celts were found in groups of 7, 9, 13, 6, and 3. By these numbers, the first three groups — 7, 9, and 13 — are idols of the Olmec antecedents of the gods of the calendar which we referred to in Chapter 27 as the Lords of the Earth, the Lords of the Night, and the Lords of the Day. The group of 6 and 3 are certainly idols of the antecedent gods whose images were carved on the tablet in the Temple of the Sun and on piers b and c in the Temple of the Inscriptions at Palenque. We will consider them later. The association of the numbers is proof that they were gods of the combined diurnal movements of the Moon and Sun.

What is especially significant is the association of the 28 celts with the 9 in the sepulcher in the large court on the north of the pyramid, and the association of 7 and 13 with the 9 in Monument Number 10. As calendrical gods, they could only have been gods in the pre-world of nonexistence of the Eurasian planetary doctrine; because, mathematically, it

*Page 387, below.

would have been impossible for them to have been days of created life — either in the underworld, or on earth — and have created or constituted the yearly cycles of Mesoamerican life.

In the Mesoamerican calendar, the divisions of the days of the creation cycle were: 260; 2,920; 18,980; and 37,960. None of these numbers are divisible by all the numbers 7, 9, and 13. The days in the cycles of created life were numerically divided into groups of 9, 20, 360, and 5; groups not divisible by 7 or 13. The numbers were the numbers of the gods in the Eurasian planetary creation cycles and, as the numbers of the gods represented by the idols in the La Venta courts, identify the idols with the Eurasian planetary gods. With the group of 9, they are the gods of the 9-year cycle of creation whose count was recorded in the divinatory tables in the Maya codices as the 819-day count, and as the 7–28–364 day count in the *Dresden Codex.* In this combination, the planetary Moon spirit would necessarily have been Mercury and, as we have seen, the serpent Moon spirit who was known as Quetzalcoatl in later cultures, had an identity with Mercury.

This enables us to read the meaning of the jaguar mosaic and the celts buried in the sepulcher under the mound. The jaguar mosaic is the planetary Moon spirit and Sun-bearer. The mound is his mountain body as the Moon. The sepulcher within the mound, like the tomb in the mountain image of Hathor, represents the underworld region of nonexistence beyond the borders of the created world.

The 28 gods were the Moon incarnations of the Moon spirit as it moved in its cycle of life creation. The Moon spirit was the new Moon in the death state of nonexistence and the celts were idols of the nonexistent bodies of its motion. The symbolism is an abstract expression of the Jaguar God as the power of creation in the darkness that was before the beginning of the world.

We should note here that the sepulcher is a feature of the last construction phase of the pyramid complex which began, presumably, some

centuries after La Venta was first laid out. This does not change the symbolic nature of the court — the island in the swamp on which La Venta was built was itself the roof over the otherworld region in which new worlds were created.

CHAPTER 31

La Venta North: The Ceremonial Court

1100 through 400 B.C.

The axis along the centerline of the first court continues along through the center of the Ceremonial Court adjacent to it on the north. The gods of the combined motion of the Moon and Sun formed as a world-man in the platform mound stations at the southeast, northeast, and southwest corners of the court in order to come into existence in a single death. These stations are directionally related to the Temples of the Foliated Cross, the Cross, and the Sun at Palenque. An opening at the north end of the court between the northeast and northwest platforms was closed on the outside by a pyramid mound across the centerline. This pyramid or mound was the station at which the gods died in their world-man image and came into existence in the underworld of the created world.

The Southeast Platform

In the southeast corner of the court, they formed the world-man as the inchoate Moon. Celts were laid under the southeast platform in a pattern forming a kan cross, with five in each arm. The cross was set over a jaguar mosaic. A hematite mirror was placed in the center of the cross. While the significance of their number is not clear, here, as in the sepulcher, the celts must have represented the gods of the joint motion of the Moon and Sun. The cross is the key to the meaning of their arrangement in relation to the jaguar mosaic. As we have seen, the kan cross was a sign of the divine nature of the Fifth Sun as vegetation. In the Temple of the Foliated Cross, it formed the root from which a maize tree grew out of the head of the earth

Itzam Na. In the head of the earth Itzam Na, the divinity of the Moon formed the maize and the divinity of the Sun gave it life. (The symbols of Olmec iconography are generally so much the same as those of the later cultures that we may be sure the kan cross in the southeast platform has the same meaning as the kan cross in the Temple of the Foliated Cross.) In their arrangement as a cross, the celts represent the Moon. The jaguar mosaic represents the planetary Moon spirit with the Sun. The Moon and the jaguar spirit are in union; but the placement of the celts on the mosaic means that the life spirit of the Moon is bound by death and the Moon is dead. The tablet in the Temple of the Foliated Cross portrays the death state of the Moon in which the gods began forming in their world-man image. Pacal, the Moon spirit, is pictured on the right or death side of the maize tree of life, while Chan Bahlum, the Moon, is on the left and life side. The relative positions mean that Pacal as the life spirit is bound in death and the life signified by Chan Bahlum's place on the left is only potential. In the vertical arrangement, the death side is above the life side, as we shall see in the southwest platform.

The mirror symbolizes the forces of creation. The mirror was a symbol of the planetary doctrine and probably was adopted when the Sumerians charted the zodiac by the constellations which rose at sunset when the Moon was new. In making their observations, the astronomer-priests recognized that the Moon and Sun were then in conjunction and that, in their relative motions, when the Moon became full, the two bodies were in opposition. Since they imagined that at conjunction the Moon was dead and that the Moon spirit had cast off his dead Moon body, they pictured the new Moon as the Moon spirit renewing its Moon body. The renewal was an act of creation which was performed in death. Death and life are opposites. The full Moon which grew from the new Moon was its opposite and the new Moon came to be regarded as the mirror of the life which it created.

Tezcatlipoca's mirror foot is a graphic expression of this concept. His mirror foot was pictured synonymously as the serpent image of the Moon

spirit. In the center of the kan cross, the mirror combines the celts and the mosaic into the incipient resurrection of the Moon; thus the celts laid on the jaguar mosaic symbolize the state of the Moon in death.

The Northeast Platform

The next station in the formation of the world-man was the northeast platform. A group of figurines and celts was buried just west of the platform. The group, designated as Offering Number 4, consisted of 16 figurines and 6 celts, making 22 in all. The figurines were of standing human forms with jaguar characteristics, and they were grouped with the celts as though all were assembled to watch some special event or some important ritual. All the celts were jade. Two of the figurines were jade, and the rest were serpentine, except one which was a conglomerate of granitic sand [**Figure 36**].

The celts were set upright with the bits at the top, standing in a row on one side of the group. The conglomerate figure was placed standing near the center of the row with his back to one of the celts and facing the other figurines, thus placing him at the center of interest. There was another figurine whose position and composition also made him a center of interest. This figurine was bright green jade mottled with black — its place in relation to the conglomerate figurine coupled the two as a pair.

The conglomerate figurine fits the character of the Moon. While the surface of the stone in which it had been carved had deteriorated, it had originally been smooth and polished. The original color was dark buff, the sandy color of earth with which the Mesoamerican Moon had a theistic identity. The bright green jade of the companion figurine gives him the character of the Moon spirit.

The other jade figurine was light gray in color with a slight blue tinge which distinguished it from the bright green of the first jade figurine. The light gray figurine was placed facing the bright green figurine on the opposite side of the conglomerate figurine.

Figure 36. Offering Number 4, La Venta [photograph courtesy of Smithsonian Institution].

La Venta North: Ceremonial Court

Out of the context of the mysticism of the Ceremonial Court, the figures convey no meaning. But when we study them in relation to the place in the creation of a new cycle of world life, we see that they are gods gathered before the union in which they formed into a world-man as the new Moon.

The platform is in the northeast corner of the court, corresponding to the location of the Temple of the Cross in relation to the Temples of the Foliated Cross and the Sun at Palenque. In the Temple of the Cross, the gods of the Sun and Moon generated a new year of life.

North and east are the directions in which ancient peoples in Middle America believed that life was created and came into being.

The Nahuatlan creation myth sheds another light on the nature of the offering. The myth describes the beginning of life and movement of the Sun and Moon: all the gods assembled and stood watching in the four directions for the rising of the Sun and Moon. When the Sun and Moon had risen, the Wind God set them in motion. From immemorial times, going back to when the hunters began to formulate religion, the northeast was regarded as the beginning point of life.

The figurines were grouped in an assembly facing in four directions. Their buried place to the west of the platform suggests that they were assembled to watch for the rising of the Sun and Moon as the beginning of life. The west was the region of death; northeast was the point of direction in which the Sun rises in summer when life has returned to the earth.

In this light, let us consider the nature of the celts and the three distinctive figurines. Leaving aside the figurines for the moment and turning to the celts, their number was six. This is the number of the gods who constituted the life stages of the Moon's month cycle. In the Temple of the Sun at Palenque, they were God C as the dying Moon, the Sun God, 7-Jaguar, the rising God C, Pacal, and Chan Bahlum. While the gods in the Temple of the Sun were gods in being — forming as a world-man in the underworld as a prelude to coming on earth — if we turn back to the *Epic of Gilgamesh*, we find that Enkidu and Gilgamesh were the gods of the six stages of the Moon's month cycle who formed as the world-man in the nonworld before the beginning. They were the planetary gods: Saturn, Sun, Moon, Mars, Mercury, and Jupiter.

Returning now to the three figurines, we should bear in mind that the divinity of the Moon was composed of three spirit forms — the Moon God, the Moon Goddess, and their joint corporeal spirit. The Moon in death was transformed into the three spirits who recombined as the new Moon. The composition of the second jade figurine relates it to the first and, since the Moon spirits were of the same divinity, the second must be the goddess spirit. Thus the three figurines constitute the gods of the death stages of the Moon's cycle and the new Moon. Together with the six celts, they are the gods of the month cycle of the Moon.

The life and death sides of the cycle are distinguished by the difference in the iconic forms of the idols. The jade which composed the celts constituted the life divinity of the Moon. Each god was the life of the Moon for a stage which ended in death and the beginning of a new stage. As axes they were gods of sacrifice and their placement with the bits up signified diurnal deaths and resurrections. The arrangement of the celts is a plastic representation of the planetary cycle.

The other figurines numbered 13. Their number identifies them with the 13 new Moon forms of the Moon spirit in which his movement created the year cycles of the Moon.

Thus we see that Offering Number 4 is the station in which the gods gathered in a union for the creation of a new span of earthly life constituted as the body of the new Moon. It is the stage represented by the Temple of the Cross.

La Venta North: Ceremonial Court

The Southwest Platform

The course of creation as it was set by the four temples at Palenque led from the Temple of the Cross in the northeast, to the Temple of the Sun in the southwest. The buried idols in the Ceremonial Court show that the next station in the court was the platform in the southwest corner. The idols buried under the southwest platform and related to it show the gods forming in the world-man image of the new Moon. To see why they do, we must review the portrayal of gods forming as the world-man image of the new Moon and their single death which followed in the Temples of the Sun and the Inscriptions.

The tablet in the Temple of the Sun portrays the Mesoamerican gods of the Moon cycle forming as the new Moon. There the Moon God is shown forming in the underworld, first as the dying God C, then as the Sun God and 7-Jaguar, and then coming to the border of the life region above, forming as the rising God C. In the above, the Moon appears embodied as the planetary spirit Pacal and then as the full Moon Chan Bahlum.

Four idols were buried in the southwest corner of the Ceremonial Court. One was a small, kneeling, headless statue. Two were under the platform. They were combined as though they were a two-fold god like the addorsed spirit jaguar and Moon God in Relief Number II on the mountain at Chalcatzingo. One was a jaguar mosaic like the one under the southeast platform; it was set on top of the other, which was constructed as a series of 28 layers of stones laid in rows and set in clay. The stones were, for the most part, serpentine and were carefully arranged in each layer. The fourth was a kneeling figure holding a metate.

When the significance of the jaguar mosaic and the 28 layers of serpentine and other stones is understood, the relation of the kneeling headless figure and the figure with the metate to the two God C's in the Sun Temple tablet appears very clearly. The mosaic was the same as the one associated with the sepulcher in the first court and, as noted, the one in the southeast platform; it is the planetary Moon spirit with the Sun [**Figure 37**]. The block of 28 layers of stone rows is certainly an abstract image of the Jaguar God as the Moon. It is, in effect, a platform mound beneath the platform which covered it and fixed its location in the underworld of the nonworld.

The block of stones represents the mountain which was the death shape of the Moon. The physical composition of the stones symbolizes the life which is locked in the death of the Moon mountain, and the 28 layers symbolize the cyclical motion of the Moon in its monthly course of life creation.

The relative position of the mosaic to the Moon idol is the reverse of that in the southeast platform. The reversal means that the spirit is on the life side of the Moon cycle and the body of the Moon is on the death side. The spirit is, therefore, released from the bonds of death and is infusing life into the dead body of the Moon. The symbolism is the same as that of the addorsed jaguar and the Moon in the Chalcatzingo relief.

The burial of the four idols represents the underworld where the life first forms as the waxing new Moon. The world of prelife above is the floor of the Ceremonial Court. As we have noted, there is a circular mound which closed the opening between the northeast and northwest platforms. A monument designated as Stela 3 stood at the center of a line between the southwest platform and the mound. Idols of the gods of the planetary Moon spirit and the full Moon were carved in the stela. The stela was fashioned from a large stone block, 14 feet high, rounded at the top, and set vertically in the ground facing north [**Figure 38**].

Two human figures are carved standing in front of an arch on a ledge facing each other. The one on the left wears a high fantastic headdress, the one on the right has an aquiline nose and a pointed beard which looks false; archaeologists call him "Uncle Sam." His headdress is a large fish. Human forms appear around and above the two figures, seemingly floating. Some wear beards similar to Uncle Sam's.

La Venta North: Ceremonial Court

Figure 37. Jaguar Mosaic, La Venta [photograph courtesy of Smithsonian Institution].

Figure 38. Stela 3, La Venta [photograph courtesy of Smithsonian Institution].

La Venta North: Ceremonial Court

The headdress — of a fish — on the figure on the right identifies the Uncle Sam figure as the Moon God. In Eurasian religious imagery, the fish was an embryo body of the Sun, which is to say, a Moon. The ancients of Mesoamerica adopted this solar Moon image. The *Popul Vuh* tells how the Lords of Xibalba sacrificed the two boys, Xbalanque and Hunahpu, and threw their ground-up bones in the river. After 5 days, Hunahpu and Xbalanque appeared in the water as fish-men and then rose transformed into the Sun and Moon. Xbalanque was the jaguar Moon spirit and, hence, the Morning Star.

The beard also identifies the figure as the Moon. In Relief Number II at Chalcatzingo, the Moon figure has a beard. In Asia, hair growing on a god symbolized the growth of vegetation and identified the nature of his divinity.

The relative positions of the two figures are the same as those of Pacal and Chan Bahlum, and prove the identity of the figure on the left as the planetary Moon spirit. The structure of his headdress cannot be surely identified; it is probably ornamented with maize kernels. Maize was associated with the planetary Moon spirit as the Morning Star because the star brought the Sun which brought the maize.

The two figures are carved as portraits. Although the facial features of the Moon spirit (on the left) have been destroyed, those of the Moon figure are so individual and different from the features which mark the Jaguar God that they must compose a portrait of the ruler. Similarly, the bodily features and attire of the planetary Moon spirit are those of a living person dressed in the manner of nobility. While the bodily and clothing features of the Moon figure have been destroyed, it may be presumed that he is similarly represented.

As portraits, they represent rulers of La Venta, but since La Venta endured for centuries and must have had a long succession of rulers, they must represent a dynasty such as the dynasty of Pacal. The founder of the dynasty would have been the incarnation of the Moon spirit which was

immortal, and the successors would have been his incarnation as the Moon which was mortal and which constituted the life body of the spirit.

According to Stirling, Stela 3 represents the open jaws of a jaguar. The ledge on which the two gods stand is the lower jaw and they are, therefore, inside the Jaguar God's mountain form. Being gods of the full Moon, they stand in the jaws of the death which was the next stage of the Moon cycle and the resurrection of the world-man.

At La Venta, another idol was found in association with the southwest corner of the Ceremonial Court. It had been moved and left by loggers who had been unable to carry it away, so exactly where it stood is not known. The idol has been designated as Stela 1 and it represents a goddess standing in the open jaws of the Jaguar God. If it relates to the figures in the southwest corner, it corresponds to the skeletal and jaguar masks of Itzam Na on the tablet in the sanctuary of the Sun Temple at Palenque; in that relation, it would represent the Supreme Jaguar God and the place of emergence of the gods from the underworld of creation.

The record of the gods coming on earth as created life would properly begin with Stela 3 and continue with idols which follow. The key to the symbolism of Stela 3 can be found in the reliefs at Chalcatzingo. The reliefs associated with Relief Number I at Chalcatzingo show the spirit forms of the Jaguar God descending in death from the back of the cave which forms the open jaws of the Jaguar God. The figures circling around and above the heads of the two gods in Stela 3 are surely the spirit forms of the two gods moving in the death cycle of the Moon.

Although much of the top of the stela has been destroyed or is badly weathered so that the figures cannot be fully identified, the body parts of seven full figures can be distinguished. Two of them resemble the addorsed fetal jaguar spirit and Moon God in Relief Number II at Chalcatzingo [Figure 31]. They are the two floating horizontally over the two in the center over the headdress of the Moon God in the stela. Four others can be easily recognized, but they have no identifying characteristics. The seventh, although hard to distinguish, is characterized by a face with a false beard to the right of the addorsed figures.

Since the addorsed figures must represent the Moon spirit as the Sun and the Moon God, all seven must be the gods of the Moon cycle. The positions of the figures suggests that they are swimming, although there is no sign to indicate water. But in the symbolism of resurrection from death, the sacrificed god had to pass through the waters of creation. In order to go to their joint death in the Temple of the Inscriptions, Pacal and Chan Bahlum had to cross the Otulum River. The belief that the new Moon was the manifestation of life creation as it can be deduced from the structure of the Ceremonial Court is comparable to the beliefs of the later Mayas as it is shown by the temples of Palenque. It also follows generally the same theme as the mythology of the Great Goddess in the ancient Middle East. In the Sumero-Babylonian *Epic of Gilgamesh*, Gilgamesh united with Ishtar as consort and crossed the waters of death with the new Moon spirit Urshanabi; when Hercules died as the Moon, Nessus, he swam the Evenus River with his Moon Goddess consort Deianeira; and in the sacrifice rites in later Aztec times, the prisoners who were to be sacrificed were ritually bathed.

The line from the southwest platform through Stela 3 joined the centerline of the axis at the base of the mound which closed the north opening to the Ceremonial Court. This point was on the south edge of the mound. A monument at that point — designated Monument 13 — is called the "Ambassador" because on it there is a relief of a bearded man holding what purports to be a flag attached to a short staff. The man is obviously in motion and an outline of a footprint behind him indicates that he is dancing. Logically the flag is a sacrificial banner such as the dancers carried in the dance of the "leap of the month of Toxcatl." The monument denotes the sacrificial death of the world-man.

An offering designated as Number 10 was buried on the centerline under the Ambassador [**Figure 39**]. This offering consisted of 38 celts

Figure 39. Offering Number 10, La Venta [photograph courtesy of Smithsonian Institution].

arranged so that they formed a Latin cross. The number of celts in each arm and in the center were different and formed five groupings. In the groupings, there were 9 in the east arm, 7 in the west arm, 3 in the north limb, 6 at the crossing in the center, and 13 in the south limb. The celts were all laid with the bits toward the north.

Offering Number 10 shows that the world-man died as the combined form of the planetary gods of the Eurasian Moon cycles. The groups of 7, 9, and 13 are readily recognized. The 6 at the crossing in the center correspond to the 6 which formed the world-man as the new Moon, and the 3 at the head of the cross in the north limb correspond to the Eurasian gods: Mercury, Jupiter, and Venus. In the epic, those gods were Gilgamesh, Enkidu, and Ishtar; in the Temple of the Inscriptions at Palenque, they are portrayed in the resurrection as Pacal, Chan Bahlum, and Lady Zak-Kuk.

The Sarcophagus and the Tomb

The mound which closed the opening on the north side of the Ceremonial Court was on the outside of the court. Originally it had been a low stepped pyramid platform. Buried within it along the projection of the centerline were two parallel arrangements of celts, one on each side and equidistant from it. These two groups of celts are designated as Offerings 9 and 11. Each consisted of a concave mirror and three rows of celts with bits toward the north. In each group, one celt formed one row and each of the other two rows were formed with four celts. Some cinnabar was placed behind the rows, i.e., toward the south, with a large number of scattered beads.

On the continuation of the centerline inside the mound, there was first a stone sarcophagus and then a rectangular enclosure which is thought to be a tomb. The sarcophagus — with carving to represent a jaguar — is of the size and shape to receive a body; jade earspools and other ornaments were in position as though they had been on a body, but the bones had disappeared.

The sides of the enclosure were formed with basalt columns set vertically in the manner in which the columns around the sides of the Ceremonial Court were set. The cover was also formed with basalt columns which were laid horizontally across the width of the enclosure. The remains of two sacrificed infants were found inside, along with jade ornaments, figurines, and other offerings.

The sarcophagus is designated as Monument 6 and the enclosure as Monument 7 [**Figure 40**].

When Enkidu died in the epic, Gilgamesh and Ishtar came into being in the underworld with the planetary gods. As it was metaphorically described in the epic, Gilgamesh ran about the steppe land for 7 days and 7 nights. Then he buried Enkidu and descended into the Abyss in search of Utnapishtim.

In the diffusion of the planetary doctrine, the seven gods became nine. The arrangement of celts in Offerings 9 and 11 shows that they were the idols of the nine planetary gods who came to be called the Lords of the Night in Mesoamerica. The direction of the bits and the mirror signify that they represented the gods in motion and that their motion was along the path of creation.

In the planetary doctrine, the movement of the planetary gods alternated between the formation of life and the daily stages of the Moon's motion. Each day a god moved through a full Moon cycle, forming a stage in the life of the year during daytime and a day in the cycle of life during the night. The diurnal alternation was from full Moon to new Moon, from Moon life to Moon death; hence, the new Moon was the planetary Moon spirit. In the parallel grouping of the celts in Offerings 9 and 11, one group represents the full Moon as the annual cycle of life, the other represents the new Moon as the movement of time. Since, in the doctrine, life was counted as daytime and days were counted as nights, the offerings have the symbolism of Gilgamesh on the steppe. The two groups represent the two gods in Stela 3 — one, the Moon God with the fish headdress; the other, the

Figure 40. Monuments 6 and 7, La Venta [photograph courtesy of Smithsonian Institution].

planetary Moon spirit.

Here the theme of the La Venta monuments seems to merge the theme of the epic into the theme of the Temple of the Inscriptions. The sarcophagus, carved as a jaguar idol, and the body which had lain within it were like the sarcophagus of the deceased Pacal with the idol of his life form carved on the lid. Offerings 9 and 11 are symbolic counterparts of the images of Pacal and Chan Bahlum portrayed descending to the tomb of the deceased Pacal on the piers of the temple.

The offerings mark the personage who had been buried within the sarcophagus as the Moon God whose image is carved on Stela 3 and who was, we may surmise, the founding ruler of a La Venta dynasty. The correspondence of this La Venta sarcophagus with Pacal's tomb in the Temple of the Inscriptions tells us that the body which had lain within it must have represented a dynasty of rulers, for surely, the relation of the sarcophagus and tomb to the monuments in the courts leading from the main pyramid would not be a single one-time ruler.

The basalt columns which formed the sides and top of the "tomb" contained the divinity of the Jaguar God as a volcanic mountain. The emblem of the Jaguar God carved on the sarcophagus and the human body which it had contained gave it the character of the Jaguar God. The relation of the sarcophagus to the "tomb" inside the pyramid combined the two monuments into the mountain image of the Jaguar God as the gateway from the underworld region of death and creation to the beginning of life. The sacrifice of the infants whose remains were in the "tomb" necessarily implies resurrection. Between the sarcophagus and the "tomb" were a number of basalt columns piled horizontally across the centerline suggesting a cosmogonic band. The band was a sign of the boundary between nonbeing and being, between death and life; it signifies the entrance of the infants into the underworld of created life.

The theology of the infant sacrifices is illustrated on the piers of the Temple of the Inscriptions. These show two infants as body spirits rising

in the person of the ruler bringing a new year of life on earth. Theologically, the sacrifice of the infants was a rite of passage in which the spirits of the two gods in Stela 3 passed through the jaguar mountain gateway out of the underworld region of death to the beginning of life. The monuments which mark the path of creation on the north side of the main pyramid end north of Monuments 7 and 6 as a row of three colossal heads. Between the colossal heads and the mound covering Monuments 7 and 6, the path is broken by an airstrip which was built when oil was discovered under the land around La Venta. Offerings 9 and 11 and the sarcophagus and "tomb" are idols of gods forming in the underworld as a world-man through whom they will come on earth bringing the life of the new year. In the construction of the airstrip, the monuments of the last stage of the world-man's development were displaced; logically they show the completion of the world-man image.

The monuments and offerings in the Court of the Sepulcher and the Ceremonial Court, when considered in light of the Temple of the Inscriptions at Palenque, show the earth underworld of creation because they show the annual cycle of life in which the gods were in being and which, as the motion of the Mercury Sun spirit and the Moon spirit, came on earth in the person of the ruler. Furthermore, they are all placed on the north of the main pyramid on a line running southeast-northwest, which was the direction of creation, as proven by the monument at Palenque and the placement of the reliefs at Chalcatzingo.

North was the direction of life and south the direction of death. There are a number of monuments on the south side of the main pyramid which can only be interpreted as showing an earlier creation that brought the gods into being. Such a creation shows that the Olmecs had adopted the Eurasian creation beliefs along with the planetary doctrine.

Since the airstrip construction breaks the physical connection between the Ceremonial Court and the displaced monuments with the colossal heads in its northerly extension, let us turn our attention to the south side of the

main pyramid. By doing so, we will be able to more easily understand the meaning of the colossal heads, since there is a similar head on the south.

CHAPTER 32

La Venta South

1100 through 400 B.C.

Altar 5, where the path of creation through the outer world begins on the south side of the main pyramid, faces west. It stands on the west side of a long mound which runs north and south. Behind it, on the other side of the mound with its back toward Altar 5 and facing east, is a similar altar. This second altar is designated Altar 4. The two are not known to be altars and are actually idols of the Jaguar God.

The front of west Altar 5 represents the cave mouth of a jaguar mountain which is formed as a niche in the center of the altar base flanked by stylized jaguar fangs [**Figure 41**]. The human aspect of the Jaguar God is carved as a seated man leaning forward out of the niche. He wears a helmet in the shape of a truncated cone which is decorated with the u-sign of the earth. Rain symbols are carved beneath the "u" and a band with a jaguar mask at the center and St. Andrew's crosses on either side encircles the base of the helmet crown.

The helmet shows other markings which are too eroded to identify or the meanings of which are obscure. A gorget, which is probably a mirror, is fastened to a collar around his neck and shoulders. His arms are bent at the elbows and extended; in the cradle of his forearms and hands, he holds a dead infant child — in the same way that the Las Limas Supreme Jaguar holds the dead infant.

Seated tailor fashion in the cave mouth of the jaguar mountain, he is a composite of the Las Limas and Cerro de la Canterra Relief Number I images of the Olmec Jaguar God.

Figure 41. Altar 5, La Venta [photograph courtesy of National Geographic Society].

Reliefs carved on the sides of the altar block portray, on either side, two men, each holding infants who are kicking and struggling. The men wear fantastic headdresses, of unknown symbolism; one wears a mirror pectoral showing his earth nature.

In the group on the right side of the god figure, the top of one infant's head is formed in the shape of the jaguar fang symbol, which is the shape of the top of the infant's head in the Las Limas statue; otherwise the infants appear in human form, although the carving makes them somewhat grotesque [**Figure 42**].

The opposite side of the altar has been broken so that the carving shows two Earth Gods wearing mirror pectorals, but only one infant's head is represented. The face of that infant has a feline cast; but presumably, one of the two was human and the other was jaguar in nature.

Let us now have a look at Altar 4 facing east [**Figure 43**]. There is a niche in the altar which matches the niche in the west altar. The niche represents the cave mouth of the jaguar mountain opening out of the underworld.

The Jaguar God in his anthropomorphic aspect is carved seated tailor fashion and wearing a birdhead-and-feather headdress emblazoned with an Ollin sign on each side. He is holding a rope which extends around the base of the altar block on two ends.

The edge and top of the stone slab, which is the altar table, is carved to represent a jaguar face and pelt. There is a St. Andrew's cross in the front of the jaguar's mouth, between the fangs and flaming fire pots on the lips. In his mountain image, the Olmec Jaguar God was a volcano. His jaguar image was sometimes represented with a serpent tongue hanging between the fangs. This is the meaning of the symbols.

On the south side of the altar, the viewer's right, there is a carving of a seated man secured by a rope tied to his left wrist which the Jaguar God holds in his hands [**Figure 44**]. The north side of the altar has been reworked, but seems to have been originally carved in low relief, probably

Figure 42. Side Altar 5, La Venta [photograph courtesy of National Geographic Society].

La Venta South

Figure 43. Altar 4, La Venta [photograph courtesy of National Geographic Society].

Figure 44. Side Altar 4, La Venta [photograph courtesy of National Geographic Society].

to portray a figure complementing the one on the south side.

The two altars constitute a double image of the Jaguar God as a world-man with the attributes of the Las Limas idol. Altar 5, facing west, portrays the Jaguar God as the death state of the new Moon; in the Las Limas idol, the death state was represented by the godheads incised on the Jaguar God's knees and the infant in his arms. In the altar, the death state is revealed by the god's headdress. The band around the base of the crown has the symbolism of the cosmogonic band in the Temple of the Sun [Figure 10]; the cosmogonic band, it will be remembered, terminated as the head of a fire-serpent at each end, the jaguar mask or head of the earth (skeletal) Itzam Na was at the center, and a *bil*, the sign of maize that signified the god's power of creation served as a plume on Itzam Na's headdress. The St. Andrew's crosses on the headband of the Jaguar God in Altar 5 were signs of fire-serpents; and the raindrops over the cartouche in the center of the band which frames his face can be read as a symbol of his power of life creation. In the Temple of the Sun, the cosmogonic band was above the Sun God and 7-Jaguar who were combined as the new Moon to which Itzam Na was giving life. In Altar 5, the infant is the spirit of the new Moon, and the manner in which the Jaguar God holds it signifies that he is giving it new life.

Now if we think of the sides of the altar as wing panels of a triptych folded back and then imagine them unfolded so that they form a single plane with the front of the altar, the composition of the figures on the sides shows them as gods of the Moon cycle turned to face the Jaguar God seated in the niche. The three panels of our triptych show the Jaguar God as he was represented by the Las Limas idol without the god images on the upper part of his body.

The two figures on each side, where there is only one godhead on each knee of the Las Limas idol, make an apparent difference; but the two figures on the sides of the altar represent the planetary Moon spirit and the Moon, each holding an infant. They are like Pacal and Chan Bahlum on the piers of the Temple of the Inscriptions, each with a serpent-footed infant in his arms. The infants on the sides of the altar are the spirit forms which will become incarnate in the two adult figures. They are, surely, the infants sacrificed in the "tomb" under the mound at the north opening of the Ceremonial Court. Thus, the figures equate the Death God and Xolotl whose images are incised on the left and right knees of the Las Limas idol. The equation is confirmed by the serpent in the headdress of the first figure on the right side of the altar; Xolotl was the underworld fire-serpent.

As in Altar 5, the headdress of the god in the niche in Altar 4 is revealing. The birdhead-and-feather headdress in combination with the Ollin sign signifies the life which the Sun brings on earth. When the side of the altar, imagined as a triptych, is turned forward to form a single plane with the front, it shows the seated figure facing the Jaguar God in the center. The rope symbolism identifies the seated figure with the image of Xipe incised on the right shoulder of the Las Limas idol. Xipe was the god who wore the flayed skin of the god sacrificed as Xolotl. When he cast off the flayed skin, he appeared transformed into the Morning Star as Xolotl's twin, Quetzalcoatl. The rope symbolizes his sacrifice as Xolotl.

This symbolism of the rope is pictorially described in the *Madrid Codex.* The pictograph is of a scorpion with a hand in place of a stinger at the end of its tail. The hand holds a rope which is fastened to the foreleg of a deer. In the symbolism of the codices: the hand signifies sacrifice, the scorpion is a sign of death, the deer is an animal form of the Sun and Maize God, and the leg is a symbol of movement and the sign of the deer's ascension.

While the figure on the opposite side of the altar has been destroyed, it would certainly have completed the cycle of gods as a figure of the Moon God. The jaguar face and pelt carved on the front and top of the altar match the human figure to the double face of the Las Limas idol, and the St. Andrew's cross between the fangs accords with the serpent nature of the gods incised on the Las Limas idol's limbs.

La Venta South

Altar 5 (facing west) is back-to-back with Altar 4 (facing east), the directions of death and life. Together, the two altars are the Jaguar God in a divided image of a world-man in the waxing new Moon stage of his development.

The features of the seated god on the side of the altar with the rope around his wrist are too eroded to compare them to the planetary god-spirit in Stela 3. Because the figure of the Moon God on the opposite side of the Altar 5 is missing, it is impossible to know if his features were those of the Moon God portrait of the ruler on that stela. Whether or not the features would have identified the two, it is reasonable to conclude that symbols would have identified them with the two gods on Stela 3.

CHAPTER 33

La Venta: Colossal Heads

Altars 5 and 4 portray the formation of the world-man as the waxing new Moon. Three monuments between those two altars and the main pyramid portray his death and resurrection as the god coming into being in the underworld. The symbolism of the monuments is obscure, but when we study them in the light of the planetary doctrine, we can see that they represent the resurrection which brings the gods to their being in the underworld. They are Stela 2, Altar 1, and Monument 1. They were placed between Altars 5 and 4 on the long mound and the main pyramid. To these, we should add the main pyramid itself.

Stela 2 is a large naturally formed slab over 11 feet in height and nearly 7 feet at its greatest width [**Figure 45**]. A standing male figure is carved in the center, facing toward the front. He is shown holding a long scepter or staff diagonally across his chest and wearing a high and elaborate headdress. Three smaller figures are carved on each side, one above the other. Their bodies are turned toward the center and they appear to be in motion. The three on the left of the central figure (observer's right) are looking forward toward the center while the three on the opposite side are looking backward over their shoulders away from the center.

Altar 1 is a huge stone block over 9.5 feet in length and approximately 7 feet wide, and slightly more than 6 feet high. Carved as a human head, the shape of the altar block makes the head rectangular.

Monument 1 is a colossal stone bodiless head, 8 feet 1 inch high and some 20 feet in circumference.

Figure 45. Stela 2, La Venta.

La Venta: Colossal Heads

Monument 1 stands at the base of the main pyramid at the southwest corner. Stela 2 is on a line between the long mound which separates Altars 5 and 4 and a point on the base of the pyramid close to Monument 1. Altar 1 is just east of Stela 2.

Altar 1, like Monument 1, is a bodiless head. The significance of these and the three colossal heads on the north side of the main pyramid has completely escaped students of the Olmec culture. Consequently, we shall treat the subject of severed heads at sufficient length to understand how the heads at La Venta relate to the cycles of creation.

The severed head has had a fundamental place in religion from its beginnings. When hunters, who regarded animals as gods, killed a bear or deer, they fixed the head on a stake set in the ground or in a lake. They believed that the life spirit lodged in the head; after the death of a god, the spirit traveled through the stake to the underworld, where it was reembodied — then returned to the hunting grounds, bringing new game animals with it. When hunting gave way to agriculture, the planters buried severed heads in the soil — believing that the spirit would return in their crops.

The belief that the god's head was the source of created life became a doctrine of the Great Goddess religion. The Sumerians made it the source of the combined motion of the Moon and Sun which created life on earth. The *Epic of Gilgamesh* describes the beheading of the monster Huwawa by Gilgamesh and Enkidu. In consequence of their act, the solar life spirit lodged in each of them. The doctrine of the severed head was part of the Eddic mythology and that of the ancient Greeks. For instance, Mimir (whose spring contained the knowledge of the past and future, and watered the tree of life) was killed in a war between the gods. Odin embalmed and kept Mimir's head, which provided prophesies. When the Greek god Orpheus died, his head was cut off and thrown into a river where it floated and sang. The Celts had a cult of the severed head. Helmeted heads of warriors were found in the tombs of Shang kings, showing that the cult was part of the religious practices of ancient China.

Ann Ross in her book *Pagan Celtic Britain* describes a scene from an Elizabethan play, "The Old Wives Tale," which explains the nature of the bodiless head.* A woman named Zantippa goes to the well of life to fill her pitcher, whereupon a head appears in the well. After a brief colloquy with the head, Zantippa breaks the pitcher on it. This brings thunder and lightning and then a head appears in the well with ears of corn, and then another, filled with gold.

In the cult, the head was divine and the fact that it was without body meant that it represented a god who had been sacrificed. The god sacrificed in the Divine King cult was the god of vegetation or the Corn God — whose sacrifice meant that he would return in new corn body as a new crop. In "The Old Wives Tale," the well was the well of life and the head with ears of corn was the sacrificed Corn God returning in his new corn body. The meaning of the gold which filled the other head is explained by the belief that the seat of the divine spirit of the god was in his head. The divinity incarnate in corn was the golden Sun, which explains why the god's head lived on when his body died, for the Sun was immortal. Here we may note that cult heads from the La Tene phase of Celtic history and the earlier Bronze Age in Europe were used as solar symbols and that the head could represent the god in different aspects. The ears of corn which appeared with the one head was the body spirit of the Moon; the gold which filled the other head was the Sun as the life spirit of the Moon.

In the doctrines of the Great Goddess religion, the substance of life was formed from the divinity of the Moon and the severed heads were theistically lunar. The head cult was brought to Mesoamerica with the Great Goddess religion and there is evidence of the cult in the cultures of all the periods of Mesoamerican civilization. For example, the Aztecs in the Postclassic Period carved the image of the Moon Goddess Coyolxauhqui as a severed head nearly 4 feet in height. In the sacrifice rites centered on the gods of the Moon cycle, a girl representing the Moon Goddess was

*Ross, pg. 110.

decapitated. In the Feast of Tititl, the sacrificer priest (who by virtue of his function represented the Moon God) danced backward carrying her head. The action clearly shows that while he danced, her spirit was transferred to and lodged in the priest. In the Tlacaxipeualiztli rites, warriors (representing the maize brought by the returning Sun of spring) danced carrying the severed heads of warriors sacrificed as divinities of the Moon.

Sacrifices were celebrated at the end of each 52-year Calendar Round. Bundles of reeds representing the years were burned in holocausts associated with human sacrifices. At Cerro de las Mesas in the Gulf region of Vera Cruz, 52 urns from the Classic Period were found — each containing the remains of the severed head of a sacrificed youth. Obviously, the bundles and severed heads were believed to have the power to renew the 52-year cycle.

The heads incised on the knees and shoulders of the Las Limas idol show that the Olmecs associated severed heads with the lunar cycle, and a stela from Tres Zapotes testifies to the cult in the form in which it was followed in later cultures. The Zapotes stela, designated by the letter A, is some 8 feet in height. Although broken and partly destroyed, the relief shows the bodies of three figures. One holds a severed head in the manner in which the priest in Tititl carried the Moon Goddess' head when he danced. The carving on top of the stela is a mask of the Jaguar God.

Masks could have the same quality as severed heads. This is evident from the tablet in the Temple of the Sun at Palenque. In the symbolism of the tablet which portrays the Moon cycle, the mask of the skeleton Itzam Na is shown giving life to the Moon God 7-Jaguar. The mosaic masks of the Jaguar God in the Ceremonial Court at La Venta are idols of the Jaguar God moving as the Moon with the Sun in the creation of life.

The doctrine of the severed head remained unchanged in Eurasian and Mesoamerican religious cultures from earliest times to the Spanish conquest. The colossal heads were, quite certainly, idols of the Jaguar God in his aspect as the Moon moving the Sun in the cycles of creation. With

this key to understanding, we can interpret the symbolism of Stela 2, Altar 1, and Monument 1 in their relation to each other.

Stela 2 surely represents the planetary spirit Mercury. The composition of the principal figure with the three smaller figures on either side is similar to that of Stela 3; the figure itself, with its elaborate headdress, resembles the figure of the planetary spirit on that stela. The manner and style in which the figures on Stela 2 are carved with the central figure holding what may be a scepter, makes it a prototype of the later Maya stelas on which the Mayas carved images of their rulers.

The three small figures on each side of the principal figure must represent his corporeal form as the Moon. In the representation of the life and death sides of the Moon cycle in Sumero-Babylonian rituals and iconography, right was the death side and left was the life side. The same symbolic division of right and left was part of Mesoamerican iconography, as we have seen in the temples at Palenque and the pictograph of the Birth Tree of Apoala. We may be sure that the Olmecs used this same iconographic device. The little figures are all in motion, so we may surmise that the three figures on the right are descending in death, and the three figures on the left are moving upward toward life.

This is confirmed by the action of the figures on the left, who are shown looking backward over their shoulders. The backward action is the symbolism of the backward dance of the priest with the severed head of the Moon Goddess in Tititl. He danced toward life. It was also the symbolism of the march of the warriors in Ochpaniztli when they turned backward, then forward, thereby carrying the mirrors on their backs forward as they carried the life of the new year to the earth above. The life which had formed in the underworld was in the mirrors. From the number in each group (three) on Stela 2, we can identify them as the three gods of the full Moon, the Moon spirit, and the Moon God and Goddess.

Altar 1 was almost completely buried when discovered. Although rectangular, the corners were rounded and its platform shape is symbolic of

the platform mounds which represented the Jaguar God in his aspect as a mountain. The Moon, in its nature as the earth, was represented as a mountain. When the Moon died, it descended to the underworld where death gave it the inert character of stone. We may conclude, therefore, that since Altar 1 was buried, it represents the dead body of the Moon.

There is, however, a feature of the head which symbolizes the immortality of the Moon's power of regeneration immanent in its death state. Carved on the back is a broad headdress. Hair symbolized growing vegetation.

The new Moon was half-death, half-life. Where Altar 1 represents the death half, Monument 1 represents the life half. This is evident from its placement at the base of the main pyramid. The pyramid was built as a replica of a volcano, a mountain filled with fire. Fire, which was the essence of the Sun, was the spirit form of life. The pyramid, therefore, represents the living mountain, and the setting of the head at the base made the head the source of life.

The carvings of the colossal heads do not reveal their sex, which could be either or both — for the Moon was both. The severed head of 9-Reed from which the Birth Tree of Apoala grows in the picture in the *Codex Vindobonensis* is both female and male. Covarrubias, in *Mexico South,* published a photograph of a Totonac Indian woman in conjunction with a photograph of Monument 1.* The monument could be a portrait of the woman. The hairdress on the back of Altar 1 seems to suggest the head of a female.

Within the half-death, half-life nature of the new Moon, there was movement and life constituted by the spirit Sun-bearer Mercury. The spirit motion was in the direction of life, the Sun's course as the day, from east to west. The motion joined the two sides of the new Moon and made them one. In the mystic area of the pyramid, Stela 2 joins Altar 1 and Monument 1. The relative locations of the three monuments symbolizes the union.

*Plate 1.

East was the direction in which the Sun rose and signaled the resurrection. In the Nahuatlan creation myth, Quetzalcoatl (the god of the Morning Star) watched toward the east for the rising of the two Suns and the beginning of created life. Altar 1 was buried just east of Stela 2. The Stela was on the floor of the court above it. The Stela was on a line between the world-man image of the Jaguar God in the two altars on the long mound, and the place where Monument 1 stood at the base of the pyramid. In its setting, it was the Morning Star bringing the Sun out of the Moon's death state in the underworld into its life state in the heart of its mountain.

The combination of the three monuments foreshadows the iconography of the Temple of the Inscriptions at Palenque. There, in the death of the Moon, the Moon spirit Pacal descended to the sarcophagus of the deceased Pacal, where his body and life as the Moon were renewed.

Then he rose as a new Moon to the top of the pyramid where he came on earth as the ruler. In the La Venta combination, Stela 2 shows the descent and ascent of the Moon spirit. His body was renewed in Altar 1 and his life in Monument 1.*

In the Temple of Inscription, the symbolism of the sarcophagus repeats the symbolism of Altar 1 and Monument 1. The body of the deceased Pacal in the sarcophagus and the burial of Altar 1 have the same symbolic meaning. The mask covering Pacal's face gives it the character of the head which constitutes the altar. It is in itself a bodiless head. Its jade composition is of the divinity of the Moon as vegetation in the dormant state of death. It represents the Moon's power of regeneration and its symbolism is synonymous with the hairdress on the back of Altar 1.

Where death was inside the sarcophagus, life was on the outside. The image of Pacal on the cover was his idol as the Moon spirit at the point of being reembodied and rising. The image of Zak-Kuk carved on the outside

*In the opinion of many students, the colossal heads are portraits of rulers. If so, Altar 1 must be an exception, but in Mesoamerican religion, rulers were divine; it is clear from the reliefs at Palenque that their portraits as gods in the lunar cycle of creation are consistent with the theme of the iconography.

end of Pacal's coffer unites her to him as the goddess half of the new Moon.** She is also the life half because she is shown again united to Chan Bahlum on the pier of the temple at the top of the pyramid. Chan Bahlum was Pacal's life form on earth and, in the union with Chan Bahlum, Lady Zak-Kuk was the Moon Goddess ascending to earth.

Thus the physical character of the sarcophagus is formed on the pattern of the La Venta monuments. Where Altar 1 is below the ground and Stela 2 above it, the deceased Pacal is inside, beneath his life image on the cover; and, where Monument 1 is at the base of the pyramid, the image of Lady Zak-Kuk is on the outside of the sarcophagus in the tomb chamber at the bottom of the pyramid.

The gods in the precincts of the pyramid at La Venta were not yet in being on its south side; but, since the monuments depict the Jaguar God, they must have been envisioned as combining into all the gods in one and then dying and coming into being in the sarcophagus in the court on the north side.

**The dynastic succession of the dynasty of Pacal was formed by the union of the Moon God and Goddess.

CHAPTER 34

La Venta: The World-Man

Let us now go back to the north side of the main pyramid and the new Moon stage of the formation of the world-man. We have mentioned the colossal heads, which were designated as Monuments 4, 2, and 3. The largest is Number 4, on the west, which measures 8 feet 5 inches high. Number 2, in the middle, measures 6 feet 2 inches. Number 3 is 6 feet high.

Three monuments were found when the airstrip was constructed between the "tomb" and the three heads. These can be read with the heads as idols in which the gods formed the new body of the Moon. They are designated as Monuments 19, 20, and 21. The first would seem to be Monument 19 **[Figure 46]** which is a large boulder with a flatish surface on one side.

This surface forms the face of the monument, and the figures of a seated man and a rattlesnake are carved on it. The body of the rattlesnake is curved around the edges of the face with its head raised above the seated figure. The head forms the top of the composition. The snake's tail and rattle curve around the bottom and upward toward the head. The curve of the body with a space between the tail and head forms a cross section outline of a cave.

The human figure sits underneath the snake's head in the curve at the end of its body. His legs are extended straight in front with the snake's rattle above the feet. He wears a headdress that combines the features of a serpent, a jaguar, and a bird of prey. He wears a nose ornament and what

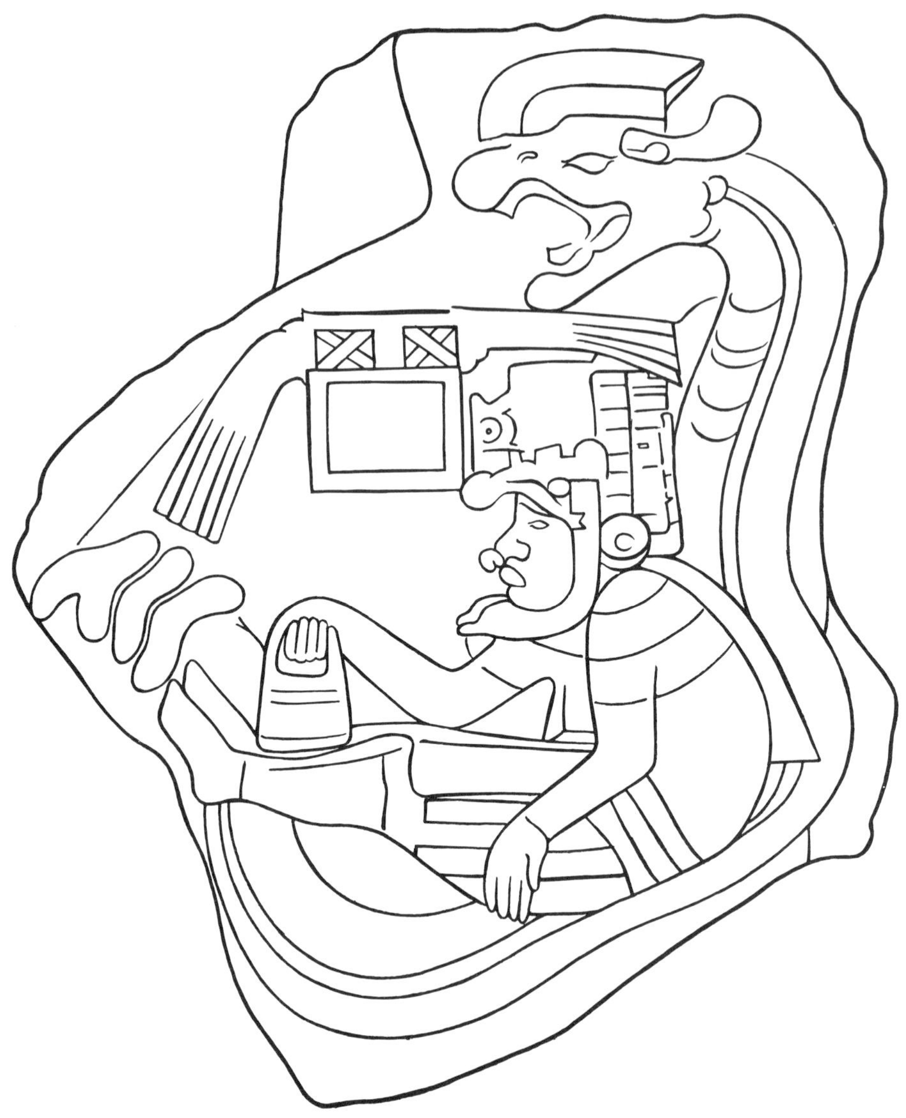

Figure 46. Monument 19, La Venta.

appears to be a beard. A bag in his right hand, held in front of him, is thought to hold copal, a substance which is ritually burned to represent the fire of the Fire God.

The man faces toward the opening in the cave contour of the serpent's body. Over his head and covering the cave opening is a band which flares slightly at the ends. Parallel lines are incised in the flaring, suggesting tassels. There are two St. Andrew's crosses in the center of the band and a u-sign of the earth underworld beneath the St. Andrew's crosses. The band is a cosmogonic band dividing the realm of the underworld into regions of life in formation beneath, and life in being above. The snake head is above the band, the human figure beneath. Both face toward the left.

The cosmogonic band in the tablet of the Sun Temple sanctuary at Palenque terminates in a serpent head at each end. In the sarcophagus cover, the cosmogonic band is rendered as serpent branches of the maize tree, or tree of life, growing from the skeletal head of the creator god Itzam Na. On Monument 19, the lines which form the tassels at the ends of the cosmogonic band make four divisions on the right and five on the left.

The divisions logically represent the nine planetary gods. The four on the right, which is the death side, are the gods of the new Moon — which were represented at Palenque by Chalchiuhlicue (Venus), Tlazolteotl, Tepeyolotl, and Tlaloc (the three aspects of Saturn). The five on the left, the life side, are represented by Xiutecuhtli (Sun), Itztli (Moon), Piltzintecuhtli (Mars), Centeotl (Jupiter), and Mictlantecuhtli (Mercury). These gods constituted the joint motion of the Sun and Moon pictured as a serpent.

The headdress and serpent in association with the human figure identify Monument 19 as an image of the Jaguar God. While the cave symbolization of the Jaguar God's mountain aspect is usually formed as a jaguar mouth, the serpent was as much a part of the god's image as the human and the jaguar, and would be used as a sign of the cave. The jaguar mouth symbol of a cave was used to represent the entrance to the death region of the

underworld, while the serpent image logically represents the opening of the way back to life.

This was certainly the symbolism of the boulder on which the rattlesnake was carved. Apparently, the boulder was partly buried in the earth so that only the carved face was visible. The composition of the figures places the head of the snake in the region of life. The head is formed with the same serpent-jaguar-bird features as those forming the headdress of the man. Those features mark it as the fire-serpent, and its rearing body signifies that it is the Morning Star bringing the Sun out of the underworld. In this imagery, the human figure represents the earthly form of the planetary Moon spirit.

A comparison of Monument 19 with the sarcophagus in the tomb of Pacal in the Temple of the Inscriptions confirms this interpretation and shows that the symbolism of the tomb must have evolved from the concept of the monument. In the evolved symbolism of Palenque, the boulder has become the sarcophagus. The earth in which the boulder was set has become the tomb chamber, and the opening to life between the snake's rattle and its head has become the serpent-shaped spirit duct leading from inside the sarcophagus to the summit of the pyramid.

There is a good deal more. In the evolution, the face of the boulder has become the cover of the sarcophagus and, in the carvings on the face and the sarcophagus cover, the man seated in the body of the snake has become the figure of Pacal in the open jaws of the skeletal serpent. The copal which he holds in the bag is changed to the net garment of the Sun God worn by Pacal. The opening between the rattle and the head of the snake is pictured as the opening between the fangs of the skeletal serpent. The tassels at the ends of the cosmogonic band are rendered as the serpent branches of the maize tree. Finally, both figures face left; both wear nose ornaments; and both are identified with the image of the jaguar — the one by his headdress, the other by the god who will become his Moon body, Chan Bahlum, whose glyph is a snake-jaguar.

La Venta: The World-Man

The sarcophagus of Pacal in the tomb beneath the Temple of the Inscriptions was an idol of the Maya Supreme God Itzam Na in his aspect as the new Moon. Monument 19 was likewise an idol of the Olmec Jaguar God in his aspect as the new Moon. In the *Epic of Gilgamesh*, the Sumero-Babylonian counterpart was Utnapishtim whose house was on the shore of the waters of life where the way to the earth above began.

Monument 19 portrays the Moon spirit at the point of renewing its Moon body as all the gods. In the epic, the renewal is portrayed by Gilgamesh when he puts on his new Moon garment and casts off the old one.

Monument 20, representing the new Moon body, is a stone figure of a whale 6.5 feet in length. The whale was a natural symbol for the new Moon. In ancient iconography, the embryo Moon body of the Sun was commonly represented as a fish. To the ancients, a whale was a creature of the sea and the air — part-fish and part-animal of the earth. The sea was a manifestation of the waters of creation and the air over the sea was the sky. The whale, emerging from the sea, became a body of the sky and a manifestation of the Moon coming into being in the workings of creation.

Now, when we consider the nature of the whale in relation to the epic, we can see that it compares with Urshanabi who became Gilgamesh's body as the new Moon. Urshanabi was lunar motion implicit in Utnapishtim as the new Moon. He was Utnapishtim's ferryman across the waters of death and his guide along the road to life. The waters of death were the depths of the sea and the ferry crossing to Utnapishtim's was metaphorically like a whale swimming on the surface. In the metaphor of the epic, Urshanabi rose from the waters of death when he washed Gilgamesh and gave him a new garment at the direction of Utnapishtim. The garment was his vestment as the Moon, and the washing was a sacrificial rite in which the giver and receiver were one.

Gilgamesh put on the new garment and cast off the skins which had been his dress as the body of the dead Enkidu. In their joint action,

Urshanabi was united to Gilgamesh as his new Moon body; in their unity, they set out for Erech. Their journey to Erech was the waxing new Moon stage in the formation of the world-man as the Moon cycle.

At La Venta, Monument 21 must represent the cast off body of the dead Moon. The monument is a stone statue of the upper part of a headless human figure. The two arms are resting on a flat base which divides the statue into two halves. The lower half is formed as a roughly worked tenon. The tenon was apparently buried in the earth, leaving visible the body on its base. The stone is very weathered and the details have disappeared; but the missing head indicates that the figure represents a body beheaded in sacrifice.

Decapitation was the way by which the Mesoamerican ancients sacrificed the representatives of the Moon Gods. The full Moon was represented in human form and its death and transformation into the new Moon was theologically by sacrifice. The upper half of the human body would logically have represented the life half of the Moon cycle, while the lower half would have been associated with the new Moon half — the one being the Moon's cycle through the sky, the second its cycle through the underworld. From the headless nature of the monument and its placement (half above and half within the earth), we may take it that the monument represents the cast off body of the dead Moon.

When Gilgamesh left Utnapishtim's, he left in the Moon body given him by Utnapishtim; but the life which had formed within him was given to him by Utnapishtim's wife. Her gift was signified by the loaves which she baked while he slept. In the theme of the La Venta monuments, the life of the new Moon was infused by the three idols carved as the colossal heads. Within them were the life spirits of the Moon God and Goddess and the Moon's moving spirit united to the Sun.

Gilgamesh brought the Sun and Moon into the created form of life in being in an underworld realm of creation by passing through the realm of death; Monument 21 shows the death state through which the gods

represented by the idols in the Ceremonial Court came into being. They took their form as the three colossal heads. The three heads do not negate a single being in the Hercules mythology. In the Hercules mythology, Hercules became Geryon on the island of death by killing him. Geryon had three bodies with heads. Cernunnos, the Celtic Moon-Sun God, was constituted as three gods; and there are figurines from later Mesoamerican cultures that were tripartite gods. The three heads combined represented the Jaguar God as a single god; it makes no difference whether one of the heads was female, both sexes were quite regularly joined in a single being in Mesoamerican iconography.

The world-man was an abstract image of the gods combining to form the cycles of earthly life and time, conceived as the changing phases of the Moon moving in its synodic life cycle. The stages of the cycle formed the parts of his body. His development was gradual and the part of him which became the new Moon formed first as the spirit, then as a new body in the dead body of the old Moon, like a chrysalis in a cocoon. His new Moon part became complete when it broke from death and entered life with an infusion from three gods of the full Moon. Thus, the colossal heads completed the formation of the new Moon stage of the world-man.

At this point, when we consider the archaeological site of La Venta, we see that the pyramid which closed the north opening of the Ceremonial Court and the monuments in the adjacent area beyond are coupled with the area north of the principal pyramid; and that together they mark the stages in the formation of the world-man's cyclical image. The succession of the nine parallel rows of celts, the sarcophagus, and the "tomb" buried beneath the pyramid, mark his formation as the inchoate Moon. Monument 19 with the human figure wrapped in the body of the rearing rattlesnake, the stone whale, the headless statue, and the three colossal heads, all in combination, mark his development as the new Moon bringing life into the living world on earth, doubtless through the person of the La Venta ruler. La Venta is a complete expression of the creation and planetary doctrines of the Great

Goddess religion.

La Venta asks the riddle, only the Great Goddess can give the answer.

CHAPTER 35

The Culture Bearers

ca. 13th through 12th Century B.C.

What peoples brought the culture of the Great Goddess religion to America and how?

One clue to their ethnic origin is Stela 3. The false beards on the figures on the stela make it evident that they believed beards to be essential to divine incarnation. They must, therefore, have been beardless people from eastern Asia. The evidence for this is a Scythian king who was a Mongol. He was buried with a false beard. The aquiline nose of the Stela 3 Moon God is not significant.

In Maya times, rulers wore false beards and aquiline nose masks. The reason, no doubt, was identification with the Moon and the eagle Sun-bird. The nose of the god on Stela 3 is doubtless a mask. We can only say with reasonable certainty that the culture-bearers came out of China, from its hinterland where peoples had adopted the religion of the Great Goddess.

Whoever the Asian culture-bearers were, they must have been an organized group, large enough to establish themselves in the country as overlords and small enough to make their way and leave no imprint of their passage. They would have had to include among their number men who were warriors, as well as members of the priest class who had been trained in the sciences and rituals of religion.

A land route must be ruled out because it passes through country which is difficult to cross from a starting point in China, blocked by the Bering Strait. Moreover, because of weather, an overland route is not suitable for supporting any but small hunting parties. It also would have been a very long route that crosses deserts before reaching any of the regions in Mexico where the Olmec culture arose.

There is no reason why such a group could not have traveled by sea. The climate of the period between the beginning of the third millennium B.C. and the middle of the second millennium B.C. was favorable for sea voyages. Men with horses and livestock had crossed the sea and settled in Japan by the beginning of the third millennium or shortly thereafter. By 1500 B.C., Asians had discovered and settled the Micronesian Marianas, tiny islands in the midst of the ocean.

During the third and the first half of the second millennium, men had made their way by ship through the Mediterranean Sea and the Atlantic Ocean, and had discovered and founded settlements in Britain and Ireland, and the Orkneys and Shetlands in the far north beyond.

At the beginning of the third millennium, the Egyptians were importing timber from Phoenicia in ships which sailed in fleets of 40 vessels. Early in the next millennium, the Phoenicians, the Minoans, and the Mycenaean Greeks rose as great sea powers in the Mediterranean Sea, and the Egyptians extended their sea trade to Punt at the southeastern end of the Red Sea.

Ancient monuments and archaeological records reveal this Mediterranean Sea trade, but there is no reason to think that ships did not ply the Persian Gulf from Mesopotamia to India, or that peoples who could reach and settle Japan and the Marianas were incapable of long sea voyages.

Ships leave no trace of their passage and there are few written records of ancient voyages. We know of some which are particularly significant. In the next millennium, sometime between 609 and 593 B.C., the Phoenicians made a periplus (i.e., a journey of circumnavigation) sailing around Africa.

They went south along the east coast and up the west coast to the Straits of Gibraltar, then back through the Mediterranean. The voyage took 3 years and the men stopped each year to plant and harvest crops.

The Culture Bearers

In the fourth century, the Carthaginian Hamilcar sailed through the Straits of Gibraltar and, turning north, continued across the Atlantic to northwest France and Brittany and, probably, to Cornwall in England. A few years later, his grandson Hanno made another periplus in the opposite direction — southward around the bulge of Africa to Senegal and, it is thought, to the Cameroons. As many as 60 ships may have sailed in Hanno's periplus and perhaps 30,000 men were involved. A century or more earlier, the Chinese kings of Wu sent out naval expeditions which returned with thousands of prisoners.

A periplus around the lands bordering the Pacific Ocean, starting in China, would have found favorable winds and currents which would have enabled ships to reach Mexico. Junks have very often been driven by storms from Japanese waters onto the coast of North America. Around 3000 B.C., a form of pottery was introduced into Ecuador from Japan. It is guessed that it was brought by fishermen blown to the South American coast by storms, but there is reason to believe that the boat from Japan belonged to an exploring and colonizing expedition involving a number of individuals of both sexes and having appropriate skills.

The world stage was set in the second millennium B.C. for such a periplus. The discovery of bronze had given the nations possessing it superior weapons which enabled them to conquer and plunder their neighbors. Bronze is made from tin and copper, which was obtainable only in certain places, usually in distant and foreign parts. Rulers, therefore, sent out exploratory expeditions to find sources. For instance, the center of the early bronze industry was the Middle East — in explorations from there, men discovered and exploited the tin deposits of Cornwall at the southwest tip of England, using the sea route through the Mediterranean Sea and the Atlantic Ocean in their journeys.

The Bronze Age — a time when weapons, utensils, and various implements were made of bronze — began at different times in different parts of the ancient world, starting in Mesopotamia. With it, there began an

era of discovery and imperial expansion which has continued down to the present. In the first one thousand years, starting around the middle of the third millennium, this expansion carried the Great Goddess religion westward across the Mediterranean Sea and around the shores of the Atlantic to Brittany in France, then on to Britain, and eastward across the steppes to China and the shores of the Pacific.

By the early part of the second millennium, the pastoral tribes of the central steppes had begun pushing outward, displacing the tribes around them. This outward movement is thought to have resulted from desiccation of the vegetation, which forced the nomads to find new pastures for their stock. The displaced tribes, in turn, drove out those beyond and they, in their turn, overran the lands of their outer neighbors — until the tribes farthest from the center invaded the lands of the settled farmers where advanced civilization had become established. The nomad tribes were bred to fighting and many were able to overpower the peaceful farmers, in which event they established themselves as overlords and assimilated the civilizations of their subject peoples. The new rulers in these situations, stimulated by the power and wealth which they had gained, embarked on wars of conquest and plunder — and created regional empires with individual cultural styles, such as the Hittite and Indo-Aryan.

The outward movement came in waves, sweeping over one or another part of the borders from the steppe lands. Many of the larger island groups off the coast of southeast Asia were known from early times. For example, the Marianas were probably discovered by Melanesian Islanders driven off course by storm — then the waves of migrants coming out of the Asian hinterland would have naturally stimulated movement to the islands and voyages of further exploration.

While there is no evidence of a periplus such as we have hypothesized, there are factors which, when considered in conjunction with the appearance of the Eurasian religious culture at the beginning of the Olmec period in Mexico, support the presumption of a planned voyage of discovery and conquest which would, of necessity, have included warriors and soothsayer-priests to read the auspices and determine favorable times for action.

Men undertaking journeys of exploration seek to learn all that they can about the unknown regions into which they are going. Knowledge of the existence of America could have been obtained in the second millennium from fishermen and hunters of sea animals, and from reindeer hunters. The evidence of the Japanese fishing boat reaching Ecuador attests a fishing industry in those times. The region comprised by eastern Siberia and Alaska was a single culture area and, from time immemorial, reindeer hunters have crossed the winter ice on the Bering Strait between Asia and Alaska. Men dwelling along the coastal regions of the north were sea animal hunters whose quarry took them to the shores of the islands and coasts of Alaska. Features in the culture of the Native Americans of the northwest coast of North America reflect the culture of ancient Asia. They are the same as features in cultures of ancient China and of Melanesia which were carried to those islands from the Asian mainland and which show the lineage of the steppe culture. The Native Americans of the Pacific Northwest coast have a maritime economy and their culture is distinct from that of their inland brethren. The similar features, therefore, show that there were early contacts by sea which originated in eastern Asia.

For some unknown reason, our hypothetical periplus ended in Mexico. The winds and currents which aided in its outbound voyage could have made a return impossible, or other factors could have made the leaders of the expedition determine to remain and establish themselves as rulers in a new land. Whatever the reason, the ending of the periplus would have marked the beginning of a new civilization in the New World. A periplus was a highly possible way by which the Asian culture-bearers could have come to Mesoamerica. There may have been other possible routes and different culture traits that may have been brought at different times; but, however they came, they brought the seeds of Eurasian civilization, which grew into the Olmec religious culture.

BIBLIOGRAPHY

Alexander, H.B., "North American Mythology," *The Mythology of All Races*. Vol. X, Marshall Homes Co., 1916.

Anderson, J.O. and Charles E. Dibble, translation and annotation, *Florentine Codex: General History of the Things of New Spain*. Fray Bernadino de Sahagún. The School of American Research. Santa Fe, NM: Museum of New Mexico and University of Utah.

Anthes, R., "Mythology in Ancient Egypt," *Mythologies of the Ancient World*. Edited by S.N. Kramer. Doubleday & Co., Inc., 1961.

Armillas, Pedro, "Northern Mesoamerica," *Prehistoric Man in the New World*. Published for William Marsh Rice University by University of Chicago Press, 1964.

Aveni, Anthony F., *Archaeoastronomy in Pre-Columbian America*. Austin and London: University of Texas Press, 1975.

Aveni, Anthony F., *Skywatchers of Ancient Mexico*. Austin and London: University of Texas Press, 1980.

Baudez, C.F. and P. Matthews, "Capture and Sacrifice at Palenque," *Tercera Mesa Redonda de Palenque*. Vol. IV, Pre-Columbian Art Research, Herald Printers, Monterey, California, 1978.

Benson, Elizabeth P., *The Maya World*. Thomas Y. Crowell Company, New York, 1967.

Bernal, I., *Mexico Before Cortez: Art, History, and Legend*. Translated by Willis Barnstone. Garden City, New York: Dolphin Books, Doubleday & Company, Inc., 1963.

Bernal, I., *The Olmec World*. Translated by Doris Heyden and Fernando Horcasitas. Berkeley and Los Angeles: University of California Press, 1969.

Bjerre, Jens, *The Last Cannibals*. New York: Morrow, 1957.

Bober, P.P. "Cernunnos: Origin and Transformation of a Celtic Divinity," *American Journal of Archaeology*. 1955.

Bodde, D. "Myths of Ancient China," *Mythologies of the Ancient World*. Edited by S.N. Kramer. Doubleday & Company, Inc., 1961.

Borhegyi, Stephan F. de, "Wheels and Man," *Archaeology*. Vol. 23, No. 1, January 1970.

Bouquet, A.C., *Comparative Religion*. Melbourne, London, Baltimore: Penguin Books, 1953.

Brown, W.N., "Mythology of India," *Mythologies of the Ancient World*. Edited by S.N. Kramer. Doubleday & Company, Inc., 1961.

Brundage, Burr Cartwright, *The Fifth Sun – Aztec Gods, Aztec World*. Austin and London: University of Texas Press, 1979.

Burland, C.A., *The Four Directions of Time: An Account of Page One of Codex Fejérváry-Mayer*. Santa Fe, New Mexico: Museum of Navajo Ceremonial Art, 1950.

Burland, C.A., *The Seldon Roll: An Ancient Mexican Picture*. Manuscript in the Bodleian Library at Oxford. Berlin: Verlag Gebr. Mann., 1955.

Burland, C.A., *Introduction to Codex Fejérváry-Mayer, Codices Selecti*. Vol. XXVI. Graz, Austria: Akademische Druck- und Verlagsanstalt: 1971.

Campbell, J., *The Masks of God: Primitive Mythology*. The Viking Press, 1959.

Campbell, J., *The Masks of God: Oriental Mythology*. The Viking Press, 1962.

Campbell, J., *The Masks of God: Occidental Mythology*. The Viking Press, 1964.

Bibliography

Carraseo, P., "Social Organization of Ancient Mexico," *Handbook of Middle Amerian Indians*. Vol. 10. University of Texas Press, 1971.

Carnoy, A.J., "Iranian Mythology," *Mythology of All Races*. Vol. 6. New York: Cooper Square Publishers, Inc., 1964.

Caso, A., *Explicacion del Reverso del Codex Vindobonensis*. Edicion de el Collegio National, Mexico D.E., 1951.

Caso, A., *The Aztecs, People of the Sun*. Norman: University of Oklahoma Press, 1958.

Caso, A., "Mixtec Writing and the Calendar," *Handbook of Middle American Indians*. Vol. 3, University of Texas Press, 1965.

Caso, A., "Zapotec Writing and Calendar," *Handbook of Middle American Indians*. Vol. 3, University of Texas Press, 1965.

Caso, A., *Los Calendrios Prehispanicos*. Universidad Nacional Autonoma de Mexico, Instituto de Investigaciones Histórica, Mexico, 1967.

Caso, A., "Calendrical Systems of Central Mexico," *Handbook of Middle American Indians*. Vol. 10, University of Texas Press, 1971.

Chang, Kwang-Chih, "China: Courses Toward Urban Life," *Archaeological Considerations of Some Cultural Alternates*. Edited by Robert J. Braidwood and Gordon R. Willey. Chicago: Aldine Publishing Co., 1962.

Chang, Kwang-Chih, *The Archaeology of Ancient China*. New Haven and London: Yale University Press, 1971.

Chêng, Tê-K'un, "Shang China," *Archaeology in China*. Vol. II. Cambridge: W. Heffer & Sons, Ltd., 1960.

Childe, V. Gordon, *What Happened in History*. Baltimore, MD, U.S.A.; Mitcham, Victoria, Australia; Harmondsworth, Middlesex, Great Britain: Penguin Books, Ltd., 1942.

Childe, V. Gordon, *The Prehistory of European Society*. Bàltimore, MD, U.S.A.; Mitcham, Victoria, Australia; Harmondsworth, Middlesex, Great Britain: Penguin Books, Ltd., 1958.

Childe, V. Gordon, *New Light on the Most Ancient East*. New York: Groves Press, Inc.

Clerke, A.M., "Zodiac," *The Encyclopedia Britannica*. Eleventh Edition. New York: Encyclopedia Britannica Company, 1910-1911.

Codex Mendoza. Aztec manuscript, with commentaries by Kurt Ross. CH-Fribourg: Miller Graphics, Productions Liber, S.A., 1978.

Codex Vindobonensis Mexic, I. Faksimileausgabe der Mexikanischen Bilderhandschrift der Nationalbibliothek in Wien. Eingeleitet durch Walter Lehmann und Ottokar Smital. Verlag für Nord - U Südamerika Kunstanstalt Max Jaffeé; für alle übrigen länder; Verlag Von Anton Schroll & Co., 1929.

Coe, Michael D., *The Jaguar's Children: Pre-Classic Central Mexico*. New York: The Museum of Primitive Art, 1965.

Coe, Michael D., "The Olmec Style and its Distribution," *Handbook of Middle American Indians*. Vol. 3, University of Texas Press, 1965.

Coe, Michael D., *The Maya*. New York and Washington: Frederick A. Praeger, Inc., 1966.

Coe, Michael D., *America's First Civilization*. American Heritage Publishing Co., Inc., in association with the Smithsonian Institution, D. Van Nostrand Company, Inc., 1968.

Coe, Michael D., "Olmec Jaguars and Olmec Kings," *The Cult of the Feline: A Conference in Pre-Columbian Iconography*. October 31 and November 1, 1970. Washington, D.C.: Dumbarton Oaks Research Library and Collections, Trustees for Harvard University.

Coe, Michael D., "Death and the Ancient Maya," *Death and the Afterlife in Pre-Columbian America: A Conference at Dumbarton Oaks*. October

27, 1973. Washington, D.C.: Dumbarton Oaks Research Library and Collections, Trustees for Harvard University.

Coe, Michael D. and Richard A. Diehl, "The Archaeology of San Lorenzo Tenochtitlan," *In the Land of the Olmec*. Vol. I. Austin and London: The University of Texas Press, 1980.

Coon, Carlton, *The Story of Man, From the First Human to Primitive Culture and Beyond*. New York: Alfred A. Knopf, 1954.

Corcoran, John X.W.P., "Celtic Mythology," *Larousse Encyclopedia of Mythology*. London: Paul Hamlyn, 1959.

Covarrubias, Miguel, *Mexico South: The Isthmus of Tehuantepec*. New York: Alfred A. Knopf, 1946.

Covarrubias, Miguel, "Eagle, Jaguar and the Serpent: Indian Art of the Americas," *North America: Alaska, Canada, the United States*. New York: Alfred A. Knopf, 1954.

Covarrubias, Miguel, *Indian Art of Mexico and Central America*. New York: Alfred A. Knopf, 1957.

Davies, Nigel, *The Toltecs Until the Fall of Tula*. Norman: University of Oklahoma Press, 1977.

Davis, Whitney, "So-called Jaguar-Human Copulation Scenes in Olmec Art, " *American Antiquity*. Vol. 43, No. 5. July 1978.

Doran, Edwin, Jr., "The Sailing Raft as a Great Tradition," *Man Across the Sea: Problems of Pre-Columbian Contacts*. Austin and London: University of Texas Press, 1971.

Dixon, R.B., "Oceanic Mythology," *The Mythology of All Races*. Vol. IX, Boston: Marshall Jones Co., 1916.

Dresden, M.J., "Mythology of Ancient Iran," *Mythologies of the Ancient World*. Edited by S.N. Kramer. Doubleday & Company, Inc., 1961.

Drucker, P., R.F. Heizer, and R.J. Squier, *Excavations at La Venta Tabasco, 1955*. Smithsonian Institution Bureau of Amer. Ethnology, Bulletin 170. Washington: U.S. Govt. Printing Office, 1959.

Dumbarton Oaks Conference on the Olmec. Elizabeth P. Benson, Editor. Washington, D.C.: Dumbarton Oaks Research Library and Collections, Trustees for Harvard University, 1968.

Dumézil, G., *Archaic Roman Religion*. Translated by Phillip Krapp. Chicago and London: University of Chicago Press, 1970.

Dumézil, G., *Gods of the Ancient Northmen*. Edited and translated by Einar Haugen. Berkeley, Los Angeles, London: University of California Press, 1973.

Duran, Fray Diego, *The Aztecs, the History of the Indies of New Spain*. Translated with Notes by Doris Heyden and Fernand Horcasitas. New York: Orion Press, 1964.

Durkheim, Emile, *The Elementary Forms of Religious Life*. London: 1964.

Eggeling, H.J., "Brahman, Bráhmana, Brahmanism," *Encyclopedia Britannica*. Eleventh Edition. New York: The Encyclopedia Britannica Company, 1910-1911.

Ekholm, Gordon F., "Transpacific Contacts," *Prehistoric Man in the New World*. Published for William Marsh Rice University by University of Chicago Press, 1964.

Ekholm, Gordon F., "Diffusion and Archaeological Evidence," *Man Across the Sea: Problems of Pre-Columbian Contacts*. Austin and London: University of Texas Press, 1971.

Ekholm, Susanna, M., "A Three-sided Figure from Izapa, Chiapas, Mexico," *American Antiquity*, Vol. 33, pg. 376, 1968.

Fairservice, Walter A., Jr., "The Origins of Oriental Civilization," *Mentor Ancient Civilizations*. New York: New American Library of World Literature, Inc., 1959.

Bibliography

Ferguson, J.C., "Chinese Mythology," *Mythology of All Races*. Vol. 8. New York: Cooper Square Publishers, Inc., 1964.

Ford, James A., "A Comparison of Formative Cultures in the Americas: Diffusion or the Psychic Unity of Man." *Smithsonian Contributions to Anthropology*. Vol. 2. Washington: Smithsonian Institution Press, 1969.

Frankfort, Henri, *Kingship and the Gods: A Study of Ancient Near Eastern Religion as Integration of Society and Nature*. Chicago and London, The University of Chicago Press, 1948.

Frazer, Sir James G., *The Golden Bough, A Study in Magic and Religion*. Abridged Edition. New York: The Macmillan Company, 1958.

Furst, Jill Leslie, *Codex Vindobonensis Mexicanus I: A Commentary*. Institute for Mesoamerican Studies, Publication No. 4. Albany: State University of New York at Albany, 1978.

Furst, Peter T., "House of Darkness and House of Light: Sacred Functions of West Mexican Funerary Art," *Death and the Afterlife in Pre-Columbian America: A Conference at Dumbarton Oaks*. October 27, 1973. Elizabeth P. Benson, Editor. Washington, D.C.: Dumbarton Oaks Research Library and Collections, Trustees for Harvard University.

Furst, Peter T., "Morning Glory and Mother Goddess at Tepantitla, Teotihuacan; Iconography and Analogy in pre-Columbian Art," *Mesoamerican Archaeology, New Approaches*. Edited by Norman Hammond. Austin: University of Texas Press, 1974.

Furst, Peter T., "Jaguar Baby or Toad Mother: A New Look at an Old Problem in Olmec Iconography," *The Olmec and Their Neighbors*. Washington, D.C.: Dumbarton Oaks Research Library and Collections, Trustees for Harvard University, 1981.

Gay, Carlo T.E., *Chalcacingo*. Graz, Austria: Akademische Druck- und Verlagsanstalt, 1971.

Gallenkamp, C., *Maya, The Riddle and Rediscovery of a Lost Civilization.* New York: David McKay Company, Inc., 1959.

Ghirshman, R., *Iran: From the Earliest Times to the Islamic Conquest.* Baltimore: Penguin Books, 1954.

Gibson, C., "Structure of the Aztec Empire," *Handbook of Middle American Indians.* Vol. 10. University of Texas Press, 1971.

Gordon, C.H., "Canaanite Mythology," *Mythologies of the Ancient World.* Edited by S.N. Kramer. Doubleday & Company, Inc., 1961.

Graves, Robert, *The Greek Myths.* Baltimore: Penguin Books, 1955.

Gray, John, *The Canaanites,* New York and Washington: Frederick A. Praeger Publishers, 1964.

Grove, David C., "Chalcatzingo, Morelos, Mexico: A Reappraisal of the Olmec Rock Carvings," *American Antiquity.* Vol. 33, No. 4, 1968.

Grove, David C., "Olmec Felines in Highland Central Mexico," *The Cult of the Feline: A Conference in Pre-Columbian Iconography.* October 31 and November 1, 1970. Washington, D.C.: Dumbarton Oaks Research Library and Collections, Trustees for Harvard University.

Grove, David C., "The Highland Olmec Manifestation: A Consideration of What Is and Isn't," *Mesoamerican Archaeology, New Approaches.* Proceedings of a Symposium on Mesoamerican Archaeology held by the University of Cambridge Center of Latin American Studies in August of 1972. Austin: University of Texas Press, 1972.

Grove, David C., "Olmec Monuments: Mutilation as a Clue to Meaning," *The Olmec and Their Neighbors.* Washington, D.C.: Dumbarton Oaks Research Library and Collections, Harvard University, 1981.

Gurney, O.R., *The Hittites.* Baltimore: Penguin Books, 1961.

Guterbock, H.G., "Hittite Mythology," *Mythologies of the Ancient World.* Edited by S.N. Kramer. Doubleday & Company, Inc., 1961.

Bibliography

Haeberlin, Herman Carl, "Fertilization in Indian Pueblo Culture," *Memoirs Anthropological Assn.* Vol. 3, 1916.

Hamilton, Edith, *Mythology: Timeless Tales of Gods and Heroes.* New York and Toronto: A Mentor Book, The New American Library; London: The New English Library, Ltd. 1942.

Harner, Michael J., "Jívaro Souls in Gods and Rituals," *Middle American Source Books in Anthropology.*

Hays, H.R., *In the Beginnings: Early Man and His Gods.* New York: G.P. Putnam's Sons, 1963.

Heidel, Alexander, *The Gilgamesh Epic and Old Testament Parallels.* Chicago and London: University of Chicago Press, 1946.

Heine-Geldern, R., "The Problem of Transpacific Influences in Mesoamerica," *Handbook of Middle American Indians.* Vol. 3. University of Texas Press, 1965.

Heizer, R.F. and J.E. Gullberg, "Concave Mirrors from the Site of La Venta, Tabasco: Their Function, Minerology, and Optical Description," *The Olmec and Their Neighbors.* Washington, D.C.: Dumbarton Oaks Research Library and Collections, Trustees for Harvard University, 1981.

Heroditus, *The History of Heroditus.* Translated by George Robinson, edited by Manuel Komroff. New York: Tudor Publishing.

Holmberg, V., "Siberian Mythology," *Mythologies of All Races.* Vol. 4. New York: Cooper Square Publishers, Inc., 1964.

Hopkins, E. Washburn, *Origin and Evolution of Religion.* New York: Cooper Square Publishers, Inc., 1969.

Hubert, Henri and Marcel Mauss, *Sacrifice: Its Nature and Function.* Translated by W.D. Halls. Chicago: The University of Chicago Press, 1964.

Jacobsen, Thorkild, *Toward the Image of Tammuz and Other Essays on Mesopotamian History and Culture*. Cambridge: Harvard University Press, 1970.

Jacobsen, Thorkild, *The Treasures of Darkness: A History of Mesopotamian Religion*. New Haven and London: Yale Univesity Press, 1976.

James, E.O., *Myth and Ritual in the Ancient Near East, An Archaeological and Documentary Study*. New York: Frederick A. Praeger, 1958.

Jensen, A.E., *Myth and Cult among Primitive Peoples*. English translation by Choldin and Weissleder. Chicago and London: University of Chicago Press, 1963.

Jisl, Lumír, *Mongolian Journey*. Translated by Till Gottheiner. London: Batchworth Press, 1960.

Joralemon, Peter D., *A Study of Olmec Iconography, Studies in Pre-Columbian Art and Archaeology*. Washington, D.C.: Dumbarton Oaks Research Library and Collections, Trustees for Harvard University, 1971.

Joralemon, Peter D., "The Olmec Dragon: A Study in Pre-Columbian Iconography, *Origins of Religious Art and Iconography in Preclassic Mesoamerica*. Edited by H.B. Nicholson. Los Angeles: University of California at Los Angeles, Latin American Center Publications, 1976.

Joralemon, Peter D., "The Old Woman and the Child: Themes in the Iconography of Preclassic Mesoamerica," *The Olmec and Their Neighbors*. Washington, D.C.: Dumbarton Oaks Research Library and Collections, Trustees for Harvard University, 1981.

Keith, A.B., "Indian Mythology," *Mythology of All Races*.Vol. 6. New York: Cooper Square Publishers, Inc., 1964.

Kelley, David H., "The Birth of the Gods at Palenque," *Sobrietiro de Estudios de Cultura Maya*. Vol. V. Mexico: U.N.A.M., 1965.

Bibliography

Kelley, David H., "American Parallels," *The Alphabet and the Ancient Calendar Signs*. By Moran and Kelley. Part II. Palo Alto, CA: Daily Press, 1969.

Kelley, David H., "Diffusion: Evidence and Process," *Man Across the Sea: Problems of Pre-Columbian Contacts*. Austin and London: University of Texas Press, 1971.

Kelley, David H., "The Nine Lords of the Night," *Contributions of the University of California Research Facility No. 16*. October 1972. University of California Dept. of Anthropology.

Kelley, David H., "Eurasian Evidence and the Mayan Calendar Correlation Problem," *Mesoamerican Archaeology, New Approaches*. Edited by Norman Hammond. Austin: University of Texas Press, 1974.

Kelley, David H., "Maya Astronomical Tables and Inscriptions," *Native American Astronomy*. Edited by Anthony F. Aveni. Austin and London: University of Texas Press, 1977.

Kelley, David H. and K. Ann Kerr, "Mayan Astronomy and Astonomical Glyphs," *Dumbarton Oaks Conference on Mesoamerican Writing Systems*. Washington, D.C.: Trustees for Harvard University, 1974.

Kelley, J. Charles, "Archaeology of the Northern Frontier: Zacatecas and Durango," *Handbook of Middle American Indians*. Vol. 11. University of Texas Press, 1971.

Kindatai, *Ainu Life and Legends*. Board of Tourist Industries, Japanese Government Railways, 1941.

Kirk, G.S., *Myth, Its Meaning and Function in Ancient and Other Cultures*. Berkeley and Los Angeles: University of California Press, 1970.

Kramer, S.N., *History Begins at Sumer*. Garden City, NY: Doubleday & Co., 1959.

Kramer, S.N., "Mythology of Sumer and Akkad," *Mythologies of the Ancient World*. Garden City, NY: Doubleday & Co., 1961.

Kramer, S.N., *The Sumerians, Their History, Culture and Character*. Chicago and London: The University of Chicago Press, 1963.

Kramer, S.N., *The Sacred Marriage Rite: Aspects of Faith, Myth and Ritual in Ancient Sumer*. London and Bloomington, IN: Indiana University Press, 1969.

Kubler, George, "The Iconography of the Art of Teotihuacan," *Studies in Pre-Columbian Art and Archaeology*. No. 4. Washington, D.C.: Dumbarton Oaks Research Library and Collections, Trustees for Harvard University, 1967.

Kubler, George, "Studies in Classic Maya Iconography," *Memoirs of the Connecticut Academy of Arts and Sciences*. Vol. XVIII. New Haven, CN: Anchor Books, 1969.

Kubler, George, "Jaguars in the Valley of Mexico," *The Cult of the Feline: A Conference in Pre-Columbian Iconography*. October 31 and November 1, 1970. Washington, D.C.: Dumbarton Oaks Research Library and Collections, Trustees for Harvard University.

Kühn, H. *On the Track of Prehistoric Man*. Translated from the German by Alan Houghton Brodrick. New York: Random House, 1955.

Kühn, H., *The Rock Pictures of Europe*. Fair Lawn, NJ: Essential Books, Inc., 1956.

Lamberg, Karlovsky C.C. and Martha, "An Early City in Iran," *Scientific American*. June 1971.

Legrain, Leon, *The Babylonian Collections of the University Museum*. Revised Edition. Philadelphia: The University Museum of Pennsylvania, 1950.

León-Portilla, Miguel, "Mythology of Ancient Mexico," *Mythologies of the Ancient World*. Edited by S.N. Kramer. Doubleday & Company, Inc., 1961.

Bibliography

León-Portilla, Miguel, *Aztec Thought and Culture, A Study of the Ancient Nahuatl Mind.* Translated from the Spanish by Jack Emory Davis. Norman: University of Oklahoma Press, 1963.

Levy, G.R., *Religious Conception of the Stone Age and Their Influence upon European Thought.* New York and Evanston: Harper and Row, The Cloister Library, Harper Torch Books, 1963.

Linné, S., "Mexican Highland Cultures," *Archaeological Researches at Teotihuacan, Calpulalpin, and Chalchicomula in 1934/35.* Stockholm: 1942.

Linton, Ralph, *The Tree of Culture.* New York: Alfred A. Knopf, 1957.

Littleton, C. Scott, "An Anthropological Assessment of the Theories of Georges Dumézil," *The New Comparative Mythology.* Berkeley, Los Angeles, and London: University of California Press, 1973.

Lloyd, Seton, *Early Anatolia.* Baltimore: Penguin Books, 1956.

Luckert, Karl W., *Olmec Religion: A Key to Middle America and Beyond.* Norman: University of Oklahoma Press, 1976.

Lumholtz, Carl, "Symbolism of the Huichol Indians," *Memoirs of the American Museum of Natural History.* Vol. III, Anthropology II. New York: 1900.

Lumholtz, Carl, *Unknown Mexico*, London: Macmillan Co. Limited, 1903.

MacCana Proinsias, *Celtic Mythology.* Hamlyn, 1970.

MacCulloch, J.A., "Eddic Mythology," *Mythology of All Races.* Vol. 2. New York: Cooper Square Publishers, Inc., 1964.

MacCulloch, J.A., "Celtic Mythology," *Mythology of All Races.* Vol. 3. New York: Cooper Square Publishers, Inc., 1964.

Marinatos, S. and Max Hirmer, *Crete and Mycenae.* New York: Harry N. Abrams, Inc.

Maringer, Johannes, *Gods of Prehistoric Man*. Edited and translated from the German by Mary Ilford. Alfred A. Knopf, 1960.

Maudsley, A.P., *Biologia, Central-Americana, Archaeology 1889-1902*. Facsimile edition. Milpatron Publishing Corp., 1974.

Meggers, B.F., Cliford Evans, and Emilio Estrada, "Early Formative Period of Coastal Ecuador: The Valdivia and Machalella Phases," *Smithsonian Contributions to Anthropology*. Washington: Smithsonian, 1965.

Mexico: Pre-Hispanic Paintings. Preface by Jacques Soustelle and Introduction by Ignacio Bernal. New York: New York Graphic Society by arrangement with U.N.E.S.C.O., 1958.

Miller, Arthur G., *The Mural Painting of Teotihuacan*. Washington, D.C.: Dumbarton Oaks Research Library and Collections, Trustees for Harvard University, 1973.

Money, Kyrle, *The Meaning of Sacrifice*. Published by Leonard and Virginia Woolf at the Hogarth Press, 52 Travistock Square, London, W.C. and the Institute of Psycho-Analysis, 1930. Reprinted by Johnson Reprint Corporation, New York and London.

Moreno, Wigberto Himénez, "Mesoamerica Before the Toltecs," *Ancient Oaxaca: Discoveries in Mexican Archaeology and History*. Stanford: Stanford University Press, 1966.

Morley, Sylvanus G., *The Ancient Maya*. Revised by George W. Brainerd. Stanford: Stanford University Press, 1946.

Moscati, Sabatino, *Ancient Semitic Civilization*. New York: G.P. Putnam's Sons, 1957.

Moser, Christopher L., "Human Decapitation in Ancient Mesoamerica," *Studies in Pre-Columbian Art and Archaeology*, No. 11. Washington, D.C.: Dumbarton Oaks Research Library and Collections, Trustees for Harvard University, 1973.

Bibliography

McEwan, G.F. and D.B. Dickson, "Valdivia, Jomon Fisherman, and the Nature of the North Pacific: Some Nautical Problems with Meggers, Evans, and Estrada's (1965) Transoceanic Contact Thesis," *American Antiquity*. Vol. 43, No. 3. July, 1978.

Needham, J. "Science and Civilization in China," Vol. 3, *Mathematics and the Sciences of the Heavens and the Earth*. Cambridge, London, New York, and Melbourne: Cambridge University Press, 1959.

Nicholson, H.B., "Religion in Pre-Hispanic Central Mexico," *Handbook of the Middle American Indians*. Vol. 10. University of Texas Press, 1971.

Nicholson, H.B., "Preclassic Mesoamerican Iconography from the Perspective of the Postclassic: Problems in Interpretational Analysis," *Origins of Religious Art and Iconography in Preclassic Mesoamerica*. Edited by H.B. Nicholson. Los Angeles: University of California at Los Angeles, Latin American Center Publications, 1976.

Nicholson, Irene, *Mexican and Central American Mythology*. London: Paul Hamlyn, 1967.

Nilsson, Martin P., *Mycenaean Origin of Greek Mythology*. Berkeley and Los Angeles: University of California Press, 1972.

Norman, V. Garth, "Izapa Sculpture, Part 1," *Album Papers of the New World Archaeological Foundation*. No. 30. Provo, Utah: Brigham Young University, New World Archaeological Foundation, 1973.

Nuttall, Zelia, "The Fundamental Principles of Old and New World Civilizations: A Comparative Research Based on a Study of the Ancient Mexican Religious, Sociological, and Calendrical Systems," *Archaeological and Ethnological Papers of the Peabody Museum*. Vol.II. Cambridge: Peabody Museum, 1901.

Paddock, John, "Oaxaca in Ancient Mesoamerica," *Ancient Oaxaca: Discoveries in Mexican Archaeology and History*. Stanford: Stanford University Press, 1966.

Pasztory, Esther, "The Iconography of the Teotihuacan Tlaloc," *Studies in Pre-Columbian Art and Archaeology*. No. 15. Washington, D.C.: Dumbarton Oaks Research Library and Collections, Trustees for Harvard University, 1974.

Paulsen, Allison C., "Patterns of Maritime Trade Between South Coastal Ecuador and Western Mesoamerica, 1500 B.C. to A.D. 600," *The Sea in the Pre-Columbian World*. Conference at Dumbarton Oaks, October 26 and 27, 1974. Elizabeth P. Benson, Editor. Washington, D.C.: Dumbarton Oaks Research Library and Collections, Trustees for Harvard University.

Phillips, P., "The Role of Transpacific Contacts in the Development of New World Pre-Columbian Civilization," *Handbook of Middle American Indians*. Vol. 3. University of Texas Press, 1965.

Pickands, M., "The 'First Father' Legend in Maya Mythology and Iconography," *Third Palenque Round Table, 1978*. Edited by Merle Greene Robertson. Austin and London: University of Texas Press, 1980.

Piggott, Stuart, *The Druids*. New York and Washington: Praeger Publishers, 1968.

Pina Chan, Roman, *Mesoamerica, Memorias*. Vol. VI. I.N.A.H. Mexico: 1960.

Pina Chan, Roman, and L. Covarrubias, *El Pueblo del Jaguar (Los Olmecas Arqueologicios)*. Consejo Para la Planeacion e Instalacion del Museo National de Antropologia Sep. Mexico: 1964.

Popul Vuh: The Sacred Book of the Ancient Quiché Maya. English version by Delia Goetz and Sylvanus G. Morely, from the translation of Adrian Recinos. Norman: University of Oklahoma Press, 1950.

Porada, Edith, "The Art of Ancient Iran," *Pre-Islamic Cultures*. New York: Crown Publishers, Inc., 1965.

Puhvel, Jaan, *Myth and Law Among the Indo-Europeans: Studies in Indo-European Comparative Mythology*. Berkeley, Los Angeles, London: University of California Press, 1970.

Quirarte, Jacinto, "Izapa-Style Art, A Study of its Form and Meaning," *Studies in Pre-Columbian Art and Archaeology*. No.10. Washington, D.C.: Dumbarton Oaks Research Library and Collections, Trustees for Harvard University, 1973.

Quirarte, Jacinto, "Tricephalic Units in Olmec, Izapan Style and Maya Art," *The Olmec and Their Neighbors*. Washington, D.C.: Dumbarton Oaks Research Library and Collections, Trustees for Harvard University, 1981.

Radin, Paul, *Winnebago Hero Cycles: A Study in Aboriginal Literature*. Indiana University Publications in Anthropology and Linguistics, Memoir 1 of the International Journal of American Linguistics. Baltimore: Waverly Press, 1948.

Radin, Paul, *The Trickster: A Study in American Indian Mythology*. With commentaries by Karl Kerenyi and C.G. Jung. New York: Philosophical Library, 1956.

Radin, Paul, *Primitive Religion: Its Nature and Origin*. New York: Dover Publications, Inc., 1957.

Rice, Tamara Talbot, *The Scythians*. New York: Frederick A. Praeger, 1957.

Rivet, Paul, *Maya Cities*. New York: G.P. Putnam's Sons, London Elek Books, 1960.

Robertson, M.G., "An Iconographic Approach to the Identity of the Figures on the Piers of the Temple of the Inscriptions, Palenque," *Tercera Mesa Redonda de Palenque*. Vol. IV. Monterey, CA: Pre-Columbian Art Research, Herald Printers, 1978.

Robertson, Merle Green, *The Sculpture of Palenque*, Vol. I, *The Temple of the Inscriptions*. Princeton, Princeton University Press, 1983.

Robicsek, Francis, *Copan, Home of the Mayan Gods*. New York: Museum of the American Indians, Heye Foundation, 1972.

Robicsek, Francis, "The Mythical Identity of God K," *Tercera Mesa Redonda de Palenque*. Vol. IV. Monterey, CA: Pre-Columbian Art Research, Herald Printers, 1978.

Rose, H.J., *Religion in Greece and Rome*. New York: Harper & Brothers, Harper Torchbooks, 1959.

Ross, Ann, *Pagan Celtic Britain: Studies in Iconography and Tradition*. London: Routledge and Kegan Paul; New York, Columbia University Press, 1967.

Ross, Ann, *Everyday Life of the Pagan Celts*. London: B.T. Batsford Ltd.; New York: G.P. Putnam's Sons, 1970.

Royes, R.L., *The Book of Chilam Balam of Chumayel*. Norman: University of Oklahoma Press, 1967.

Rudenko, Sergi I., *Frozen Tombs of Siberia*. Translated with preface by M.W. Thompson. Berkeley and Los Angeles: University of California Press, 1970.

Ruppert, K., J.S. Eric Thompson, Tatiana Proskuriakoff, *Bonampak, Chiapas, Mexico*. Publication 602. Washington: Carnegie Institution, 1955.

Saggs, H.W.F. *The Greatness That Was Babylon: A Sketch of the Ancient Civilization of the Tigris-Euphrates Valley*. New York: Hawthorn Books, Inc., 1962.

Sanders, W.T. and J. Marino, *New World Prehistory, Archaeology of the American Indian*. Englewood Cliffs, NJ: Prentice Hall, Inc., 1970.

Satterthwait, L., "Calendrics of the Maya Lowlands," *Handbook of Middle American Indians*. Vol. 3. Austin: University of Texas Press, 1965.

Schávelzon, Daniel, "Temples, Caves or Monsters? Notes on Zoomorphic Facades in Pre-Hispanic Architecture," *Third Palenque Round Table, 1978*. Part 2. Edited by Merle Green Roberston. London and Austin: University of Texas Press, 1980.

Schele, L., "Palenque: The House of the Dying Sun," *Native American Astronomy*. Edited by Anthony F. Aveni. London and Austin: University of Texas Press, 1977.

Schele, L., "Genealogical Documentation of the Tri-Figure Panels at Palenque," *Tercera Mesa Redonda de Palenque*. Vol. IV. Monterey, CA: Pre-Columbian Art Research, Herald Printers, 1978.

Séjourné, Laurette, *Burning Water, Thought and Religion in Ancient Mexico*. New York: The Vanguard Press, 1956.

Séjourné, Laurette, *Un Palacio en la Ciudad de Los Dioses (Teotihuacan)*. Mexico: Instituto de Antropologiá & Historia, 1959.

Seler, Eduard, *Codex Fejérváry-Mayer, Eine Altmexicánische Bilderlaudschrift der Free Public Museum in Liverpool*. English translation. Berlin and London: 1901-1902.

Seler, Eduard, *The Tonalmatl of the Auban Collection*. Berlin and London: 1901-1902.

Seler, Eduard, *Observations and Studies in the Ruins of Palenque, 1915*. Translated by Gesela Morgner, edited by Thomas Bartman and George Kubler, compiled by Merle Greene Robertson. Monterey, CA: Herald Printers, 1976.

Shao, Paul, *Asiatic Influences in Pre-Columbian American Art*. Ames, IA: The Iowa State University Press, 1976.

Sharp, Andrew, *Ancient Voyagers in the Pacific*. Baltimore; Mitcham; Harmondsworth: Penguin Books, Ltd., 1957.

Smith, W. Robertson, *The Religion of the Semites: The Fundamental Institutions*.New York: Meridian Books, The Meridian Library, 1956.

Sorenson, John L., "The Significance of an Apparent Relationship between the Ancient Near East and Mesoamerica," *Man Across the Sea: Problems of Pre-Columbian Contacts*. Austin and London: University of Texas Press, 1971.

Soustelle, Jacques, *Arts of Ancient Mexico*. New York: The Viking Press, 1967.

Spencer, R.F., J.D. Jennings et al., *The Native Americans*. London, Evanston, and New York: Harper and Row, 1965.

Spores, R. *The Mixtec Kings and Their People*. Norman: University of Oklahoma Press, 1967.

Stern, Theodore, *The Rubber Ball Games of the Americas*. Monographs of the American Ethnological Society, No. 17. London and Seattle: University of Washington Press, 1949.

Stirling, Matthew W., "Stone Monuments in Southern Mexico," *Smithsonian Institution Bureau of American Ethnology*. Bulletin 138. Washington: U.S. Government Printing Office, 1943.

Stirling, Matthew W., "Monumental Sculpture of Southern Vera Cruz and Tobasco," *Handbook of Middle American Indians*. Vol. 3. Austin: University of Texas Press, 1965.

Stocker, T., S. Meltsoff, and S. Armsey, "Crocodilians and Olmecs: Further Interpretations in Formative Period Iconography," *American Antiquity*. Vol. 45, No. 4. October, 1980.

Suggs, Robert C., "The Island Civilizations of Polynesia," *Mentor Ancient Civilizations*. New York: The New American Library of World Literature, Inc., 1960.

Sumerian Art, Illustrated by Objects from Ur and Al-Ubaid. London: The British Museum, 1969.

The Holy Bible. Authorized King James Version. New York, Toronto, and London: Oxford University Press.

Bibliography

The Peoples of Siberia. Edited by M.G. Levin and L.P. Potapov. London and Chicago: The University of Chicago Press, 1964.

Thompson, J.S. Eric, *Folklore of San Antonio*. San Antonio, TX: Field Museum of Natural History Publications.

Thompson, J.S. Eric, *The Rise and Fall of Maya Civilizations*. Norman: University of Oklahoma Press, 1954.

Thompson, J.S. Eric, *Maya Hieroglyphic Writing*. Norman: University of Oklahoma Press, 1960.

Thompson, J.S. Eric, *Maya History and Religion*. Norman: University of Oklahoma Press, 1970.

Tonnelar, E., "Teutonic Mythology: Germany and Scandanavia, *Larousse Encyclopedia of Mythology*. London: Paul Hamlyn, 1959.

Tozzer, Alfred M., translator and editor. *Landa's Relación de las Cosas de Yucatan*. Papers of the Peabody Museum of American Archaeology and Ethnology. Vol. XVIII. Cambridge: Harvard University and the Peabody Museum, 1941.

Troike, Nancy P., "Fundamental Changes in the Interpretations of the Mixtec Codices," *American Antiquity*. Vol. 43, No. 4, 1978.

Von Cles-Reden, Sibylle, *The Realm of the Great Goddess: The Story of the Megalithic Builders*. Englewood Cliffs, NJ: Prentice-Hall, Inc., 1962.

Von Winning, Hasso, and O. Hammer, *Anecdotal Sculpture of Ancient West Mexico*. An Ethnic Arts Publication and Exhibition Sponsored by the Ethnics Arts Council at the Natural History Museum of Los Angeles County, 1972.

Von Winning, Hasso, "Late and Terminal Preclassic: The Emergence of Teotihuacan," *Origins of Religious Art and Iconography in Preclassic Mesoamerica*. Edited by H.B. Nicholson. Latin American Center Publications, 1976.

Wauchope, Robert, "Southern Mesoamerica," *Prehistoric Man in the New World*. Published for William Marsh Rice University by the University of Chicago Press, 1964.

Weaver, Muriel Porter, "The Aztecs, Maya and their Predecessors," *Archaeology of Mesoamerica*. London and New York: Seminar Press, 1972.

Westheim, Paul, *The Art of Ancient Mexico*. Translated from Spanish to English by Ursula Bernard. Garden City, NY: Doubleday & Company, Inc., Anchor Books, 1965.

Weyer, Edward, Jr. *Primitive Peoples of Today*. Garden City, NY: Doubleday & Company, Inc.

Wheeler, Sir Mortimer, "The Indus Civilization," *The Cambridge History of India, Supplemental Volume*. Cambridge: University Press, 1960.

Wicke, C.R. *Olmec: An Early Art Style of Pre-Columbian Mexico*. Tucson: University of Arizona Press, 1971.

Willets, W., *Chinese Art*. Baltimore: Penguin Books, Inc., 1958.

Willey, G.R., *Mesoamerica, Courses Toward Urban Life: Archaeological Considerations of Some Cultural Alternates*. Edited by Robert J. Braidwood and Gordon R. Willey. Chicago: Aldine Publishing Co., 1962.

Willey, G.R., *An Introduction to American Archaeology*. Vol. 1, North and Middle America. Englewood Cliffs, NJ: Prentice-Hall, Inc., 1966.

Zimmer, Heinrich, *The Art of Indian Asia: Its Mythology and Transformations*. Completed and edited by Joseph Cambell. Bollingen Series XXXIX. New York: Pantheon Books, 1955.

GLOSSARY

Abhijit, a *nakshatra* (asterism) in the constellation Lyra featuring the bright star Vega.

Aditi, in Vedic mythology, the universe as Mother of the World and all things and life within it; all gods.

Aditya, offspring of Aditi, Asuras representing the forces of life in the creation of Vedic mythology.

Adonis, the Greek form of the god Dumuzi [Tammuz] as consort of the Great Goddess in her aspects as the planetary Venus and the Death Goddess.

Agdistis, the hermaphrodite form of Atlas and Cybele united as one. Attis was the Phrygian form of the god of vegetation and animal life and Cybele is the Death Goddess and Earth Mother; in the planetary doctrine, their bisexed form was the new Moon forming as the year of new life on earth.

Agni, Indo-Aryan (Vedic) Fire God; the earth in the dynastic succession of creation; the Sun in the planetary cycle; in his complete aspect, all the gods.

Ahrensburg hunters, deer hunters living in northern Germany circa 10,000 B.C. whose cult remains were found at Stellmoor.

Aillil, in the Celtic mythology of Ireland, god-king of Connacht.

Ainu, a primitive tribe living in Japan whose culture is hunting and whose religion is the Bear Cult in which the bear is held to be a god.

***Akitu* festival**, the New Year festival in ancient Babylon.

Altai, a mountain district in central Asia.

An, Sumerian Sky God.

Anu, Babylonian, Hurrian, and Hittite name for the Sky God.

Aphrodite, the Greek form of the Sumero-Babylonian goddess Inanna-Ishtar, goddess of the planet Venus.

Apsu, [Abzu], Sumero-Babylonian progenitor god, the Abyss, and the primordial fresh waters.

Ares, Greek name for Mars.

Argonauts, in Greek mythology, a group of Greek god-kings and heroes led by Jason on his voyage to secure the Golden Fleece.

Artimpasa, the Scythian name of the Great Goddess in her life aspect, the Scythian Ishtar.

Astarte, Canaanite name for Ishtar.

Asuras, in Vedic mythology, supernatural spirit forms of potential life existing at the time of the creation of the world.

Attis, Phrygian name for Dumuzi [Tammuz] as god of vegetation. In his underworld aspect, he was merged with the Earth Mother as Cybele [the Sumerian equivalent is Ereshkigal] as the hermaphrodite Agdistis; on earth, he was incarnate in a high priest who took the name Attis.

Aztecs, one of the Chichimec tribes living north of the border of Mesoamerica which migrated southward during the last half of the twelfth century A.D. and settled in the Valley of Mexico at the site of present-day Mexico City. They adopted Mesoamerican culture and had established themselves as masters of most of central Mexico at the time of the Spanish conquest (circa 1520 A.D.).

***Bil* sign**, Mayan symbol for maize.

Birth Tree of Apoala, a pictograph in the *Codex Vindobonensis* representing the annual reincarnation of the god of maize and life-sustaining plants in the person of the Mixtec ruler. In the pictograph, the god is shown as the god of sacrifice, Xipe, descending as 7-Rain in

death through the trunk of the tree of life; receiving new life from the Death Goddess and Earth Mother as 9-Reed in her aspect as the new Moon; rising as new maize and good crops as 7-Eagle through the trunk of the life tree; and coming on earth as the godhead of the ruler through its flowering branches.

Bolon Dz'acab, in Maya religion, the immortal spirit as the combined divinity of the Moon and Sun as the life of vegetation.

Brahmana, Sanskrit texts elaborating and explaining the Vedic sacrificial rituals.

Celts, a group of Indo-European tribes which moved out of the Eurasian steppes in the second millennium B.C. spreading westward across Europe and crossing to the British Isles.

Centeotl, the Aztec Maize God, one of the Lords of the Night.

Cernunnos, Supreme God of the Celts.

Chalchihuites, the form of Mesoamerican culture as it developed in the northwesterly region of Mesoamerica around 300 A.D.

Chalchiuhlicue, a Moon and Earth Goddess, spouse of Tlaloc. She was one the Nahuatlan creator gods, as the Fourth Sun. Her title was "Goddess of Waters" which related her to the waters of creation.

Chan Bahlum, son of Pacal and Moon, godhead of the divine rulers of Palenque.

Chichimecs, barbarian tribes living north of the border of Mesoamerica toward the end of the Classic and the beginning of the Postclassic Periods (700 – 1300 A.D.).

Chicomecoatl, 7-Serpent, a name for the Earth Mother as maize in Nahuatlan religion.

Chou Period, a dynastic period in ancient China, circa 1027 – 221 B.C.

Cihuacoatl, Snake Woman. One of the names of the Earth Mother. Also the title of the head of the Aztec warriors and the First Lord under the Aztec supreme ruler.

Coatlicue, one of the names of the Earth Mother, the mother of the Aztec god of the Sun and of war, Huitzilopochtli.

Codex, a pictograph manuscript painted on alternating folds of strips of deer hide or comparable backing material, with covers fastened at the ends to hold the folds in book form.

Cosmogonic band, in Maya iconography, a bar or band shown on icons, usually terminating at each end in a serpent head and marked with x-signs of the fire-serpents. It is used to mark the division between the realms of life formation and life in the underworld.

Cybele, Phrygian name of the Great Goddess, the Babylonian Ishtar.

Damkina, Babylonian name for Ninhursag, spouse of Ea.

Danavas, Asuras representing the mortal forces of death in the Vedic creation myth.

Deianeira, one of Hercules' wives. In the planetary doctrine as it was contained in the mythology of Hercules, Deianeira was the goddess Ishtar.

Dumuzi, Sumerian god of vegetation and animal life, and spouse of Inanna, with combined divinity of Sun and Moon. The godhead of Sumerian kings.

Dyaus, *Dyaus Pitar*, the Indo-Aryan (Vedic) progenitor god, the Sky Father.

Dyavaprithivi, the Indo-Aryan (Vedic) progenitor couple united as one. Corresponding to the Sumero-Babylonian Anshar and Kishar.

Ea, the Babylonian Enki.

Glossary

Earth-lion, the serpent which stole the old-man-becomes-young plant from Gilgamesh, the immortal form of Gilgamesh as the Mercury Moon spirit.

Ehecatl, the Nahuatlan Wind God, an aspect of the planet Venus as the twin gods Quetzalcoatl and Xolotl, the gods of the morning and evening stars.

Enki, Sumerian god of the Earth and underworld, dispatcher of life to the world above.

Enkidu, the companion of Gilgamesh in the story of creation described in the *Epic of Gilgamesh*; a personification of the Moon.

Enlil, Sumero-Babylonian Storm God, god of the region of life on earth.

Epic of Gilgamesh, an account of the creation and coming of life on earth through the medium of divine kings. The epic is best known from a late Babylonian version but was originally composed in Sumer and was accepted as a statement of the planetary doctrine of the Great Goddess religion by the peoples of ancient Mesopotamia.

Erech, city in ancient Mesopotamia whose kings were divine rulers of Sumer.

Ereshkigal, Sumerian Death Goddess and Earth Mother.

Erytheia, in Greek mythology, the island of death in the western ocean, seat of the three-bodied Geryon.

Eurystheus, Divine King of Mycenae, or according to some accounts of Tiryns, for whom Hercules performed the twelve labors.

Fifth Sun, a Mesoamerican term for the world in being, also called Sun of Movement.

Flood and Fire, a symbolic term for the creation of a new cycle of vegetation as life on earth.

Flowering War [Flower War, War of Flowers], a limited action of religious warfare between neighboring states, fought for the purpose of taking prisoners for sacrifice to maintain Ollin (the continuing order of world life). The name relates to the return to life of vegetation from its winter death.

Geryon, in Greek mythology, the personification of the Moon dying in the last quarter and coming to life in its death state as the new Moon. Geryon had three heads and bodies. He lodged on Erytheia, the island of death, where Hercules killed him in the performance of his tenth labor.

Geshtinanna, aspect of Inanna as Death Goddess and Earth Mother in Sumero-Babylonian religion.

Gilgamesh, Divine King of Sumer, circa 2600 B.C. The protagonist in the *Epic of Gilgamesh* which describes the creation of his godhead as king. Gilgamesh's immortal godhead was constituted by the divinity of the planet Mercury and the Sun.

Gilyaks, a primitive tribe living in Siberia whose culture is hunting and whose religion is the Bear Cult in which the bear is held to be a god.

God C, a Moon incarnation of the Sun, as a god of vegetation in Maya religion.

God K, Bolon Dz'acab, a Maya form of the Nahuatlan god, Tezcatlipoca.

God L, in Maya religion, the Sun incarnate in the Moon dying in the last quarter and reviving as the new Moon; the dead Sun, the new Moon as 7-Jaguar.

Greeks, a group of Indo-European peoples who settled in western Asia Minor and the peninsula of Greece during the third and second millennia B.C.

Hades, in Greek mythology, Death God and ruler of the underworld.

Halach uinic, title of the Maya supreme ruler.

Glossary

Hathor, the Egyptian Mother Goddess or Earth Mother. She was imagined as a cow living in the mountains of Upper Egypt where she received the deceased at their burial. She also had a sky aspect as the heavenly cow, and a death aspect as the destroyer of mankind, in which aspect she was the Eye of the Sun God Re; the Eye identified her with the ancient concept of the Sumero-Babylonian planetary goddess Venus as the immortal spirit of the mortal Moon Goddess.

Heavenly Bull, in Sumero-Babylonian mythology, the animal sent by the Sky God, Anu, at the request of Ishtar, to destroy Gilgamesh and Enkidu, also the spouse of the Death Goddess and Earth Mother, Ereshkigal.

Helius, the Greek divinity of the Sun.

Hera, wife of Zeus in the Olympian pantheon, originally a Moon Goddess and the Earth Mother.

Hercules (Roman) or **Heracles** (Greek), a god worshiped in the countries of the eastern Mediterranean whose godhead was incarnate in the kings. He was the progenitor of the Scythians. In Greek mythology, he was cast as a hero with extraordinary strength who was deified and added to the Olympian pantheon. In the planetary cycles, Hercules was the Sun-bearer Mercury with a Moon incarnation.

Hermes, Greek name of the planetary god Mercury. In Greek religion, the messenger of the gods and conductor of souls to the underworld. In the planetary doctrine, he was the Sun-bearer; in the planetary cycles, he was the Sun and, in combination with the Sun, the life spirit which gave the Moon its motion.

Hittites, a group of Indo-European peoples who invaded and settled in Asia Minor during the second millennium B.C.

Horus, son of Osiris and Isis, god incarnate as the living king of Egypt on Earth. His godhead was a composite divinity of the morning star, the Sun and Moon.

Huehueteotl, "Old God," a name for the Nahuatlan Fire God.

Huichols, an Indian tribe now living in western Mexico in the mountains of Nayarit, whose culture at the turn of the nineteenth and twentieth centuries was essentially the same as that of their pre-Columbian ancestors.

Huitzilopochtli, the tutelary god of the Aztecs, the Fifth Sun (quod vide) as life on Earth.

Huwawa, a monster under the guardianship of the Sun God in Sumero-Babylonian mythology.

Illamatecuhtli, a name for the Death Goddess and Earth Mother as the Moon in Nahuatlan religion.

Inanna, the Sumerian Great Goddess in her cosmic form as the planet Venus and the divine spirit of all forms of earthly life.

Indo-Aryans, a group of Indo-European peoples who established themselves in northwest India in the middle of the second millennium B.C.

Indra, the Indo-Aryan (Vedic) Storm God. The fourth god in the dynastic succession of creation who brought the world into existence by cleaving the body of the cosmic serpent Vritra, the Vedic counterpart of the Sumerian Enlil.

Ishtar, the Babylonian name of Inanna as the divinity of the Great Goddess.

Isis, in Egyptian religion, spouse of Osiris, and Egyptian form of the Great Goddess.

Itzam Na, Supreme God of the Mayas.

Itzpapalotl, Obsidian Butterfly, Nahuatlan Moon Goddess of Death, one of the name forms of the Earth Mother.

Itztlacoliuhqui, death aspect of the Aztec god of maize, Centeotl, and a variant of Tezcatlipoca, god of frost.

Itztli, the Nahuatlan god Flint Knife, one of the Lords of the Night as the new Moon.

Ixteucale, a god form of the planet Venus as the Sun-bearer, companion of Tezcatlipoca in the year ritual of Toxcatl of the Aztec calendar.

Janus, Roman god of beginning. Janus was commonly represented with two heads or faces turned in opposite directions, he was comparable to the Babylonian god Ea, ruler of the death region of the underworld and giver of life, and his servant Isimud with two addorsed heads.

Jason, Divine King of Corinth, leader of the Argonauts on a fabulous voyage from Greece to Colchis on the eastern shore of the Black Sea to secure the Golden Fleece. Jason represents the survival of the planetary doctrine of Divine Kingship in Greek mythology. In his divinity as king, he was the Sun-bearer Mercury incarnate as the Mood God and consort of the Moon Goddess, Medea.

Jupiter, Supreme God of the Roman pantheon identified with the Greek Zeus; in the planetary cycles, the planetary god Jupiter was the full Moon.

Khepri, an alias of Atum, the Egyptian god of beginning who emerged from the primeval waters of creation as a serpent, or a beetle, on a flaming hill, the primordial form of all the gods combined.

Lords of the Day, the 13 gods of the new Moon as days of creation in the Nahuatlan calendar.

Lords of the Night, gods of the days of earthly life, nine in number, in the Nahuatlan calendar.

Maat, the order of world life established by the gods in the creation of the Egyptian world.

Marduk, tutelary god of Babylon with attributes of the Storm God Enlil, and the god of vegetation and animal life, Dumuzi; the godhead of the king.

Mars, Roman name for Ares, the god of war in the Olympian pantheon; god of spring. In the planetary cycles, Mars was the Moon in its first quarter.

Medea, in Greek mythology, daughter of Aeëtes and heiress to the throne of Corinth. A Moon Goddess counterpart of Ishtar, and spouse of Jason.

Medhbh, in the Celtic mythology of Ireland, spouse of Aillil, Queen of Connacht, the incarnation of the Earth Goddess.

Meiendorf, an ancient site in northern Germany containing the archaeological remains of deer hunters living circa 15,000 — 10,000 B.C.

Me's, in Sumerian religion, the laws established by the gods for maintaining the order of world life.

Mictlantecuhtli, the Aztec god of death, one of the Lords of the Night.

Mimir, in Teutonic mythology, boon companion of Odin and his aspect as the evening star.

Mitra, in Vedic mythology, the planetary god Mercury as the Sun-bearer.

Mixtecs, a tribal group living in southern Mexico immediately north and west of the Zapotecs. Mixtec culture flourished following the decline of the Zapotecs at the beginning of the eighth century A.D.

Moctezuma, the ruler of the Aztecs at the time of the Spanish Conquest.

Moira, the decrees of the Fates in the religious beliefs of the ancient Greeks.

Mother-Eagle-Young-Girl, the Huichol Tate Velike Uimale, the upperworld or earthly life aspect of the Huichol Earth Goddess.

Mt. Mashu, a mountain in the Sumero-Babylonian underworld; the gateway to the death region was through Mt. Mashu.

Mycenae, ancient Greek city in Argolis in the Peloponnesus, a center of Mycenaean civilization which flourished circa 2800 – 1100 B.C.

Nabu, Babylonian planetary god Mercury, son of Marduk.

Nahuatlan, the Postclassic culture (circa 900 – 1500 A.D.) of central Mexico, including the Toltec and Aztec.

Nakawe, the Huichol Earth Mother and Mother of the Gods. In one of her aspects, she was the Moon with the animal form of a serpent.

Nakshatras, asterisms or star groups in the Hindu lunar zodiac, also termed lunar mansions.

Nanauatzin, the god who became Sun in the Nahuatlan (Aztec) creation myth.

Nanna, also Nanna-Sin, Sin, Sumero-Babylonian Moon God.

Nemontemi days, the Aztec term for the 5 days of the solar year at the end of the Mesoamerican calendrical year of 360 days. They were days when life was believed to depart from the earth and so were regarded as unlucky days.

Nera, the planetary god Mercury in the Celtic myth of Samhuin.

Nergal, Sumerian god of death, the planetary god Mars.

Nessus, a centaur and form of Hercules as the full Moon. In the myth of Hercules and Nessus, Hercules saw Nessus ravishing his wife, Deianeira, and killed him with an arrow shot. The killing describes the full Moon changing to the new Moon.

Ningal, Sumero-Babylonian Moon Goddess.

Ninhursag, Sumerian Earth Goddess, spouse of Enki.

Ninlil, spouse of Enlil in Sumero-Babylonian religion.

Ninurta, Sumerian name of the planetary god Mercury.

Ochpaniztli, in the Aztec calendar, the eleventh month (August 31 – September 19) feast portraying the creation in the underworld of the maize crop of the new year on earth.

Odin, the Teutonic planetary god Mercury and Supreme God.

Ollin, in Nahuatlan religion, the motion of the Moon combined with the Sun as the power of creation and maintenance of the order of world life; the Fifth Sun or Sun of Movement.

Olmecs, peoples living in the southeastern part of Mexico and neighboring Guatemala during the last half of the second millennium B.C. The Olmec culture became the mother culture of Mesoamerican civilization.

Olympus, highest mountain in Greece, its cloud-shrouded summit was held to be the home of the Olympian gods.

Omecihuatl, the Nahuatlan name of the progenitor goddess.

Ometecuhtli, the Nahuatlan name of the progenitor god.

Ometeotl, the Nahuatlan name of the Mesoamerican Supreme Being, as the universe. In his various aspects, he was the Creator-Maker, the progenitor couple, and all the gods. His name means "Two Lords."

Osiris, the first King of Egypt; also the Moon, growing grain and vegetation, the deceased king, lord of the dead; principle god of ancient Egypt.

Pacal, divine ruler of the Mayan center of Palenque 615 – 683 A.D. After his death, he was buried in a crypt under the pyramid of the Temple of the Inscriptions. As the living ruler, he was the Moon and in death, the Moon spirit Venus combined with the Sun. His body in its sarcophagus became the new Moon as the creator of the annual cycles of the life of Palenque.

Palenque, a classic Maya ceremonial center in southern Mexico.

Persephone, Greek goddess of death, spouse of Hades.

Phryxus, in Greek mythology, the spirit of deceased god-king of Boeotia which descended to the underworld place of death on a winged ram with a golden fleece. Phryxus sacrificed the ram and on a tree hung its fleece — the object of Jason's voyage as leader of the Argonauts.

Planetary cycle, the cyclical succession of the planetary gods in their lunar motion.

Planetary gods, seven Moon Gods uniting the Sun to the motion of the Moon. In the union, they were gods of the Moon's phases in its cyclical motion through the course of the solar year. In their cosmic forms they were: Saturn, Sun, Moon, Mars, Mercury, Jupiter, Venus — the known planets of ancient times with the Sun and Moon counted as planets. As the motion of the Moon, they were gods of time as days. In an extended cycle, their number was increased to nine and their order changed to begin with the Sun. In the nine-god cycle, they were: Sun, Moon, Mars, Mercury, Jupiter, Venus, and three aspects of Saturn.

Pleiades, an asterism in the constellation Taurus, originally consisting of a cluster of seven stars, only six of which are now visible.

Popul Vuh, the sacred book of the Quiché Maya containing the description of the creation of the world.

Prajapati, in Indo-Aryan (Vedic) mythology, the divinity of the universe from which the world came into existence, an aspect of Purusha as the world-man; in the planetary cycle, Saturn.

Pre-Columbian, a term denoting the higher civilizations of Mexico, Central and South America before Columbus' discovery of America.

Prithivi, Indo-Aryan (Vedic) progenitor goddess, the Earth Mother.

Purusha, in Vedic mythology, all the gods combined as an anthropomorphic cosmos or world-man. In the creation myth, Purusha died in an archetypal sacrifice and his body parts came into being as the elements of the created world.

Quetzalcoatl, in Nahuatlan religion, the plumed serpent, the planet Venus, chiefly as the morning star, one of the two fire-serpents as carrier of the Sun, twin of Xolotl, the second Sun of creation.

Quiché Maya, a Mayan tribe living in the highlands of Guatemala.

Quincunx, an arrangement of five things with one in each corner and one in the middle of a square, e.g., the five face on playing dice. The quincunx was a sign of the Venus god in Mesoamerican iconography. It was formed either as five dots or variously as an abstraction such as a Maltese cross with a dot in the center or a geometric figure with volutes in lieu of dots.

Rig Veda, a collection of Indo-Aryan hymns in praise of gods. The *Rig Veda* dates from around the middle of the second millennium B.C. and constitutes the basis for Indo-Aryan mythology as it is presently known.

Rita, the order of world life established by the Vedic gods of ancient India.

Sahagun, Bernardino de, Franciscan friar who lived in Mexico during the sixteenth century, author of the *Codex Florentine* describing the Indian civilization at the time of the Spanish conquest.

Samhuin Feast, November 1, the beginning of Celtic underworld creation year and the beginning of winter on earth.

Savitir, in Vedic mythology, the Sun giving the light of day, the active power of the Sun.

Scythians, culturally related nomadic tribes living in the steppe regions of central Eurasia.

Scythus, founder of the Scythian race and first king, son of Hercules and the Scythian Earth Mother.

Seth, brother of Osiris. In the theology of Egyptian kingship, he was the spirit form of the Divine King Horus and the carrier of the Sun through the underworld.

Glossary

7-Jaguar, God L.

Shamash, Babylonian Sun God.

Shang Period, a period in ancient China circa eighteenth – fourteenth century B.C., named for the Shang dynasty.

Sin, Sumero-Babylonian Moon God.

Soma, in Indo-Aryan (Vedic) religion, the juice of the soma plant having divine properties, the Moon God identified with vegetation.

Stellmoor, an ancient site in northern Germany containing the archaeological remains of deer hunters living circa 15,000 – 10,000 B.C.

Sun of Movement, in Mesoamerican religion, the Sun and Moon combined and moving in lunar cycles, their joint motion created the seasons of life on earth. The current period of world existence.

Tabiti, the Death Goddess and Earth Mother aspect of the Great Goddess in Scythian mythology.

Tammuz, Babylonian form of Dumuzi, god of vegetation and animal life identified with the Moon and having solar attributes.

Tanist, in orthodox rites of the institution of Divine Kingship, two men were appointed to rule for a fixed term. One ruled for half the term and was then sacrificed, the other ruled for the second half and was sacrificed at the end of the term. As used in the text, the first is called the Divine King and the second, the tanist. The term is taken from the early Irish law of succession, by which the successor was appointed during the lifetime of the reigning chief.

Tartarus, the underworld of death in Greek mythology.

Tatevale, the Huichol Fire God, consort of Nakawe, the Mother of the Gods.

Tecuciztecatl, the god who became the Moon in the Nahuatlan (Aztec) creation myth.

Tenochtitlan, capital of the Aztec state, located in central Mexico, the site of present-day Mexico City.

Teotihuacan, the city and imperial state in the central Mexican highlands which flourished between the last centuries B.C. and the eighth century A.D.; it became the dominant cultural center of the Mexican region of Mesoamerica during the Classic Period.

Tepantitla Tlaloc, a fresco in the palace of Tepantitla in Teotihuacan picturing a god identified as Tlaloc.

Tepeyolotl, in the Nahuatlan region, "Heart of the Mountain," a spirit form of Tezcatlipoca as the Moon, also of the Mountain God Tlaloc as vegetation.

Tezcatlipoca, the Nahuatlan name for a god form of the Moon. One of the creator gods as the First Sun; chief god in Mesoamerican religion.

Tiamat, Sumero-Babylonian progenitor goddess, the primordial salt waters, the ocean transfigured as a serpent.

Tititl, in the Aztec calendar, seventeenth month (December 29 – January 17) feast portraying the death of the Moon as the goddess Illamatecuhtli and her resurrection as the god of the new Moon.

Tlacaxipeualiztli, in the Aztec calendar, second month (March 4 – March 23) feast portraying the coming of the new year bringing life-sustaining maize.

Tlahuizcalpantecuhtli, in Nahuatlan religion, Quetzalcoatl as the morning star of Venus.

Tlaloc, one of the Nahuatlan creator gods as the third Sun. Rain and Lightning God.

Tlalocan, the land of Tlaloc in the afterworld in Nahuatlan religion.

Tlatoani, title of the Aztec supreme ruler.

Tlaxcala, a tribal state neighboring the Aztec center at Tenochtitlan.

Tlazolteotl, Nahuatlan Death Goddess and Earth Mother.

Toci, in Nahuatlan religion, a name for the Death Goddess and Earth Mother as the Moon and the mother of the god of maize, Centeotl.

Toltecs, a people of legendary origins who established an empire in central Mexico with its center at Tula, north of present-day Mexico City. They reached the height of their power circa 1000 – 1100 A.D.

Tonalpohualli, in the Nahuatlan calendar, the count of the days. A calendrical cycle of 260 days constituting a period of world creation in which the time divisions are days and nights. The day divisions are registered in 13 series of 20 days and the night divisions are in 20 series of 13 nights. The day count is the Moon's month cycle and the nights are the count of the months of the 260-day period of creation.

Tonatiuh, in Nahuatlan religion, the Sun, as Piltzintecuhlti, he was the rising Sun and one of the Lords of the Night.

Torquemada, Juan de, Spanish author of an eighteenth-century work describing the culture of pre-Columbian Mexico.

Toxcatl, feast in the fifth month of the Aztec calendar (May 3 – May 22). The feast was the climax of a year-long ritual in which the lives and movements of two youths, one consecrated as the Moon (Tezcatlipoca), and the other as the planet Venus combined with the Sun (Ixteucale), constituted the motion of the Fifth Sun creating the life of the following year.

Trickster, the primordial divine life spirit, a universal figure in ancient religions.

Uraeus, an emblem in the shape of a serpent fastened on the crown of the king of Egypt, or worn by the ruler as a fillet over the forehead. The uraeus was the manifestation of the king's divinity.

Urshanabi, in Sumero-Babylonian mythology, servant of Utnapishtim and ferryman across the waters of the Abyss.

Utnapishtim, in Sumero-Babylonian mythology, personification of the regenerative powers of the new Moon. Like the Biblical Noah, Utnapishtim loaded forms of life on an ark when a Flood covered the earth and so preserved life for subsequent generations.

Uto-Aztecan, an Indian linguistic stock relating diverse tribes of North America and Mexico including the North American Utes and Shoshones and the Aztecs.

Utu, Sumerian Sun God.

Varuna, Indo-Aryan (Vedic) Sky God with the Moon as one of his aspects.

Vishnu, in pre-Hindu religion during the Vedic period, the aspect of the Sun moving in its annual cycle. In the Vedic and later Hindu planetary cycle of gods, Vishnu took the place of Mercury as the god of the Sun's movement. In Hindu religion, he became one of the three supreme gods.

Vritra, in Vedic religion, the cosmic serpent which Indra slew by cleaving it with a lightning bolt, thereby releasing the waters of creation. The Moon serpent.

Winnebago, a Native American tribe living in the present-day state of Wisconsin in the United States.

Xibalba, in Mayan religion, the death region of the underworld.

Xilolen, Nahuatlan goddess of young maize.

Xipe, Nahuatlan name of the god of maize and plant life returning on earth in the springtime. Xipe had an animal and a human form. As an animal, he was a serpent — each year his body died and when a new one had fully formed within it, he cast it off. As a human, he was sacrificed and when his flayed skin was put on a living human, his

divinity lodged in the body of the wearer; when the body of the wearer was fully incarnate, the wearer cast off the flayed skin. Xipe was, consequently, called "The Flayed One." He was also a mountain which came to life each spring in the vegetation covering the inanimate rock beneath.

Xiutecuhtli, Aztec name for the Fire God.

Xochiquetzal, Nahuatlan goddess of flowers, a goddess of maize, spouse of Centeotl.

Xolotl, in Nahuatlan religion, the planet Venus as the evening star. One of the two fire-serpents as the carrier of the Sun through the death region of the underworld. Xolotl had the physical forms of a dog, a serpent, and a jaguar, as well as a larva. He was the twin of Quetzalcoatl who, as the other fire-serpent, carried the Sun through the sky.

Yggdrasil, in Teutonic mythology, the tree of life which constituted the universe. Odin sacrificed himself by hanging on one of its limbs and rose in resurrection after 9 days, bringing life to the earth.

Zak-Kuk, also **Lady Zak-Kuk**, a ruler of the Mayan center Palenque, Mother of the Palenque god-ruler Pacal. In her divinity, she was a Moon Goddess whose cyclical aspect in the death state of the Moon was the Earth Mother spouse of the deceased Pacal, and in the stages of its life state was the spouse of Pacal's son, Chan Bahlum.

***Zet*-serpent**, in Egyptian religion, the transfigured form of Osiris as the embodiment of the gods, the morning star, also the Moon.

Zeus, Greek Storm God, chief god of the Olympic pantheon, Greek counterpart of Sumerian Enlil.

Ziusudra, the Sumerian name of Utnapishtim.

INDEX

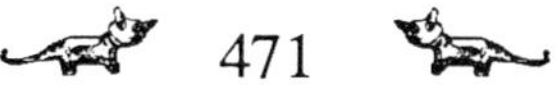

Index

Index

Index

Index

Index

Index

Index

Index

Index

Index

COLOPHON

The Olmec Riddle was produced in late 1986 and early 1987 using a Macintosh Plus computer, Radius full-screen display, two 20-megabyte fixed disks, a Laser Writer Plus printer, MacWrite word-processing software, and Pagemaker 1.2 composition software.

The typeface is Times, with the text set in 12 point type on 15 point leading.

The paper is 70-lb. Vintage Velvet text, with 100-lb. end-papers of Vintage Velvet text, and a flysheet of 20-lb. Patapar.

The printing was accomplished by Neyenesch Printers, Inc. in San Diego, California. The Smyth-sewn bindery reflects the work of Stauffer Edition Binding Company, Inc. in Monterrey Park.

One thousand copies were printed of this First Edition, First Printing.